Trinity & All Saints

ACCREDITED BY THE UNIVERSITY OF LEEDS

LIS LIBRARY

This book is due for return on or before the last date
stamped below

THE POLITICS OF
THE PAST

ONE WORLD ARCHAEOLOGY
Series Editor: P. J. Ucko

THE POLITICS OF THE PAST

Edited by

Peter Gathercole
Darwin College, Cambridge

David Lowenthal
University College London

London and New York

First published by Unwin Hyman in 1990

First published in paperback 1994
by Routledge
2 Park Square, Milton Park, Abingdon, Oxon, OX14 4RN

Simultaneously published in the USA and Canada
by Routledge
270 Madison Ave, New York, NY 10016

Reprinted 2001 (twice)

Transferred to Digital Printing 2005

Routledge is an imprint of the Taylor & Francis Group

© 1990, 1994 Peter Gathercole, David Lowenthal and contributors

Typeset in 10 on 11 point Bembo by Computatape (Pickering) Ltd, Pickering,
North Yorkshire

British Library Cataloguing in Publication Data
   The politics of the past. – (One world archaeology: 12).
   1. Archaeology
   I. Gathercole, Peter   II. Lowenthal, David
   III. Series 930–1

Library of Congress Cataloging in Publication Data
   The Politics of the Past/edited by Peter Gathercole, David Lowenthal
       p. cm. – (One world archaeology: 12)
   Papers from the session of the World Archaeological Congress.
   Bibliography: p.
   Includes index.
   1. Archaeology – Political aspects – Congresses. 2. Archaeology – Political
aspects – Developing countries – Congresses. 3. Archaeology and state –
Congresses. 4. Archaeology and state – Developing countries – Congresses.
5. Ethnocentrism – Congresses.
I. Gathercole, Peter II. Lowenthal, David. III. World Archaeological Congress
(1986: Southampton, England) IV. Series.
CC175.P65 1989
930.1–dc20 89–9099

ISBN 0–415 09554–9

List of contributors

Peter V. Addyman, York Archaeological Trust, UK

Ronald Belgrave, Local Government Race Equality Office, London, UK

Michael L. Blakey, Department of Sociology and Anthropology, Howard University, Washington, DC, USA

David J. Butts, Faculty of Social Sciences, Massey University, Palmerston North, New Zealand

Howard Creamer, National Parks and Wildlife Service, Armidale, New South Wales, Australia

Lawrence Foanaota, Solomon Islands National Museum, Honiara, Solomon Islands

Peter Gathercole, Darwin College, Cambridge, UK

Joan Gero, Department of Anthropology, University of South Carolina, Columbia, South Carolina, USA

Sandy Grant, Phuthadikobo Museum, Mochudi, Botswana

Sian Jones, Museum Education Service, Southampton City Museums, UK

Carl Kuttruff, Department of Geography and Anthropology, Louisiana State University, Baton Rouge, Louisiana, USA

David Lowenthal, Department of Geography, University College London, UK

W. J. McCann, Department of German, University of Southampton, UK

Robert MacKenzie, National Association of Citizens Advice Bureaux, London, UK

Andrzej Mikołajczyk, Archaeological and Ethnographical Museum, Łódź, Poland

Keith Nicklin, Horniman Museum and Library, London, UK

Nwanna Nzewunwa, Office of the Dean of Student Affairs, University of Port Harcourt, Nigeria

Stephen O'Regan, Aoraki Consultant Services, Wellington, New Zealand

Sharon Pay, Archaeology Section, Southampton City Museums, UK

Robert Paynter, Department of Anthropology, University of Massachusetts at Amherst, USA

Sergio Rapu, Office of the Provincial Governor, Easter Island (Rapa Nui), Chile

Dolores Root, Department of Anthropology, University of Massachusetts at Amherst, USA

Chris Scarre, Department of Archaeology, University of Cambridge, UK

Helga Seeden, Department of History and Archaeology, American University of Beirut, Lebanon

Matthew Spriggs, Department of Prehistory, Australian National University, Canberra, ACT, Australia

Nicholas P. Stanley Price, Getty Conservation Institute, Marina del Rey, California, USA
Frank Willett, Hunterian Museum, Glasgow, UK

Foreword

This book is one of a major series of more than 20 volumes resulting from the World Archaeological Congress held in Southampton, England, in September 1986. The series reflects the enormous academic impact of the Congress, which was attended by 850 people from more than 70 countries, and attracted many additional contributions from others who were unable to attend in person.

The *One World Archaeology* series is the result of a determined and highly successful attempt to bring together for the first time not only archaeologists and anthropologists from many different parts of the world, as well as academics from a host of contingent disciplines, but also non-academics from a wide range of cultural backgrounds, who could lend their own expertise to the discussions at the Congress. Many of the latter, accustomed to being treated as the 'subjects' of archaeological and anthropological observation, had never before been admitted as equal participants in the discussion of their own (cultural) past or present, with their own particularly vital contribution to make towards global, cross-cultural understanding.

The Congress therefore really addressed world archaeology in its widest sense. Central to a world archaeological approach is the investigation not only of how people lived in the past but also of how, and why, changes took place resulting in the forms of society and culture which exist today. Contrary to popular belief, and the archaeology of some 20 years ago, world archaeology is much more than the mere recording of specific historical events, embracing as it does the study of social and cultural change in its entirety. All the books in the *One World Archaeology* series are the result of meetings and discussions which took place within a context that encouraged a feeling of self-criticism and humility in the participants about their own interpretations and concepts of the past. Many participants experienced a new self-awareness, as well as a degree of awe about past and present human endeavours, all of which is reflected in this unique series.

The Congress was organized around major themes. Several of these themes were based on the discussion of full-length papers which had been circulated some months previously to all who had indicated a special interest in them. Other sessions, including some dealing with areas of specialization defined by period or geographical region, were based on oral addresses, or a combination of precirculated papers and lectures. In all cases, the entire sessions were recorded on cassette, and all contributors were presented with the recordings of the discussion of their papers. A major part of the thinking behind the Congress was that such a meeting of many hundreds of participants that did not leave behind a published record of its academic discussions would be little more than an exercise in tourism.

Thus, from the very beginning of the detailed planning for the World Archaeological Congress, in 1982, the intention was to produce post-Congress books containing a selection only of the contributions, revised in the light of discussions during the sessions themselves as well as during subsequent consultations with the academic editors appointed for each book. From the outset, contributors to the Congress knew that if their papers were selected for publication they would have only a few months to revise them according to editorial specifications, and that they would become authors in an important academic volume scheduled to appear within a reasonable period following the Southampton meeting.

The publication of the series reflects the intense planning which took place before the Congress. Not only were all contributors aware of the subsequent production schedules, but also session organizers were already planning their books before and during the Congress. The editors were entitled to commission additional chapters for their books when they felt that there were significant gaps in the coverage of a topic during the Congress, or where discussion at the Congress indicated a need for additional contributions.

One of the main themes of the Congress was devoted to 'Archaeological "Objectivity" in Interpretation', where consideration of the precirculated full-length papers on this theme extended over four and a half days of academic discussion. The particular sessions on 'Archaeological "Objectivity" in Interpretation' were under my overall control, the main aim being to focus attention on the way that evidence of the past – including archaeological evidence – has been used and viewed by particular groups (whether local, regional or national) at different times. Essential to this aim was the exploration of the reasons why particular interpretations might have been chosen, or favoured, by individual societies and traditions at specific points in their development, or at certain stages in their activities. The whole theme attempted, therefore, a unique mix of critical assessment of the basis of archaeological methodology with critical awareness of the social contexts of the use (and possible manipulation) of the evidence of the past.

Central to this re-evaluation of the strengths and weaknesses of archaeological approaches to the interpretation, and indeed 'display', of the past – whether through academic articles or by means of formal or informal curricula, or through museums or site presentation – is an assessment of the methodologies and approaches to the significance of material culture. This has long been a core issue in archaeological discussion, but it badly needed re-examination. Throughout the history of archaeology as a discipline, material culture, or at least the repetitive association of distinctive material culture objects, has been taken to reflect activities of specific social groups or 'societies' whose physical movements across a geographic stage have often been postulated on the basis of the distribution patterns of such objects, and whose supposed physical or ethnic identity (see also *State and society*, edited by J. Gledhill, B. Bender & M. T. Larsen) have often been assumed to correlate with such artefactual groupings. More recently archaeologists have been forced to recognize, often through lessons gained from ethnography, that a distinctive material culture complex may represent the activities of a vast variety of social groupings and subgroups, and that archaeological classification may often serve to camouflage the subtle messages of style and technique (see also *Animals into art*, edited by H. Morphy, and *Domination and resistance*, edited by D. Miller, M. J. Rowlands & C. Tilley) which probably symbolize complex patterns of behaviour, as well as individual aspirations, within any society.

If the very basis of the equation between a material culture complex and a social grouping is ambiguous, then much of archaeological interpretation must remain subjective, even at this fundamental level of its operations. Whenever the archaeological data of material culture are presented in museums, on sites, in literature, in schools or in textbooks, as the evidence for the activities of 'races', 'peoples', 'tribes', 'linguistic groups' or other socially derived ethnic amalgamations, there should be at least scepticism if not downright suspicion. In a large number of such cases, what we are witnessing is the none-too-subtle ascription of racial/cultural stereotypes to static material culture items.

The overall theme therefore took as its starting point the proposition that archaeological interpretation is a subjective matter. It also assumed that to regard archaeology as somehow constituting the only legitimate 'scientific' approach to the past needed re-examination and possibly even rejection. A narrow parochial approach to the past which simply assumes that a linear chronology based on a 'verifiable' set of 'meaningful' 'absolute' dates is the only way to tackle the recording of, and the only way to comprehend, the past completely ignores the complexity of many literate and many non-literate 'civilizations' and cultures. However, a world archaeological approach to a concept such as 'the past' focuses attention on precisely those features of archaeological enquiry and method which archaeologists all too often take for granted, without questioning the related assumptions.

Discussions on this theme during the Congress were grouped around seven headings, and have led to the publication of five books. The first subtheme, organized by Stephen Shennan, Department of Archaeology, University of Southampton, which lasted for almost a day, was concerned with 'Multiculturalism and Ethnicity in Archaeological Interpretation' and the second, under the control of Ian Hodder, Department of Archaeology, University of Cambridge, which occupied more than a day, was on 'Material Culture and Symbolic Expression'. The fourth subtheme, 'The Politics of the Past: Museums, Media, and other Presentations of Archaeology', was organized by Peter Gathercole of Darwin College, Cambridge, and also lasted for more than a day. Each of these subthemes has led to a separate book: *Archaeological approaches to cultural identity* (edited by S. J. Shennan), *The meanings of things*, edited by I. Hodder, and this particular volume. The fifth subtheme, on 'The Past in Education', was organized by Robert MacKenzie, Training Manager, National Association of Citizens' Advice Bureaux, and discussion of this topic (which lasted formally for half a day at the Congress and informally throughout the week by means of displays and educational events) has been expanded into the book *The excluded past*, under the editorship of Peter Stone (of English Heritage) and R. MacKenzie. David Bellos of the Department of French, University of Manchester, was responsible for a short discussion session on the sixth subtheme, 'Mediations of the Past in Modern Europe', and contributions from this subtheme have been combined either with those from the third on 'Contemporary Claims about Stonehenge' (a short discussion session organized by Christopher Chippindale, Museum of Archaeology and Anthropology, University of Cambridge), or with those from the seventh subtheme on 'Indigenous Perceptions of the Past' which lasted for almost a day. Robert Layton of the Department of Anthropology, University of Durham, was in charge of this seventh topic and has also edited the two resulting books, *Who needs the past?* and *Conflict in the archaeology of living traditions*. The latter also incorporates several contributions from a one-day discussion on 'Material Culture and the Making of the Modern United States: Views from Native America', which had been organized by Russell Handsman of the American Indian Archaeological Institute, Washington, Connecticut, and Randall McGuire of the Department of Anthropology of the State University of New York at Binghamton.

The whole of the 'Archaeological "Objectivity" in Interpretation' theme had been planned as the progressive development of an idea and the division of it into subthemes was undertaken in the full knowledge that there would be considerable overlap among them. It was accepted that it would, in many ways, be impossible, and even counter-productive, to split, for example, education from site presentation, or literary presentations of the past from indigenous history. In the event, while each of the books resulting from this overall theme has its own coherence, they also share a concern to make explicit the responsibility of recognizing the various ways of interpreting humanly created artefacts. In addition they recognize the social responsibility of archaeological interpretation, and the way that this may be used, consciously or unconsciously, by others for their own ends. The contributions in these books, directly or indirectly, explicitly or implicitly, epitomize the view that modern archaeology must recognize and confront its new role, which is to address the wider community. It must do this with a sophisticated awareness of the strengths and the weaknesses of its own methodologies and practices.

A world archaeological approach to archaeology as a 'discipline' reveals how subjective archaeological interpretation has always been. It also demonstrates the importance that all rulers and leaders (politicians) have placed on the legitimization of their positions through the 'evidence' of the past. Objectivity is strikingly absent from most archaeological exercises in interpretation. In some cases there has been conscious manipulation of the past for national political ends (as in the case of Ian Smith's Rhodesian regime over Great Zimbabwe, or that of the Nazis with their racist use of archaeology). But, apart from this, archaeologists themselves have been influenced in their interpretations by the received wisdom of their times, both in the sort of classificatory schemes which they consider appropriate to their subject, and in the way that their dating of materials is affected by their assumptions about the capabilities of the humans concerned. Nowhere is archaeological explanation immune to changes in interpretive fashion. This is as true of Britain as of anywhere else – Stonehenge especially has been subjected to the most bizarre collection of interpretations over the years, including all sorts of references to it having been constructed by Mycenaeans and Phoenicians. Although, at first sight, it is tempting to assume that such contentions are different from attempts by politicians to claim that the extraordinary site of Great Zimbabwe was constructed by Phoenicians using black slaves, the difference is not very easy to sustain.

Realization of the flexibility and variety of past human endeavour all over the world directs attention back to those questions that are at the very basis of archaeological interpretation. How can static material culture objects be equated with dynamic human cultures? How can we define and recognize the 'styles' of human activity, as well as their possible implications? In some contexts these questions assume immense political importance. For example, the archaeological 'evidence' of cultural continuity, as opposed to discontinuity, may make all the difference to an indigenous land claim, to the right of access to a site or region, or to the disposal of a human skeleton to a museum, as against its reburial.

All these factors lead in turn to a new consideration of how different societies choose to display their museum collections and conserve their sites. As the debates about who should be allowed to use Stonehenge, and how it should be displayed, make clear, objects or places may be considered important at one time and 'not worth bothering about' at others. Who makes these decisions and in what contexts? Who is responsible, and why, for what is taught about the past in schools or in adult education? Is such education based on a narrow local/regional/national framework of archaeology and history, or is it oriented towards multiculturalism and the variety of human cultural experiences in a worldwide context? What should the implications be for the future of archaeology?

The main themes in *The politics of the past* are discussed in its several introductory sections. My aim in what follows is to examine points which strike me as particularly noteworthy, for the overall contents are, in my opinion, central to future discussions about the very nature of a discipline of archaeology.

Most archaeologists still appear to believe that an objective study of the past is both possible and what they themselves are engaged in. They seem unaware of those 'prejudices and passions' by which all their interpretations are likely to be 'unconsciously biassed' (Childe 1933, p. 418 n.), and of those 'sentimental considerations [which] are liable to disturb the objectivity of scientific judgement' (Childe 1934, p. 68). In fact, archaeology is a highly political practice. *The politics of the past* brings together a unique set of case studies which illuminates the nature of those political influences and concerns within which the practice of archaeology is normally carried out.

Archaeology has on occasion become a vehicle for racial oppression and the abuse of human rights. Another book in this series, *Archaeological approaches to cultural identity* (edited by S. J. Shennan), has examined some of the deficiencies and weaknesses of methodology and interpretation which may have allowed archaeology to assist in the exploitation of its own data and conclusions. As Gordon Childe said when discussing the role of pre-history in Nazi Germany, in the wrong hands it 'may have disastrous effects' (1933, p. 410). Contrary to Childe's view, however, such abuses are not simply overt political distortions of an 'objectively studied Prehistory' whose results demonstrate the fallacy of selective qualitative judgement in the building of an 'exclusive nationalism' (Childe 1933, p. 418). As *The politics of the past* records, Nazi archaeology was not just a matter of distortion by politicians or of manipulation of evidence by German archae-ologists who were Nazis; many non-political archaeologists also played a part by accepting the overall Nazi interpretive context of the past (see McCann, Ch. 6). It was not only the evidence of archaeology, as the unique study of the remote past, that was distorted under the Nazi regime. Some categories of ethnographic objects from Poland were sold to German museums, but those deemed Slavic were destroyed in order to remove them (and the culture they represented) from the record (see Mikołajczyk, Ch. 19).

Childe examined the political role of archaeology and prehistory in a national framework in the context of a particular nationalism. More recent studies (e.g. Madrid 1986), as well as several chapters in this book, shift the emphasis to demonstrate that archaeology is an active agent in everybody's present. Part of the importance of the *One World Archaeology* series is to establish that this was no less true of the ideologies and practice of *past* nations (cf. *Centre and periphery*, edited by T. C. Champion; *State and society*, edited by J. Gledhill *et al.*; and *Domination and resistance*, edited by D. Miller *et al.*). This use of the past as a visible symbol of previous excellence continues unabated today – an overt, political conjuring act which often results in the complexities of the archaeological evidence being transformed into simple messages about national cultural identity. Thus 'Iraq restoring Babylon to former glory' (*Guardian*, 6 October 1986) was only partly, if at all, about a concerted international archaeological research enterprise – it was more about an open-cheque effort by Iraq's president to attract tourists and 'to inspire his people in the costly and gruelling war with Iran'. Several contributions to this book describe the way that archaeology is normally financed by central government agencies, whose interests may be far removed from the concerns of local cultural groups with the closest ties to sites (which are often under threat of destruction or of being resurrected in the 'national interest').

Given the overtly political nature of so much archaeological practice, it is remarkable that examination of the relationships between archaeology and politics has generally been avoided (Madrid 1986, p. 222). *The politics of the past*, however, tackles the nature of such relationships. In many countries funding agencies are part of government or government-controlled authorities which in almost all cases define what is, and what is not, deemed relevant for study (Kohl 1989). As several chapters in this book show, the perceived needs of national development and tourism often determine site-recording policy and associated conservation activities, including legislation dealing with environmental impact statements and preservation (see also *Archaeological heritage management in the modern world*, edited by H. F. Cleere). In too many cases the policies resulting from the perceived priorities have totally ignored the effect on local communities, policies that deny the fact that 'If you ain't got nothing to worship at, you ain't got a culture' (Spriggs, Ch. 9, p. 127).

It is paradoxical that archaeologists have often found themselves aligned against such perceived national interests, at least in situations where governments have not yet recognized that heritage protection must form part of national cultural identity. This book is full of examples, sometimes disturbing, of archaeologists' failures to appreciate the importance of the wider context of archaeological interpretation.

Despite the complexity of many of the actual situations and choices facing archaeologists, much of the recent history of the discipline demonstrates its acceptance, tacit or not, of a social and political conformity (Patterson 1986) leading to clashes of interpretation, and of interest, between archaeologists working in foreign areas and indigenous archaeologists. In addition, indigenous archaeologists themselves may become isolated within their own communities, where, all too often, archaeology and other studies of the past are viewed as manifestations of imperialism (cf. Gidiri 1974).

The politics of the past places in a wider context studies published in other volumes of the *One World Archaeology* series (*Who needs the past?* and *Conflict in the archaeology of living traditions*, both edited by R. Layton; and *The meanings of things*, edited by I. Hodder), which show that however concerned people are with the interests of their own and their children's generations, they may still not be interested in the practice of archaeology, as defined, organized, and practised nationally. This book examines in a variety of ways issues concerning the development of local museums and cultural centres (see also *World Archaeological Bulletin*, 1989). It is in the context of such local (and often ethnic) concerns with the past that conflict with archaeologists often emerges, and in this context archaeology often appears to be an uncaring discipline, typical of a dominant elitist society.

This book presents evidence about why this conflict so often occurs. Sometimes, for complex reasons, academic accounts of art works have been published even when doing so would lessen museum security and enhance sale-room prices. On other occasions, the increased employment of local or indigenous people by organizations such as parks services is applauded because it provides opportunities for these people to determine the practices and uses of sites within such parks. In fact, such employment may deny them the possibility of participating in the more fundamental decision about whether such sites should be exploited at all or be excluded from 'foreign' interventions. This book starkly presents a range of current strategies – for example, the employment of Australian Aborigines, which has been far from successful in allaying fears about the disturbance of sites.

Only occasionally are archaeologists seen to be on the side of those whose remains they study. In many cases, those whose sites are under investigation see archaeologists as the enemy, because archaeologists insist they have the right to disturb and desecrate burial sites and to make decisions about the disposal of other people's dead (Hubert 1988, 1989, Ucko 1989, p. 12). Even in West Africa, where most archaeologists are Africans and the infra-structure of academic positions and museums is relatively well developed, the aspirations among archaeologists during the 1970s concerning the role archaeology should play in cultural revival have largely come to nothing, and it is clear that archaeology is still regarded as an elitist occupation.

All these issues reflect one fundamental question: Who has ownership rights to the remains of the past? The answer has to be sought in analysis of political organizations, where struggles for influence and domination are played out in both informal and formal contexts. Such power struggles may take place at local, regional, or national levels (Ucko 1983), but more and more frequently these struggles are acquiring an international dimension. No archaeologist can afford to ignore the explicit concerns of international agencies, such as the World Council of Indigenous Peoples (WCIP), which question the social and political context of academic enquiry, the control of access to archaeological and historical sites, and particularly museum displays including the messages they convey (e.g. Burgess 1986). Not surprisingly, the approaches of such agencies to the study and exploitation of the past are similar to many of those considered in this book. The international level of concern – whether to indigenous peoples through WCIP, to museums through the International Council on Museums (ICOM), or to prehistorians, archaeologists, and historians through Unesco – is, however, only one aspect of the problem.

Many people who are struggling in local political contexts to keep their cultures alive and well are unaware of this international concern. It is easy enough to talk about the world, including 'the cultures of the Indigenous Peoples [that] are part of the cultural heritage of all mankind. Indigenous cultures, like all cultures, deserve dignified treatment and proper respect of all peoples of the world' (Burgess 1986). But as *The politics of the past* makes clear, the world may be a dangerous and ambiguous place for a substantial proportion of the population. In the United Kingdom, for example, immigrants are denied any significant role in public statements about the nation's cultural past, or its present identity. In many countries an issue of prime political, social, and humanitarian concern is whether only the sites of selected religious groups will be legally protected and their objects and creations glorified in museum displays. In so-called developing countries museums and sites may have powerful and crucial roles in the development of nationalism, particularly when they become vehicles for education and instruction (see also *The excluded past*, edited by P. Stone & R. MacKenzie).

Part of the complexity of the politics of the past lies in the fact that the apparent congruence of interests of those agencies which deal with events at a pan-level can swamp all other interests. It is easy to ignore agonizing local dilemmas of principle and action by invoking a putative 'world' identity and interest. Who would wish, for example, to be embroiled in disputes about the access of hippies, tourists, and Druids to Stonehenge if an alternative were to declare it a World Heritage site and to deny close access to everyone by insisting on protection? Part of the complexity of the whole situation becomes clear when one realizes how much easier it must be for legislators and politicians to recognize the significance of a specific archaeological or historical site than to come to terms with claims for the sanctity of whole *areas* of land, let alone for the sanctity of the earth itself.

Local versus national or even world conflicts over heritage will not simply go away. Struggles over ancestral remains have intensified in recent years despite efforts by archaeologists to make their enquiries acceptable to the local cultures concerned. Indigenous minorities such as the Australian Aborigines have been employed in archaeology or archaeology-related activities. They have also been 'educated' about their own cultures and the supposedly forgotten activities of their own cultural antecedents. *The politics of the past* shows that some cultures have welcomed the care and attention paid to their material culture and art objects by archaeologists, anthropologists, and museums so that these are protected for posterity, especially at times when their own younger generations are absent or preoccupied with non-indigenous cultural activities. However, the assumption that indigenes need to be taught about their cultural backgrounds and histories by (usually foreign) academics has sometimes provoked resentment. On occasion, such cultural instruction has resulted in the 'newly' acculturated demanding the return of their cultural property, often from the very archaeologists, anthropologists, and museum curators who had removed cultural objects into their own care in central depositories, usually in capital cities.

There is often a genuine dilemma. On the one hand, by retaining cultural objects in a safe physical environment, such as a national museum, archaeologists may be called imperialist and racist. On the other hand, if sacred objects are returned to the spots in which they were found (where, often thanks to archaeological endeavours, their symbolic local cultural significance is now ensured), traditional methods of guarding their spiritual essence may result in their physical destruction.

No less difficult are those (probably still rare) cases where successful teaching, employment, or research funding has led to a renewal of indigenous cultural interest which then changes the received 'academic wisdom' concerning the nature of the sites or objects found. As this book shows, any participation by young Maori in traditional cultural affairs is considered a success: 'benefits of [participation] involving the young far outweighed the dangers of ethnological error' (p. 104). Archaeologists and anthropologists who recognize that culture and cultural interpretation are never static (see also *The meanings of things*, edited by I. Hodder) would probably agree with the Maori view and would perhaps recall archaeological evidence suggesting that artistic depictions and objects have often been retouched by succeeding cultures (see also *Animals into art*, edited by H. Morphy). However, when monuments of one's own supposed cultural heritage or of the material culture of others, which are considered to be works of art, are involved, attitudes often appear to be different. When members of the public adorn Stonehenge with graffiti, these are swiftly erased, and barriers are erected to prevent the re-occurrence of such defacement. When young Australian Aborigines, divorced from their own cultural backgrounds, were taken to rock art sites by older Aboriginal people in order to be taught about their culture, the young repainted faded paintings. The result was a furore, including 'shock and horror among those who do not share the same cultural traditions' (Mowaljarlai *et al.* 1988, p. 693; see also Mowljarlie & Peck 1987, Horton 1987, Bowdler 1988). The contextless nature of Western concepts about art have sometimes led to conflict between archaeologists and indigenes (Ucko 1985), which demonstrates the often intensely political nature of archaeological and anthropological enquiry and reinforces the view 'that the arts, both sacred and profane, have . . . often stood at the very eye of social, political and religious controversy . . . not only as symbols of cultural heritage, but also as mediators for cultural communication, and as mechanisms for social and political protest' (Vastokas 1987).

Such examples lend support to Peter Gathercole's introductory comments: the past – and the heritage of any particular group or nation – can be viewed either as an amorphous ragbag of trappings and attitudes or ordered into a coherent picture of legitimized events. Which particular view or interpretation is favoured depends on the perspectives and interests of the protagonists. Michael Blakey (Ch. 3) draws attention to a comparable point about the nature of archaeological enquiry. It can offer to different peoples a heritage through which they can claim association with one another. We must therefore recognize that, in any particular situation, archaeologists may be seen as agents in the prevention of perceived advantages of allegiance and groupings. Thus archaeologists' assertions that Tasmanian Aborigines had been totally annihilated were seen by their descendants as attacks on their status in modern Australian society.

Access to any past (or pasts) may be crucial. The future of Britain as a multicultural society, for example, may well be affected by the way the past is made accessible and meaningful to the various cultural components of society, or the extent to which the past is kept as a commodity for the enjoyment of a white elite. In a country such as New Zealand, for example, where the establishment's controls are less dominating, it is not the future of multiculturalism and multicultural education which is under threat but the very nature of Maori and white biculturalism. The Maori could react to the continued elitism of academic archaeology by no longer recognizing the special skills of archaeologists and by demanding exclusive Maori control not only of their own local cultural remains but also of all teaching about the Maori past.

Given the intricacies of these diverse political situations, it is probably not surprising that archaeologists and anthropologists, at least in Fourth World contexts, are finding themselves in situations which threaten the respectability, and perhaps the very existence, of their discipline. In several countries, they are now being called into courts of law to give alternative interpretations of the archaeological evidence, for the defence and for the prosecution. The nature of the political enquiry that constitutes the activity of archaeology is now being opened to public scrutiny.

This discussion inexorably leads from the initial question of who may legitimately claim to own the past to the basic question whether there really is a *single* past. In *Conflict in the archaeology of living traditions* (edited by R. Layton), some contributors contend that despite the numerous ways of approaching and interpreting the same data, facts about the past do indeed exist. These facts cannot be, and should not be, explicated within a single analytic and interpretive parameter. At the opposite extreme are those contributors who argue that all views of the past are equally meaningful and correct. It is certainly true, as Patterson has maintained (1986, p. 21), that archaeologists have no reason to be complacent:

> The accumulation or acquisition of more empirical facts does not provide the basis [to engage in productive dialogue], for the members of one community frequently reinterpret certain facts produced by their opponents and ignore others . . . The assumptions and constraints of one period or place are not necessarily applicable in another. Instead, archaeology is constituted, its various communities linked, not by the questions archaeologists ask but rather by what they take for granted: the presuppositions or antecedent logical conditions of those questions.

Archaeologists have inevitably developed their interpretations of data within the context of the received wisdoms of their own times; for example, that American Indian and Australian Aboriginal societies had been dispersed (Patterson 1986, p. 11) and were on the verge of dying out (Ucko 1985, p. 63), and that the brilliance of Maya culture had been completely destroyed with the arrival of the Spanish (Patterson 1986, p. 13). Until recently academics did not allow such wisdoms to be questioned by those who were the most affected by them. Now serious challenges are being made to all such assumptions.

Does this mean that archaeology is no different from fictional literature and that 'not only "anything goes" but archaeology can be used to support any cause' (Trigger 1986, p. 4)?

Archaeology, like historiography, appears to develop in complex, rapidly-changing societies. In these societies an understanding of past changes is used to give meaning to the present. Highly subjective factors influence the interpretation of the past. The available evidence suggests that archaeology is neither simply a reflection of society nor fully independent of it. Archaeology is influenced by the inherent limitations of the archaeological record and the interpretation of this record is influenced in major ways by social processes. Yet the data of archaeology are not entirely constructions of our own mind, even if their recording and analysis are coloured by our presuppositions. (Trigger 1986, pp. 13, 15)

Trigger can do no more than assert his belief in the existence of real archaeological data. As *The politics of the past* stresses, the problem confronting archaeology today is an acutely moral one. If the essential question about the nature of the past cannot be answered satisfactorily, how can the preoccupations, aims, and practices of archaeologists be allowed to prejudice those of others? The *One World Archaeology* series, and *The politics of the past* in particular, provide the means whereby archaeologists can gain deeper understanding of the nature of archaeological enquiry. Only through such self-awareness and the close analysis of the assumptions and practices of the discipline is there any hope that the evidence of the past will be made accessible to all and that specific aspects will be allowed to retain their significance for those for whom they have a useful role to play.

Peter Gathercole and David Lowenthal make it clear in *The politics of the past* that archaeologists can no longer afford to remain unaware of at least two forces competing for their services – the rulers and the ruled. Inevitably archaeologists will find themselves caught up in controversies and will have to confront complex dilemmas. As the editors also say, archaeologists, and indeed everyone involved in the heritage industry, must be aware that archaeology is now 'an intensely political calling' not just in theory but in practice (p. 92).

Archaeologists, through analyses such as those which characterize this book, must come to terms with contemporary demands on the profession and with the complex setting in which it operates. Otherwise, as Stephen O'Regan (Ch. 7) so eloquently puts it, archaeologists will simply continue to be seen by those who do not form part of an exploitative elite, as 'little more than birds of prey feasting on the carcases of [someone else's] culture'.

P. J. Ucko
Southampton

References

Bowdler, S. 1988. Repainting Australian rock art. *Antiquity* **62**, 517–23.
Burgess, H. F. 1986. On museums and indigenous cultures (unpublished ms.). Jokkmokk, Sweden.
Childe, V. G. 1933. Is prehistory practical? *Antiquity* **7**, 410–18.

Childe, V. G. 1934. Anthropology and Herr Hitler. *Discovery*, March, 65–8.

Gidiri, A. 1974. Imperialism and archaeology. *Race* **15**(4), 431–59.

Horton, D. 1987. Editorial. *Australian Aboriginal Studies* **2**, 1.

Hubert, J. 1988. The disposition of the dead. *World Archaeological Bulletin* **2**, 12–39.

Hubert, J. 1989. A proper place for the dead: a critical review of the 'reburial' issue. In *Conflict in the archaeology of living traditions*, R. Layton (ed.), 131–66. London: Unwin Hyman.

Kohl, P. L. 1989. The material culture of the modern era in the ancient Orient: suggestions for future work. In *Domination and resistance*, D. Miller, M. Rowlands & C. Tilley (eds), 240–5. London: Unwin Hyman.

Madrid, A. 1986. Archaeology in a political context: examples from four Latin American countries. *Archaeological Review from Cambridge* **5**(2), 222–5.

Mowaljarlai, D., P. Vinnicombe, G. K. Ward & C. Chippindale 1988. Repainting of images on rock in Australia and the maintenance of Aboriginal culture. *Antiquity* **62**, 690–6.

Mowljarlie, D. & C. Peck 1987. Ngarinjin cultural continuity: a project to teach the young people the culture including the repainting of Wandjina rock art sites. *Australian Aboriginal Studies* **2**, 71–8.

Patterson, T. C. 1986. The last sixty years: toward a social history of Americanist archaeology in the United States. *American Anthropologist* **88**(1), 7–26.

Trigger, B. G. 1986. Prospects for a world archaeology. *World Archaeology* **18**(1), 1–20.

Ucko, P. J. 1983. The politics of the indigenous minority. *J. Biosoc. Sci. Suppl.* **8**, 25–40.

Ucko, P. J. 1985. Australian Aborigines and academic social anthropology. In *The future of farmer foragers*, C. Schrire & R. Gordon (eds), 63–73. Cambridge, Mass.: Cultural Survival Inc.

Ucko, P. J. 1989. One world archaeology. *History Today* **39**(3), 10–12.

Vastokas, J. [J. V.] 1987. Art and politics. *Native Art Studies. Association of Canada Newsletter* **2**(4), 1.

World Archaeological Bulletin **3**, 1989. Oxford: Oxbow Books.

Contents

POLITICS AND ADMINISTRATION

ARCHAEOLOGY AND THE PEOPLE

Preface

The session of the World Archaeological Congress from which this book derives contained 29 papers, of which all but 7, together with one by W. J. McCann given at another Congress session, have been extensively revised for this book. At the Congress contributions were arranged on a regional basis, with separate panels on Africa and North America, Oceania and Australia, and Europe and on media presentations of the past. Panels on general aspects of archaeology and politics prefaced and concluded the whole. The regrouping of the papers for publication emphasizes such political issues as the influences of race, class, and gender on archaeological thought and practice and other topical themes that transcend regional considerations.

We thank the contributors for responding so constructively to our often protracted and vexatious editorial queries. Our thanks go also to the Southampton organizers, especially Caroline Jones and Paul Crake, who with Peter Ucko brought the participants together for a memorable meeting; to Stephen O'Regan, Dolores Root, and Helga Seeden, who with us chaired panel discussions; to Peter Ucko, who saw the need for such a session; and to Mary Alice Lamberty for her constructive, indispensable, and indefatigably cheerful help in editing the text.

Peter Gathercole
David Lowenthal

Introduction

PETER GATHERCOLE

'History is written by the winners', says Robert Paynter in 'Afro-Americans in the Massachusetts historical landscape' (Ch. 4). This is frequently the case; those in power often write accounts of the past to justify the status quo. What has actually taken place, an amorphous ragbag of happenings and attitudes, becomes in the eyes of its interpreters the logical and smoothed-out antecedent of things as they now are. But historical interpretations are never absolute. The struggles between contending versions therefore offer great opportunities for archaeology, which can often reveal new evidence about the past. In theory and, as much of this book demonstrates, increasingly also in practice, archaeology can help to ensure that history is not written only by the winners. It is said that when Jack Golson, an archaeologist at the Australian National University, advertised a lecture in Port Moresby entitled '50000 years of Papua New Guinea history' (the evidence for which was mainly archaeological), people trekked for miles to hear him. Hitherto, history had been about white people. Now it would be about everybody.

It is the existence of archaeology worldwide, particularly its growing practice in the Third and Fourth Worlds, that makes discussion of 'the politics of the past' so fruitful. The topic is inherent in any comprehensive examination of archaeological interpretation which extends beyond Eurocentric models; megalithic comparisons are no longer based on Stonehenge, ethnographic parallels do not require a Greenwich meridian. This book draws much on material from Africa, North America, Oceania, and Australia, and only to a lesser extent from Europe. It is divided into four parts, entitled 'The Heritage of Eurocentricity', 'Rulers and Ruled', 'Politics and Administration', and 'Archaeology and the People'. Each has a short introduction summarizing its contents. David Lowenthal's concluding chapter highlights some of the interconnections among these four themes.

One issue common to many chapters is how social, cultural, political, psychological, and ideological factors constrain archaeological objectivity, especially when the results of research are put before the public. An instructive example is the view of history offered by the *National Geographic Magazine* over the past 100 years (Gero & Root, Ch. 2). Here the orientation, aimed largely at North American readers, essentially reflects the assumptions of the magazine's readership. But constraints placed on archaeology can be directly economic. Thus archaeology on Easter Island (Rapu, Ch. 18) is undertaken primarily for its money-earning capacity in the growing tourist market. In the Solomon Islands (Foanaota, Ch. 17), the extent to which the National Museum can maintain its National Site Survey (the bedrock of its archaeological research) depends much on aid from international agencies such as Unesco and from such friendly governments as Australia and Japan. Culture queues up for assistance, just as do public works. Money or the lack of it also helps determine the effectiveness of museums in Botswana (MacKenzie, Ch. 15, Grant, Ch. 16). Cost-effectiveness lay behind the decision to create the Jorvik Viking Centre in York (Addyman, Ch. 20), and determines the areas emphasized in archaeological atlases (Scarre, Ch. 1).

Another general theme, transcending our categories, is the nature of historical knowledge. When Butts (Ch. 8), then curator of the Hawke's Bay Museum, New Zealand, redisplayed its Maori collection, he fully involved members of the Ngati Kahungunu tribe to ensure that their own conception of their history was presented. Conflicting interpretations of historical realities are considered under several heads. Blakey (Ch. 3) and Paynter (Ch. 4) discuss bias against Afro-Americans in museum displays and in American historical archaeology, and Belgrave (Ch. 5) deplores the absence of Anglo-Caribbeans from areas of British history. From a feminist stance, Jones & Pay (Ch. 12) criticize male control of the archaeological and museum professions, which restricts the status of women within their ranks, and interprets history in ways that marginalize women's roles.

Several chapters are concerned to a greater or lesser extent with the effects of wars: in Europe in the 1940s, in Nigeria between 1967 and 1970, and today in the Lebanon. Partisan interpretations of history to justify each side's actions can be instanced in Biafra (Nicklin, Ch. 23) and Beirut (Seeden, Ch. 11). But in this century partisanship finds its most ruthless expression in fascism. As Mikołajczyk explains (Ch. 19), in 1939 the Łódź Museum in central Poland became an explicit instrument of pan-German propaganda. The wider political and ideological settings of Nazi interpretations of the Germanic past are discussed by McCann (Ch. 6).

The use of the media to publicize, inform, educate, cajole, and elucidate is another interconnecting topic. In West Africa, according to Nzewunwa (Ch. 14), all the media are under-utilized in the development of the role of archaeology in education. Spriggs (Ch. 9) argues that Hawaiian newspapers have politically crystallized rescue archaeology, attitudes towards burial sites, and the bearing of archaeological discoveries on indigenous traditional beliefs. Besides informing the public and influencing politicians, the press has given a platform to Hawaiian nationalists and forces archaeologists to reconsider their interpretations in the context of contemporary political issues.

Given this array of influences on the constituents and expression of historical knowledge, the reader might wonder whether archaeological interpretation is any more than a recurrent exercise in subjectivity. This issue certainly shaped Ucko's original conception of the World Archaeological Congress:

I wanted to show that a world archaeological approach to archaeology as a 'discipline' revealed how subjective archaeological interpretation has always been . . . Discussion would focus not only on the conscious manipulation of the past for national political ends (as did Smith's Rhodesian regime with Great Zimbabwe or the Nazis with their racist use of archaeology), but also on the way archaeologists themselves have been influenced in their interpretation by the received wisdom of their times. (Ucko 1987, pp. 31–2)

To be sure, many outside influences, emotional as much as intellectual, are bound to affect all interpretation. But these influences do not deprive archaeologists of choice. Certain preconceived attitudes may condition interpretation in a restrictive and negative fashion, but others can have a reverse effect, offering insights of great potential value. It is wrong to regard archaeological interpretation as little more than subjective idiosyncrasy. Interpretation is an active process of mind, in which evidence is tested against current theories. Practice and theory continually interrelate to generate fresh hypotheses.

Thus although hypothetically one interpretation may be as valid as another, their relative validity can be subjected to unlimited testing. Although some archaeologists might argue that subjectivity makes the discipline unstable or even directionless, in my view the co-existence of a wide range of interpretations indicates vitality and signals future growth. The global scope of the subject, of which this book is one indication, enhances this view. The more interpretive options available, the greater the likelihood of correcting bias and eliminating error. Hence it is important, on both philosophical and pragmatic grounds, to emphasize archaeology's links with anthropology and history, since they all draw on a common stock of cultural experiences. This emphasis is particularly relevant to the charge, often reiterated in this book, that archaeology's historical origins and pro-Western roles deprive it of integrity. 'There can be no doubt that your science of archaeology is white organised, white dominated, and draws its values and techniques from a European and Anglo-American culture and devotes much of its time to the study of non-white people,' says the Australian Aborigine, Rosalind Langford. 'As such it has within it a cultural bias which has historically formulated an equation between non-white races and primitiveness' (quoted in Creamer, Ch. 10, p. 133).

It is undeniable that archaeology's biases derive from its Western origins and inherited preconceptions. But is it so constituted as to be incapable of learning from experience to correct them? As this book makes clear, some archaeologists now welcome the challenge of alternative explanations to received wisdoms. The recognition as well as interpretation of archaeological evidence will always be biased and incomplete. There can be no archaeologically achieved final truths or wholly objective interpretations. But to recognize such limitations is not to reduce the subject to a set of mere perceptual constructs. Archaeology is a societal activity that embodies both the residues of its past and its changing attitudes towards that past. We call the residues evidence and the attitudes interpretations. The continuing dialogue between the two enables archaeology, always open to new questions, at the same time always to reveal new knowledge.

Reference

Ucko, P. J. 1987. *Academic freedom and apartheid: the story of the World Archaeological Congress*. London: Duckworth.

THE HERITAGE OF
EUROCENTRICITY

Introduction

Archaeology began by viewing Europeans and Western European civilization as a realm of existence apart from the rest of the world. European artefacts and enterprise, along with Europeans themselves, were understood in terms unlike those of other cultures. Where the two impinged – through conquest or other forms of contact – the interaction was also seen from a profoundly Eurocentric viewpoint. This perspective, enshrined in the 1884 international agreement that made Greenwich the standard prime meridian, still shapes the mental image of most people throughout the world. Asked to sketch the world from memory, 80 per cent of almost 4000 students from 49 countries located Europe at the centre, even when it meant placing their own country at the edge of the map. Europe remains the supposed hub of the world (Saarinen 1988).

In basing their professional behaviour on these views archaeologists have not been unique or even original. They have simply elaborated hypotheses and stereotypes that are widely disseminated within Western thought generally. Long implicated in the furtherance of Western hegemony, the profession is to this day predominantly Western (European and North American) in personnel, resources, and *raisons d'être*. Archaeologists from non-Western backgrounds (e.g. Latin America, the Pacific), also usually trained in Western academic institutions and often dependent on Western sponsors for funding and promotion, have largely absorbed Western academic norms; in consequence, they too have until recently been no less Eurocentric in their approach.

Eurocentric views have taken several forms, with varying impact on archaeological thought and practice. Four clusters of pervasive beliefs merit attention here.

(a) *Eurocentricity as a Christian crusade.* Religious conversion was the first and fiercest rationale that accompanied European explorers and conquerors to the ends of the inhabited world. The Eurocentricity inherent in the Christianizing mission acquired an archaeologically significant context with heathen conversion and/or extirpation. The disparate treatment often accorded to Christian and traditional non-Christian burial practices and relics, and the implications of such discrepant veneration for the politics of the past, are touched on in Chapters 7, 8, and 9.

(b) *Eurocentricity as chauvinism.* Self-approval – the normative, unreflective stance of virtually all peoples – is the most pervasive expression of Eurocentrism embodied in archaeological interpretation. *We* are good, wise, right, beneficent, powerful; *they* are bad, stupid, wrong, evil, impotent. Singled out by self-praise, Europeans also allocate to themselves the lion's share of attention. What we have done in past millennia underscores our manifold superiority; what they have left behind are exotic curiosities, if not unintelligible or disgusting relics of interest only to ethnographers. Allying practice to prejudice, and prejudice to the market, Europeans have purloined or destroyed relics of non-European cultures, subsequently ignoring or denigrating their surviving remnants, unless they could fantasize European origins for them, as at Great Zimbabwe and the Ohio Valley mounds. To such selective preservation and Eurocentric misreadings, archaeologists have often lent their technical skills and expert imprimaturs.

(c) *Eurocentricity as evolutionary superiority.* Accustomed to viewing themselves as the most highly evolved living beings, 19th-century Europeans amplified their divergence from non-Europeans in increasingly genetic terms. For 18th-century savants, Europeans had simply been the most advanced of mankind's several races, but all were thought capable of evolutionary progress. By the late 19th century, non-Europeans were consigned to inherited, ineradicable inferiority. In this view, documented by Gero & Root (Ch. 2) from a century of archaeological stereotypes in the *National Geographic Magazine*, and by Blakey (Ch. 3) and Belgrave (Ch. 5) from stereotypical museum presentations, only Europeans had advanced over time; indeed, only Europeans have *had* a history in any intelligible sense. Incapable of progress, other peoples were seen as permanently stalled at lower levels of culture through which Europeans had evolved millennia before. The 'living proofs' of this static inferiority were such contemporary primitives as the Australian Aborigines, who had survived in a state of savagery from which any efforts to lift them were doomed to failure and further degeneration.

Where Europeans and non-Europeans co-existed in hierarchical societies, as in North America, the Caribbean, and South Africa, the maintenance of Eurocentric hegemony was felt to be both a moral and a political necessity for civilized life. Slavery, lynch law, and apartheid were condoned in defence of European values against regression to African 'savagery' or 'barbarism', of which Haiti served, and continues to serve, as a salutary warning.

Social science led the way in developing and buttressing these views. And archaeological interpretations and presentations at sites and museums, as shown by Blakey (Ch. 3) and Paynter (Ch. 4), have reinforced distinctions that linked Europeans with civilization and spirituality, non-Europeans with all that was implied by brute creation.

(d) *Eurocentricity as The White Man's Burden.* Imperial rulers often felt obliged to ameliorate the lot of the peoples they controlled. Echoing the Christian mission, this view was adumbrated in a framework of secular nationalism. The non-European native was a child requiring parental guidance both for his sake and for theirs, partly for benevolence (European knowledge and statecraft alleviating primitive misery and tyranny) and partly for security and safety (checking volatile primitive passions). Unlike actual children, however, these non-Europeans would never grow up, would always need European tutelage. Even among professed admirers of 'native' tradition, ultimate control by European caretakers remained a *sine qua non* of imperial thought and practice.

This part of the book explores several salient aspects of these Eurocentric themes. Scarre (Ch. 1) and Gero & Root (Ch. 2) describe the profoundly Eurocentric world reflected in popular archaeological publications, both in emphasizing European cultures and sites and in distinguishing 'progressive' Europeans from 'static' and 'backward' other peoples. The superior marketability of European data partly dictates their preponderance in the archaeological atlases surveyed by Scarre. Gero & Root show that Western biases in the *National Geographic* – following an editorial policy that has been remarkably consistent over the past century – both amplify and distort mainstream perspectives, including those of archaeologists themselves. That magazine's prehistoric world is one of brilliant and unique discoveries made by heroic archaeologists, usually male and muscular.

The Eurocentric heritage also embraces racism and fascism. Examining racism in museum presentations of American ethnology, Blakey (Ch. 3) shows how Eurocentric norms shape public exhibits that explicitly differentiate American whites from non-whites, especially Afro-Americans. A similar bias emerges in the relative neglect of the birthplace of W. E. B. DuBois, a black academic and activist, a site whose archaeological history Paynter (Ch. 4) traces. Belgrave (Ch. 5) discusses problems raised, both for newcomer minorities from the Caribbean and for the white British majority, by misinterpretation or neglect of the West Indian heritage in Britain. The long saga of British involvement with Africans as slaves, cheap labour, and generators of capital wealth is viewed from the perspective of descendants of slaves from former British plantation colonies. But the history of these black Britons, now resident in Britain, is ignored alike by the white British and by themselves. In the light of British racial biases that are analogous, though not identical, to those explored by Blakey and Paynter for the United States, this ambivalent heritage urgently requires re-examination.

Finally, McCann (Ch. 6) traces how German archaeologists under Nazi rule revived earlier Eurocentric racist stereotypes, interpreting sites and artefacts accordingly. Among many unanswered questions are how far their racist attitudes pervaded European archaeology generally before 1945, and how far these still persist in Western archaeological preoccupations.

Reference

Saarinen, T. F. 1988. Centering of mental maps of the world, *National Geographic Research* **4**, 112–27.

1 The Western world view in archaeological atlases

CHRIS SCARRE

Recent years have seen the publication of an increasing number of lavishly illustrated archaeological atlases. Some are designed principally for the academic or serious researcher. Many recent atlases, however, are intended for a wider audience. Most of these popular or semi-popular volumes are devoted to particular regions, especially to well-trodden areas with impressive ancient remains, such as Egypt or the classical Mediterranean. Several recent atlases, however, cover the archaeology of the whole world, and these enable us to compare the ways in which different peoples and civilizations of the past are presented to general audiences. The content and nature of six such atlases of world archaeology produced in Britain and France since 1974 provide detailed evidence of the cultural lenses through which European scholars and the public view the prehistoric world.

The perils of geographical imbalance and cultural bias inevitably beset any overview of world archaeology. The high cost of preparing world archaeological atlases exacerbates these problems, for they must appeal to a wide readership if they are to be profitable. Coverage of countries and monuments must also cater to the reasonable expectations of the ordinary reader, even if that means emphasizing certain topics, say, the Nile Valley, more than academics might think suitable.

Although these atlases of world archaeology exhibit considerable variation in scale and approach, their global coverage and popular appeal are characteristic of public interest in archaeology in the 1970s and 1980s. This vogue seems to be linked with the growth of popular tourism; in some atlases individual sites are described almost in the manner of a guidebook. In Britain, the fashion began in 1974 with Jacquetta Hawkes's *Atlas of ancient archaeology*. This consists principally of single-page descriptions of important sites, with plans and line drawings, but no photographs and only a few regional maps. In contrast, David and Ruth Whitehouse's *Archaeological atlas of the world* (1975), intended as a site location reference book, consists entirely of maps and contains no site plans or descriptions. Regional maps, site plans, and photographs, many in colour, illustrate the substantial text of Andrew Sherratt's *Cambridge encyclopedia of archaeology* (1980). Intended for a more popular readership, Keith Branigan's *Atlas of archaeology* includes a number of living reconstructions of ancient buildings as they might originally have appeared, complete with human figures. Like Hawkes's volume, Branigan's is essentially a series of site descriptions. The last two atlases to be considered here, Christine Flon's *World atlas of archaeology* (published in both Britain and France in 1985) and the present writer's *Past worlds: The Times atlas of archaeology* (1988), include lavishly illustrated site descriptions and regional accounts.

Varied though they are, these six works show much about how world archaeology is currently being presented to the Western European public. Geographical balance is the primary difficulty that faces all their authors or editors. None manages to do equal justice to every region. All give Europe the greatest coverage, with the Near East close behind. Major areas such as China and sub-Saharan Africa tend to be marginalized. It is in the space allocated to different parts of the world that the Eurocentricity of these volumes is most immediately apparent. The aim of the present enquiry is to assess how much this Eurocentricity stems from the European world view of the editors and publishers and how much from such practical constraints as the availability of material and the demands of potential markets.

First of all, however, these atlases must be placed in historical perspective. Let me sketch how ideas of a world archaeology have developed in Western Europe over the last four centuries.

The development of world archaeology

The emphasis these atlases give to the European past partly reflects the fact that archaeology is in origin a largely European discipline. Antiquarianism, it is true, has a long history outside Europe as well as within it. An illustrated catalogue of Chinese bronzes dates to AD 1092 (Chang 1981), and a museum of antiquities may have been established by the Babylonian princess Ennigaldi-Nanna at Ur in the 6th century BC (Woolley 1954 [1982]). But the field techniques and analytical procedures of modern archaeology are products of the European tradition, and European colonialism and cultural influence have played a major role in spreading the subject throughout the world.

Surveys of national antiquities published in the 16th and 17th centuries, such as Camden's *Britannia* (1586), may truly be termed archaeological. They reflected the search for identity and nationalist aspirations of the young states of Western Europe, notably Tudor England (Daniel 1975, p. 20).

A second strand of antiquarian interest, based on the study of Greek and Roman remains, emerged in northwestern Europe at about the same time. Writers and painters such as Winckelmann, Chandler, Stuart, and Revett introduced classical architecture and sculpture to large audiences. By the early 19th century educated Western Europeans had come to regard ancient Greece as the root of Western civilization and themselves as its cultural heirs (Tsigakou 1981, p. 48). The appreciation of Greek and Roman art assumed tangible form in the wholesale acquisition of classical antiquities for private collections, which in turn formed the basis of such major museums as the Louvre and the British Museum. Greece was particularly ripe for such spoliations, for the governing Turkish authorities did not oppose, and sometimes facilitated, the export of classical remains by Western collectors (St Clair 1983). Thus Western appropriation of the physical remains of ancient Greece buttressed the claim to the cultural heritage. Similarly in Egypt and the Near East plunder, collecting, and the shipment of antiquities back to Western Europe became standard practices (Daniel 1975, pp. 21–2, 68ff).

Nineteenth-century innovations in field techniques and the progressive replacement of treasure-hunting by controlled excavation and recording led to the birth of modern archaeology in Western Europe. Under European guidance, the new discipline was soon carried far afield to colonies and elsewhere in Africa, India, Australasia, and the Far East. The Indian Archaeological Survey was established under British rule in 1861 (Chakrabarti 1982); the first excavation in Japan was carried out by the American Edward S. Morse at the Omori shell midden in 1877 (Ikawa–Smith 1982); and the Swedish geologist J. Gunnar Andersson's investigations at Yang-shao (Yangshao) and Chou-kou-tien (Zhoukoudien) in 1921 first introduced field archaeology to China (Chang 1981).

However, the motivation and approach of these two types of exotic inquiry significantly differed. The Greek and Roman remains were regarded as part of the cultural heritage of Western civilization; but no European came forward to claim the cultural remains of the exotic territories as part of the Western heritage. On the contrary, the archaeology of the colonial world was invoked to demonstrate the superiority of the supposed mainstream of human cultural development, the tradition that had culminated in white European and North American society. Elsewhere, impressive ancient ruins were seen as evidence of subsequent native cultural degeneration or of the submergence of an earlier European civilization by more barbarous present-day peoples.

European views about the origins of Great Zimbabwe offer a classic instance of such reasoning. Rather than accept the site as the work of the local people, white settlers led by Cecil Rhodes favoured the wildly improbable view that it had been built at the behest of the Phoenicians, or even the Queen of Sheba (Garlake 1973, pp. 15–16). They assumed that black people were fundamentally incapable of civilized effort, and that outsiders must have created these great monuments. Similar theories denigrating the native Indian inhabitants of North America led European settlers to misinterpret archaeological evidence there. Thus the Mound Builders of the Ohio Valley, with their huge earthworks and sophisticated ornaments, were seen as a peaceful and civilized people who had been overrun by the 'savage' ancestors of the present-day Indians (Trigger 1985). By these and similar arguments, European colonists took over the past of native subjects and manipulated it to demonstrate white cultural superiority and also to justify white hegemony. The spread of archaeology under European imperialism was thus bound up with theories of white supremacy, which continued to suffuse archaeological perspectives even after the post-war withdrawal of European suzerainty.

It was the spread of colonial archaeology that first made possible the writing of world prehistory, whose development in the early part of this century Glyn Daniel presents as a consequence of Western discovery:

> These European and Near Eastern beginnings, which so much influence still the balance of prehistory in textbooks and lectures, became transformed into a world prehistory by two main events, first the discovery of the ancient prehistoric civilisations of India, China and America, and secondly by the expansion of Palaeolithic studies all over the Eurafrasian landmass, particularly to South and East Africa, and parts of Asia.   (Daniel 1950, p. 259)

Presenting the story mainly in terms of new discoveries, Daniel implies that world prehistory came into being simply by tacking accounts of Asian, African, and New World development on to the European and Near Eastern core. World archaeology had not yet begun to become anything more than the story of European development in its broader context. 'In those days the task of the antiquary was evidently to carry back the story of his own society, or at any rate of the traditional civilization in which he shared,' said Grahame Clark in his 1959 presidential address to the Prehistoric Society. 'Other people's histories and antiquities were no vital concern of his and might well be left to other peoples' (Clark 1959). The publication two years later of Clark's *World prehistory* marked the first serious attempt to recount cultural development on a world scale that was not unquestioningly Eurocentric. Europe still loomed large – indeed, more than half of the first edition of Clark's volume was devoted to Europe and the Near East – but the danger of regional bias was explicitly recognized and the extensively revised third edition (1977) reflected still more strongly Clark's goal of even-handed treatment. It is against this developing post-war, post-colonial intellectual awareness that the imbalance of recent world atlases of archaeology must be measured.

Geographical imbalance

Western accounts of world archaeology, whether in atlases, encyclopedias, or academic works, vary considerably in the amount of space they devote to different regions and continents.[1] But the general imbalance of our atlases is apparent from a simple page count. Excluding the Palaeolithic (10 per cent worldwide), Europe receives on average some 30 per cent of their total space, and the Near East (including Egypt) a little over 23 per cent. Thus more than half the coverage is devoted to the European cultural heritage and its Near Eastern roots. Other parts of the world – the Far East (10 per cent), the Americas (13.5 per cent), Africa south of the Sahara (5 per cent) and India (4.5 per cent) – are given scanty treatment, while Central Asia and Oceania (each 2.4 per cent) are virtually (in two atlases totally) ignored.

This simple analysis shows how these six publications emphasize European and Near Eastern archaeology and marginalize that of other parts of the world, but does not quantify the degree of imbalance. There is unfortunately no perfect model of balanced geographical treatment with which comparison can be made. An arbitrary yardstick such as absolute geographical size is of limited validity, and merely confirms the impression of European and Near Eastern dominance. Thus Africa receives, on average, only one-sixth the amount of space devoted to Europe, although it is three times as large; the Far East, approximately one and a half times the size of Europe, is given roughly one-third Europe's coverage; and the Americas, four times as large, less than one half.

Even though the richness and importance of the archaeological record of each region cannot be similarly quantified, the overemphasis given to Europe and the Near East is abundantly clear. What are the reasons for it?

Let us first examine the practical considerations underlying the production of these volumes. 'Today there is no region in the world where archaeological work does not exist in some form and with more or less ambitious aims,' writes René Ginouvès (Flon 1985, p. 11). But the extent of archaeological discovery and knowledge varies enormously from country to country, and the variance severely constrains compilers of world archaeologies. The text space a region receives depends heavily on the richness of its archaeological record. This naturally favours areas that have had the most archaeological excavation and research, among which Europe and the Near East are obviously leaders.

The varying accessibility of archaeological work in different parts of the world also affects coverage. It is much easier to obtain information from France, Germany, or the United States than from countries that are politically, culturally, and linguistically more isolated, such as China and Japan. To obtain good-quality photographs and other illustrative materials from such countries is especially difficult, and these atlases necessarily rely heavily on such illustrations. These facts naturally restrict the coverage given to such countries.

Publishers' commercial imperatives furnish a second set of constraints, not only proscriptive but prescriptive, requiring that certain favoured sites or regions be given special treatment. To be profitable, large format full-colour volumes such as *Past worlds: The Times atlas of archaeology* and the *World atlas of archaeology* require a wide circulation, and serious consideration is given to potential markets abroad when page space is allocated. Within Europe, France is a particularly good market for semi-popular works of this kind. Farther afield, the book club readership of the United States and Japan can be highly profitable markets. But few sales are made in sub-Saharan Africa. These differences in market potential inevitably influence the regional balance of at least some world archaeological atlases. For example, the growth of the Japanese market is reflected in the increased space devoted to the archaeology of the Far East in the two most recent atlases.

The emphasis these atlases give to European and Near Eastern archaeology is partly explicable by the amount of fieldwork carried out there, the relative accessibility of the results, and the expectations of potential markets. How much then does the Eurocentric emphasis of these volumes owe to the ideological persuasions of their authors, editors, and publishers? And how conscious are they of the issue? Eurocentricity is perhaps only to be expected in volumes produced in Western Europe. The question is one of intention: what kind of world atlas of archaeology do these writers and publishers aim to produce? Do they really seek a balanced presentation that will do justice to most parts of the world, and fall short of this aim only owing to practical constraints? Or are they unaware, or even pleased, that their coverage is strongly Eurocentric?

This question can be answered only by examining the atlases themselves. Of the six editors, only Jacquetta Hawkes expressly discusses the problem of geographical balance in world coverage. Frankly admitting the imbalances in her volume, she justifies them by the varying richness of the archaeological record:

> There is a vast difference in size between the regions, and in particular it might appear that relative to other continents, Europe has so much more space in the Atlas than on the globe that a strong bias of interest must be manifest. No doubt there would be some shift in balance if the Atlas were being prepared in another place, but I find this more nearly inevitable than it is objectionable. The solid justification is that western and southern Europe is very rich in ancient monuments and has enjoyed generations of men eager to explore, record and conserve them. In other equally favoured regions, such as the Nile and Tigris-Euphrates valleys, Mesoamerica and Peru the space allowance is comparably generous.   (Hawkes 1974, p. 7)

It is encouraging to find the issue discussed at all, but Hawkes does not explain why other areas of the world that are also rich in monuments, for example, China and Polynesia, receive so little coverage; is it perhaps because they are considered less significant? The regional bias inherent in the European world view may well provide the explanation.

The other atlases pass over their Eurocentricity in silence. While page allocation can give no clue to the intentions of authors and publishers, the Eurocentric imbalance cannot be explained away simply as a product of practical constraints; the distorting influence of traditional Eurocentricity must be at work here as well. Yet at the same time these atlases reflect the post-war European trend toward wider world consciousness. One-third of the first (1961) edition of Grahame Clark's *World prehistory* was devoted to Europe; by the third (1977) edition this had fallen to a little over a fifth. The mid-1970s atlases of world archaeology gave Europe some 40 per cent of their total coverage; the atlases of the early 1980s cut this to around a quarter, and the most recent one (1988) to just over 20 per cent. This trend may partly reflect increased archaeological activity and the wealth of important new discoveries outside Europe. It also relates to the increased general awareness of non-European heritages and to their role in the development of human society.

Conclusion

Western society has been globally dominant over the past three centuries. This has enabled Western views of the world to become widely established. At the same time, economic power has aggrandized archaeology in Europe and North America, providing resources for extensive field work both at home and abroad. Coupled with colonialism, archaeology gave Western scholars the initiative in investigating and interpreting the early remains and antiquities of non-Western cultures. The resultant strongly Eurocentric view of human development only began to be re-assessed and modified within the past 30 years. Indeed, as recently as 1965 the distinguished British historian Hugh Trevor-Roper (now Lord Dacre) could summarily dismiss undergraduates' requests to be taught African history:

> Perhaps in the future, there will be some African history to teach. But at the present, there is none, or very little . . . The history of the world, for the last five centuries, *in so far as it has significance*, has been European history. (Trevor-Roper 1965, p. 11; my emphasis)

Trevor-Roper considered unworthy of serious attention what he termed 'the unrewarding gyrations of barbarous tribes in picturesque but irrelevant corners of the globe'.

Some twenty years earlier the archaeologist Gordon Childe, whose political convictions were far removed from Trevor-Roper's, had similarly divided world prehistory into important or relevant and unimportant or irrelevant areas, concentrating on Europe and the Near East and paying little attention to the archaeology of the Americas or his native Australia. The opening chapter of *What happened in history* refers to 'our own [i.e. European] culture' as 'on the main stream', Chinese and Indian civilizations as 'placid and unchanging backwaters', and the civilizations of the Mayas and Incas as virtual dead-ends (Childe 1942, p. 21).

The decline of European hegemony and the growth of overseas tourist travel have changed both academic and popular attitudes toward other regions of the world and their cultural remains. But European world archaeologies still pay undue attention to European prehistory. Practical considerations, market forces, and enduring traditions of archaeological research and discovery in Europe and the Near East continue to dictate the extensive coverage these areas receive. At least in terms of geographical balance, we are still far from achieving a true 'world archaeology'.

Note

1   In the six atlases with which we are here concerned, geographical imbalance is
compounded by differences in chronological range. All begin with the earliest
hominids, but only two continue as far as the Industrial Revolution; the others
stop at various dates between the dawn of the classical world and the 15th or 16th
century AD.

References

Branigan, K. (ed.) 1982. *The atlas of archaeology*. London: Macdonald.

Camden, W. 1586. *Britannia*. London.

Chakrabarti, D. K. 1982. The development of archaeology in the Indian sub-
continent. *World Archaeology* 13, 326–44.

Chang, K. C. 1981. Archaeology and Chinese historiography. *World Archaeology* 13,
156–69.

Childe, V. G. 1942. *What happened in history*. Harmondsworth: Penguin.

Clark, J. G. D. 1959. Perspective in prehistory. *Proceedings of the Prehistoric Society*
25, 1–14.

Clark, J. G. D. 1961. *World prehistory: an outline*. Cambridge: Cambridge University
Press.

Clark, J. G. D. 1977. *World prehistory: in new perspective*. Cambridge: Cambridge
University Press.

Daniel, G. E. 1950. *A hundred years of archaeology*. London: Duckworth.

Daniel, G. E. 1975. *A hundred and fifty years of archaeology*. London: Duckworth.

Flon, C. (ed.) 1985. *The world atlas of archaeology*. London: Mitchell Beazley (English
edition of *Le grand atlas de l'archéologie*. Paris: Universalis, 1985).

Garlake, P. S. 1973. *Great Zimbabwe*. London: Thames & Hudson.

Hawkes, J. (ed.) 1974. *Atlas of ancient archaeology*. London: Heinemann.

Ikawa-Smith, F. 1982. Co-traditions in Japanese archaeology. *World Archaeology* 13,
296–309.

St Clair, W. 1983. *Lord Elgin and the Marbles*, 2nd edn. London: Oxford University
Press.

Scarre, C. (ed.) 1988. *Past worlds: The Times atlas of archaeology*. London: Times
Books.

Sherratt, A. (ed.) 1980. *Cambridge encyclopedia of archaeology*. Cambridge: Cambridge
University Press.

Trevor-Roper, H. 1965. *The rise of Christian Europe*. London: Thames & Hudson.

Trigger, B. G. 1985. The past as power: anthropology and the North American
Indian. In *Who owns the past?* I. McBryde (ed.), 11–40. Melbourne: Oxford
University Press.

Tsigakou, F.-M. 1981. *The rediscovery of Greece*. London: Thames & Hudson.

Whitehouse, D. & R. Whitehouse. 1975. *Archaeological atlas of the world*. London:
Thames & Hudson.

Woolley, L. 1954 (1982). *Ur 'of the Chaldees'* (revised and updated by P. R. S.
Moorey). London: Herbert Press.

2 Public presentations and private concerns: archaeology in the pages of National Geographic

JOAN GERO & DOLORES ROOT

This study attempts to understand how archaeology participates in the formation of the dominant political ideology of America. We start with the
premise that the way in which any group of people charts its past, and what
is valued from that past, are social practices, embedded in a larger logic and
broader set of actions (Gero in press). The prehistoric past, like other aspects
of knowledge, is mediated and constrained by a contemporary social context
which provides an ideology for interpretation. At the same time, interpretations of the past play an active function, a *political* function, in legitimating
the present context, naturalizing the past so that it appears to lead logically to
present social practices and values (Conkey & Spector 1984, Leone 1984). In
this chapter, we inspect how archaeology is presented in the pages of
National Geographic Magazine and how, in this particular context, archaeology is touted, exploited, and capitalized upon to reinforce the dominant
ideology that produced it. Thus, we hope to demonstrate the closeness of fit
between archaeology as a particular means of organizing and presenting the
past and the North American industrialized, capitalist state whose past it so
effectively tells.

National Geographic Magazine, which in 1988 celebrated its hundredth year
of publication, has enjoyed a particularly long history and wide circulation
record in comparison with other popular American magazines. In fact, it is
hardly an exaggeration to say that the sum total of what many Americans
know about archaeology comes directly from its pages, or at least that it has
often served as an introduction to and stimulus for learning more about the
subject. Evidently the version of archaeology it presents is extremely
effective in fixing images and transmitting messages about the past into
American homes. Moreover, the origins, intellectual ancestry, and social
lineage of the *National Geographic Magazine* are all peculiarly American,
advancing the democratic principles on which the USA was founded and
embodying the contradictions inherent in a capitalist class society. How then
do images and accounts of archaeology in the magazine perpetuate the ideological interests and perspectives of American expansionism and capitalism?

The history of *National Geographic Magazine*

Before we delve into the familiar yellow-covered, glossy-paged magazine, some history is essential. The founding of the National Geographic Society in 1888 coincided with a transformed world view. There was a growing American faith in the production and distribution of goods as a primary means of improving the human condition. At the turn of the century, when *National Geographic Magazine* was modernized and assumed its present publication form, America's quest for new frontiers, new markets, and a knowledge of the world expanded in the larger context of a developing capitalist world order. Education, science, and research were promoted as the paths to American progress and to the growth of American power and influence (see Arnove 1980, Cawleti 1968, Harris 1978, Oleson & Voss 1979). The recognition that American progress depended on trained experts, together with an abundance of surplus capital, led to the formation of universities as we know them today and to national organizations of specialists and philanthropic foundations that sponsored scientific research. By the late 19th and early 20th centuries, once-isolated regional learned societies had become centred in an expanding network of national organizations dedicated to the advancement of specialized knowledge. These new organizations were seen as 'fundamental instruments of material and cultural progress' (Oleson & Voss 1979, p. ix). The formation of the National Geographic Society, dedicated to the advancement and dissemination of specialized geographic knowledge, was part of this movement.

National Geographic and the democratic ideal

The National Geographic Society's origins were exclusive and intellectual, growing out of a meeting between a group of genteel avocational scholars and a few celebrated geographers and explorers in January 1888, in the prestigious Cosmos Club in Washington, DC. Gardiner Greene Hubbard, a well-known lawyer and financial underwriter of the newly invented telephone, became the Society's first president; on his death in 1897, Alexander Graham Bell, a distinguished inventor, a founding father of the Society, and Hubbard's son-in-law, assumed the presidency of the Society, along with its then floundering publication. Bell's first step was to hand-pick and personally subsidize a new publications editor, choosing a recent Amherst College graduate and son of a close friend, Gilbert Hovey Grosvenor, who proceeded in 1900 to marry Bell's daughter Elsie May. In 1903, the Hubbard and Bell families presented the society with a permanent facility, Hubbard Memorial Hall, laying the foundations for a tight family venture that rapidly became a popular national institution.

In 1899, in a climate of increasing professionalism and specialization of knowledge, the educational distance between elite scholars and general readers was thought to be unbridgeable; the idea of making geography or any other scholarly pursuit accessible to a general audience was revolutionary in this context. One of Gilbert Hovey Grosvenor's first battles was to convince the Board of Managers that the best way to fulfil the mission of the Society's founding fathers – and the key to the magazine's solvency – was to take geography into the homes of the American people. He reasoned:

Why not transform the Society's magazine from one of cold geographic fact, expressed in hieroglyphic terms which the layman could not understand, into a vehicle for carrying the living, breathing, human interest truth about this great world of ours? Would not that be the greatest agency of all for the diffusion of geographic knowledge? It was my job to change that bright vision into fact. But how to do it? Where to start? . . . Finally I was convinced I had the answer: each [article] was [to be] an accurate, eyewitness, firsthand account. Each contained simple, straightforward writing – writing that sought to make pictures in the reader's mind. (Grosvenor 1957, pp. 23–4)

Along with non-technical language, pictorial illustrations became the hallmark of the *National Geographic* making faraway places and people real and immediate while also humanizing them. The success of the first series of exotic photographs (1903), featuring Filipino women naked from the waist up, quickly confirmed Grosvenor's conviction of the power of pictures to make geography come alive and initiated a long-standing interest on the part of American male readers in the geography of foreign women.

As Grosvenor gained greater control over the magazine, becoming in 1907 its chief executive and a trustee of the Society, he increasingly asserted his populist vision of a magazine for large masses of people: 'We [felt we] should give our members what they wanted, not what some specialist thought they should have' (Grosvenor 1957, p. 34). A wide variety of natural phenomena, including plants and animals, prehistory and exotic peoples, became subjects of *National Geographic* articles and extended the life of the old rubric of 'natural history' into a time when scholars were parcelling it up among their various specialities (Pauly 1979, p. 527).

In the spirit of popularization and entrepreneurship, Grosvenor's second battle involved opening up membership of the National Geographic Society to anyone and everyone regardless of education, occupation, or social status, and using membership subscriptions to sponsor expeditions and underwrite publication costs. No distinctions were to be made between scholars and laymen, nor were there to be special fellows who alone would discuss and decide technical matters: 'Class distinctions of this kind, which are very well in a monarchial country where aristocratic distinctions are recognized . . . [are] somewhat out of place in a republic like the United States, (Bell 1912, pp. 274–5).

At the same time, while assuring the membership that a professional elite did not dominate the Society, Grosvenor made membership appear special and exclusive. Membership was only to be by sponsorship, and if someone did not personally know a member, the Society would provide a list of people living close by who might become sponsors (Grosvenor 1957). In advising Grosvenor on this procedure, Alexander Graham Bell noted in 1904:

> I think therefore the applicant should not be asked to enclose a check in payment of his dues as this suggests OF COURSE he will be elected a member if he sends his money. Such an impression should be avoided as tending to lower the dignity of the Society. (cited in Pauly 1979, p. 529)

Yet the membership has no voice in policy-making nor in the selection of research projects, which are partly funded through annual membership dues.

As recounted by Grosvenor (1936, 1957), it took several difficult years for his ideas of popularizing geography and subscription by membership to win the full support of the Board. By 1910, however, *National Geographic*'s mission of increasing membership subscriptions had become a frequent theme of editorial statements in the magazine that proudly asserted the financial independence of the democratic institution:

> The society has no endowment, nothing coming to it but the membership fees. No millionaire has since come forward to help us out, yet the society today has a great endowment raised by its own efforts . . . We have never had to take off our hats to any multi-millionaire for having endowed the society with a million dollars; we have done it ourselves. (Bell 1912, p. 273)

The reiterated myth of a membership of common people building their own society and responsible for their own fates has undoubtedly contributed to the outstanding success of the National Geographic Society; we trace its growth from 900 members in 1899 to more than 750 000 in 1920, to over a million in 1930, to two million by 1950, with membership topping 10 500 000 in 1981.

From the time of its populist reorganization, then, the National Geographic Society embodied a set of contradictions. On the one hand, we note its obviously elitist and intellectual foundations within a network of inter-related, intermarrying American blue-blood families who are closely aligned with the political and financial interests of the American capitalist establishment. On the other hand, we see in *National Geographic Magazine* the consistent promulgation of an ideology replicating the most sacred ideals of American democracy: participation by the common man on an equal footing in all endeavours, and the image of the rugged individual making it on his own. This was clearly stated in 1938: *National Geographic Magazine* 'helps to open up the highways and by-ways of the world . . . [and] the janitor, plumber and loneliest lighthouse keeper share with kings and scientists the fun of sending an expedition to Peru or an explorer to the South Pole' (Ross

1938, p. 24). Here, congruent with widely shared American values, the ideology of democracy has been used to mask the reality of elite control within the Society. This marked parallelism suggests that the magazine's popularity may depend in part on its ability to replicate American ideology so ingenuously, selling back to its readers what they already believe.

National Geographic and American expansionism

The growth of *National Geographic Magazine* also parallels the growth of American global influence. The turn of the century marks the beginning of economic and political expansionism beyond American continental borders, a strategy promoted in humanistic terms by the magazine. The National Geographic Society recognized that it 'could assist the nation in dealing effectively with its new global responsibilities through research in political and economic geography' (Pauly 1979, p. 521), and undertook to advertise the benefits of colonialism in a format that could be broadly embraced and widely understood. After building up military strength in the late 19th century, the United States moved to forge a confederation of North and South America in the so-called Pan American Union. The Spanish–American War of 1898 yielded new US possessions: the Philippines, Cuba, and Puerto Rico; Latin American countries and customs suddenly became of great interest and concern to Americans (Abramson 1987, p. 57).

National Geographic Magazine monitored territorial acquisitions and reported on geographical areas where changes of power seemed imminent. But it was the coverage of the First World War that really consolidated its readership around a national policy concern: each issue of the early war years summarized the preceding month's military highlights and plotted the combatants' positions; every article in 1917 and 1918 related directly to the war effort. Moreover, the National Geographic Society's maps were placed at the service of the military and when the draft law was passed, the Society offered the use of its stencil machines to help mail out the ten million notices, and its employees volunteered to run the machines. Copies of *National Geographic Magazine* were sent free to all army bases, camps, YMCAs, and to American soldiers fighting in Europe (Abramson 1987, p. 118).

When the war began in 1914, the National Geographic Society had 285 000 members; by the armistice in November 1918, membership had reached 650 000 (Abramson 1987, p. 119). Thereafter, the acquisition of territory, cheap labour, and political influence was inextricably linked to the acquisition of knowledge for American readers, all packaged together in winning smiles and hearty handshakes as *National Geographic* editors travelled the world, acting as self-proclaimed US goodwill ambassadors.

In aligning the interests of the Society with those of the nation, the editors associated themselves (and continue to do so) with the political and military leaders of the nation. Like large corporations and philanthropic foundations with their interlocking directorates, the Society has always invited policy-makers, captains of industry, statesmen, heads of government bureaus, and high-ranking military officials to serve as directors, extending its influence considerably beyond the realm of geographic research into the sphere of national and international policy.[1] For many years, most contributors to *National Geographic Magazine* enjoyed official positions with various departments of the government and included United States presidents and vice-presidents, congressmen, justices of the Supreme Court, and members of the cabinet (Mott 1957, p. 625). It is the President of the United States who bestows the Society's Hubbard Medal for exceptional achievements in geography, although the head of state is obviously not involved in less politically relevant lines of scholarship.

Not only is the Society linked to national policy through its board of directors, but it has served the government in various ways. Its maps and photographs have provided 'a veritable goldmine' of information to the government and to intelligence sections of the armed services (1943, Vol. 83: 277[2]), and articles such as 'Maps for victory: National Geographic Society's charts used in war on land, sea and in the air' (1942, Vol. 81: 667) are typical wartime entries. Many articles assume a strong editorial tone, directly asserting US foreign policy in the framework of geographic concerns, as suggested by such titles as: 'Wards of the United States: notes on what our country is doing for Santo Domingo, Nicaragua, and Haiti' (1916, Vol. 30: 143); 'Germany's dream of world domination' (1918, Vol. 33: 559); 'The Hawaiian Islands: American's strongest outpost for defense – the volcanic and floral wonderland of the world' (1924, Vol. 45: 115); 'New map reveals the progress and wonders of our country' (1933, Vol. 63: 650); 'Your Society aids war effort' (1943, Vol. 83: 277); 'Pacific wards of Uncle Sam' (1948, Vol. 94: 80); and, 'Iraq – where oil and water mix' (1958, Vol. 114: 443).

National Geographic expressly perceives its role as an extension of American diplomacy. During the First World War, Grosvenor wrote, 'The months that lie ahead are pregnant with opportunities for national service and for achievements in the increase and diffusion of geographic knowledge . . . With the sustaining support of each individual member, the Society cannot fail to prove equal to and worthy of these opportunities' (1918, p. 375). In a letter to a friend in 1918 (1957, p. 5), he explicitly stated, 'I intend to use *National Geographic Magazine* to the best of my ability to promote a better understanding between Great Britain and the United States.'

National Geographic, then, is all-American, as American as Mom, apple-pie, and industrial capitalism. Its themes are expansion and discovery, homage to boundless American ability, ambition, and resourcefulness, showing that Americans can go anywhere and do anything, and that strategic resources for some is knowledge for all. Here is geography at the service of society, promoting America, democracy, and internationalism through exploration, expansion, and imperialism:

The clerk in the store or the mechanic in a mill may not consciously engage in any enterprise [of discovery], but when he learns that the government of which he is a part has . . . opened a town on the shores of the North Pacific . . . and has driven a railroad nearly 40 miles inland toward the Arctic Circle on its way to the coal fields of the Matanuska and the gold fields of the Tanana, he has a feeling that he, too, is participating in the making of this new world. (Secretary of the Interior Franklin Lane in *National Geographic Magazine*, 1915, Vol. 28: 590)

National Geographic readers are swept along in the expansionist, imperialist enterprise, given gorgeous pictures and thrilling undertakings in the name of American goodwill, accepting the ideology of a collective good derived from a course of national imperialism. Yet official editorial policy maintained (and maintains) a contradictory neutrality. Clearly formulated the same year as Lane's expansionist pronouncement, it was encapsulated in 'Seven [editorial] principles' (Vol. 28: 318–20):

1 The first principle is absolute accuracy;
2 An abundance of beautiful, instructive and artistic illustrations;
3 Everything printed in the Magazine must have permanent value;
4 All personalities and notes of a trivial character are avoided;
5 Nothing of a partisan or controversial character is printed;
6 Only what is of a kindly nature is printed about any country or people, everything unpleasant or unduly critical being avoided;
7 The contents of each number is planned with a view of being timely.

These same principles were reaffirmed almost verbatim in the magazine in 1936 and again in 1957, during the second half of Gilbert Hovey Grosvenor's 54 years as editor and director, and then again by his son Melville Bell Grosvenor in 1967, ten years after assuming the editorship, and yet again by his grandson, Gilbert M. Grosvenor, the Society's current president, in 1974 and in 1978. The bloodline continuity of leadership underscores the remarkable consistency of editorial policy and publication programme maintained by the magazine throughout its existence. As the principles are repeated, they reiterate a journalistic honour code, insisting on the impartiality of the magazine. It is the disavowed propaganda which we now examine in seeing how archaeology is treated in its pages.

Analysis of archaeology in *National Geographic Magazine*

The archaeological content of *National Geographic Magazine* reveals various ways that archaeology is used to build and promote a nationalist ideology. The information presented here is based on a survey of the distribution of all the magazine's archaeological articles from 1900 to 1985, and on a more intensive systematic sample of archaeology articles that appeared every third year of publication, supplemented by additional volumes when historically needed. In total, more than 50 per cent of the volumes published between 1900 and 1985 were researched. We discuss our findings under three broad categories that delineate ways in which we believe the magazine used archaeological research to further its goals.

The thrill of archaeology

J. O. LaGorce, G. H. Grosvenor's first paid employee and a long-time *National Geographic* editor, recognized the power of glamourized knowledge: 'Behind the term geography is exploration. Behind that is adventure and just over the hill is romance' (Hellman 1943, p. 29). Behind archaeology in the magazine is an intensification of drama that portrays archaeology as a process of exploration and discovery, emphasizing resource extraction and a search for treasure. Archaeology validates the exploration of exotic landscapes in the name of scientific enterprise, using tales of archaeological discovery to heighten knowledge into super-drama, entertaining a popular fascination with the remote and the spectacular while progressive inroads are made to extract the resources of foreign lands. Archaeological sites are overtly cast as reservoirs of enormous riches, as seen in article titles spanning decades of publication:

1912   'Forgotten ruins of Indo-China: the most profusely and richly carved group of buildings in the world' (Vol. 10: 392)
1930   'A new alphabet of the ancients is unearthed: an inconspicuous mound in northern Syria yields archaeological treasures of far reaching significance' (Vol. 58: 477)
1942   'Finding jewels of jade in a Mexican swamp' (Vol. 82: 635)
1955   'Fresh treasures from Egypt's ancient sands' (Vol. 108: 611)
1965   'Drowned galleons yield Spanish gold' (Vol. 127: 1)
1978   'Regal treasures from a Macedonian tomb' (Vol. 154: 55)

The hint of treasure is always gleaming behind the edge of the archaeologists' shovel or trowel, as *National Geographic* systematically blurs the distinction between 'treasures of scientific value' and items that would bring huge prices on the international art and antiquities market.

There is one significant caveat to acquiring archaeological treasure: in contrast with other geoscientific endeavours, archaeology offers rewards of data, artefactual and associational, only to the investigator who arrives *first* at the site. Subsequent scholars who come to study find little but architectural foundations, backdirt piles, and debitage. The difference between actually opening the tomb/raising the galleon/finding the jewels of jade *versus* getting to the site even shortly after the excavations are closed underscores archaeology as the particular kind of all-or-nothing enterprise that demands

Americans be quick and aggressive, daring and venturesome. First-person accounts emphasize the drama of personal risk:

1924 'Discovering the oldest statues in the world! A daring explorer swims thru subterranean river of the Pyrenees and finds rock carvings made 20,000 years ago' (Vol. 46:123)

1933 'Air adventures in Peru: cruising among Andean peaks, pilots and cameraman discover wondrous works of an ancient people' (Vol. 63:81)

1942 'Discovering Alaska's oldest Arctic town: a scientist finds ivory eyed skeletons of a mysterious people and joins modern Eskimoes in dangerous spring whale hunt' (Vol. 82:319)

1953 'Hunting prehistory in Panama jungles' (Vol. 104:271)

The implicit involvement of the magazine in promoting these ventures, and the almost universal domination of American archaeologists at these scenes, dramatically illustrate that these riches are Americans' for the taking, and shows Americans as 'right for the job'.

The appeal of exploration and treasure seeking in the magazine depends heavily on high-quality, close-up photographs that heighten the impact of discovery and convey the immediacy of being at the scene. Photographs, too, abbreviate and intensify action, obviating the textual narration for 'readers' who want a fast and dramatic skim of the material. Although most archaeologists recognize that data collection requires patient planning and the often tedious conducting of fieldwork, the archaeologists pictured in *National Geographic Magazine* exhibit extraordinary hyperactivity. Photographs depict archaeologists crawling, clambering, climbing, scaling, burrowing, swimming, diving, slinging sledgehammers, driving dog teams, and more, all in the direct line of duty. A particularly splashy piece in 1963, 'Relics from the rapids' (Vol. 124: 412–35), illustrates the recovery of historic artefacts from a voyageur canoe dump site; the archaeologists are shown splashing and tumbling in the rapids, holding artefacts above their heads and bobbing through chutes and standing waves, an absurdly improbable dramatization of doing archaeology.

But this ruggedness ties archaeologists to other explorers and exemplifies the bold, competitive spirit that made the United States a world power. Moreover, the explorer-archaeologist in *National Geographic Magazine* equates spatial frontiers with scientific frontiers, as Secretary of the Interior Franklin K. Lane suggested (1915, p. 595): The 'absorbing determination [of the American people] to "go forth and find"' is directly linked to learning 'what this land is, what it will yield to research, and *how it may best be used*' [emphasis ours]. Archaeology argues that to gain new knowledge you have to get to new places, and to get there first you have to be tough.

To dramatize the lengths to which archaeologists will go to acquire knowledge, archaeological photographs in *National Geographic* regularly feature context or overview shots that situate sites in the most remote and challenging locations, surrounded and isolated by jungle or desert, or in the middle of vast spaces without roads or airstrips. Aerial views of Angkor Wat show it standing inviolate in its remote jungle setting (Vol. 161: 554–5); Pueblo Bonito is dwarfed by mesas and buttes stretching in unbroken vastness in all directions (Vol. 162: 555); Mayan caves are photographed from across the river, suggesting one more barrier to their exploration (Vol. 160: 223). Knowledge, again, consists of covering (or uncovering) new ground; greater remoteness means greater knowledge.

National Geographic's coverage of archaeology never dwells on explanations of prehistory or technical aspects of excavation. Rather, the editorial emphasis is on the quest: the quest in which one must be first, and for which one must traverse great distances in order to acquire artefacts, and, above all, the unique artefact. The most frequent photographic image in its articles on archaeology displays the *unique artefact*, torn from its original production and use context and cleared from its recent archaeological matrix. These hand-held or free-standing treasures abound from the earliest to the most recent volumes of the magazine, almost invariably representing whole artefacts (fragments, sherds, flakes, or parts are seldom illustrated). The beauty and costliness of items, the intensity of labour involved in their production, are highlighted; especially common are pieces of jewellery (necklaces, brooches, rings, pins, pendants), elaborately decorated vessels, pots or amphorae, pieces of technological paraphernalia (watches, measuring instruments, tools used in production) – the finest, the first, the biggest, the best. These are the possessions of elite consumers and specialist producers; other classes of material culture from which an archaeologist could construct a typology or derive a seriated sequence are virtually never included. Image after image makes it clear that unique artefacts are the hunted treasure, exaggerating but also distorting the archaeological tendency towards an entirely material representation of the past. Long after the professionals have declared scientific explanation to be the goal of archaeology, *National Geographic Magazine* still promotes an object-centred view of the past.

Humanizing and homogenizing the past

National Geographic also manipulates prehistory and archaeology by investing prehistoric individuals with feelings, personalities, and thoughts, offering 'portraits' of past ways of life, emphasizing first-person narratives of the archaeologist, and juxtaposing photographs of archaeological research with modern natives. Early archaeologists often patronizingly describe the foreign places in which they worked; W. M. Flinders Petrie (1903, p. 359) characterizes Egypt for its 'lawlessness . . . bribery and the suppression of truth'; Hiram Bingham (1915, 1916) notes the prehistoric simplicity of present-day Peruvian primitives. Now increasingly written by staff reporters, articles endeavour to capture professional personalities, scholarly passions, or strong emotions at the time of discovery. In a 1978 article on Minoan and Mycenean civilizations, Dr Heinrich Schliemann and Sir Arthur Evans come alive as 'two brilliant, eccentric and rich men [who] almost single handedly revealed the Bronze Age origins of European civilization to a stunned world' (Vol. 153: 148). Readers are invited to experience the past directly through *National Geographic*'s reporting, as when Mary Leakey projects her emotions upon discovering preserved Pliocene footprints:

> At one point, and you need not be an expert tracker to discover this, the traveler stops, pauses, turns to the left to glance at some possible threat or irregularity, then continues to the north. This motion, so intensely human, transcends time. Three million seven hundred thousand years ago, our remote ancestor – just as you or I – experienced a moment of doubt. (1985, Vol. 168: 592)

Frequently, the past is made more accessible through the lens of contemporary American concepts, categories, and social relations, homogenizing all pasts to look like ours, and marking all prehistoric events along a timeline of the rise of Western civilization. The ruins of Tiahuanacu in Bolivia are compared to Stonehenge and other European dolmens (1927, Vol. 51: 218); the timescale of strata from Russell Cave in Alabama is correlated to great events in Western civilization, including the landing of the Pilgrims in 1620, the birth of Christ, the construction of Egypt's pyramids, etc. (1956, Vol. 110: 542–58). A 1936 article on Mexican archaeology is entitled 'In the empire of the Aztecs: Mexico City is rich in relics by a people who practiced human sacrifice, yet loved flowers, education and art (Vol. 71: 725), as though sacrifice and flowers were incongruous in any terms but our own. Everyday life at Russell Cave, Alabama, is depicted in the following terms:

> Naked children dash hither and yon about the mouth of the cave, playing the boisterous games of youth. As sunset nears, the men return to divide their kill . . . Soon each family gathers around its fire to eat, laugh, and boast of the day's experiences . . . Only the glow of dying embers testifies that humans are here asleep. Generation after generation life goes on . . . (1958, Vol. 113: 430)

Skeletons are given flesh and evaluated accordingly, as in an article on Herculaneum, where the caption beneath an artist's reconstruction reads, 'Beauty more than skin deep . . . in life she was about 35 years old . . . with a lovely face of rare proportion, perfect teeth and a dainty nose' (1984, Vol. 165: 588–9). Again and again, present-day American values are extended into the past, onto the peoples of the past, appropriated by us to represent us in an earlier state.

The photographs of modern natives also humanize archaeological landscapes, again connecting the past with the present. In the 91 archaeology

Figure 2.1   Maya man, used almost as a scale against a sculptured figure from his glorious past. (Carnegie Institution – *National Geographic Magazine*, January 1925, p. 86.)

articles canvassed in our survey, close to one half of the photographs show modern natives of the country in which the site is located. Natives are often pictured associated with excavations, as workmen or labourers, or used for scale or to point out artefacts or site features. Early photographs of workmen usually cast them as children: 'The men's vitality is remarkable, after a hard day's work excavating they will run home singing and dancing' (1930, Vol. 57: 111), and as exotics: 'A neat hand with a dagger is often a neat hand with a pick. The workmen in the Near East cannot always be selected according to European standards of reliability' (ibid.). Since large-scale archaeological projects seem to be *National Geographic*'s preference, photographs characteristically feature hundreds of workmen, necessitating some assurance to readers that scientific methods are still in use. Beneath the photograph of an archaeologist perched on a high tower is the caption: 'Though the 250 native workers, soldiers and prisoners displayed habitual good humor, constant diligence was needed to prevent careless handling of precious ancient objects unearthed' (1933, Vol. 64: 126).

Readers are also bombarded with photographic images of 'the Other', the *non*-American, often manipulated to maximize contrast with American lives and values. Frequently, natives with no apparent connection to the archaeological project are posed either standing or striding in front of ruins, human scales for more than the size of archaeological features – scales, too, for differences in the human condition (Fig. 2.1). We are told explicitly that

Figure 2.2 Europeans in suits and hats at the Theseum, Athens. (Keystone Press
– *National Geographic Magazine*, September 1916, p. 272.)

these modern natives represent the living, breathing descendants of a glorious past, but the photographs reveal a present-day material impoverishment
far below our level of modern American technology. 'Though kingdoms
rise and fall, these Kurdish ferrymen carry on' (1930, Vol. 57: 103). Again
and again, the equation is made between what is unearthed and a native
material culture, between the indigenous technology and what was practised
millennia before, between a modern physiognomy and physical characteristics depicted in antiquity. A contrastive photograph juxtaposes dancing
figures on a painted prehistoric vessel against modern Cretans: 'Across the
gulf of countless generations, the Minoan love of dance still finds expression
in Crete where villagers at Lasithi (right) need little excuse to take to their
feet' (1978, Vol. 153: 146).

The emphasis is always on the changelessness of backward peoples, even in the face of modernization coming from the West; picture the photograph with this caption: 'Bedouins, camels, goats, sheep, a happy desert family camp beside a well at Al Jauf . . . A pipeline, gift of Americans who drilled here for oil, leads to a diesel pump. Black goat-hair tents of nomads date back to Biblical times' (1948, Vol. 93: 492). Rich Clarkson (1986), director of photography for the magazine, tells of hiring a camel train and directing its route in front of Egyptian pyramids for one published cover. The message from *National Geographic* is clear: over time, 'they' have progressed so little (or have even retrogressed), while 'we' have come so far, superseding and by implication surpassing the ancient civilizations which they represent. Are not these innocents *with* their ruins quite '*in ruins*' themselves?

One significant exception to the patterned pairing of ruins and natives can be observed. In pictures of classical Greek and Roman sites, or clearly Eurocentric sites, raggedy Greek or Italian children or backward-looking natives are notably absent. Instead, a highly evolved European type is consistently paired with his architectural origins, standing in suit and top hat at the Temple of Jupiter at Baalbeck (1912, Vol. 23) or in front of the Theseum in Athens (1916, Vol. 30). These images stress the evolutionary progress of Europeans by contrast with the evolutionary arrest of Others (Fig. 2.2). Decade after decade, classical sites of Greece record changing American fashions as tourists are posed with their 'origins' (1963, Vol. 124; 1980, Vol. 157), while non-European sites exhibit the exotic native in timeless garb. This same distinction is reflected in the treatments accorded to jewellery recovered from the African site of Jenne Jeno, modelled by an indigenous African woman, and the jewellery from Herculaneum adorning the neck, arm, and finger of a modern high-fashion blonde model. Supposedly primitive natives are matched with remains from African countries; whites are paired with remains of our own self-declared heritage. In all these comparisons, archaeology becomes a convenient vehicle for examining the exotic 'Other' in relation to ourselves, and for promoting self-congratulatory American well-being. Moreover, by reiterating the primitiveness of peoples from backward lands, and by posing Americans beside the cultural remains they claim as their heritage, the right of Americans to excavate everywhere, to dig anyone's past, is proclaimed and validated.

Selective slants in National Geographic archaeology

Archaeological reporting and imagery in *National Geographic Magazine* are also slanted by systematic geographic, topical, and chronological emphases. Selections are ostensibly guided by Grosvenor's seven sacrosanct editorial principles: topics are to be accurately reported, photogenic, impersonal, of permanent value, non-partisan, non-critical, timely. In fact, the magazine's ideological and nationalistic bent overrides these concerns, distorting archaeological inquiries in various ways.

Throughout the magazine's history, whole continents and subcontinents – Australia, India, China, Southeast Asia and Africa – receive little attention.

Except for the Leakeys' contributions, our sample contains only two archaeological articles on Africa exclusive of Egypt[3] (one treats the Roman site of Carthage). South American archaeology is largely restricted to Hiram Bingham's work at Macchu Picchu; Central American archaeology is almost entirely devoted to the Maya. Preponderant coverage is given to archaeological investigations in the Middle East (23 per cent) and Europe (15 per cent). Within these geographic areas, Middle Eastern archaeology in *National Geographic* focuses on biblical history and other antecedents of Western civilization, while European prehistory emphasizes classical Greek and Roman sites. The magazine gives disproportionate attention to the cultural development of Western civilization and to the origins of the Judaeo-Christian tradition.

In highlighting these aspects of the archaeological record, it is not surprising that the magazine concentrates on the archaeology of state-level societies. To be sure, early seafaring, temple-building, and biblical states leave behind dramatically photogenic monuments, tombs, and artefactual evidence. But such images make the past appear to be like the present and lead the public to believe that the state has always existed and is the norm as well as the most successful form of social organization. This misrepresentation of the past conveniently gives a time-depth to the American state, underwriting a logic that portrays this system of governance as innately human and intrinsic to the human condition.

The archaeology presented is also dominated by the actions and images of males, reiterating the sexual bias that makes exploration and discovery unambiguously man's work in a man's world. Out of the 74 articles in which the gender of the archaeologist could be identified, only two articles feature female archaeologists, with another five recognizing females as co-partners with males. The naked eye of the camera shows the occasional female participant in archaeology in postures of near repose, seated in the laboratory or sometimes in an excavation unit, often merely observing what is being pointed out to her (Gero 1983, 1985) and never engaged in the frenzied physical action characteristic of males doing 'proper' archaeology. Photographs of male and female co-investigators poring over data show the females recording dictated notes or being shown the niceties of artefacts indicated by the males; yet the captions ('Two doctors look for disease in ancient bones from Crete') clarify that both individuals are in charge of the research (Vols 148: 769 & 159: 219). Inevitably, it is the rugged adult male with his virile vitality who best exemplifies the ethic of aggressive American expansionism that is part and parcel of the *National Geographic* image of the archaeological endeavour.

Images of natives in *National Geographic Magazine* serve to humanize and interpret the past well into the present. After 1950, however, they are overshadowed by images of technological prowess in archaeology, emphasizing a new reliance on scientific technology for uncovering the secrets of the human past. Technological innovations appear soon after their earliest applications in archaeological research: radiocarbon dating is reported in

1950; deep-sea diving advances are frequently presented and continually updated after the early 1960s; computer applications to archaeological reconstructions are featured in 1970. In the international arena, *National Geographic* asserts America's technological superiority, which enables, and even guarantees, accurate interpretation of the archaeological record. The primacy given to scientific technology confirms that those nations possessing sophisticated technology must be at the forefront of geographic and archaeological research. Moreover, images of technological prowess underscore these nations' right to extract and to interpret the archaeological resources of the world, thereby legitimizing American expansionism and the accompanying asymmetrical social relations.

Conclusion

For close to one hundred years, *National Geographic* has played an active role in promulgating a nationalist ideology, presenting a view of the past that promotes technological progress as cultural superiority, expansionism as scientific inquiry for the benefit of humankind, and democratic state systems as inevitable and normative outgrowths of the great civilizations of the ancient Western world. Beginning with Gilbert Hovey Grosvenor in 1915, the editors have claimed an unbiased, objective reporting of the facts; in 1978 Gilbert Melville Grosvenor reasserted that the magazine 'will continue to travel the world unencumbered by ideology . . . as the world goes its way, we will record it, accurately and clearly' (Vol. 153: 1). But the articles identified here reverberate with messages that naturalize the material and social conditions of an expanding capitalist society: the past is represented in objects, particularly exquisite objects associated with prehistoric elites; the lavish material conditions enjoyed by Americans are contrasted with those of other times and other peoples; and prehistory is concentrated into those parts of the globe that illuminate the cultural antecedents of Western industrial society.

Photography is *National Geographic*'s principal medium of communication, crucial to its interpretation of archaeology. It is not used, as in archaeological scholarship, to record strata, assemblages, fragments of artefacts, or architectural detail. Instead, it brings into the American living room the exotic 'Other' together with the romance of the undiscovered past, making American expansionism and imperialism picturesque. *National Geographic* graphically illustrates archaeology-as-exploration, turning the discovery of rare resources into high drama and humanistic exchange. Implicitly building on the assertion that photography is precise and accurate, the magazine's photographs guilefully assert the inherent superiority of Euro-American males and the morality of cultural progress. Lessons of power, of national and racial hierarchies, and of the social relations of domination are frozen in the hardware and logic of the photograph (after Haraway 1984–5).

In popularizing archaeology for an American audience, *National Geogra-*

phic distorts archaeological practice by stressing exploration in remote places and the physical demands of field archaeology, overemphasizing the discovery of 'lost' civilizations, opulent artefacts, and bizarre social practices. Its analysis and interpretation of the archaeological record are generally limited to depictions and descriptions of the spectacular remains of prehistory, frequently embellished with characterizations that promote the American mythos. Filtered through a contemporary vision and rationale, *National Geographic*'s telling of the past replicates and extends back in time the values and structures of our dominant ideology: Eurocentrism, nationalism, racism, materialism, sexism, and emphasis on state-level society.

It was the opening premise of this chapter that our constructions of the past are mediated by present social contexts and serve a political function in legitimating our social and material conditions of existence. We have argued that *National Geographic*'s popularization of archaeology advances a nationalist ideology and legitimizes American expansionism abroad. But how much of this promulgation of American ideology stems from *National Geographic*'s popularization of archaeology? And, conversely, how much does the American ideology promulgated by the magazine overlap with the agenda of archaeological scholarship?

North American archaeology and *National Geographic* share a common heritage: both grew out of industrial capitalism and prospered with American imperialism. Archaeology as practised in North America (and Western Europe) is fundamentally a Western science (Hall 1984); its approach to understanding the past is part and parcel of the objectified and commoditized view of the world inherent in the capitalist mode of production. The artefact-laden past portrayed in *National Geographic Magazine* only slightly exaggerates the role of archaeology in Western industrialized society, where units of production and labour and time are measured against a value standardized the whole world over. The material record, the central focus for most archaeological investigations, is often held to represent a distillation of individual, material solutions to problems, such that the past is universally measured in terms of rational utility. The embeddedness of persons and objects in a social world is disjoined by a Western ideology that maintains a natural discontinuity between social and material spheres (Comaroff 1985). It is these commoditized views of the world, integral to scientific archaeology, that are sold to the public by *National Geographic Magazine*.

The past we construct, then, is more than passively conditioned by our political and economic system; it is a direct product of, and an effective vehicle for, that system's ideological messages. As a product of Western logic controlled by Western practice, archaeology reduces the cultural distance between past and present by reifying a commoditized view of the world and the values that support that view. Archaeology as an enterprise legitimizes the hegemony of Western culture and Western imperialism and imposes a congruent view onto the past, one that is ably promoted by successful media such as *National Geographic*.

Acknowledgements

We wish to thank James Faris for lending enthusiasm to the undertaking. The content and images of many *National Geographic* archaeology articles were creatively and systematically researched by Kimberly Grimes. Richard Handler made important contributions to this chapter after a careful, critical reading of an earlier draft, and Stephen Loring's powers of perception produced important insights. In the end, however, we acknowledge full responsibility for the final form our argument has taken.

Notes

1   The Board of Trustees for the National Geographic Society in 1960, for example, included the Director of the National Park Service, the Deputy Administrator of the National Aeronautics and Space Administration, the Director Emeritus of the National Bureau of Standards, the Vice Chief of Staff of the U.S. Air Force, the former Director of the U.S. Coast and Geodetic Survey, and the Secretary of the Smithsonian Institution, as well as the Chairman of the Board of Riggs National Bank, the Honorary Board Chairman of Chesapeake & Potomac Telephone Co., and the Vice President (retired) of the American Telephone and Telegraph Co. This roster of military, economic, and scholarly interests is typical of decades of National Geographic Society Boards of Trustees.

2   Throughout this chapter, all references to volumes without authors are citations from particular issues of *National Geographic Magazine*.

3   Egypt is considered here as part of the Middle East.

References

Abramson, H. S. 1987. *National Geographic: behind America's lens on the world.* New York: Crown.

Arnove, R. (ed.) 1980. *Philanthropy and cultural imperialism.* Boston: G. K. Hall.

Bell, A. G. 1912. History of the magazine. *National Geographic Magazine* 23, 273–4.

Bingham, H. 1915. The story of Machu Picchu: the Peruvian expeditions of the National Geographic Society and Yale University. *National Geographic Magazine* 27, 172–217.

Bingham, H. 1916. Further explorations in the land of the Incas by the National Geographic Society. *National Geographic Magazine* 29, 431–73.

Cawleti, J. G. 1968. America on display: the World's Fairs of 1876, 1893 and 1933. In *The age of industrialism in America: essays in social science and cultural values*, F. C. Jaher (ed.), 317–63. New York: Free Press.

Clarkson, R. 1986. 'Mediocrity and the Golden Age'. The Niels Lauritzen Lecture, presented at the University of South Carolina, Columbia, 22 September.

Comaroff, J. 1985. *Body of power, spirit of resistance.* Chicago: University of Chicago Press.

Conkey, M. W. & J. Spector 1984. Archaeology and the study of gender. In *Advances in archaeological method and theory, Vol. 7*, M. B. Schiffer (ed.), 1–38. New York: Academic Press.

Gero, J. M. 1983. Gender bias in archaeology: a cross-cultural perspective. In *The socio-politics of archaeology*, J. M. Gero, D. M. Lacy & M. L. Blakey (eds), 51–7.

Amherst: University of Massachusetts, Department of Anthropology Research Report No. 23.

Gero, J. M. 1985. Socio-politics of archaeology and the woman-at-home ideology. *American Antiquity* **50**, 342–50.

Gero, J. M. In press. Producing prehistory, controlling the past: the case of the New England Beehives. In *Critical traditions in archaeology*, V. Pinsky & A. Wylie (eds). Cambridge University Press.

Grosvenor, G. 1936. The National Geographic Society and its magazine. *National Geographic Magazine* **69**, 123–64.

Grosvenor, G. 1957. *National Geographic Society and its magazine: a history*. Washington, DC: National Geographic Society.

Hall, M. 1984. The burden of tribalism: the social context of southern African Iron Age studies. *American Antiquity* **49**, 455–67.

Haraway, D. 1984–5. Teddy bear patriarchy: taxidermy in the Garden of Eden, New York City, 1908–1936. *Social Text* **11**, 20–64.

Harris, N. 1978. Museums, merchandising and popular taste: the struggle for influence. In *Material culture and the study of American life*, M. G. Quimby (ed.), 140–74. New York: Norton.

Hellman, G. 1943. Geography unshackled – part I. *New Yorker Magazine*, 25 September, 26–34.

Lane, F. K. 1915. The nation's pride. *National Geographic Magazine* **28**, 589–606.

Leone, M. L. 1984. Interpreting ideology in historical archaeology: using the rules of perspective in the William Roca Garden in Annapolis, Maryland. In *Ideology, power, and prehistory*, D. Miller & C. Tilley (eds), 25–35. Cambridge: Cambridge University Press.

Mott, F. L. 1957. *A history of American magazines, volume IV: 1885–1905.* Cambridge, Mass.: Harvard University Press.

Oleson, A. & J. Voss 1979. Introduction. In *The organization of knowledge in modern America, 1860–1920*, A. Oleson & J. Voss (eds), vii–xxi. Baltimore: Johns Hopkins University Press.

Pauly, P. 1979. 'The world and all that is in it': The National Geographic Society, 1888–1918. *American Quarterly* **31**, 517–32.

Petrie, W. M. Flinders 1903. Excavations at Abydos. *National Geographic Magazine* **14**, 358–9.

Ross, I. 1938. Geography, Inc. *Scribner's Magazine* **103**, 23–7 and ff.

3 American nationality and ethnicity in the depicted past

MICHAEL L. BLAKEY

The archaeological record presents us with an historical stream of social relationships, of causes and effects, and of the norms, limits, consequences, and options of empirical behaviour. Social perspectives are partly formulated by this knowledge, which influences political and social decisions in the here and now. Theological knowledge, though acquired differently, is largely historical and performs a similar function. Both archaeological and theological perspectives on the past help explain behaviour and in so doing influence it.

Archaeology describes a heritage. One's own social past or background, familial, ethnic, and national, constitutes much of who we think we are. Heritage conveys a sense of social worth and meaning. Like lineage, heritage conveys relationships through kinship and tradition. Archaeology creates meaning by interrelating the heritages of associated peoples.

Archaeologists speak for a past that cannot represent itself. Hence developments in archaeological theory and method have changed the human past, often dramatically. As with biological anthropology (Allen 1975, Gould 1981, Blakey 1987) and cultural anthropology (Gough 1968, Willis 1974, Leacock 1978, Drake 1980), archaeological views of the past are reshaped by changing cultural biases. The 'common sense' mentality of the present, popular and scientific alike, tends to conform these various disciplines' understanding of the past with that of the present. Archaeologists' particular values and interests must affect what they consider important in, and how they view, that past. And these interpretations then influence how we view ourselves and others in the present. Thus archaeology helps shape ideological knowledge that has far-reaching political implications (Gero *et al.* 1983).

This chapter examines the biases with which the past is displayed to the public in museum settings. Since a major function of museums and reconstructions is to socialize the public, the ideological content of their archaeological messages has an especially pronounced impact.

Archaeologists are as involved in bias as museologists. In a previous study (Blakey 1983), I considered sociopolitical biases in the production and extraction of evidence. Self-reported research interests among North American and Western European archaeologists have shown a pervasive emphasis on Judaeo-Christian (Middle Eastern) and European heritage (Tax 1975). The relative lack of American interest in African and Asian studies reflects the absence of American colonial involvement on those continents. Western Europeans have expressed far greater concern with African and Asian studies, second only to their interest in the Middle East. Extensive European colonial and neocolonial relations with Africa and Asia substantially account for the preponderance of European research there. Yet despite the salience of the African heritage in the United States, Africa plays little role in the interests of American archaeologists.

As these data suggest, American archaeologists exhibit an ethnic bias that 'whitens' national heritage and identity. If such a bias plays a role in American ideology, it should appear in the public depiction of the past. Indeed, Eurocentrism emerges strikingly in the reconstruction of the Hugo Reid Adobe site (Schuyler 1976), where non-Western elements of heritage were eliminated from public exhibition. The archaeological evidence suggested that Reid had lived in an Amerind-acculturated frontier culture. But at the Reid site the cultural influence of local California Indians was played down, and Reid's home misrepresented as an affluent European's house, uncontaminated by contact with Native Americans. The museum exhibits discussed below similarly include virtually no depictions of the acculturation of whites by non-whites, though both the archaeological and historical record confirm its prevalence. Acculturation by Afro-Americans in the South deeply affected white sociolinguistic development (Wood 1974, Joyner 1984).

Museum exhibits typically depict American national identity as definitively Euro-American. Moreover, white and non-white prehistory and history are exhibited in separate contexts, obscuring the exploitative nature of their relationship. (The particular cultural characteristics emphasized in the depictions of various ethnic groups reflect still other biases.)

At the start, non-whites were entirely omitted from depictions of national heritage and identity. As time went on, Euro-Americans and non-whites appeared in separate or segregated contexts. Today, exhibits increasingly display all groups, stereotypically portrayed, within a common context of national history. These changes reflect increased awareness resulting from the racism–antiracism dialectic. But the ideology of white racial supremacy remains institutionalized in the public delineation of nationalism.

Man, nation, and nature

The National Museums of the Smithsonian Institution are located on the Mall in Washington, DC, between the Capitol building and the Washington Monument, which memorializes the nation's founding father. The Smithsonian museums are among the nation's official symbols.

The National Museum of American History and the National Museum of Natural History depict the pasts of Europeans and of the colonized respectively. Native Americans and Third World peoples are exhibited in

the Natural History museum. Like plants, animals, and geological speci-
mens, they are contextually defined as part of *nature*. By association, Native
Americans become part of that vast wilderness 'tamed' in the name of
'American' (Euro-American) expansion or 'progress'.[1] While the Native
American past has traditionally been displayed in the National Museum of
Natural History, the Euro-American past is exhibited in the National
Museum of *American* History (formerly the Museum of History and Tech-
nology). The latter museum also stresses technological development and
social progress (Meltzer 1982).

Delaware's Island Field (Native American) Museum is in the countryside;
the Delaware State Museum in the state capital, Dover, has no permanent
exhibits devoted either to Afro-Americans or to the native Delmarva
Indians, though both have co-existed with whites throughout Delaware's
history (Weslager 1943, Blakey 1988). In the 1790 census black Dela-
wareans, of whom nearly a third were free farmers, were about 30 per cent
of the population.

Archaeologists, along with museologists, are implicated in the process of
disjunction. The Native/Euro-American distinction, for example, is intui-
tive among many North American archaeologists. Native American society
is often approached from the perspective of natural and cultural ecology,
even in the historical (colonial and national) period when American Indian
history is substantially one of cultural, economic, and political interaction
with Europeans and other Americans. Instead of being viewed in the
context of adjustment to Euro-American expansion and imperialism,
Native American history is cast as pristine articulation between traditional
culture and natural ecology. Treatment of the decimation of the Powhatan
population in post-contact Virginia is representative of the politics of the
ecological emphasis. Natural ecological and demographic factors have been
highlighted by the 'New Archaeology', as opposed to explanations based on
the lethal effects of European invasion (Fitzhugh 1985, pp. 187–92).

'American' history, broadly aligned with international politics and
economics, is seen as motivated by initiative, productivity, and 'a struggle
for freedom'. By contrast, Native Americans are portrayed as having
'struggled for survival' (like fauna) and stood in the way of 'American'
expansion. But of the dire consequences of their failure to adapt (war- and
disease-afflicted contact sites, refugee areas, and reservations) museum representations have little to tell.

Exclusively associated with civilization, technology, and moral, social,
and technological progress, whites alone are portrayed as 'Man'. And these
characteristics came to be stressed as distinctive of humankind in Euro-
American interpretations of the past during the industrial period. White and
non-white remain sharply dichotomized along lines of 'man' and 'nature' in
museum contexts.

Portrayals of modern sapiens in illustrations of hominid phylogeny offer
further evidence of the 'white as man' stereotype. A Western European type

is typically used to represent *Homo sapiens sapiens* (the Smithsonian's 'Tower of Time' poster is a rare and recent exception), although they are much less numerous than, for example, Asians, and a composite, intermediate physiognomy would more accurately reflect modern humanity in toto (see Cobb 1943, pp. 132–3, for the use of an 'American Negro' as a 'Composite Modern' type on the hominid phylogenetic tree).

Consider the meanings conveyed by the spatial layout of evolutionary exhibits at the Natural History Museum. From marine fossils and dinosaurs in the Fossils Hall one enters the Hall of Mammals, at the end of which is an exhibit of hominid evolution, beginning with afarensis and ending with neandertalensis. Ethnographic exhibits follow immediately, first of Africans and then Asians; across the hallway from Asia the North American Indian, Inuit, and Pacific exhibitions converge at a stairway, leading on the next floor to 'Western Civilization'. A powerful evolutionary ranking by race immerses the viewer within an implicitly unilinear phylogenetic framework.

The ethnographic exhibitions do not show societies developing over time; they are static, locked within a timeless ethnographic present. Only the Asian exhibit ends with rudimentary farm mechanization, elevating Asians above other Third World peoples depicted as utterly without industrial development. In Africa even the historical development of chiefdom and state receives little attention. Each region has had diverse cultures, many of which in fact developed simultaneously rather than in the order they are exhibited, and with various kinds and degrees of diffusion among them. That the whole Third World has for centuries been part of a global political and economic system, involving the diffusion of complex developments to every nation and continent, is almost totally neglected in the museum depictions. 'Western [white] Civilization' is the only exception to this static pre-industrial culture. This is the only exhibit that has 'civilization' in its title rather than 'cultures of . . .'. Furthermore, the appropriation of Egypt exclusively within the European context obscures the African and Asian origins of this early civilization.[2] Within unilinear levels of evolution, 'races' are ranked in terms of supposed superiority and inferiority, truly human whites linked with future–progress, dehumanized non-whites with past–extinction.

Non-white exclusion and segregation in museum presentations

Social inequality and conflict commonly accompany exploitative capitalistic production. To legitimate capitalism, production and expansion are emphasized as progressive goals, while their attendant inequality, oppression, and conflict are symbolically submerged. Museum exhibits hide inequality and conflict in a variety of ways that reflect and foster a skewed concept of 'American' identity. North American history is portrayed simply as Euro-

American history; other groups are represented in separate contexts that neglect or conceal the exploitative interface with whites.

Even where ethnic or cultural diversity is acknowledged in the National Museum of American History, social inequality and conflict are obscured. Depicted in that museum's 'Nation of Nations' exhibition along with other American 'ethnics', Afro- and Native Americans share these ethnics' museum role as separate groups, set apart from the general context of evolving 'American' (Euro-American) culture.[3]

For Afro-Americans, museum treatment even as a separate group has been rare. At the Smithsonian prior to 1985, only the Anacostia Neighborhood Museum, which opened in 1967 (distant from the Mall and from national tourism), and the Nation of Nations exhibit, beginning in the 1970s, portrayed Afro-Americans at all. (The State Museums of Delaware have until recently given blacks, unlike Native Americans, no exhibit space.)

Museum neglect is part of a broader pattern of racial prejudice that devalues the importance and neglects the pursuit of Afro-American archaeology. Maroon and free-black sites that reflect resistance to slavery, and black communities that demonstrate the independent initiative of Afro-Americans during and after slavery have received scant attention. Afro-American indignation and initiative are alike excised from the history of the United States.

Only when the histories of Native, Afro- and Euro-Americans are examined within a common framework of political and economic analysis and displayed in a single interactive context can the historical inequalities and inter-group conflicts integral to the American story become comprehensible to museum visitors.

Current trends in museum ethnic presentations

While the more overt forms of racism are being excised from anthropological and historical theory, texts, and museum exhibits, the role of non-white cultures in American history is increasingly being represented in more sophisticated pluralistic contexts. This stems directly from sociopolitical movements of the 1960s rather than from advances in scientific understanding. The outrage expressed by Afro-Americans over biased depictions of history and prehistory attests the power of those symbols and the alienation fostered by their own exclusion from the definitive symbols of 'American' history and the history of civilization (Gough 1968; Paynter, Ch. 4, this volume).

At the Delaware State Museums between 1979 and 1982, five short-term Afro-American exhibits (four on art and music, one on women) were put on; in 1983 another dealt with black involvement in the Civil War. Along with references to abolitionism and the inclusion of black slaves and servants in interpretive programmes at historic sites, these displays represent a significant improvement over the previous exclusion of Afro-Americans from historical representations. They reflect growing black social and political influence in the state since the late 1960s. The black historical record remains highly skewed, however, with undue emphasis on song and art, servitude, the abolitionist movement, and, perhaps, women. The emphasis on the ending of slavery rather than the long-term effects of that system is especially evident. The breadth and richness of Afro-American occupational, religious, educational, and other institutional experiences have yet to be represented.

The topics currently represented reflect a racially slanted Euro-American view of the strengths of Afro-American society. Entertainment, including sport, is the main aspect of Afro-American culture that whites, rather than blacks, generally experience. The emphasis on art confirms the achievements of blacks in a non-threatening role and their stereotypically emotive character. The temporary nature of these exhibits suggests the non-integral significance of Afro-Americans, even thus narrowly depicted. In 1985 there were again no exhibits on Afro-Americans throughout the Delaware museum system.

A broader portrayal of blacks in American history features at the National Museum of American History's 'After the Revolution: Everyday Life in America, 1780–1800' exhibit, which opened in 1985 and depicted blacks, Indians, and whites in its sequence of separate exhibits. The exhibition deals in a balanced way with important Afro-American institutions, including the church. Although this period antedated some of slavery's worst iniquities, the exhibit does deal with it at length. But while slave escape and black freemen are described, the Afro-Indian alliances, so significant for refuge and rebellion, are not (Porter 1932, Willis 1963). Generally the full scope of the interrelationships between these two groups is not shown. Nor is much attention given to organized black militant rebellion, which accelerated after 1800. Afro-American history is bound to be distorted when displayed in selective bits and pieces within a restricted time period.

Yet the Afro-American perspective emerges clearly in 'After the Revolution'. The influence of extensive Afro-American consultation in its design contrasts sharply with the depiction of Afro-Americans (often still termed 'Negro') in the Nation of Nations exhibit. There the history of blacks in entertainment is most prominent, reflecting what whites in a racist society value of Afro-American culture. Louis ('Satchmo') Armstrong's portrait is the largest and most impressive associated with Afro-America. Yet his significance in black history is much greater for Euro-Americans than for Afro-Americans. One of several outstanding jazz innovators, he seems more popular among whites than blacks.

Edward ('Duke') Ellington, whose music embraces the popular and the cerebral, would have made a better choice than Armstrong, for he is held in higher regard by Afro-Americans. That he was not chosen is consistent with the museum's tendency, in line with the bias of white Americans generally, to omit black intellectuality from its depiction of the black experience. As in the Delaware museums, the over-emphasis on black entertainment is dramatic throughout. No black scientists and intellectuals, no black political figures, and no persons of letters appear in this exhibit; yet when I ask Afro-American college students whom they would choose for the place of prominence, they offer a long list of intellectuals and political activists, and never an entertainer, artist, or musician.

Contrasting stereotypes of Euro-Americans and people of colour

Six dichotomies emerge in depictions of Euro-American and non-Euro-American pasts:

Euro-American	Other
national	natural
American	ethnic (or tribal)
technological	artistic
intellectual	emotional
donor	recipient
powerful	passive

The *national–natural* dichotomy applies principally to differences between colonizers and colonized. The *American–ethnic* distinction is applied to Afro-Americans, formerly colonized peoples, and some Euro-Americans only recently emerging from subordinate American social strata. Selective emphasis on *art* and *entertainment* as central to Afro-American culture stresses their *emotional* as opposed to *intellectual* and *technological* role in American life, while the church emphasizes their spirituality. It is not that art and spirituality lack a profoundly important place among Afro-Americans. But the rich and influential tradition of Afro-American literature, exploration, statesmanship, labour, scholarship, invention, and medicine is virtually ignored by white America.[4]

The paucity of material on organized slave rebellion and the ceaseless struggle against racial discrimination serve to characterize blacks as *passive*. To view them as such one must indeed omit the bulk of Afro-American history, a history of a culture honed by struggle. Through such successive omission, the museum fosters passivity in those it socializes.

The bias toward a *donor–recipient* relationship, as exemplified at the Hugo Reid Adobe site, is also associated with passivity and power. Acculturation has no doubt affected colonized and enslaved peoples more than their oppressors. But the influence has operated in both directions, although it is depicted as exclusively one-way.

Similarly, historical simplifications misrepresent Afro- and Native Americans to the point of stereotyping them. Depicting the full range of historical interaction could show how imposition of restricted options has limited the social and economic positions of Afro-Americans and could help to convey the continuing prospects for reciprocal exchanges of ideas and culture. But the museum visitor, influenced by museum depictions that misconceive the past, learns to expect inter-ethnic relationships that are untenable in the present.

Conclusion

In the reverberations of cause and effect, wrote David Hume, there emerges a point 'after which 'tis difficult to distinguish the images and reflections, by reason of their faintness and confusion' (Hume 1739, p. 36). In the depictions of the past discussed above it is often difficult to separate cause from effect, past from present, real from reified. Catering to an ideology shaped by stereotypical Eurocentric notions of identity, such depictions alike create and reflect current biases.

Social and political behaviours are influenced by these notions of self and other, of racial rank and role, and the expectations they engender. As long as Euro-Americans manifest such limited and self-centred understanding, their relations with other Americans will remain incongruous and conflict-ridden. The very meaning of self derives from how we understand and relate to others. The racism that continues to distort Euro-American understanding of others, as exemplified in these museum displays of the nation's history, simultaneously distorts their views of themselves.

Ultimately the reasons for decisions about what will be exhibited are not and probably cannot be objective. Exhibits can, however, become more balanced through plural class and ethnic representation at all levels of archaeological and museological enterprise. The 'After the Revolution' exhibition represents the nascence of balance in museology; elsewhere, the participation of Afro-, Asian, Hispanic, and Native Americans in the practice of archaeology is barely discernible.

Since 1986, criticism of the Smithsonian Institution's Eurocentrism by minority academics, museologists, and members of the United States Congress has become more pronounced. A handful of Afro-American scholars within the Smithsonian Institution had been urging it to become more inclusive ever since the 1960s. Civil rights legislation provided leverage for a more inclusive exhibition and hiring policy under the Smithsonian's new Secretary, an archaeologist who brought with him an awareness of a need for change and openness. Among the results were a mandate for greater ethnic diversity in hiring, the development of outreach programmes for non-Euro-American communities, and several exhibitions.

Long-planned museums of African and Asian art were at length built on the Mall. The appropriate location for exhibiting American Indian history was debated within the American History and Natural History museums. Native Americans pushed for changes in their ethnographic depiction in the Natural History Museum and for the reburial of skeletons. 'From Field to

Factory', an American History Museum exhibition on Afro-American rural–urban migration, gained immediate popularity, and the Smithsonian's Afro-American artefact holdings were catalogued for the first time by one of the few black archaeologists. Afro-Americans and Native Americans from various organizations are now exerting pressure for special museums to represent them on the Mall.

Asian-American pressure has also yielded significant results. A special exhibition on the treatment of Japanese-Americans in American internment camps during the Second World War marked the bicentennial of the United States Constitution in 1987. For once, here was Asian-American history on the Mall, as well as a serious portrayal of the harmful effects caused by the concept of a 'national race' and by American racism. Bernice Johnson Reagon, head of an Afro-American culture programme, aptly expressed the significance of the exhibit:

> When I walked through that exhibition, it was the safest I felt in the Smithsonian since I came. I said to myself, a place that can explore in this way the point at which the Constitution slipped and failed to protect, is exhibiting some real health about its history. (*New York Times*, 17 June 1988, p. B6)

It will require extensive study to evaluate adequately the meanings and effects of these changing depictions of human relations. The segmentation of racial categories mentioned throughout this chapter persists in museum displays and public perceptions. The older exhibits remain little altered despite the recent pressures noted above. Nonetheless, the signs of reform on Washington's Mall are an encouraging reflection of a nation's struggle with its identity.

Acknowledgements

I should thank H. Martin Wobst of the University of Massachusetts–Amherst, and C. Jones and W. Montague Cobb of Howard University for comments on the ideas in this chapter. Dominique C. Wester of the Delaware Bureau of Museum and Historic Sites is appreciated for sharing data on recent exhibits, as is Fath Ruffins of the Smithsonian Institution for information on the 'After the Revolution' exhibition. Patricia Jones-Jackson, Howard University (whose death is sorely felt by her colleagues), contributed data on the acculturation of Euro-Americans. I am grateful to Michael Blake for pointing out the importance of the context of the Mall itself.

Notes

1 The disjunction between 'history' and 'protohistory' by definition removes Native Americans from historical analysis and representation. Given that Native

American oral tradition interacted extensively with European written tradition, that many if not most European settlers and early Euro-Americans were illiterate, and that the history of all these groups was written by an elite literate minority, the protohistoric–historic distinction makes little sense. Moreover, oral history is history no less than written chronicle.

2 The ubiquitous appropriation of ancient Egypt (and the 'origin of civilization') exclusively within the Western heritage, like so many of the most influential ideas, generally goes beyond notice, much less beyond question. Yet Egypt has throughout its entire development been culturally and biologically integrated with many societies on the African continent, most intensively with those along the Nile. Egypt's roots and branches spread also along the rivers of the Middle East, and north to Mediterranean Europe. Egypt was indeed at the centre of *its* world, in which Western Europe was more peripheral than, for example, Ethiopia or Nubia. By whose authority and for what reason has Egypt been extracted from the heritage of its own continent to represent the past of Western Europeans exclusively? For what 'objective' purpose has the 'Western Civilization' exhibition become exclusively the proper context for the depiction of *our* Egyptian roots? It should be clear that the ideology of white supremacy is responsible. Egypt's relationship to our world is conceived and created by *our* sciences of archaeology and history. In some Afro-American and African scholarship, by contrast, Egypt has long been viewed in terms of African heritage (Rogers 1957, Cobb 1981, van Sertima 1983; see also Bernal 1987, pp. 433–7, and the survey of Cheikh Anta Diop's work in van Sertima 1986).

3 'American' and 'ethnic' are widely used euphemisms for 'Anglo-American' or 'white American' and 'everyone else'. Euro-Americans also commonly distinguish 'ethnics' from 'ordinary people'.

4 Afro-Americans invented the traffic light and self-lubricating machinery, made the first American clock and supplied key contributions to the electric light bulb, storable blood plasma, and successful open heart surgery. As Belgrave (Ch. 5, this volume) points out with respect to the Caribbean contribution to Britain's development, black labour was crucial to the material and industrial development of the West.

References

Allen, G. 1975. Genetics, eugenics, and class struggle. *Genetics* **79**, 29–45.

Belgrave, R. 1990. Black people and museums: the Caribbean Heritage Project in Southampton. In *The politics of the past*, P. Gathercole and D. Lowenthal (eds), Ch. 5. London: Unwin Hyman.

Bernal, M. 1987. *Black Athena: the Afroasiatic roots of classical civilization, vol 1. the fabrication of ancient Greece 1785–1985*. New Brunswick, NJ: Rutgers University Press.

Blakey, M. L. 1983. Socio-political bias and ideological production in historical archaeology. In *The socio-politics of archaeology*, J. M. Gero *et al.* (eds). Research Report no. 23. Department of Anthropology, University of Massachusetts, Amherst.

Blakey, M. L. 1987. Skull doctors: intrinsic social and political bias in the history of American physical anthropology, with special reference to the work of Aleš Hrdlička. *Critique of Anthropology* **7**(1), 7–35.

Blakey, M. L. 1988. Social policy, economics, and demographic change in Nanticoke-Moore ethnohistory. *American Journal of Physical Anthropology* **75**, 493–502.

Cobb, W. M. 1943. Education in human biology: an essential for the present and the future. *Journal of Negro History* **28**, 119–55.

Cobb, W. M. 1981. The black American in medicine. *Journal of the National Medical Association* **73**, Supplement, 1190–9.

Drake, St. C. 1980. Anthropology and the black experience. *The Black Scholar* **11**, 2–31.

Fitzhugh, W. W. (ed.) 1985. *Cultures in contact: the European impact on native cultural institutions in eastern North America, AD 1000–1800*. Anthropological Society of Washington Series. Washington, DC: Smithsonian Institution Press.

Gero, J. M., D. M. Lacy & M. L. Blakey (eds) 1983. *The socio-politics of archaeology*. Research Report no. 23. Department of Anthropology, University of Massachusetts, Amherst.

Gough, K. 1968. Anthropology and imperialism. *Monthly Review* **19**(11), 12–17.

Gould, S. J. 1981. *The mismeasure of man*. New York: Norton.

Hume, D. 1739. *A treatise of human nature*. (Reprinted from the original 1968, L. A. Selby-Bigge, ed.) London: Oxford University Press.

Joyner, C. 1984. *Down by the riverside: a South Carolina slave community*. Urbana: University of Illinois Press.

Leacock, E. 1978. Women's status in egalitarian society: implications for social evolution. *Current Anthropology* **19**, 247–75.

Meltzer, D. J. 1982. National museums and the reification of the Jacksonian myth. Paper presented at the 12th Annual Middle Atlantic Archaeological Conference, Rehoboth, Delaware.

Paynter, R. 1990. Afro-Americans in the Massachusetts historical landscape. In *The politics of the past*, P. Gathercole & D. Lowenthal (eds), Ch. 4. London: Unwin Hyman.

Porter, K. W. 1932. Relations between Negroes and Indians within the present limits of the United States. *Journal of Negro History* **17**, 287–367.

Rogers, J. A. 1957. *100 amazing facts about the Negro*. St Petersburg, Fla.: H. M. Rogers.

Schuyler, R. 1976. Images of America: the contribution of historical archaeology to national identity. *Southwestern Lore* **42**, 27–39.

Tax, S. 1975. *Fifth international directory of anthropologists*. Chicago: University of Chicago Press.

van Sertima, I. (ed.) 1983. *Blacks in science: ancient and modern*. London: Transaction Books.

van Sertima, I. 1986. *Great African thinkers, vol. 1: Cheikh Anta Diop*. New Brunswick: Transaction Books.

Weslager, C. A. 1943. *Delaware's forgotten folk: the story of the Moors and Nanticokes*. Philadelphia: University of Pennsylvania Press.

Willis, W. S. 1963. Divide and rule: red, white, and black in the Southeast. *Journal of Negro History* **48**, 157–76.

Willis, W. S. 1974. Skeletons in the anthropological closet. In *Reinventing anthropology*, D. Hymes (ed.), 121–52. New York: Vintage Books.

Wood, P. 1974. *Black majority: Negroes in colonial South Carolina from 1690 through the Stone Rebellion*. New York: Alfred Knopf.

4 Afro-Americans in the Massachusetts historical landscape

ROBERT PAYNTER

Leafing through *New England reflections*, a book of pictures from the late 19th century, one comes upon a familiar but discordant image (Newman 1981, image 19). The picture is of a uniformed police officer of the Victorian era (Fig. 4.1). What is out of place is the fact that the person is an Afro-American. To see an Afro-American in a position of authority that entitles him to use physical force on any citizen regardless of colour, in an era when white Americans regularly brutalized Afro-Americans without legal redress, is astonishing. It is no less odd, at first glance, to find such an image in a book about rural New England. After all, had not Afro-Americans only come North to live in urban ghettos in the 20th century in order to pursue opportunities unavailable to them in the racist South? The answer is in fact no, but persisting contemporary stereotypes would scarcely prepare one to encounter an Afro-American cop in a 19th-century rural New England town.

The unexpected apparition raises two questions: what was the Afro-American presence in the New England landscape and culture, and why is the picture a surprise? The former is a topic of current research among historical archaeologists and other scholars. The latter is generally ignored by an archaeological community that regards itself as constrained by scientific objectivity to remain aloof from the politics of the present.

This chapter examines what light the contemporary historical landscape – those places that today call our attention to the past – throws on the role of Afro-Americans in New England's past. Controversy surrounding the W. E. B. DuBois Boyhood Homesite in Massachusetts, in particular, shows how profoundly politicized our understanding of the past, especially of issues involving race and colour, is bound to be.

The Afro-American experience in Massachusetts

Massachusetts is a major cultural and political hearth of the United States. It is the site of the first permanent English settlement in the non-plantation colonies, of the first vigorous protest against English imperial policies, and of the first mass industrialization in North America. Its statesmen and

Figure 4.1   A black policeman in turn-
of-the-century western Massachusetts.
(Ashfield Historical Society, Ashfield,
Mass.)

scholars led in forging the new nation and in shaping its dominant culture
and ideals.

Afro-Americans were an integral part of this story, having arrived in
Massachusetts Bay Colony as early as 1638. They actively sought their own
freedom, as evidenced by the mid-17th century Afro-American farmer in
Dorchester who purchased slaves to set them free (Bower 1985, p. 5).
During the 17th and 18th centuries Afro-Americans, slave and free, worked

in agriculture, commerce, crafts, and maritime activities, as well as in service, throughout rural and urban Massachusetts (Greene 1942). During the 19th century, Afro-American numbers declined in the industrializing neighbourhood of Boston but increased in maritime areas and the rural interior.

Along with history books and historical novels, lectures, and films, numerous historical sites in Massachusetts inform millions of visitors about the nature of life in the Commonwealth in times past and the formative role of its residents. Museums and sites on the National Register of Historic Places are presently the two major components of Massachusetts' historical landscape. Federal museums include National Parks commemorating battles and other events that precipitated the American Revolution and patterns of life under early industrialization. State Heritage Parks throughout the Commonwealth also commemorate these developments. Privately run outdoor museums re-create such aspects of the past as European colonization, a typical 19th-century rural village, and the utopian lifestyle of the Shakers. To these may be added hundreds of small-town museums and private historic houses.

The National Register of Historic Places includes some 30 000 properties in the state. Such listing, which requires scholarly justification of local, regional, or national significance, helps to protect a property's historical integrity and promotes its inclusion by museums, tourist agencies, and guidebooks as a site to be visited. In sum, museums and historic sites in Massachusetts provide a highly detailed and tangible sense of the local, regional, and national past.

What would one learn about Afro-Americans by visiting such places? At these museums and historic sites one scarcely encounters Afro-Americans (Blakey, Ch. 3, this volume). The overwhelming and erroneous impression conveyed is that Afro-Americans are absent from Massachusetts history.

The Museum of Afro-American History in the African Meeting House in Boston is the state's only major museum devoted to black history. Except for the National Park Service's Black Freedom Trail, calling attention to the history of Afro-Americans in colonial Boston, the Afro-American presence is negligible or non-existent at major outdoor museums. Only a handful of sites on the National Register, probably no more than 30 in the 30 000, commemorate Afro-American history (James Bradley pers. comm. 1987). And very few of these, e.g. the DuBois Homesite, Monroe Trotter's House, Paul Cuffe's House, the aforementioned African Meeting House, and Parting Ways (Deetz 1977), bear directly on Afro-Americans; most, such as the William Lloyd Garrison House and the Elijah Burt House, which sheltered fugitive slaves en route to Canada on the Underground Railroad, commemorate the abolitionist activities of whites.

Few as they are, these Afro-American sites have a public visibility more proportionate to Afro-American participation in the Massachusetts past than do most museums. If the *American heritage guide: great historic places* (Hilowitz & Green 1980) virtually ignores Afro-American history in Massachusetts, the American Association for State and Local History's guide directs particular attention to the Museum of Afro-American History and to Parting Ways (1986, pp. 240–2). Of 119 places in Eastman's *Who lived where* (1983, pp. 21–54) five relate to Afro-Americans: Frederick Douglass, W. E. B. DuBois, Booker T. Washington, James W. Johnson, and Sojourner Truth. But visitors to these places would not come away well informed. The sites associated with Douglass and Truth are unmarked private residences, the Johnson site is an unmarked barn, the Washington site has been razed, and the DuBois site is a cellar in the woods.

Notwithstanding the Museum of Afro-American history, the Black Freedom Trail, and Parting Ways, the advertised historical landscape of Massachusetts is a flawed text. The story it tells is one of a small number of Afro-Americans, most of them in the Boston area, and of whites who generally supported emancipation and helped Afro-Americans gain their freedom. The only figures of national prominence associated with Afro-American history are those whites involved in anti-slavery activities. Afro-Americans are portrayed as relative newcomers who have made no major contribution to that history, and who are now supported by white welfare in their inner-city ghettos.

The story told by this landscape suffers from numerous distortions. The impression given that Afro-Americans were largely absent in the past ignores their presence in virtually every Massachusetts locale and way of life over 350 years.

Afro-Americans of national prominence in Massachusetts include Crispus Attucks, shot in one of the incidents leading up to the Revolution; Prince Hall, who led Boston's Afro-American community during the Revolution and the Commonwealth's abolition of slavery; the poet Phyllis Wheatley; the whaling entrepreneur and crusading reformer Paul Cuffe; and activist philosopher, historian, and scientist W. E. B. DuBois.

The under-representation of Afro-Americans in the Massachusetts historical landscape is symptomatic of a larger neglect of the black presence in the North, a neglect that serves northern misrepresentations of the causes and cures of racism. Although most northern whites today practise racism, they perceive it as wrong and unrelated to their own background. In their view racism was born in the slave plantations of the South, and persisted in the South until the Civil Rights movement of the 1960s; the North's small-scale subsistence farms and industrial cities are seen as having been antithetical to slavery and racism. The modernizing forces of urbanization and the free wage market, long found in the North and only penetrating the South after the Civil War, are seen as dissolving racism. Thus, the way of life of northern whites is assumed to have been the solution to racism, not one source of the problem (Reich 1981, Omi & Winant 1986, pp. 19–20).

The historical landscape of Massachusetts as currently shown presents no challenge to this story. A more accurate delineation of the significant Afro-American rural presence would raise useful questions about the depth and centrality of racism in American culture generally. The demonstration of a tangible Afro-American historical presence would help to show that the North was no less a source of racism than the South and would help to account for its widespread continuance in American society.

The Afro-American presence in the North has received somewhat more attention from historical archaeology than from historical narrative. Black Lucy's Garden (Baker 1978), the African Meeting House (Bower & Rushing 1980), Parting Ways (Deetz 1977), and, in nearby New York, Sandy Ground (Schuyler 1980) and Skunk Hollow (Geismer 1982) all disclose northern Afro-American ways of life. Studies at these sites contribute to an understanding of Afro-American material culture and shed light on the nature of northern racism. Other crucial issues, however, remain little explored by archaeologists.

In what ways, if at all, were Afro-Americans exploited by whites in the North? Was the colour line drawn as it is today, or has it shifted over time? Has the earlier experience of Afro-Americans in the North much continuity with that of today, or did the great 20th-century migration to the North mark a major watershed? Only when such questions have been addressed can we begin properly to understand what it has meant to live in Massachusetts, as either a white or an Afro-American, over the past 350 years.

Theoretical perspectives

Before examining the circumstances and political implications of a specific Afro-American site, the W. E. B. DuBois Boyhood Homesite in Great Barrington, western Massachusetts, I shall briefly outline the theoretical perspectives that guide Afro-American historical archaeology. Three basic perspectives have been salient in recent research: the culturalistic position, the status position, and the race–class position. The culturalistic position is exemplified in Deetz's view (1977, pp. 138–54) that a distinctive Afro-American mindset produced the material culture found in Afro-American sites. That mindset and its associated material culture contrast markedly with those of white culture. For instance, Afro-American buildings reflect basically different spatial units, Afro-American ceramic assemblages reflect lower socioeconomic status or African survivals, Afro-American settlements reflect different gender relationships, and Afro-American 'foodways' are variously distinctive. Though not explicitly discussed, Deetz leaves one with the sense that this Afro-American mindset seems to pass from generation to generation little affected by white culture. White hegemony over Afro-Americans impoverishes the surface features of the Afro-American material assemblage but leaves its essential structure unaltered. Moreover, these different mindsets may contribute to a failure of communication, overt and covert, between members of these groups, thereby providing the basis for deleterious stereotypes.

White and Afro-American mindsets and associated cultures, in this view, arise and evolve owing to spatial and social segregation. Cultural differences stem from geographical isolation. Even if isolation ceases, cultural conservatism continues to maintain different mindsets. Thus owing to segregation, both past and present, whites and Afro-Americans continue to participate in basically different cultures.

A second approach to Afro-American archaeology is the status perspective (e.g. Geismar 1982, Schuyler 1980). Like the culturalistic approach, this emphasizes the differences between white and Afro-American material culture. But in the status perspective, the mechanisms of differentiation stem not from culture but from positioning within a hierarchical society, which gives groups different life chances and experiences. The mechanisms in North American society that distribute these positions are the market and racial prejudice. Racial prejudice distorts market operations, excluding Afro-Americans from upper echelons in the hierarchy. Racial differentiation persists not because of the isolation due to different mindsets, but because mainstream social institutions restrict interracial interactions.

A third position is the race–class perspective exemplified in the work of Otto (1984), Bower (1985), and Ferguson (1985). They argue that racial differentiation is used to justify unequal access to strategic resources. Colour categories may shift, but the colour line persists as a fundamental feature of the political economy.

As with the status approach, the race–class approach sees racism arising out of people's market interactions as slaves or as wage earners and consumers. But, like the culturalist argument, it holds more than the market responsible for distinctive racial ways of life in capitalist society. In particular, it emphasizes how the cultural material of the African past is used to construct viable Afro-American communities in the face of divisive white racism. Racial categories are fundamental to North American society, not simply the result of group isolation or market distortion.

These three positions have their analogues in three social perspectives on racism: the cartel theory, the market theory, and the radical theory (Gordon 1977, Reich 1981). According to the cartel theory, all whites benefit from association with other whites and from excluding Afro-Americans through a variety of mechanisms. The market theory attributes racism to social forms that preceded the institution of the market and views its continuance under the operation of a free market as irrational. The logic of the market will punish racists who ignore labour and sales markets and will eventually dissolve racism. Meanwhile, it persists only owing to the self-perpetuation of a culture of poverty. The radical perspective sees racism as necessary to sustain capitalist growth. Racism helps to divide the work force against itself, thereby enhancing owners' profits.

These perspectives parallel the historical archaeology approaches outlined above. The cartel theory, pitting whites against Afro-Americans, echoes the culturalist model differentiating two mutually isolated cultures. The status perspective and the market model similarly position racial groups in the social hierarchy and share an expectation that the free operation of the market should dissolve racial categories as it has other ethnicities. The race–class and radical views regard race–class interactions as fundamental features of American culture.

Do the material conditions of Afro-Americans approximate to those of whites earning similar incomes? Can persisting differences best be understood as the consequences of durable mindsets? Do rapid capital accumulation and the extraction of profits from a divided labour force exacerbate the divergence between Afro-American and white material conditions? Data on everyday life from historical archaeology can provide fuller insights into the nature and consequences of the colour line than documents alone can yield. But the very questions we pose about the past are influenced by how we view the present. Which questions we choose to ask, as well as the answers we obtain, depend in considerable part on our approach to the politics of racism in the present.

The W. E. B. DuBois Boyhood Homesite: a case study in the politics of historical archaeology

William Edward Burghardt DuBois was one of the most important scholar-activists of the late-19th and early-20th centuries. Born in the western Massachusetts town of Great Barrington in 1868, he died in Ghana in 1963 at the age of 95, his life spanning the history of Afro-America virtually from slavery through Jim Crow to the modern Civil Rights movement (Figs 4.2–4). Living during this period as an Afro-American makes DuBois an important source on American history; he also prominently shaped this history, yet he remains relatively little known.

His intellectual and political accomplishments were numerous. His dissertation, *The suppression of the African slave trade to the United States of America, 1638–1870* (1896), gained the first Ph.D. awarded by Harvard to an Afro-American and was the first publication in Harvard's *Historical Studies*. His *The Philadelphia Negro* (1899) was the first scientific sociology and urban ethnography of Afro-Americans. He helped to initiate the Niagara Movement which set the agenda for the National Association for the Advancement of Colored People, of which DuBois was also a founder. From 1910 to 1934 he was the influential editor of the NAACP's magazine, *The Crisis*. He wrote more than 20 books and hundreds of periodical articles.

Among Afro-Americans, DuBois is best known for his eloquent critique, in *The souls of black folk* (1903), of Booker T. Washington's limited vision of freedom, and for his two autobiographies, written in his 70th and 90th years (DuBois 1940, 1968, Lester 1971). Among many whites, if recognized at all, he is remembered as a Communist agitator hounded by Senator Joseph R. McCarthy for promoting world peace and pan-African unity. Clearly establishing the link between class and race struggles, his intellectual work and political life are set in the tradition of a distinctive and cogent 'black radicalism' (Robinson 1983). Throughout his career, DuBois shaped the American and global crusade against racism.

Figure 4.2 W. E. B. DuBois (back row, extreme left) in the graduating class of the High School, Great Barrington, Massachusetts. (Archives, University of Massachusetts, Amherst.)

Figure 4.3 W. E. B. DuBois (aged 41) when Professor of History and Economics, Atlanta University. (Archives, University of Massachusetts, Amherst.)

Figure 4.4 W. E. B. DuBois and Shirley Graham DuBois visiting what was to become the W. E. B. DuBois Boyhood Homesite. (Photograph from the 1950s.)

The site at which DuBois spent his boyhood and vacations later in life today contains about five acres of woodlot and gravelly field (Fig. 4.4). The house and barn were torn down in the 1950s, and from the main road it is impossible to discern that the lot was once inhabited. In the early 20th century a small parcel was taken out of the middle of the DuBois lot, so that the remainder is U-shaped. A house built in this notch is at present inhabited by a white family. In the 1960s some landscaping work was done on the DuBois lot by Afro-Americans. In the summers of 1983 and 1984, the University of Massachusetts Summer Field School investigated the archaeological and documentary data pertaining to the site.

Politics and archaeology are intimately interwoven at the DuBois site. DuBois's writings promote a political understanding of the colour line, in sharp contrast to the supposedly apolitical theories predominantly used in historical archaeology. Our own excavations show politics to be inextricably implicated in the conduct of archaeological research and the interpretation of its results.

At the most mundane level, the white owner of the small parcel of land in the middle of the DuBois site expressed his relief that my field crew had no Afro-Americans. This mean-spirited personal prejudice seemed to have no consequence for the site, but other Yankee racism had more drastic repercussions.

In 1969, six years after DuBois's death, the site became a National Landmark. This was towards the end of the period of civil rights activism, a year after the assassination of Martin Luther King, Jr, a time when inner cities were in rebellion. The dedication ceremony attracted international dignitaries, including the Ambassador of Ghana, a representative of the People's Republic of China, and such prominent figures of the civil rights movement as Julian Bond, Horace Mann Bond, and Ossie Davis.

The local Great Barrington community was not particularly pleased with the attention given its famous son, nor with the people coming to honour him, nor with DuBois himself. Local veterans' groups tried to block the dedication. The town government questioned the legality of using the site as a park. Physical violence and disruption of the ceremony were threatened, and the dedication took place in the presence of many state and local police. An editorial in the local *Berkshire Courier* (1969) condoned the townspeople's hostile sentiments and, though it counselled against violence at the ceremony, suggested that they take revenge on the site after the dedication.

What for those who admire DuBois amounts to desecration, for the archaeologist also raises a question about the site's integrity. Was the site substantially trashed, making recovery of the lifeways of this Afro-American community impossible? Two summers of fieldwork suggest otherwise. Numerous domestic features, such as two large surface middens, numerous rubbish pits, the house foundations, and the well were uncovered. None show evidence of systematic destruction, either to desecrate the site or to hunt for bottles. I suspect that the vandalism urged by the local paper was not carried out because by 1969 there really was nothing to vandalize, especially no standing structures. It was just a lot in the woods. The threat from the community seems to have passed. The same editorialist who suggested vandalizing the site in 1969 retracted this idea in 1979 in another editorial in the *Berkshire Courier* recognizing DuBois's prominence.

The racial politics of Great Barrington figure less dramatically in DuBois's own writings about the site. His autobiographies sketch Afro-American life and work in the town and the racism that accompanied the segregation of Afro-Americans in service industries. In an essay of 1928 he describes his own house and home lot, along with those of his uncles, as clear havens from the harsher realities of the northern colour line. The DuBois archives contain drawings of his renovation plans, largely unrealized owing to the financial burden of his defence during his prosecution in the McCarthy era.

Other DuBois writings both complicate and clarify our understanding of mixed Afro-American and white involvement in the site. Oral history indicated that after one of DuBois' uncles sold the site in the 1870s, it came into the hands of poor white families. Title research by Richard Gumaer and Nancy Milligan (1984) identified these white families as headed by William Piper and Edward Wooster. Thus it looked as if most of the late 19th-century and early 20th-century material might relate to rural whites, not to rural Afro-Americans such as the DuBois family.

Two DuBois documents dissuade me of this view. At the age of 15 DuBois became the Great Barrington correspondent for New York and Springfield, Massachusetts, newspapers. His reports are basically social notes describing life in Great Barrington. His communication of 14 March 1885 to the *The Freeman* notes that 'last Friday night a surprise party from this place, took a sleigh ride to Sheffield, and visited Mr. William Piper. There were about thirty present, and festivities were continued till an early hour' (Lester 1971, p. 168). So, DuBois is somehow a friend of the Piper family; the Wooster family also appears in these social notes.

The second document is a partial DuBois genealogy, extended by Pomerantz, Gumaer & Paynter (1984). Both Piper and Wooster appear on this genealogy, married to DuBois cousins. Because Great Barrington residents remembered only connections through male lines, they assumed the site had passed out of the DuBois family's hands. DuBois's own writings show that it stayed in the family through female descendants for over a century.

Though family continuity is clear, the racial identities of Piper and Wooster are not yet known. Western Massachusetts had a reputation for abolitionist sentiments, refugee populations, and rest and recreation for social activists. Did this liberalism extend to interracial marriages? If Piper and Wooster were white, does this constitute an exception to general northern apartheid? The DuBois context makes these questions especially cogent. More generally, how did an Afro-American community survive American apartheid in the 19th century in a way that nurtured one of the significant shapers of recent American and world culture? And how might this National Landmark site best serve to empower the Afro-American community today?

Conclusion

History is written by the winners, and the same holds true for the residue of the past left in the historical landscape. Afro-Americans are in general omitted from the facet of contemporary Massachusetts that purports to tell how and where the present came into being. This omission is consistent with northern white misunderstandings of racism as an evil attributed solely to the outmoded production system of southern slavery, now in process of dissolution thanks to the modern, urban-industrial production system of the North. A more complete picture of the historical landscape reveals the presence of Afro-Americans, free and slave, some well-to-do, but most exploited in menial tasks in northern cities and countrysides well before the 20th century. It confirms a racism as endemic to the northern way of life as to the southern.

Racism and its denial by whites make research on Afro-American sites unavoidably political. The practical aspects of archaeology at the DuBois site – reading the documents, arranging fieldwork logistics, preserving the site's integrity, planning its future development – all entangle the present in the production of the past.

It is not only at Afro-American sites that past and present thus commingle. Little in the foregoing distinguishes Afro-American from any other archaeology. The import of numerous sites is revealed in provocative documents, be they the explicitly political writings of a Thomas Jefferson or the political meaning implicit in the mortality statistics of grinders of a cutlery (Eyer & Sterling 1977, Blakey 1985). In an age when most archaeology has become a form of cultural resource management, politics inevitably plays a role in assessing site significance and decisions involving interpretation and conservation. And all archaeology tells people stories about the past, stories that suggest what the present should do about the future. But in Afro-American archaeology it is especially easy to see these issues for what they are, and how contemporary politics impinge upon our understanding of the past.

In studying Afro-American sites, archaeologists should seek a better understanding of the realm of racism and resistance to it. Historical archaeologists have begun to document the material connections on Afro-American sites but still pay too little attention to the implications of racism when studying white sites. Such perspectives can help prepare us for the surprising truths that include an image of an Afro-American policeman in rural, 19th-century Massachusetts.

Acknowledgements

Tom Patterson, Michael Nassaney, Randy McGuire, Patricia Mangan, Dolores Root, and Joan Gero have all helped me to formulate my ideas of scientific objectivity, and Linda Morley my social sensibility. Beth Bower and my colleagues at the University of Massachusetts, especially John Bracey, William Strickland, Arlene Avakian, Linda Seidman, Nancy Muller, and John Kendall, have supported and guided my research into Afro-Americans. Michael Blakey, Homer Meade, and Johnnetta Cole, first-rate scholars and activists in the DuBois tradition, have set standards, challenged my understandings, and sharpened my awareness of socially responsible research.

References

American Association for State and Local History 1986. *A historical guide to the United States.* New York: Norton.
Baker, V. 1978. Historical archeology at Black Lucy's Garden, Andover, Massachusetts. *Papers of the Robert S. Peabody Foundation for Archeology,* Vol. 8.

Berkshire Courier 1969. Keeping cool. 16 October.

Berkshire Courier 1979. Changing attitudes. 18 October.

Blakey, M. L. 1985. Stress, social inequality and culture change. Ph.D. Dissertation, Department of Anthropology, University of Massachusetts, Amherst. University Microfilms International, Ann Arbor, Michigan. No. 13912059.

Blakey, M. L. 1990. American nationality and ethnicity in the depicted past. In *The politics of the past*, P. Gathercole & D. Lowenthal (eds), Ch. 3. London: Unwin Hyman.

Bower, B. 1985. Material culture in Boston: the black experience. Paper presented in symposium on the archeology of domination and resistance, organized by R. Paynter and R. McGuire, Annual Meeting of the Society for Historical Archeology. Boston, Mass.

Bower, B. & B. Rushing 1980. The African Meeting House: the center for the Afro-American community in Boston. In *Archeological perspectives on ethnicity in America*, R. L. Schuyler (ed.), 69–75. Farmingdale, NY: Baywood.

Deetz, J. F. 1977. *In small things forgotten*. New York: Anchor.

DuBois, W. E. B. 1896. The suppression of the African slave trade to the United States of America, 1638–1870. Cambridge, Mass.: *Harvard Historical Studies*, no. 1.

DuBois, W. E. B. 1899. *The Philadelphia Negro*. Philadelphia, Pa.: University of Pennsylvania.

DuBois, W. E. B. 1903. *The souls of black folk*. Chicago: A. C. McClurg.

DuBois, W. E. B. 1928. The house of the black Burghardts. *The Crisis* **35**(4), 133–4.

DuBois, W. E. B. 1940. *Dusk of dawn*. New York: Harcourt, Brace.

DuBois, W. E. B. 1968. *The Autobiography of W. E. B. DuBois*. New York: International Publishers.

Eastman, J. 1983. *Who lived where*. New York: Facts on File Publications.

Eyer, J. & P. Sterling 1977. Stress-related mortality and social organization. *Review of Radical Political Economy* **9**, 1–44.

Ferguson, L. 1985. Struggling with pots in Colonial America. Paper presented in symposium on the archeology of domination and resistance, organized by R. Paynter and R. McGuire, Annual Meeting of the Society for Historical Archeology. Boston, Mass.

Geismar, J. H. 1982. *The archeology of social disintegration in Skunk Hollow*. New York: Academic Press.

Gordon, D. 1977. Race, editor's introduction. In *Problems in political economy*, D. Gordon (ed.) 143–50. Lexington, Mass.: Heath.

Greene, L. 1942. *The Negro in colonial New England, 1620–1776*. New York: Columbia University Press.

Gumaer, D. R. & N. Milligan 1984. Deed chain for the DuBois site. MS on file. Department of Anthropology, University of Massachusetts, Amherst.

Hilowitz, B. & S. E. Green 1980. *An American heritage guide: great historic places*. New York: Simon & Schuster.

Lester, J. (ed.) 1971. *The seventh son: the thought and writings of W. E. B. DuBois, vols I and II*. New York: Random House.

Newman, A. B. 1981. *New England reflections, 1882–1907*. New York: Random House.

Omi, M. & H. Winant 1986. *Racial formation in the United States*. New York: Routledge & Kegan Paul.

Otto, J. S. 1984. *Cannon's Point Plantation, 1794–1860*. New York: Academic Press.

Pomerantz, F., D. R. Gumaer & R. Paynter 1984. The black Burghardts. Exhibit panel prepared for Black History Month celebrations at the State House, Boston, Mass. On file, Department of Anthropology, University of Massachusetts, Amherst.

Reich, M. 1981. *Racial inequality*. Princeton, NJ: Princeton University Press.

Robinson, C. J. 1983. *Black Marxism*. London: Zed.

Schuyler, R. L. 1980. Sandy ground. In *Archeological perspectives on ethnicity in America*, R. L. Schuyler (ed.), 48–59. Farmingdale, NY: Baywood.

5 Black people and museums: the Caribbean Heritage Project in Southampton

RONALD BELGRAVE

Africans, Asians, and their descendants have been resident in Britain for nearly 500 years (Fryer 1984, p. 1), and, in fact, Africans were there before the Anglo-Saxons. Yet anyone roaming through the libraries and museums of Britain could be forgiven for imagining that black people had never lived in Britain in times gone by, or that black people have been resident in Britain in noticeable numbers for only the past 30 years. The rare references to black people, almost without exception, portray them as servants, as slaves, or in some other victim-oriented role.

A parallel situation in the Caribbean is referred to by Brathwaite (1983):

> Growing up in Barbados in the 1930s and 40s, a descendant of slavery, I never heard about it at home, in the street or at school. This conspiracy of silence was compounded by the 'history' we were taught, which began with the 'discovery' of the island by a noble Englishman in the name of King James I, who planted his sword as a cross in the ritual manner at the spot where a plinth now stands; a confused account of Royalists, Roundheads and Redlegs,[1] and the news that these whites, together with labour from Africa, *co-operated* in the production of sugar.

The past few years have seen the establishment of a number of organizations and projects to document and display the history of blacks in Britain. The African Peoples' Historical Monument Foundation UK (Black Cultural Archives),[2] in London, is presently trying to build a museum in Brixton. The closing exhibition of the Labour-controlled Greater London Council,[3] held at the Royal Festival Hall in March 1986, was 'A History of the Black Presence in London'.

Institutions outside London have concentrated on subjects other than history: for example, Birmingham Museums' 1984 exhibition entitled 'Change in the Inner City' was a study of the local Afro-Caribbean community from an arts perspective (Jones 1985). The exhibit was based on interviews with people from various ethnic communities. The researchers found a significant difference between working with Afro-Caribbean communities and with Asians or Europeans. Asians especially were primarily concerned with preserving their traditional cultures and social structures (arts, religions, languages, etc.) Community organization among Afro-Caribbean groups was less coherent, possibly because they had fewer strong religious and cultural agencies with which to identify.

Leicester Museum's 'Indian Arts and Crafts' exhibit, by contrast, sought material that would explain the beliefs and ways of life of Indians living in Leicestershire. Collections were made there as well as in India, focusing on the towns from which emigration to Leicestershire took place (Nicholson 1985). A West Midlands exhibition in 1982, 'West Africa, West Indies, West Midlands', was accompanied by a book produced by the Sandwell Education Authority, showing that the black presence in the West Midlands significantly predated the accepted picture of post war settlement.

Many factors have led to an increasing global emphasis on black history and its documentation. The overwhelming impact of Alex Haley's *Roots*, the efforts of W. E. B. DuBois (Paynter, Ch. 4, this volume) and other pioneering black historians, the reawakened consciousness of the 1960s, and the re-examination of a long tradition of folk and oral history have led many people to initiate quests for lost or forgotten chapters of family, institutional, and organizational histories.

Research in North America has moved beyond the traditional accounts of European explorers and the traditional date of 1619 when a Dutch frigate deposited 20 Africans at Jamestown, Virginia, to investigate evidence from ancient Olmec society suggesting that Africans may have preceded Europeans to the shores of America. While these investigations are not essential to a critique of the current status of black Americans, they do offer an opportunity to place their birthright in a new perspective (Battle 1980).

Black-oriented and black-run activities of this nature in Britain have always lagged behind the United States, owing to blacks' proportionally smaller numbers, to a history of less vicious racism by whites, and to a more extensive dispersion of the black community. But black people in Britain are now beginning to move forward. Although the Black Cultural Archives in London is the only organization currently looking at the black history of Britain on a national level, groups in such places as Southampton, Birmingham, Leicester, and Bradford are concentrating on their own resident black communities' perceptions, lifestyles, and heritage, thus contributing to an overall reappraisal and a new appreciation of black history in Britain.

Over the past decade or two the importance of oral history for the collection of historical information has become more and more widely recognized. Its application to black communities in Britain began in 1983, at the instigation of the Keeper of Museums' Education, with the establishment of Southampton's Caribbean oral history project.[4] Publicly billed as the 'Caribbean Connection', the Caribbean Heritage Project aimed to study Southampton's links with the Caribbean from the present day back as far as documents would allow (approximately 1590). It was inspired by the research of the city's Children's Librarian, who had for some time been examining papers at the City Record Office to document Southampton residents who owned property, estates, and slaves in the Caribbean. These included nearly every Southampton member of Parliament from 1747 until 1834 (when slavery in the British Caribbean was abolished) and afterwards.

During the reign of Elizabeth I, British involvement in the slave trade was officially approved and sponsored. By the late 16th century black servants were fashionable in Britain; many were employed at the court and by wealthy aristocrats. In 1592 both the mayor of Southampton and the member of Parliament for Southampton owned black servants. In 1596 the government concluded that blacks were so numerous that they were taking jobs away from whites, and Elizabeth I therefore issued a proclamation to have all black people deported. But it had become chic among aristocrats to own blacks, and the subsidy rolls of 1598–1600 show that at least ten families in Southampton still held black servants.

During the 18th century many black people lived in Southampton, although it is difficult to discover whether they were born there or came from Africa or the Caribbean. Several Southampton merchants either owned property in the Caribbean or invested money there. In 1747 Southampton elected Anthony Swymmer, son of a merchant in Jamaica, as its member of Parliament.

How many black, let alone Caribbean, people there now are in Southampton is difficult to estimate. (In Britain the term 'black' is used to denote people of African, Caribbean, and Asian origin.) The criterion used in the 1981 national census was 'place of birth of the head of household', which means that the census statistics acknowledge neither the ethnicity of those black people born in the United Kingdom nor of those households whose head was born in the United Kingdom. Of the city's population of 205 000, the Southampton Council for Racial Equality estimated the total number of blacks at about 15 000 (7.3 per cent) and the Caribbean community at about 3000 (1.5 per cent) (SCRE 1985); most of the latter have come from Jamaica and St Vincent, with others from Barbados, Trinidad, and Guyana. Approximately half of the black population lives in the inner city area (St Lukes and Bargate wards), while the Caribbean community is concentrated in the inner city's Northam, Newtown, and Nicholstown districts.

Although oral history has long been established as a research strategy within many national museums, similar activities within provincial museums have largely been confined to relatively small-scale research conducted by curatorial staff to provide information in support of already established collections. Until 1983 Southampton Museums were no exception and, apart from some individual and university-course projects, little oral research had been attempted locally. Moreover, the Caribbean community was generally neglected even by conventional collections.

The establishment of the Museums' Education Service project made it possible to set up an archive of transcribed tapes for use both by the community from which it originated and by others. Teachers' packs and portable exhibitions were devised to enable children in Southampton's primary and secondary schools to appreciate the Caribbean community as a different but equal part of Southampton society, one with trans-Atlantic links.

The project's essential aim is to counteract the paucity of historical documentation and the under-representation of black people in museums, as in the media, drama, science, and the education system in general. What little attention black people do receive, moreover, tends to be negative, taking the form of media furore over crime and riots and of history books dwelling on chattel slavery. To break down negative stereotypes, these fundamentally patronizing images need to be counterbalanced through the presentation of all aspects of black community life.

The researchers largely succeeded in triggering off a flow of life history by asking such questions as:

> When did you first come to England?
> What were your first impressions of England?
> What was life like back in the West Indies?
> What sort of employment have you had?

Many of those interviewed commented on the irony of black servitude in a 'British' context:

> Our foreparents had been slaves, yet we were made, at certain times, to stand in a congregation and sing 'Rule Britannia' . . . they were making us praise our slavery for we were singing 'Britons shall never be slaves' – yet we were slaves ourselves.

> Just let [slavery] stay in the history books . . . because some of our countrymen would really be annoyed and seek revenge.

People react realistically yet also with affectionate nostalgia:

> I started school at the age of 7 . . . we used to learn by recitation. We had inspectors come in once a year into the classroom to inspect and you had to know your lesson.

> Family relationships in the West Indies is quite close, we were brought up to respect our parents.

> Over there, living in the country, you don't worry about running to the doctor. The doctor might be too far away . . . so you just find yourself a nice tastable herb and boil it and have a drink and it is surprising, you feel better afterwards.

Large-scale settlement in Britain, beginning with the Second World War, brought to Southampton's Caribbean-born people an awareness of the racial assumptions embedded in British identity:

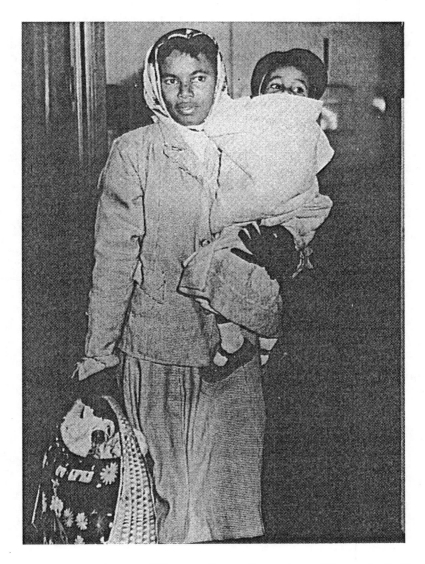

Figure 5.1   The second diaspora (the first being from Africa to the Caribbean): the S.S. *Ascania* arrives at Southampton.

When I went to war I was asked, 'What's your nationality?' . . . I said 'British' and they didn't like that. They said 'Say West Indian'.

During the war 7000 West Indians enlisted in the Royal Air Force and were stationed in Britian, and 345 'Overseas Volunteers' were recruited from the Caribbean as skilled craftsmen in British factories (Ruffell 1984, pp. 57–8). After the war some stayed, but most returned home. Finding it difficult to get employment in the Caribbean, many former service personnel and volunteers then came back to Britain.

Others came, as before, to further their education. But West Indians came on a massive scale in the late 1950s and early 1960s in response to recruitment drives for skilled labour in London Transport, British Rail, the National Health Service, and British hotels and restaurants (Fig. 5.1). These West Indians saw England as the 'Motherland', a land of opportunity, a place where the streets were paved with gold. But many settlers soon came to realize that England had little love for its 'children':

I expected to be treated the way I was treated in Jamaica, as a person, not as a second-class citizen.

So from a child we heard about England, we goes to school, we sang about Great Britain and that sort of thing. We were proud of England but when you got here it was different.

A place where people kept themselves to themselves.

It was then that I realized that although the English were polite, it was a different matter when it actually came to living with them . . . as soon as they opened the door and there was a black face, that door was slammed.

Despite disappointments, many made the best of things:

But then you get used to the weather, make new friends, get a job and slowly one day this has become your home.

Social and religious institutions sheltered West Indians in their identity. Southampton's West Indian Association opened a community centre, built from the remains of a church, in 1976, with a bar, dance floor, offices, and meeting rooms:

What's important is having somewhere to go where members of the community can feel at home.

Churches functioned both as community focal points and as magnets attracting outsiders:

Our church is not just for West Indians, it is a church of God and the door is open to who-so-ever-will. It's nice to see other people coming in.

But prejudicial stereotypes endured, and racial discrimination left the children of immigrants even more isolated and disadvantaged than their parents. From the start, they were seen as different:

My daughter was born here . . . when I leave the pram outside the shop I come out and the crowd are all over her.

When telling children at school that I was from Barbados, I was often asked 'What part of Africa is that?' or 'Did you live in a mud hut?'

It was the same in the playground . . . continuous questions . . . 'Why are you different?'

Growing up in Britain, these young people feel remote from their Caribbean roots, yet at the same time excluded from British society. Being neither one nor the other, they experience intense ambivalence and loneliness and finally are encapsulated within a third and distinct culture:

Because the child is not fully West Indian, but sort of also British, there's a conflict.

You can speak English in a formal place, but keep your own patois . . . when you're among friends.

She came home crying and said to me 'Oh, mummy, why did you ever let me be born in this country'.

Me and my sisters used to say to each other 'Did you hear what they said today? They said that we're not West Indian and we're not British', but all three of us used to say 'well we're together'.

These quotations from our interviews amply substantiate the Swann report (1985) on the education of black children, which recognized the urgent need for anti-racist strategies in textbooks, the curricula, and the classroom generally.

Both in collecting data and in disseminating the findings of the project, numerous difficulties arose. These difficulties bore on points of selectivity, resources, and bias that are instructive in themselves, further illustrating the racial and social prejudices that informed the substantive data of the project.

One set of problems stemmed from the fact that one or both of the interviewers, and for some time the only one, was white and lacked any previous links with the community. Partly as a consequence, the number of interviews carried out was significantly fewer than expected. The impression created among the Caribbean community was that not enough care and respect was being given the project, and some concern was expressed over the white researcher's dedication to the project.

The use of white researchers who did not know who to talk to and had to rely on community leaders to arrange interviews also led to a sense of distance between interviewee and interviewer that adversely affected results. And white researchers, as members of a majority community perceived to be racially discriminatory, found interviewees wary of being open with information.

Prior local experience with the media caused other problems. People in the community are all too familiar with periodic media attention of a sensational nature that leads to no beneficial results. Drawing no distinction between the media and the museum as representatives of the white establishment, they were often reluctant to step forward to be interviewed. Lack of familiarity with Caribbean creole languages made it difficult for interviewers to comprehend, interpret, and present information received, and they committed many errors. The decision reached with community leaders to publicly display interview extracts in English rather than the Caribbean patois in which interviewees frequently spoke was seen by some as a misguided and unnecessary attempt to anglicize the project.

The skewed choice of informants posed other problems. Except for a passing reference to the indigenous Amerindians, the project dealt wholly with the African aspect of the Caribbean. No mention was made of East Indian or Chinese aspects of West Indian life, either in the Caribbean or in Southampton. Thus many people whose origins were Caribbean felt excluded.

Stereotypical images of the Caribbean employed to publicize the project raised problems, especially among younger members of Southampton's Caribbean community. One such image was the use of palm trees on the poster advertising the exhibition. Having lived most of their lives in Britain, without the 'Yes Ma'am, No Sir' attitude which had been drilled into their elders, and with little evidence of colonialism around them, young people are less prepared to accept what they perceive as patronizing images such as palm trees and sunny beaches. The use of the term 'West Indies' was itself problematic. Caribbean people increasingly tend to condemn the term as an unfortunate result of Christopher Columbus's error, which culminated in the people of a whole hemisphere being misnamed 'Indians'.

Disseminating the project's findings involved still other problems. An exhibition mounted in February 1984 at Southampton's well-known Bargate Museum, and again on several occasions in 1986, displayed vocal and textual extracts from the interviews, pictures, and such fruits of historical research as records of estate and slave ownership by Southampton residents. It received some media publicity and prompted several viewers to come forward with more pictures, memorabilia, and a desire to be interviewed. But the structure of the building restricted access to the exhibit for the infirm and the elderly, the community's prime potential respondents.

Community interest in the project's archive of transcribed tapes also lagged, owing to the lack of a congenial atmosphere (brought about by the sparsity of positive and sustained media interest, and by the insecurity of sporadic institutional concern). Use seemed to be confined mainly to those already involved in traditional areas of research, and archives of significant local import were unread by local people because they were unpublicized or difficult of access.

Media coverage was disappointingly slim. BBC Radio Solent produced two programmes, one a general description of the project combined with a commentary on Southampton's Caribbean community, the other a discussion of interviews carried out by Radio Solent to gauge the Caribbean community's attitudes towards Southampton Caribbean Focus. In addition, the *Southern Evening Echo* (1986) used the archives in connection with the death of a prominent member of the Caribbean community. Most of the other local media were initially probably unaware of, or uninterested in, the project's role as a media resource. BBC Radio Solent and the *Southern Evening Echo* apart, most of the media responded in a distinctly cursory manner to approaches from Southampton Caribbean Focus.[5]

A general problem for all museums is the sense of alienation experienced by black people. This reflects the lack of representation of black history within museums as well as within the education system. The oral history project made an attempt to break through that alienation and met with some success. The fact that Caribbean people took part in the project and that the results were exhibited for them and the general public was a major step in opening up the museum to a wider audience. It helped to pave the way for a subsequent project on 'Chapel and Northam 1900–45', which focused on two staunchly working-class areas in Southampton. The huge success of this project confirmed both the relevance and the popularity of oral history research with disadvantaged groups. Attempts are being made to formalize a policy at the Southampton Museums that is positively biased towards the documentation of the lives of groups thus far inadequately represented – black people, women, and the working class.

The museum profession in Britain is increasingly aware of its duty to present the story and attract the interest of the whole population, including minority groups. In order to encourage black communities to feel linked to the British heritage (which their ancestors' labour helped to create), history must be rethought and displayed to include black contributions to literature, science, and music and to provide an awareness of Britain's indebtedness to black people in terms of wealth, labour, and civilization. White historians and archaeologists must totally abandon the old notion that 'nothing of value in the history of humankind is black'.

In thus redressing the balance, however, care must be taken not to set black history apart as a special or isolated aspect of life. The black experience needs to be incorporated within the general record of society. Projects dealing with black communities still tend to be looked upon as singular and exotic, as evidenced in this local commentary commending the project's efforts:

> Without projects like this, many fascinating chapters of Southampton's varied history could easily be lost. However, thanks to the foresight of Southampton Museums, future historians have a treasure trove waiting in store for them.   (Ruffell 1984, p. 57)

Southampton's Caribbean Heritage Project has been a great learning process for the museum itself. But the museum's commitment to researching, recording, and revealing the history of black people is of no avail without the allocation of funds on a regular basis from mainstream budgets, both for research and for the provision of prominent display space. Episodic and fleeting attention to the Caribbean community, which is all that most museums and other institutions have thus far vouchsafed, leaves neither the Caribbean community nor British society as a whole with a permanent, public, and positive awareness of the presence and role of black people in the dominant white culture.

Notes

1   'Redleg' is the term used in Barbados for 'poor white' descendants of 17th-century Europeans who lost their lands and were sent to become peasants in the windward district of the island (Sheppard 1977).
2   The Black Cultural Archives were set up in 1982 through the inspiration of Queen Mother Moore (founder of the African Peoples' Historical Monument Foundation in the United States). The site identified for the proposed museum complex is significant and appropriate, since in the late 1940s this area housed pioneer black settlers who were not allowed by the 'colour bar' to live anywhere else in Brixton.
3   Abolished in 1986 along with the other metropolitan county councils by the Conservative-controlled central government, the GLC, under the leadership of Ken Livingstone, took much initiative and gave much assistance in researching and promoting black history and culture.
4   The project was partly funded by the government's Manpower Services Commission and housed, directed, and otherwise paid for by Southampton City Council's Museums' Education Service. Two researchers devoted a full year to the project, from April 1983 to March 1984, in conjunction with two other oral history projects, one on Southampton's docks, the other on women's work in the First World War. Whenever possible, interviews were carried out in the interviewee's home. BBC Radio Solent helped with training in recording techniques. Pictures were taken of interviewees, and other pictorial evidence was gathered from local newspapers and private collections. Local newspapers, especially the *Southern Evening Echo*, were researched for data on large-scale Caribbean settlement from the 1940s to the 1960s, and the City Records Office searched for evidence about the employment of black people in Southampton households.

Further work on the project was carried out by the author on a part-time basis from July 1985, and by another employee from March 1986.
5 Southampton Caribbean Focus was in 1986 the local arm of a national project which aimed to educate Caribbean and non-Caribbean people about the broad, complex, and historical backgrounds of the societies in the Caribbean.

References

Battle, T. C. 1980. Research centres document the black experience. *History News* **36**(2), 8–11.

Brathwaite, E. K. 1983. Review of Craton, M.: *Testing the chains: resistance to slavery in the British West Indies. The Times Literary Supplement* **4212**, p. 1425.

Fryer, P. 1984. *Staying power: the history of black people in Britain*. London: Pluto Press.

Jones, J. P. 1985. Responding to a multi-cultural society: which Africa, which arts? *Museum Ethnographers Group Newsletter* **19**, 15–25.

Nicholson, J. 1985. The museum and the Indian community: findings and orientation of Leicestershire Museums Service. *Museum Ethnographers Group Newsletter* **19**, 3–14.

Paynter, R. 1990. Afro-Americans in the Massachusetts historical landscape. In *The politics of the past*, P. Gathercole & D. Lowenthal (eds), Ch. 4. London: Unwin Hyman.

Ruffell, A. 1984. Southampton's historic links with the Caribbean. *Hampshire*, June, pp. 56–8.

SCRE (Southampton Council for Racial Equality) 1985. *Annual Report*.

Sheppard, J. 1977. *The 'redlegs' of Barbados: their origins and history*. Millwood, NY: KTO Press.

Swann, Lord 1985. *Report of the Committee of Inquiry into the education of children from ethnic minority groups*. British Parliamentary Papers, Cmnd 9453.

6 'Volk und Germanentum': the presentation of the past in Nazi Germany

W. J. McCANN

In 1944, when the 'Thousand Year Reich' was already approaching its premature end, Friedrich Alfred Beck published *Der Aufgang des Germanischen Weltalters* (The rise of the Germanic world-age), which presents the racial, philosophical, and historical theories underlying National Socialism in often turgid detail.[1] What Beck saw as the meaning and historical and racial background of *Germanentum* is here set in the context of other views expressed in Germany during National Socialist rule. (*Germanentum* or 'Germanic-ness' is difficult to translate precisely: it means what is of the essence of the Germanic peoples, or their ethos.) A number of these ideas did not originate in Nazi thought, or even in the 20th century; what is interesting in this context is the application of a whole state apparatus to their propagation.

Some quotations from Beck will suggest the kinds of concepts he was trying to propagate:

> German *Germanentum* is a metaphysical form of character, derived from a Nordic racial essence, which reveals itself in a creative power based on a heroic attitude which is located in the personality as the unique representation of the national [*völkisch*] organic existence, in order, while transcending that state of being which is conditioned by space–time and causality, but still within that state of being, to achieve an infinite, eternal and free life as a perfect organic unity between the nation's conception of its essence and the form taken by the reality of the people within the order of the Reich.   (Beck 1944, pp. 45–6)

> In German *Germanentum* one group of people [*Menschentum*] within the Germanic peoples has raised itself to the level of the highest and incomparable bearer and preserver of Germanic forces and values.   (*ibid.*, p. 38)

> German *Germanentum* has the task of bringing the new world-historical order to completion. The living right to this responsibility is derived from the historical achievement of German *Germanentum* and its consti-

tutional power to create order . . . The recognition, that our group/
type of people has proved itself above all other peoples through its
history as the human type [*Menschenart*] most capable of achievement,
together with the certainty that it is . . . a more powerful force for order
than all other peoples, is likely to give the man who is called to
co-operate decisively in bringing about the coming new world-
historical order courage to face his future task.   (*ibid.*, p. 47)[2]

Through all the nebulous, pseudo-metaphysical jargon, certain key ideas
emerge: first, the importance of *race*, in this case, the Germanic race;
secondly, the 'fact' that the superiority of this race is proven by its *history*; and
thirdly, the concepts of *order* and of the *Reich*, which are both derived from
and proof of this superiority. A selection from Beck's chapter headings
suggests the further development of his ideas: 'The people [*Volk*] as the
essential community'; 'Blood and soil'; 'Race and culture'; 'The Reich and the
nations in the Germanic world-age'; 'The Germanic world-age as the
fulfillment of world history'; 'The breakthrough of the primal racial forces'.
None of these ideas is new or original; some go back to Alfred Rosenberg,
whose *Mythus des zwanzigsten Jahrhunderts* (1930) Beck quotes with approval,
others to Hermann Wirth, whom we shall meet again in the context of the
SS-Ahnenerbe, to Houston Stewart Chamberlain (1899), and even further;
but the whole complex of ideas is best summed up in this swansong of
National Socialism before its extinction as a state doctrine.

Opposed to this Germanic master race and its genius for order are the
Untermenschen (sub-humans), particularly the Jews. The Second World War
'arose from the essential opposition and the irreconcilable differences
between Germanic values . . . and Jewish values, which had sought out the
most varied forms to achieve their aims'; and 'the inherent power of German
Germanentum to create order' is explicitly contrasted with 'the equally
inherent power of Jewry to produce chaos' (Beck 1944, p. vi). (Beck here
uses two different words for 'power'. The one used for *Germanentum* is the
relatively positive [at least in Nazi eyes] *Mächtigkeit*; that for the Jews the
more negative *Gewalt*.) These Jewish values are expressed in such divergent
milieux as Bolshevism and Christianity; Christianity had played a part in the
first Germanic Empire, that of Charlemagne, but one of only peripheral
importance:

> In Charlemagne's Imperium Christianum, it was a feudal and not a
> plebeian order which prevailed, and it was determined by the higher
> racial values of noble birth. Christian thought in no way became a
> decisive part of the mode of existence and way of life of the Germanic
> peoples and tribes. It was only a means in the service of the political
> power, but not a political end in itself. In Charlemagne and his
> contemporaries the awareness of a radical opposition between Ger-
> manic and Christian never ever became conscious. (Beck 1944,
> p. 211)

Christianity was certainly of no importance in the Third Reich:

> *Deutschtum* [the term which relates to 'German' as *Germanentum* does to 'Germanic'] as Christian *Germanentum*, as many apostles of Jewry would like to see it even today, would be the most shameless betrayal of *Germanentum* which could be imagined, since Christianity is nothing more than a form of Judaism, and there is no greater contrast in terms of national [*völkischer*] essence than that between *Germanentum* and Jewry. (*ibid.*, p. 39)

This historical view of *Germanentum* and its racial contrasts with Judaism are both found in a number of contexts, including the education of young women. Margarethe Schaper-Haeckel's *Die Germanin* (1943) is a good example. Bound by ties of blood to their Germanic ancestors, modern Germans must follow social and moral rules based on their example:

> If we profess a faith in the fact that the essence of the human being is determined by his blood, and if we further – believing in the continuity of the blood – regard ourselves as successors of those great Germanic peoples who once gave the world a magnificent example of a strong and noble humanity and the glory of a great culture, then we cannot fail to appreciate the further conclusion that the laws that ruled their inner and outer lives must still also be ours. To recognize the essential nature of the Germanic woman in the characters and the lives of our foremothers means for us finding our way back to our own basic principles, gaining a yardstick and a guideline for the way we shape our own lives. (Schaper-Haeckel 1943, p. 6)

These foremothers are exemplified in the Norse sagas, whose fidelity to historical fact is 'documentary' (*ibid.*, p. 7). When needed, additional evidence is taken from classical ethnographers (in fact, almost entirely from Tacitus [*ibid.*, pp. 37ff.], without noting that his depiction of the strict morality of the Germans may be coloured by a desire to contrast them as strongly as possible with his contemporaries in Rome). The model of Germanic womanhood here depicted has equal rights with her male counterparts and a favourable position in society, in spite of the fact that her tasks are secondary to those of men, for example:

> Marriage . . . demands of the Germanic woman in the first place active comradeship and loyalty to her husband . . . The business of the man, the military [*wehrhaft*] farmer [we return to this image of the military farmer/peasant below in dealing with some of Himmler's ideas] is the heavier and harder work in the fields, the care and breeding of the stock, defence with the sword. To the farmer's wife, on the other hand, falls above all care for the home, for the whole household, for food and

drink, lodging and comfort, clothing as well as lighter work in the activity of the farm. (*ibid.*, p. 40)

In most cases the spiritual contribution of the woman lies behind the deed of the man, who obtains the success and the recognition. (*ibid.*, p. 45)

This idealized emancipated peasant woman had little relevance for woman in modern urban society, however, let alone for the real position of women in the Third Reich (Stephenson 1981). More to the point are the author's attacks on suffragette activities seen as 'the fanatical, distorted and therefore equally morbid outburst of Germanic womanhood [because of England's 'Germanic' heritage], that is desperately trying to shake off the chains imposed on it by a foreign view of things that places a value on sex' (Schaper-Haeckel 1943, p. 18). Chastity among the young is essential to preserve the racial essence:

Behind the insistence that the physically and spiritually immature young person should remain intact stands on the one hand the *will, not to endanger the purity and power of the blood and on the other the general moral principle of chastity which is valid for every aspect of Germanic life.* (*ibid.*, p. 56)

In the choice of a husband and in entering marriage [the Germanic girl] is guided by pride of blood, responsibility to her ancestors and the thought of her future children. Therefore she chooses her husband according to the value of his blood, investigates the family from which he comes and his personal honour and ability. Wealth can never outweigh blood that is, for example, of a lower value than her own. (*ibid.*, p. 32)

Germanic chastity is not to be confused with Christian chastity, based on an ideal on virginity derived ultimately from Semitic sources:

To the Jewish-oriental mind, on the other hand, the virgin appears more desirable than the woman; the word 'more desirable' is chosen deliberately here, because the fact that the virgin is held in higher esteem in oriental taste is hardly likely to be due to the moral value placed on chastity. (*ibid.*, pp. 58–9)

Using Islamic descriptions of Paradise as evidence, she asserts that this emphasis on virginity is purely for increasing male sexual pleasure, indicative of 'a sadism characteristic of the oriental' (*ibid.*, pp. 59–60). Christian virginity is then described in terms which make it seem even more perverted:

What a transformation in the Germanic personality must this foreign attitude have brought about, before it dragged Germanic farmers' daughters so far from the security of their healthy, reverent attitude to life and the world that they took the veil, as is reported to us of the girls of an entire village.   (*ibid.*, p. 61)

By contrast, the modern Germanic woman ought to remain chaste until of an age to bear children of good Germanic blood and descent for the Reich (cf. below Himmler's plans for the production of an SS elite).

With Himmler and the SS-Ahnenerbe we come to the use made of *Germanentum* by the National Socialist state (Kater 1974). Rosenberg's *Mythus des Zwanzigsten Jahrhunderts* (1930) soon became a set text of Nazi ideology in schools, universities, and party indoctrination camps (Cecil 1972, pp. 142ff.). Yet despite his position as official party ideologue, Rosenberg's view of *Germanentum*, particularly where it concerned archaeology, was opposed by Himmler and his SS (Bollmus 1970, Cecil 1972, pp. 150, 156). Nor was Hitler himself over-enamoured of the Germanic ideal, except where of some practical use: 'These professors and obscurantists who found their Nordic religions are just spoiling everything . . . They help to undermine . . . They cause unrest' (quoted in Rauschning 1940, p. 52). As Kater writes (1974, p. 23), 'the German Führer had always admired the cultures of the southern latitudes, like those of the Romans and Greeks, while he despised those relatively unimaginative peoples, who, like the Germanic peoples, lived in the "cold, damp and gloomy North"'.

Himmler's view was the opposite:

In contrast to Hitler, for whom the word 'germanic' was not an essential part of a world-view or a creed, but rather could as required, stand for 'German', 'National Socialist' or even 'free of Jews', Heinrich Himmler accepted the concept [of a 'germanic Reich'] in its original meaning . . . In Himmler's racially determined view of the world the Nordic-Germanic type counted as an extraordinary biological and historical phenomenon . . . In their Germanic ancestors he saw the vanguard of a highly developed culture and of a powerful political system. The racial character of the Germanic peoples was for him a basic precondition for their superiority; the racial purity of the German 'national comrades' [*Volksgenossen*], whom he regarded as the direct descendants of the Germanic tribes, was his most important concern, particularly in the SS . . . He inferred the necessity of a practical concern for their ancestry among his *Schutzstaffeln* and for the whole nation, and indeed . . . after conquering Christianity, in creating a neo-Germanic 'replacement religion' [*Ersatzreligion*].   (Kater 1974, pp. 170, 18)

So convinced was Himmler of *Germanentum*'s relevance for himself that he believed he was a reincarnation of the emperor Heinrich I, instrumental in

German victories over the Slavs and settlements in the East (Kater 1974, p. 18).

To obtain scientific (or pseudo-scientific) support for his theories, Himmler founded the SS-Ahnenerbe (Ancestral Inheritance) in July 1935, with Hermann Wirth as its first president. Born in 1885 in Utrecht, Wirth moved to Germany before the First World War, served in the German army, and began an academic career. He became very involved in matters Germanic, but his public academic career foundered after he was taken in by the so-called *Ura Linda-Chronik*, a forgery which purported to be a Frisian family chronicle dating from the 6th to 1st centuries BC. He became a freelance scholar, writing books such as *Vom Ursprung und Sinn des Haken- kreuzes* (On the origin and meaning of the swastika, 1933).

As its name suggests, one of Ahnenerbe's main tasks was to investigate the Germanic past, initially conceived by Wirth in terms of *Geistesurge- schichte* (Intellectual/Spiritual Prehistory). But Ahnenerbe also included sec- tions on *Geisteswissenschaften* (what, in other circumstances, one might translate as 'Humanities'), on the natural sciences, particularly medicine – the medical section was responsible, among other things, for often fatal experiments involving concentration camp prisoners (Kater 1974, pp. 231ff.) – and anthropology, confined there to *Rassenkunde* (race stud- ies).[3] Similar efforts elsewhere led to schools of 'Aryan physics' and 'Germanic mathematics' (Lenard 1938).

Like Beck, Himmler had no time for the pedantic precision of traditional science: he began not with hypotheses based on the evaluation of evidence but rather with axioms for which the evidence had to be found; awkward or contradictory facts were ignored or altered. Among the strange byways explored by Himmler and the Ahnenerbe were Atlantis, the Holy Grail, early Germanic symbols (Himmler hypothesized 'an earlier, highly devel- oped weapon of our forefathers . . . which presupposes an incredible know- ledge of electricity'), and heraldry (establishing that in 1523 a Swiss family named Himmler had a swastika in its coat of arms, and that a coat of arms existed in 1608 for a certain Michael Hitler) (Kater 1974, pp. 51, 70). Some realms of inquiry had more practical purposes: Germanic methods of birth control and marriage law (Schaper-Haeckel 1943) were intended to be of use in breeding a new Germanic race and in regulating its settlement patterns.

Even folk tales (*Märchen*) and folk studies (*Volkskunde*) were caught up in the ideological net. The *Pflegstätte für Märchen- und Sagenkunde* sought 'to distinguish what is characteristic of our nature from what is alien to it, to discover how much the narrative material continues to be believed as myth, as well as to place once again in the hands of the German mother and her children the greatest treasury of German folktales in a pure and genuine form' (*Denkschrift* 1939). The *Arbeitsgemeinschaft für deutsche Volkskunde* was intended to build folk studies into 'a bulwark for the National Socialist world-view' (Kater 1974, p. 141). In folk studies Germanic elements of the pagan past were heavily emphasized, and Christianity played down.

Rassenkunde helped shape ideas of a genetically new Germanic elite:

Figure 6.1 Senior Nazi official (Reichsarbeitsführer
Hierl) inspecting the SS excavations of Alt-Christburg
hillfort in 1937.

Himmler (a former poultry-breeder) wished to breed in such 'Germanic'
racial characteristics as a Grecian profile, even hoping to create an SS unit
solely of men with this appearance. The *Lebensborn* organization, initially set
up to deal with the children of unmarried mothers and orphans of Germanic
descent or appearance 'acquired' in the occupied territories, was to promote
the breeding of children from specially chosen parents (Kersten 1952,
p. 230). In certain Eastern territories whose inhabitants were deemed
capable of 'Germanization', non-Germanic racial characteristics were to be
bred out, Germanic ones bred in in Mendelian fashion (the German word
ausmendeln was used to describe this process) to ensure a pure Germanic
population. Attempts were made to move people of German stock from the
South Tyrol to new settlement areas including South Russia, but this was
largely a failure (Kater 1974, pp. 151–9ff.).

Figure 6.2 A chieftain's grave at Hohen-Michele (Wurttemberg) being excavated by SS men in 1937.

Another major area of Ahnenerbe involvement was archaeology (Figs 6.1–3). Some work under its auspices was scientifically respectable, even if undertaken from highly suspect motives. Not surprisingly, few archaeologists subsequently alluded to their Ahnenerbe connections. Thus Herbert Jankuhn, well known for his excavations at Haithabu in Schleswig-Holstein, refers in 1949 (p. 1) to support by the Deutsche Forschungsgemeinschaft but does not mention that these funds were directed via the SS-Ahnenerbe. Referring to Haithabu, Gustav Schwantes (1939, p. 82) had reported that 'thanks to the extraordinary interest that the Reichsführer-SS Heinrich Himmler has devoted to this wonderful site for many years, the excavations will be carried out from 1938 on more extensively than heretofore as SS-excavations'.

Jankuhn himself had previously mentioned that 'with the taking over of the excavations by the Reichsführer-SS and Chief of the German Police Heinrich Himmler and their placement under the auspices of the Ahnenerbe, the excavations and their evaluation have been removed from a state of . . . uncertainty, and placed on a secure basis which permits far larger-scale planning. The purchase of the land which is of most immediate importance for the excavations has also provided the external prerequisites for more extensive excavations' (Jankuhn 1938, p. vii). Indeed, Jankuhn himself was an SS-Sturmbannführer attached to Himmler's personal staff and owed his appointment to a senior museum position in Kiel to Himmler's influence (Kater 1974, p. 139).

Figure 6.3 Aerial photography of the ruins of the castle
of Tilsit from an SS balloon in 1938.

If the quality of Jankuhn's excavations seems beyond reproach, some of
his interpretations are extremely dubious:

> Among [Indo-European peoples] the Germanic people play a special
> role, insofar as they can trace their family tree back furthest, further
> than the Romans, Celts and Slavs . . .
> It is not just that this earliest entry on the stage of history can be
> proven on the basis of archaeological finds, but also the fact that we can
> trace back beyond this the roots out of which the organic [*geschlossen*]
> people of the Germani developed in the North of Europe at the end of
> the neolithic period.
> That we can here, as with no other individual branch of the great
> Indo-European family, go so far back, is partly due to the fact that

because of the inner power of this people [*Volkstum*] no foreign [cultural? racial? WJM] overlay took place, nor did any alteration in the direction of their development, so that . . . they developed according to their own inherent principles . . . Their geographical position played a role in this . . . but this circumstance seems to be of minor importance compared with the inner strength of this people, since we can also observe later in history that the Germani further developed their own characteristics after their conquest of central Europe, even when they no longer lived in their geographically isolated original settlement areas. (Jankuhn 1938, pp. 3–4)

Jankuhn goes on to discuss the earliest settlers in what is now northern Germany, particularly the megalith builders and the 'battle-axe people':

Particularly characteristic are the fine weapons, after which they are called the battle-axe folk. And this love for a fine weapon can be followed . . . down to the end of the prehistoric period, [thanks to] the personal relationship that exists between the man and his weapon. To the Germanic man his weapon is not a tool, but is like a living being, which can often be given a name . . . This love of weapons which is so characteristic of the Germani can thus be traced back to one of the roots from which *Germanentum* developed . . . The people of the 'battle-axe culture' seem to be almost uniformly . . . extremely tall, long-headed and long-faced, thus representatives of the Nordic race. (*ibid.*, p. 5)

No shields were found at Haithabu. Jankuhn comments that the almost total absence of protective weapons 'is probably connected with the individual nature of the Germani and their attitude to combat, which was conditioned by their blood [*blutmäßig bedingt!*], in the same way as their refusal to build fortresses' (*ibid.*, p. 123). Chain mail and helmets are explained as signs of rank, rather than protection.

Germanic remains everywhere received special and often exclusive attention. In command of the SS-Sonderkommando in Russia in 1942–3, Jankuhn's mission was to 'ensure the safety' of prehistoric (particularly Germanic) material in South Russia and the Caucasus; a large number of artefacts were taken to safety in Germany. Jankuhn sought at the time to undertake excavations that would explore 'German colonization in the East' and the 'connections between the oldest German settlers and the last remains of the Gothic population', a scheme aborted by the German defeat at Stalingrad.

All Ahnenerbe archaeological work had ulterior political or propagandistic motives, but some of their archaeological activities can only be described as looting. Besides Jankuhn's Sonderkommando, other Ahnenerbe groups operated throughout occupied territories in the East. They appropriated not simply museum objects of Germanic provenance, but whole libraries, works of art, and, according to documents permitting confiscation from private Polish and Jewish sources, valuables of every kind (Kater 1974, p. 149).

The SS not only took over excavations from Jankuhn and others but also made their own excavations, both within Germany and on its eastern borders. It was Himmler's aim to have within reach of every SS-Standarte a Germanic excavation site 'as a cultural centre of German greatness and the German past' (Kater 1974, p. 54). Those of a religious nature could be used in fashioning Himmler's hoped-for new German religion. One important site was the Externsteine in Saxony, held to have been an important cult centre (experts were uncertain whether Christian or Germanic, but those who thought the former were not very popular). The Externsteine became a place of pilgrimage for the SS, with guided tours by local archaeologists.

From the investigation of early Germanic settlement patterns, Himmler anticipated practical political advantages. Previously a farmer himself, he saw Germanic peasant stock as the basis of most that was good in *Germanen-tum* and in this he was supported by Darré, the Reichsbauernleiter (Darré 1929, 1930). Since the early Germanic peasant farmer had, he thought, both farmed the land and defended it with his arms, the need for *Lebensraum* in the East encouraged Himmler to revive this practice. Emulating their forefathers both in the early migration period and during German eastward expansion in the Middle Ages, *Wehrbauer* were to be settled in areas cleared of their Slavic population.

The dating and classifying of settlements reflected another political purpose. Attempts were regularly made to show either that Germans or Germanic tribes were the first settlers bringing civilization to areas previously inhabited only by a few nomadic Slavonic savages, or that previous settlement had been that of *Untermenschen* inferior to the incoming Germanics. Thus the SS excavations of 1940–2 at Biskupin in the province of Posen (then Urstätt in the Warthegau) attacked previous Polish archaeological conclusions that the inhabitants had left because of natural causes; rather, claimed Schleif (1942), the 'violent southward expansion of the Germani' proved the military and physical (and therefore racial) superiority of the incomers over those they had driven out (see also Lück 1934).

In a similar polemic against Czech archaeology, Leonhard Franz (1938, p. 342) concluded that 'the Germani had been settled on the land for centuries before the Slavs arrived'. Remains of those settlements were especially sacred to the Nazis. Of a Germanic royal grave discovered at Stražc in Slovakia and apparently vandalized by the locals before it could be properly dealt with, Zotz (1939) commented:

> The human skeletons – and it should be realized that these were the remains of Germanic kings – were totally destroyed . . . The terrible destruction [of the finds] is so much more to be regretted, in that new evidence of Germanic glory and Germanic power in an advanced outpost of the migration period was thereby desecrated.

An excavation at the Erdenburg, near Cologne, was held to show that Germanic culture was superior to Roman culture:

In the historical contexts of the German West, the 'Erdenburg' is an example and a symbol of the forces which defeated the universal Roman Empire . . . Precisely at the time when [the border people] were erecting this fortress the day of liberation was dawning in the Teutoburger Wald. (Langsdorff & Schleif 1936, p. 393)

In their attempt to use archaeological and anthropological material to support the myth of Germanic racial superiority, some of the Ahnenerbe staff went to extremely fanciful lengths. In 1941 Himmler saw some pictures of the 'Venus' figures of Willendorf and Wisternitz (Vestonice). Assuming them to be to some extent realistic, he was struck by the similarity of their apparent steatopygic development with that of 'some tribes of savage peoples' such as the Hottentots, and asked the Ahnenerbe to produce a distribution map for the figures, as well as to see if there was any evidence that people 'like the Hottentots' had then lived in those areas, or if those people and the Hottentots were of similar descent, and whether these people had been driven out or made extinct either by a change in climate or by the Cro-Magnon or later Nordic peoples.

Himmler's reasoning was clear: if these primitive races were similar to the Hottentots, and if they had been destroyed by the Germanic invaders in the struggle for existence, then the racial superiority of the Germanic tribes not only to the Willendorf culture but also to black Africa would be proven in an incontrovertibly Darwinian way (Heiber & von Kotze 1968, p. 95). Some members of the Ahnenerbe stressed that the Palaeolithic figurines could not be assumed to be realistic representations; the report in Germanien, the Ahnenerbe's own periodical, on the Vestonice excavations rejected this view of the racial inferiority of the Vestonice culture:

We are therefore concerned here with that famous population group which, after the destruction of the Neanderthalers . . . spread in a very short while over large parts of the European, Asian and probably also the African continents, and whose conquests are among the greatest of all times. A 'europid' form was characteristic of these people. It is very probable that the later Indo-Europeans developed out of a particular group of these people. (Bohmers 1941, p. 47)

He wrote of the Palaeolithic figures' facial features: 'We can see . . . that they are not mongoloid or negroid, but belong completely to the Indo-European racial group' (Bohmers 1941, p. 51). Despite this, at least one ethnographer, Bruno Beger, not only followed Himmler's suggestion up, but hypothesized that the Hottentots and Jews were racially related. To test this hypothesis, there was an opportunity close at hand in the concentration camps:

Perhaps the Race and Settlement Office could at the selection and inspection of groups of aliens, during which process the women are examined and inspected in an unclothed state, take an occasional look at the development of fatty deposits and where possible take some photos.   (quoted in Kater 1974, p. 95)

In the face of this last example of the manipulation of science and the perversion of the past in the service of the racial ideology of *Germanentum*, further comment is superfluous.

Acknowledgement

I would like to thank the University of Southampton Advanced Studies Committee for a grant which enabled me to visit Hamburg to carry out research for this chapter.

Notes

1   Ironically, Beck signed his foreword on 6 June 1944, D-day.
2   Linguistic differences between German (particularly Nazi German) and English sometimes make it difficult to express exactly what Beck is saying, except very clumsily. I apologize for this, and in cases where the actual wording of the German is crucial, I have included important German words or phrases in brackets; otherwise, all quotations from German authors are translated in the body of the text. The original texts of quotations from Beck on pp. 74–5 and 76 follow:

Deutsches Germanentum ist aus nordischem Rassentum entspringende metaphysische Charakterlichkeit, die sich in einer schöpferischen Gestaltungskraft auf dem Grunde einer heldischen Haltung, die durch die Persönlichkeit als der einzigartigen Darstellung des völkisch ganzheitlichen Seins getragen wird, erschließt, um, über das raumzeit-ursächliche Dasein hinausgehend, aber in ihm ein unendliches, ewiges und freies Leben als vollendete ganzheitliche Einheit von völkischer Wesensidee und völklicher Wirklichkeitsform in der Ordnung des Reiches zu gewinnen.   (pp. 45–6)

Im deutschen Germanentum hat sich innerhalb der germanischen Volker ein Menschentum zum höchsten und einzigartigen Träger und Bewahrer der Germanischen Kräfte und Werte erhoben.   (p. 38)

Das deutsche Germanentum hat die Aufgabe, die weltgeschichtliche Neuordnung zu vollziehen. Das lebendige Recht zu dieser Aufgabe folgt aus der geschichtlichen Leistung und der konstitutiven Ordnungsmächtigkeit des deutschen Germanentums . . . Die Erkenntnis, daß sich unser Menschentum in seiner Geschichte vor allen anderen Völkern als leistungsfähigste Menschenart ausgewiesen hat, dazu die Gewißheit, daß es nach seinem Wesen ordnungsmächtiger als alle anderen Volker ist, können zwar dem Menschen, der zur entscheidenden Mitarbeit an der kommenden weltgeschichtlichen Neuordnung berufen ist, Mut für sein künftiges Wirken geben.   (p. 47)

Deutschtum als christliches Germanentum, so wie es manche Apostel des Judentums auch heute noch gerne sehen möchten, wäre der schamloseste Verrat am Germanentum, der sich denken lässt, da das Christentum nichts anderes als eine Form des Judentums ist, aber kein größerer völkischer Gegensatz als der zwischen Germanentum und Judentum besteht. (p. 39)

3 A full list of the sections of the Ahnenerbe (some of which existed in little more than name) will give some idea of its intended scope:

Abteilung für Alte Geschichte   Abt. f. angewandte Geologie
Abt. f. angewandte Sprachsoziologie   Abt. f. Astronomie
Abt. f. Ausgrabungen   Abt. f. Biologie
Abt. f. Botanik   Abt. f. den Vorderen Orient
Abt. f. darstellende und angewandte Naturkunde
Abt. f. deutsche Volkskunde   Abt. f. Geologie u. Mineralogie
Abt. f. die gesamte Naturwissenschaft   Abt. für Germanenkunde
Abt. f. germanisch–deutsche Volkskunde   Abt. f. germanische Kunst
Abt. f. germanische Kulturwissenschaft und Landschaftskunde
Abt. f. germanische Sprachwissenschaft und Landschaftskunde
Abt. f. germanisches Bauwesen   Abt. f. Hausmarken u. Sippenzeichen
Abt. f. indogermanisch–deutsche Musikwissenschaft
Abt. f. indogermanisch–deutsche Rechtsgeschichte
Abt. f. indogermanisch–finnische Kulturbeziehungen
Abt. f. indogermanisch–germanische Sprach- u. Kulturwissenschaft
Abt. f. indogermanische Glaubensgeschichte
Abt. f. Innerasienforschung u. Expeditionen
Abt. f. Karst u. Hohlenkunde   Abt. f. keltische Volksforschung
Abt. f. Klassische Philologie u. Altertumskunde
Abt. f. Märchen- u. Sagenkunde   Abt. f. Mittellatein
Abt. f. mittlere u. neuere Geschichte   Abt. f. Osteologie
Abt. f. naturwissenschaftliche Vorgeschichte
Abt. f. nordafrikanische Kulturwissenschaft
Abt. f. Ortung u. Landschaftssinnbilder
Abt. f. Pflanzengenetik   Abt. f. Pflanzenpräperierung
Abt. f. Schrift- u. Sinnbildkunde (Runenkunde)
Abt. f. Tiergeographie u. Tiergeschichte
Abt. f. Urgeschichte   Abt. f. Volksmedizin
Abt. f. Wetterkunde   Abt. f. Wortkunde
Abt. f. Wurtenforschung   Entomologisches Institut
Abt. zur Überprüfung der sogenannten Geheimwissenschaften
Institut f. Wehrwissenschaftliche Zweckforschung (Kater 1974, pp. 493f.)
Abt. = Abteilung   f. = für   u. = und

References

Beck, F. A. 1944. *Der Aufgang des Germanischen Weltalters*. Bochum: Feldmuller.
Bohmers, A. 1941. 'Reiche Funde eiszeitlicher Bildkunst: Die Ausgrabungen bei Unter-Wisternitz. *Germanien*, pp. 45–57.
Bollmus, R. 1970. *Das Amt Rosenberg und seine Gegner; Studien zum Machtkampf im nationalsozialistischen Herrschaftssystem*. Stuttgart: Deutsche Verlags-Anstalt.

Cecil, R. 1972. *The myth of the master race: Alfred Rosenberg and Nazi ideology*. London: Batsford.

Chamberlain, H. S. 1899. *De Grundlagen des 19ten Jahrhunderts*. Munich: Brockmann.

Darré, R. W. 1929. *Das Bauerntum als Lebensquell der nordischen Rasse* (The peasantry as the life-source of the Nordic race). Munich: J. F. Lehmann.

Darré, R. W. 1930. *Neuadel aus Blut und Boden* (A new nobility from blood and soil). Munich: J. F. Lehmann.

Denkschrift, Die Forschungs- und Lehrgemeinschaft das Ahnenerbe [1939]. Offenbach/M [no page numbers].

Franz, L. 1938. Germanen und Slawen in den Sudetenländern. *Germanien*, pp. 341–7.

Heiber, Helmut & H. von Kotze 1968. *Facsimile Querschnitt durch das Schwarze Korps*. Munich: Scherz.

Jankuhn, H. 1937 (2nd ed. 1938). *Haithabu, eine germanische Stadt der Frühzeit*. Neumünster: Wachholtz.

Jankuhn, H. 1949. Ergebnisse und Probleme der Haithabugrabungen 1930–1939. *Zeitschrift der Gesellschaft für schleswigholsteinische Geschichte* **73**, 1–86.

Kater, M. 1974. *Das SS-Ahnenerbe*. Stuttgart: Deutsche Verlagsanstalt.

Kersten, F. [1952]. *Totenkopf und Treue*. Hamburg: Mölich.

Langsdorff, H. & H. Schleif 1936. Die Ausgrabungen der Schutzstaffeln. *Germanien*, pp. 391–9.

Lenard, P. 1938. *Deutsche Physik*. Munich: J. F. Lehmann.

Lück, K. 1934. *Deutsche Aufbaukräfte in der Entwicklung Polens*, Plauen i. Vogtland: Günther Wolff.

Rauschning, H. 1940. *Gespräche mit Hitler*. Zurich: Europa.

Rosenberg, A. 1930. *Mythus des zwanzigsten Jahrhunderts*. Munich: Hoheneichen.

Schaper-Haeckel. M. 1943. *Die Germanin: Körper, Geist und Seele*. Berlin: C. V. Engelhard.

Schleif, H. 1942. SS-Ausgrabung Urstätt im Warthegau. *Germanien*, pp. 431–6.

Schwantes, G. 1939. Das Museum vorgeschichtlicher Altertümer in Kiel. *Germanien*, pp. 78–83.

Stephenson, J. 1981. *The Nazi organisation of women*. London: Croom Helm.

Wirth, H. 1933. *Vom Ursprung und Sinn des Hakenkreuzes*. Leipzig: Koehler & Amelang.

Zotz, L. 1939. Ein neues germanisches Fürstengrab in Straže in der Slowakei. *Germanien*, p. 160.

RULERS AND RULED

Introduction

It is not only in a Eurocentric context that one finds unequal access to resources and unequal awareness of, and control over, heritage. The benefits derived from or denied by the relics of the past distinguish the few from the many, rich from poor, mainstream from minority, male from female. Archaeology, which is now called upon to understand and even to mediate such differences, plays a role as significant for shaping the present as for understanding the past. Archaeological responses to these distinctions, and to the confrontations they generate, are discussed in the chapters in this section.

Often schooled, funded, and explicitly directed by national agencies, archaeologists – especially those outside Europe and North America – now face serious dilemmas. The colonized and the dispossessed manifest mounting bitterness against scholarly inquiries into sites and artefacts sacred to them as embodiments of ancestral spirits, and they increasingly press to prohibit such invasive desecration. Conflicts over site control generate much antipathy. In this emotional climate, each archaeologist must come to terms with pressures from rulers and ruled that may affect funding, access, and partisan loyalties.

Chapters 7 to 10 deal with intensifying conflicts in New Zealand, Hawaii, and Australia, where, over the past 200 years, European conquest has overwhelmed aboriginal cultures. The earlier inhabitants have been thrust aside by expansionist, technologically advanced, and materialistic Westerners (including, in the case of Hawaii, Japanese and Chinese as well), with the Eurocentric consequences discussed in the first part of this book. Descendants of Europeans and of autochthonous peoples continue to differ fundamentally in their attitudes towards land and property and in their ideas about the nature and significance of heritage – differences of major political import.

These four chapters share a concern with efforts by native minorities to secure or confirm control over sacred sites and artefacts, to recover relics and skeletal materials taken from them by collectors and museums, and to safeguard the sanctity of their heritage against further violations. In these efforts, Australian Aborigines, New Zealand Maoris, and Hawaiians resemble many other Fourth World peoples – notably Native Americans – with whom they now seek common cause.

Several related circumstances make issues of heritage control exceptionally difficult to resolve. First, native concepts of heritage go well beyond specific, isolated sites; they include entire territories, for sacredness may inhere not simply in localities but in the movements of nomadic peoples over vast tracts, exemplified in Australian Aborigine 'Dreamtime' peregrinations discussed by Creamer (Ch. 10). Secondly, archaeological findings about such peoples are apt to conflict with their own highly elaborated and socially significant oral histories. The affirmation of these narratives of origin, migration, and genealogical interconnection owes less to analytical scholarship than to continuing tribal involvement in recollecting, commem- orating, and re-enacting such histories.

Thirdly, diverse majority concerns also conflict with one another. Land developers' interests may clash with those of tourist entrepreneurs, those of homesteaders with guardians of culture, those who treat aborigines as enemies to be denigrated or despoiled with those who seek to support, adapt to, or adopt native modes of valuing environment and history. This is especially striking in New Zealand, where O'Regan (Ch. 7) and Butts (Ch. 8) show how the reassertion of traditional Maori values, discrediting an intervening self-image more tolerant of Pakeha dominance, both chal- lenges and serves to refashion contemporary Pakeha identity.

Implications for archaeological understanding and practice of all these themes are illumined here. Attempts to reassert and reaffirm native heritage interests have generated quarrels that show how intensely political a calling archaeology now is. O'Regan, a Ngai Tahu Maori, surveys from an indige- nous standpoint Maori moves, often explicitly political, to gain control of the organs that represent their own history in New Zealand. In the local New Zealand setting, Butts discusses the significance of the lead the Ngati Kahungunu tribe has taken in shaping displays of their own heritage at the Hawke's Bay Art Gallery and Museum. The impact of archaeology on Aboriginal Australian attitudes toward their own past, and how such inter- actions might affect control over and access to archaeological sites, are examined by Creamer. Dealing with another part of the Pacific, Spriggs (Ch. 9) reviews how the archaeological discipline and its practitioners have been characterized in the Honolulu media, in the light of archaeologists' own disputes over the troubled future of sacred Hawaiian sites.

The other chapters elaborate on different views of the past held by rulers and ruled in national, international, and professional contexts. Seeden (Ch. 11) outlines the appalling consequences of differential recognition of, access to, and uses of the archaeological heritage among elites and others in war-torn Lebanon. The heritage of the Lebanese upper class is largely biblical, Eurocentric, art-historical. The general populace, mainly sub- consciously connected with its own roots, and now totally deprived of access to displays even of the elite heritage, views the past in terms of metal detectors and export commodities: it deploys archaeological expertise not to develop or cherish a cultural identity but to sell it off.

The exploitation of women by men, whether deliberate or unconscious, is addressed in Jones and Pay's discussion (Ch. 12) of gender-linked roles among archaeologists themselves, still preponderantly male. Moreover, male-oriented constructions of knowledge have overwhelmingly shaped contemporary archaeological theory, museum presentations, and public attitudes.

Surveying the roles of museums in Scotland and Nigeria, Willett (Ch. 13) provocatively compares these two lands, one anciently, the other recently, subjected to English hegemony. One case involves a people long unified by culture but for several centuries now deprived of autonomy; the other a congeries of tribal groupings brought together willy-nilly into a new nation by the exigencies of imperial boundary-making. In both, rival national, regional, and local interests assert competing identities through museum displays of polemicized pasts. The issues Willett explores here underline the institutional and administrative problems discussed later in this book.

7 Maori control of the Maori heritage

STEPHEN O'REGAN

The presence of Maori culture, history, and language in New Zealand's cultural life has been enormously enhanced over the past few decades, fuelled by a burgeoning Maori population increasingly confident of itself and its direction. Maori affairs in one form or another feature in school and university curricula and are slowly but surely becoming more prominent on radio and television; traditional and contemporary Maori arts are flourishing.

Teachers and broadcasters are not the only professional communities affected by this surge of Maori cultural identity and assertion. Ethnologists, curators, anthropologists, and archaeologists have found themselves under increasingly critical Maori scrutiny. People who have devoted their professional and scholarly careers to Maori culture, history, and prehistory are being challenged by a growing determination that Maoris should define and interpret Maori culture. The view that Maori people and tribal communities are the primary proprietors of the Maori heritage, to which Pakeha (New Zealanders of Caucasian descent) have only a secondary claim, is gaining widespread acceptance among Maori people. Some hold the position that Pakeha and the larger New Zealand society should have no role at all in managing or making decisions about Maori culture. Maori sovereignty and cultural autonomy are being asserted as goals.

The idea that primary proprietorship of Maori culture should lie with ethnic Maoris is not in itself particularly startling. Indeed, it is implicitly accepted throughout New Zealand and is reflected in legislation dealing with Maori land and language, historical places and national parks, and in the administration of arts and heritage.

But if the idea is implicitly accepted, its explicit assertion seems less welcome. Many New Zealanders perceive it as separatist and divisive. It is considered an assault on national canons of race relations. Put forward as bicultural and multicultural, these canons enthrone the idea of 'two cultures, one nation' or 'two peoples, one nation'. Under these vague umbrellas Pakeha people are exhorted and encouraged towards bilingualism, cultural competence, and cultural sensitivity.

Ironically, much of the thrust towards greater Pakeha competence in Maori culture has come from Maoris themselves. Pakeha professional and educational courses are now commonly held at Maori *marae* (see glossary). In a wide range of ways Maoridom has become welcoming to and inclusive of non-Maori people.

A significant proportion of Pakeha New Zealanders are interested in and supportive of Maori cultural and political aspirations. Some measure of competence in Maori language and a general familiarity with Maori perceptions of New Zealand history are now considered necessary ingredients in the cultural kit of the educated New Zealander. Competence in things Maori is becoming part of New Zealandness – one of the main marks that distinguish Pakeha from other peoples of European descent throughout the world.

As the Pakeha move, however hesitant, towards bicultural competence, Maori claims to primary proprietorship of Maori culture and heritage cast a cloud on prospects of bicultural amity. The insistent questions arising among both Maori and Pakeha are: To whom does Maori culture belong? Who has the right to control and manage the Maori heritage? Who can speak authentically for it?

The immediate response is 'Why, Maori, of course', but then comes the qualifier 'but this rich heritage surely belongs to all New Zealanders. Increased awareness and respect by us all enlarges and enriches our bicultural society. It strengthens the quality of our life together and enlarges the cultural potential of our common future. That's why Pakeha people are learning to speak Maori, visiting *marae*, buying books on Maori, going to Maori courses and so on.'

Many, especially younger, Maori are uneasy about this response and the vision it represents. They fear that the increasing status of things Maori in the larger New Zealand society merely portends the further removal of their heritage into those white hands with status and power. They see increasing Pakeha interest and competence in *Taha Maori* as a portent of greater Pakeha control over Maori education, resources, and decision-making. Growing Maori concern over massive and worsening disparity in educational achievement and its relationship to social and economic opportunity is a feature of social debate in New Zealand.

Disastrous Maori education statistics support those fears. Access to knowledge about Maori language, history, and art is increasingly confined to those whose education and economic position enable them to take advantage of it. While more and more Maori achieve such knowledge, far more are distanced from it by the widening social and economic gap between Maori and Pakeha. Resentment at the Pakeha takeover of things Maori is increasing in a community of which 85 per cent are under 25 and whose access to mainstream status is diminishing. As access to the Maori heritage is increasingly mediated through mainstream culture, that heritage is seen to be passing inexorably into Pakeha hands.

Few Maoris who are actually disadvantaged in terms of wealth, education, and employment are conscious of their disinheritance, however, or realize their distance from their Maori heritage. They are aware only of a general sense of resentment. The articulation of resentment on their behalf is undertaken by a small number of younger educated Maori. It is they who react with hostility to being taught Maori language by Pakeha, who rail against Pakeha authors on Maori topics. It is they who talk of Maori sovereignty and Maori command over Maori culture and would limit Pakeha participation in things Maori. They give voice to the wider sense of dispossession and loss of control over what should be part of oneself.

Thus a genuine and deeply felt will to share Maori culture with the wider New Zealand society exists side by side with resentment at Pakeha occupation of Maori heritage. The less secure culturally a Maori feels the greater the sense of personal inadequacy and potential for resentment; feelings far more potent than any bicultural logic.

Yet although resentment at cultural takeover is most outspoken among the young and the culturally inadequate, a more substantial body of concern is emerging among informed elders and the essentially conservative Maori leadership, the culturally confident, mild-mannered *paepae Maori* who dominate official relationships with the Pakeha establishment. This group is also the best informed in the heritage realm that especially involves museums, art galleries, and academe. The enormous attention focused on Maori heritage by the Te Maori Exhibition has been most troubling for this group in particular, as detailed below.

Scholarship and the Maori

Conflict and change in Maori attitudes towards Pakeha scholarship on their culture and history can be introduced by an incident in my own tribal experience of more than a decade ago, which suggests a significant shift in the Maori positions on such issues. An article in an archaeological journal reviewed the foundation *whakapapa* (genealogy) of my own people. After much speculation the author came to conclusions contrary to almost all the beliefs my own and connected tribes hold about themselves. In academic terms the article was a disaster. The archaeologist demonstrated utter incompetence both in the sources of traditional history and in his understanding of *whakapapa*. I and my tribal peers were furious that such nonsense, clad in footnotes and all the trappings of academic writing, should be allowed to stand without rebuttal in the scholarly record. My elders, however, were resolute that no comment should be made and no debate entered into. They felt that Pakeha could be countered only on Pakeha terms, and to engage in debate on such terms would further demean the heritage already so indecently interfered with. It would have meant the public discussion of ancestry in a wholly inappropriate forum. We were not merely counselled to silence but commanded.

As shown in the discussion of the Te Maori material below, those days are gone. Today the younger leadership would be sent out to do battle on the fields of academe while even the more rural, *marae*-based elders would have little compunction about publicly stating their feelings and insisting on their correction.

For the Maori, though, the refutation of academic improprieties is at best a partial solution. Published nonsense remains published. Increasing attention is given to getting it *un*published. This is possible in journals of record, because they are confined to restricted subscription lists and institutional libraries. Concerned Maoris feel that notices should be circulated and inserted stating that a given article is culturally offensive or seriously incorrect.

While such action might deter irresponsible scholarship, it is unlikely to affect the publication of more popular material. In one recent instance, a tribal Trust Board sought a High Court injunction against the publication of a book on Maori carving, only to find to its chagrin that it could not defend its heritage at law. Alternative strategies have also been discussed by Maori Trust Boards in connection with a recent book on Maori *moko* (tattooing).

Maori efforts to exert some measure of control over the world of Maori scholarship raise a number of issues of general importance. A Maori 'Council of Cultural Commissars' would pose a clear danger to genuine scholarly speculation and enquiry. And beyond the stifling of scholarly understanding, the inevitable question arises: Who will police the policemen?

Maori tribal pressure was improperly used in one recent case to get a Maori place-name altered on grounds of perceived lewdness. Here the North Island area of Urenui (meaning 'enlarged penis') was altered to 'Urinui' ('a large body of descendants'). While this change may not be sustained, it shows how Maori political action can operate to interfere with authentic elements of Maori heritage, as well as to rectify and safeguard that heritage.

In the latter spirit, Pakeha scholars themselves have been revising the theories and interpretations of earlier Pakeha scholars. A large proportion of research published over the past 30 years has been devoted to demolishing established 'truths' about Maori origins and traditions in which New Zealand children, Maori and Pakeha, have been schooled for more than two generations. Maori origins in New Zealand have been thrust back approximately 1200 years from AD 1350. Polynesian origins have been relocated from South-East Asia to South America and, more recently, the Western Pacific, and the voyaging ancestors, once the 'Vikings of the Pacific', have become storm-tossed drifters and then competent navigators again.

Yet enormous confusion on Maori matters appears in the uninformed public mind, including the bulk of Maori people themselves. Many understandably doubt that scholarship has anything to offer Maoridom at all, and see those professionally engaged in studying the Maori past as little more than birds of prey feasting on the carcases of Maori culture. One difficulty is that the carcase is very much alive. In its present state of dynamic adaptation it vigorously resents being treated as carrion for scholarly enquiry.

An essential part of living Maori culture is a driving sense of purpose that draws heavily on the past. The *wairua* (spirituality) that fuels modern Maoritanga is encompassed in the phrase 'Te ohaki o nga tupuna, tuku iho, tuku iho' (The heritage of our ancestors passing down to us, passing down through us).

It is this sense of continuity with the past that scholars are felt to encroach on. Almost without exception, scholars of Pakeha descent are seen as raiders from another culture. Coming from Pakeha academic institutions, they represent all the social and economic power of Pakeha culture.

Thoughtful and well-informed Maori leaders do, however, recognize the contributions made be Pakeha scholars to our knowledge of the Maori past. They are well aware that but for the extraordinary zeal of early ethnologists a huge amount of the Maori heritage would have disappeared in the disease-ridden aftermath of the 19th-century Land Wars. They also respect contributions of modern archaeologists and prehistorians to our understanding of a past far more remote than our traditional histories can reach. But their appreciation co-exists uncomfortably with the resentments described above. It is these leaders who must warily mediate the relationship between Pakeha scholars and increasingly self-assertive Maori culture.

One reason such mediation is required is the virtual absence of scholars within the Maori community itself. Few Maori graduates or even non-graduates are yet at work in the field of Maori heritage. It will be many years before the community can hope to produce scholars sufficient to dominate Maori studies.

Moreover, there is growing hostility among Maoris toward any professional expertise concerning the definition of their past, whether the experts be Pakeha or Maori. This suggests that Maori people in the future will be even less inclined to leave their heritage in the care of scholars, of whatever ethnic descent.

All scholars and researchers may have to run some gauntlet of tribal approval. Mere appointment to academic position in Pakeha structures by Pakeha authority is, even now, an inadequate passport for access to the Maori world. And as the general level of Maori education and heritage awareness increases, that gauntlet seems likely to become more stringent. The consent of mediating leaders may in the future be insufficient to secure popular acceptance from Maoridom.

Meanwhile Maori tribal Trust Boards, faced with widened responsibilities, are increasingly appointing special councils and committees to manage tribal heritage, control tribal archives, and deal with growing demands for Maori information from government and academics. The enhancement of Maori representation on national parks and geographical boards and in various national scholarly projects has augmented the need for tribal reference sources. Partly owing to a grave shortage of competent resource people, Maori representatives on official and academic bodies suffer considerable financial and administrative strain in meeting these demands. But such efforts have proved beneficial, thanks in part to strenuous legislative efforts to gain representation on museum boards of trustees. For example, Maoris in my own Ngai Tahu tribal area have formed effective relationships with museums and the archaeological community. These developments coincide with a marked shift in the attitudes of individual scholars.

Tribal authorities experience growing pressures from within tribal communities themselves as Maori assertiveness increases. Sub-tribal communities demand much greater consultation than previously, and several Trust Boards now convene annual *hui* to discuss matters previously left to the leadership.

Improved relations between archaeologists and Maoris are still confined to a few localities and individual scholars. The archaeological revision of New Zealand prehistory, owing in part to the restricted academic circulation of the literature, has, as yet, had only minimal impact on Maori or, indeed, on Pakeha popular understanding of the past. But failure to make an impact on public perceptions is not entirely the fault of the archaeologists. New Zealand's teaching profession has never shown marked enthusiasm for indigenous content. And any attention to Maori studies at all has focused almost entirely on contemporary Maori culture and language rather than prehistory, especially when written by Pakehas. Day-to-day demands for programmes relevant to contemporary race relations are the schools' prime determinant.

With one or two notable exceptions, Maori exposure to archaeology is limited to giving – or denying – consent for interfering with sites perceived as culturally important or tribally significant. Burials tend to be Maoris' principal concern. A deep reverence for remains of tribal ancestors marks Maori thinking.

Archaeologists have long been felt to endanger the dead. Increasingly, though, the scholar is seen as 'the good guy' and Maori ire focuses on fossickers who loot the dead for artefacts. An important agency in this change is the New Zealand Historic Places Trust, which has influential Maori representatives on its Maori Advisory and Archaeological committees. Possessing *mana* in their own tribal areas, these Maori mediate between the archaeologists and the Maori community.

One instance of tribal claims on museums for *mana* over their heritage shows how political pressure can lead to improved Maori–Pakeha relations. My own tribal Trust Board lobbied for years to be allowed to nominate a tribal representative to the Canterbury Museum Trust Board. The person eventually nominated was the leader of a *hapu* with many unemployed youths. Involvement with the museum as trustee considerably enlarged this man's understanding of Maori scholarship and directed his attention more vigorously towards his tribal heritage. He developed a government-funded labour scheme for community youth, which involved clearing, replanting, and generally refurbishing the ancient site of Kaiapohia, a fortified settlement of great importance in our history. Museum archaeologists have worked side by side with the youth workers and community elders. The continuing work and social contact have dramatically improved mutual comprehension, not only among those directly involved but in the tribe as a whole.

The *Dictionary of New Zealand biography* projected for New Zealand's sesquicentennial in 1990 further illustrates how an indigenous culture can contribute when it is accorded *mana*. The dictionary's contributing teams, based in the regions and the universities, do not include Maori. Instead, at Maori insistence, a separate tribally based Maori structure selects Maori nominations for inclusion. As a result, Maori exhibit considerable enthusiasm for the project. This would not have occurred had the Pakeha project leaders attempted to approach the tribes themselves.

Apart from the consultative contributing structure, two features of the dictionary project commend it to Maori. One is the reservation of a volume solely for pre-European Maori biographies, reaching back perhaps even to realms of antiquity that Pakeha scholars dismiss as myth. Selections will be made by Maori on Maori terms, rather than on those of Western historical scholarship. The other is a Maori-language volume comprising all Maori entries in the general volumes. There has been no direct Maori pressure for these features. That they have been built into the project from its inception reflects the acceptance of years of Maori political pressure in defence of language and claims to heritage proprietorship.

Who in the Maori world is involved in activities of this kind? It is those *paepae Maori*, the tribal leaders and elders who sit on tribal Trust Boards. Their involvement in such matters has passed largely unnoticed and unquestioned by their tribes until Te Maori, to which I now turn.

Te Maori Exhibition

The development of the Te Maori Exhibition, which was to display Maori culture all across the United States, took at least three years. Its initial impact on Maori community thinking came from consultations with elders seeking consent in the tribal regions for the *taonga* (treasures) now in New Zealand museums to travel to the United States. This consultative process diffused awareness of *taonga* as art objects, previously confined to specially concerned elders and to a few museum workers and scholars, throughout the Maori world (see Butts, Ch. 8, this volume).

The proposal to have Maori elders and cultural performers conduct ceremonies at the Te Maori venues – New York, St Louis, San Francisco (Fig. 7.1), and Chicago – soon quickened the level of awareness. As these trips were to be made at government expense, the numbers of Maori willing to pronounce knowledgeably on the exhibition selection processes and Maori heritage in general rapidly escalated.

A comparable surge of concern took place among museum and arts administrators, civil servants, and assorted academics. And Pakeha interest fuelled resumption of the old 'art or artefact' debate. This debate concerns not only the status of tribal art but also the question of who should care for it.

Up to that time, the management of Maori heritage objects had largely been confined to ethnologists in New Zealand museums. Art in New Zealand was almost entirely Western; Maori carving, painting, and weaving were termed static, imitative, and constrained. Contemporary Maori

Figure 7.1 Two Maori elders entering the M. H. de Young Memorial Museum, San Francisco, for the dawn ceremonial opening of the Te Maori Exhibition, 10 July 1985. (Photograph by R. Valentine Atkinson courtesy of de Young Museum.)

creative forms were dismissed as 'crafts' and lumped with traditional and modern Maori music, literature, and poetry in a cultural cart to be rummaged through by interested academics and the tourist industry.

Museum ethnologists' proprietorship of the Maori artistic and artefact heritage began, however, to be vigorously challenged by arts administrators. The discovery of the Maori heritage by the New Zealand art world seems to have stemmed directly from its recognition by institutions of such international status as the Metropolitan Museum of Art in New York, the first American venue for Te Maori. Quite certainly, recognition by New Zealand political and administrative circles reflected the international attention newly accorded Maori art.

Maori reactions to this shift in status included satisfaction, cynicism, and amusement. There was satisfaction that a highly visible Maori heritage had achieved general public esteem, cynicism that increased Pakeha attention derived from international interest rather than from a genuine shift in appreciation, and amusement at the spectacle of the nation's various cultural caretakers scrambling for seats on airplanes to the United States.

Underlying these sentiments, though, were several more serious questions. As a result of the Te Maori build-up, the Maori leadership was for the first time being asked to focus on the Maori content of museums. Also for the first time, leaders had to confront the fact that people with little or no *mana* in Maori terms insisted on a role in appreciating and interpreting cultural heritage. Until then, museum journals of record, scholarly papers, and even popular books on Maori history and culture had largely passed the Maori world by and were dismissed as 'Pakeha writing letters to each other'. Cultural status was reserved for orally transmitted knowledge in the *marae*.

Despite increasing familiarity with academe, tribal leaders were plunged into shock by Te Maori. They were deeply involved in the enterprise before it dawned on them that the *taonga* did not belong to them any more – that they now belonged to museum trustees. Many of them were heading off to New York and St Louis before they had any idea of what was being said and written about their heritage in connection with the exhibition. Aroused by media attention accorded Te Maori, the tribes more stridently echoed their own doubts. As a result of the Te Maori experience, Maoridom has begun to press its leadership to take more stringent positions on heritage questions.

The book produced to accompany the exhibition (Mead 1984) aroused the sharpest initial tension. Detailed descriptions of items in the exhibition included extended reference to their origins and histories. Many Maori leaders were dismayed to be publicly linked with ignorant and irresponsible historical and ethnological judgements. One of Maoridom's most respected elders paused in the middle of an oration on his *marae*, tore out certain offending pages and graphically wiped his backside with them. The trigger to his anger was not the actual description of his tribal treasure but what he considered a grossly incorrect treatment of the associated *whakapapa* and history. For Maoris the primary value of the *taonga* derives from its association with particular ancestors – the *whakapapa* – and their histories. These ancestral objects carry the spiritual bonds of Maori identity. The two qualities of *wairua* and *mana* give them life. Their artistic and ethnographic interest is seen as quite incidental and deriving from Pakeha values.

The return of the Te Maori Exhibition itself became a major cultural event christened *Te Hokinga Mai* (The Homecoming). Before being dismantled, it toured the nation's four main cities, beginning at the National Museum in Wellington in 1986 and concluding in Auckland in 1987. Heavy attendances confounded some Maori leaders' views about lack of Pakeha interest and latent Pakeha hostility, although many visitors were perhaps impelled to come more by the international recognition accorded Te Maori than by any intrinsic interest.

How much real cross-cultural understanding Te Maori provided within New Zealand is hard to guess. Certainly, many Pakeha felt better about themselves in relation to the indigenous Maori heritage than they had before and expressed greater respect for Maori heritage and culture.

Much more significant has been *Te Hokinga Mai*'s effect on the Maori community. The customary ceremonials that opened the exhibition at its American venues were repeated in New Zealand, with the spontaneous participation of great numbers of Maoris. Budding tribal leaders took full advantage of opportunities for the exercise of Maori formalities and protocol. Sub-tribal groups welcomed visitors, exposing them to a live culture keeping warm the ancient heritage represented in the exhibition.

A notable feature was the high level of involvement of young Maori as guides offering commentary to visitors. While ethnologists and curators might have cringed at some of the commentary, embodying curious understandings about traditional Maori art and belief, in my view the benefits of thus involving the young far outweighed the dangers of ethnological error.

The closing ceremonies at each venue were marked by moving and emotional scenes, as those involved took leave of their 'ancestors'. These evinced a notable sense of proprietorship among both old and young, many of whom had seldom, if ever, entered a museum prior to Te Maori. The increase of scientific or scholarly understanding of Maori *taonga* may have been minimal, but the exhibition clearly inspired a flowering of emotional and cultural identity among Maori.

While museum administrators have been delighted with such high attendance and moved by the extraordinary displays of Maori involvement, they are already having to pay a high professional price for that popularity. They now face mounting Maori demands for the return of treasures to tribal areas. In the new climate of approval of Maori identity these demands are difficult to resist. Counter-arguments based on conservation needs, continuous protection, and other grounds carry little weight with Maori claimants, fired by Te Maori with a raised awareness of a heritage and the sense of its possession.

Institutions that resist such claims risk being labelled monocultural, racist, or unresponsive to Maori values and culture; the museum or gallery in general is viewed as cold and inhospitable, an inappropriate resting place for the ancestral *taonga*. Yet too ready an agreement may well lead to the *taonga*'s destruction or at least to an attenuated lifespan.

The legacy of Te Maori may well lead New Zealanders to restructure the management and control of Maori heritage. Institutions holding Maori *taonga* will, in the long run, be very different from what those who devised Te Maori envisaged. For its part, the Maori world will have to grapple seriously with the outcome of its new sense of heritage possession and the attendant risks to the very survival of its physical heritage.

Conclusion

Media attention within New Zealand and the enhanced public status of Maori art derived from the Te Maori Exhibition have greatly increased Maori awareness of their art heritage. This has, in turn, focused Maori attention on the institutions and processes that manage and define that heritage. The spirit of the times demands that Pakeha control of Maori heritage pass increasingly to Maori hands, and that Pakeha scholars and authors come under increasing Maori constraints.

References

Butts, D. J. 1989. Nga Tukemata: Nga Taonga o Ngati Kahungunu (The awakening: the treasures of Ngati Kahungunu). In *The politics of the past*, P. Gathercole & D. Lowenthal (eds), Ch. 8. London: Unwin Hyman.

Mead, S. M. (ed.) 1984. *Te Maori: Maori art from New Zealand collections*. New York: Harry N. Abrams.

Glossary

Hapu	Sub-tribal community.
Hui	Tribal gatherings.
Mana	In this context, having the sense of traditionally derived authority.
Maoritanga	General term for Maori culture, values, and heritage.
Marae	Traditional tribal cultural centres.
Moko	Tattooing, especially of the face; a practice of enormous cultural significance and personal status.
Ngai Tahu	The tribe whose region includes the great bulk of the South Island of New Zealand.
Paepae Maori	Popular term for the leaders who 'sit on the paepae', meaning the seats set in front of the marae on special occasions; literally, a perch, e.g. of a bird, or the cross bar on a latrine.
Pakeha	A non-Maori New Zealander generally of European descent, or the characteristics of that group.
Taha Maori	The Maori direction or control of something.

Taonga   Cultural treasure, ornament, or valued thing; frequently used meta-
                phorically.
Wairua   The flow of spiritual force derived from ancestry or the Maori past;
                an essential ingredient of anything 'authentically' Maori.
Whakapapa   Personal or tribal genealogy; the traditional vehicle of history in a
                non-literate culture.

8 Nga Tukemata: Nga Taonga o Ngati Kahungunu (The awakening: the treasures of Ngati Kahungunu)

DAVID J. BUTTS

Recently an important man went from Aotearoa [New Zealand] to America, leaving his people behind him. Before he left his people brought a cloak to where he was staying and placed it around his shoulders to keep him warm.

The man's family gathered. They talked to him about many things. The older men and women were remembering his life story. The children were learning. When this ceremony was finished, they all returned home.

On the day he was to leave for his journey the family and friends again gathered at the man's home. Everyone farewelled the man. Some spoke formally. Everyone sang. Powerful words were spoken to give him protection on his journey.

This man was in America for some time. He went to several major cities. In San Francisco some of the people from his home area came to visit him. Again they spoke to him of his past and offered their love and affection.

Many people admired this man during his journey. Many words were said and written about him.

Now he has returned to Aotearoa, his island home, back to the warmth and *aroha* of his people. He has found that great changes have taken place in his old home, and that some of his relatives have moved in.

Such was the experience of the *poutokomanawa* (the carved ridge post of a meeting house) of Te Kauru o Te Rangi, who died in a battle at Ahuhuri, Hawke's Bay, more than 150 years ago (Fig. 8.1). Te Kauru o Te Rangi was a chief of Ngati Kahungunu (the descendants of Kahungunu). His people had four *poutokomanawa* carved to celebrate the *mana* (prestige, power, history) of important men killed in the battle (Buchanan 1973, p. 46), which were placed in a *whare nui* (meeting house). When the house burnt down the carvings were rescued by the people and eventually loaned to the Hawke's

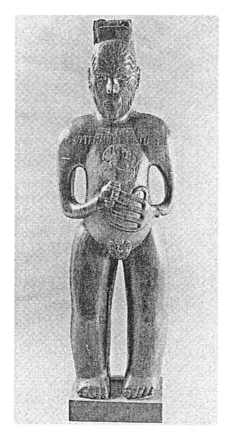

Figure 8.1 The *poutokomanawa* (carved ridge post of a meeting house) of Te Kauru o Te Rangi (144 cm). (Hawke's Bay Art Gallery and Museum, Napier, New Zealand, 37/748; after Athol McCredie [Fig. 127 in *Te Maori: Maori art from New Zealand collections*, S. M. Mead (ed.), 1984. New York: Abrams].)

Bay Art Gallery and Museum for safekeeping. In 1984 the *poutokomanawa*, Te Kauru o Te Rangi, left New Zealand with the Te Maori Exhibition for display in the United States (see O'Regan, Ch. 7, this volume). In 1986 Te Maori came back to tour New Zealand, after which the *poutokomanawa* of Te Kauru o Te Rangi returned to the museum. Eventually, he will be placed in a new *whare nui* to be built by his people.

While Te Kauru o Te Rangi was away a great change occurred in the museum with the creation of a new exhibition, Nga Tukemata: Nga Taonga o Ngati Kahungunu (The Awakening: The Treasures of Ngati Kahungunu). Along with one metropolitan and several provincial museums, the Hawke's Bay Art Gallery and Museum (HBAGM) embarked in the early 1980s on a major redevelopment of its Maori exhibitions. The pressures for the change have been both political (i.e. from Maoris) and museological.

HBAGM was established 50 years ago with considerable collections of Maori artefacts given by well-known local families, mostly European (Thomson 1981, pp. 98–100). Significant smaller collections have since been added. Until my appointment as curator in 1982 the museum had never had an anthropologist on the staff, although curators from the National Museum, Wellington, and the Auckland Institute and Museum had assisted with documentation and display. The exhibitions had portrayed a Maori culture dislocated in time and space: a case of nephrite artefacts, others of cloaks, of *waka huia* (feather boxes), of bone artefacts, and the like. In the 1960s the Simcox collection, primarily lithic and bone material from early coastal sites in Hawke's Bay and Otago, was arranged typologically for exhibition by the donor, a Hawke's Bay doctor.

These exhibitions gave no indication that the Hawke's Bay Maoris had a tribal identity, and that the people who had occupied the area for some 1000 years had a rich history. They focused on the 'classic period' of Maori culture (Davidson 1984, p. 1) before its supposed decline following the arrival of the Pakeha (European). More than half the artefacts displayed, however, dated from after the settlement of Pakeha in New Zealand.

The problem to be faced was similar to that of many other museums: how to re-display the artefacts of indigenous people, whose present context conveys more about European perceptions of an indigenous culture than about the actual culture. Various approaches to the display of these artefacts were possible. At one extreme the curator could have said, 'I am the expert employed to do this job – let me alone to get on with it.' At the other he could have maintained that only the people from whose culture the artefacts originated should decide how they should be exhibited.

The days are gone when museums in New Zealand can ignore the claims of the *tangata whenua* (people of the land, indigenous people) to control their cultural heritage, a policy that younger Maoris have been actively promoting for at least 20 years. For much longer, older Maoris have quietly mourned the loss of control over their *taonga* (treasures). Maori scholars working in museums, universities, and other institutions have expressed the need for change (O'Regan 1984, Mead 1985, Te Awekotuku 1985).

Exhibitions of Maori collections in New Zealand museums have always made statements containing implicit political messages. Some analysts suggest that these exhibitions have served Europeans as subconscious justifications for their colonization of a 'primitive' people. Whatever the validity of this view, these exhibitions have certainly never come to terms with the political reality of British colonization of Aotearoa and its impact on Maori culture. Like much of the literature on which they are based, these exhibitions present a mythical ethnography (Gathercole 1979, p. 218).

Recognition of the validity of Maori claims to control their cultural heritage in Aotearoa forces Pakeha curators to do much soul-searching and generates considerable debate (Neich 1985). In this climate of changing attitudes HBAGM faced alternative approaches to its new exhibition and opted for tribal participation instead of arbitrary professional expertise (Butts 1984).

Maori people identify strongly with regional tribal links (Kawaharu 1975, p. v). In Hawke's Bay the major tribe is Ngati Kahungunu (Mitchell 1972). A group of Ngati Kahungunu consultants was convened, covering most parts of the area. A working party of nine men and three women, with wide geographical and genealogical connections, brought to bear important individual skills; other people at local levels were consulted on specific issues. The museum director, curator, exhibitions officer, education officer, and registrar also served on the working party.

Meetings were conducted according to Maori protocol. When I began the first meeting by explaining the reason for the gathering, I was politely asked to stop so that Canon Wi Te Tau Hauata could open properly with a *karakia* (prayer). After this, each Maori member spoke in Maori and then briefly in English for those who did not understand Maori. By the fourth meeting I could greet them with a few tentative words of Maori, acknowledging the *mana* of the men and women of the working party. They were thrice welcomed to the museum, which houses important Ngati Kahungunu tribal *taonga*. The dead were greeted and farewelled. The living were greeted again and thanked for attending.

After each person had greeted the others and acknowledged their creator and their ancestors, it was then appropriate to discuss the exhibition. The meeting closed with another *karakia* followed by a meal. After the talk of ancestors and *taonga*, *whakapapa* (genealogy), and history, it is appropriate to share food. Moreover, it would be bad manners to bring people to your house and let them depart without eating and drinking.

At the first meeting the working party was told that the museum wanted to initiate a new Maori exhibition and that they had been called together to discuss what form it should take. Maori members of the working party were not being asked to rubber-stamp preconceived ideas but to advise museum staff on what type of exhibition they wanted and how, together, we could best achieve it. It was quickly agreed that Ngati Kahungunu would be the central theme. This would be one of the first attempts in New Zealand museums to focus on a local cultural reality rather than an arbitrary geographical region or on generalized, New Zealand-wide Maori history. The focus would be *Ngati Kahungunutanga* (Ngati Kahungunu culture) rather than *Maoritanga* (Maori culture in the broadest sense).

This decision had several political implications. It cut across the thrust of much national political rhetoric that recognized only racial identity, not tribal. This was in the days before government spoke so positively of the current policy of devolution of resources to *Iwi* (tribal) authorities. The decision to deal with the total Ngati Kahungunu tribal area – from Whangara, north of Gisborne, south to all of Wairarapa – meant infringing on another museum's traditional preserve. When I pointed this out, the tribal consultants simply said that this was my problem not theirs. Local government and institutional boundaries had no relevance in defining Ngati Kahungunu territory.

Only a small percentage of the HBAGM collection could be definitively attached to particular Ngati Kahungunu places and/or people, although a large proportion undoubtedly came from their tribal area. New Zealand's four metropolitan museums as well as the smaller ones were searched for artefacts with a tribal provenance. The National (Wellington) and Auckland museums proved to have large holdings of artefacts from the tribal area; Canterbury and Otago museums smaller but significant collections; the provincial ones little at all.

The co-operation of the metropolitan museums made it possible to mount a significant exhibition of provenanced Ngati Kahungunu *taonga*. Elders throughout the tribal region had lent their support to official requests for long-term loans from the museums. Formal ceremonies were held at the museum in which *kaumatua* (elders) welcomed their individual *taonga* back. These ceremonies have been important in bringing the museum and Ngati Kahungunu together.

The exhibition included *taonga* from most parts of the tribal area, so that Ngati Kahungunu throughout the area could relate directly to some part of it. However, some major Ngati Kahungunu art works still remain in each of the major metropolitan museums. The question is whether they too should be returned to the tribal area.

Both the benefits derived and the problems faced are exemplified in the meeting house, Te Poho o Kahungunu. Built at Porangahau in the mid-1870s, under the guidance of the carver Matenga Tukareaho and his son Haami Te Hau, from Nuhaka in northern Hawke's Bay, this structure was taken down about 1900. In anticipation of the exhibition, the Porangahau people loaned the Museum two carvings from this house, the *koruru* (gable figure) and the *poutokomanawa*, Te Pihi o Te Rangi, which spurred other generous acts. Window and door lintels have come on loan from family members in the Bay of Plenty and from Otago Museum.[1] Thus, for the first time in many years, the Porangahau elders have seen these carvings assembled together in one place. Many of the younger people from Porangahau had never seen these carvings before.

Much *kokero* (talk) associated with this house has been brought to the surface again by the reuniting of these carvings. This is an important learning time for the younger people and a significant stimulus to the continuity of the oral tradition associated with Te Poho o Kahungunu and the people who built it.

As facilitator, adviser, and, most of all, listener, the curator is involved in a process of past meeting present that will have far-reaching implications for the education of both Maori and Pakeha, and for future race relations in New Zealand.

Maori working party members were asked to identify a tribal designer for the exhibition and someone to co-ordinate the production of the accompanying audiovisual programme. Ngati Kahungunu painter Sandy Adsett agreed to serve as the designer at the request of his *kaumatua*. Fortunately, much of his work on the exhibition has been seen to fall within his brief as arts adviser for the Education Department in the Gisborne-Hawke's Bay region. As audiovisual project co-ordinator, Piri Sciascia brought his skills as a teacher and a tribal historian; he also was assisted by the staff of the Maori and South Pacific Arts Council.

Nga Tukemata (The Awakening) opened on Saturday, 26 July 1986. Ngati Kahungunu who gathered outside the museum in the morning had travelled from many parts of the tribal area. It was a day of high ceremony. At the beginning there were *karakia*, then *whaikorero* (speechmaking) and *waiata* (singing). The skies opened and the rain forced people to move inside. The *whaikorero* and *waiata* continued. Finally, the sacred *karakia* were chanted as the *tohunga* (priests) moved towards the entrance of the exhibition. The doors were opened and the people surged into the gallery behind the chanting *kaumatua*.

This is the statement of purpose seen by visitors after the welcome in Maori:

NGA TUKEMATA: THE AWAKENING

Nga Tukemata challenges each of us in different ways; for some there will be the discovery of Ngati Kahungunu as tangata whenua. Ngati Kahungunu are the descendants of Kahungunu and his wives. Kahungunu was an important ancestor who settled on the east coast of the North Island about 20 generations ago.

For some there will be an awakening to Ngati Kahungunu art as a tradition equal to any in the world. Consider the taonga (artworks) before you as signposts on a journey of discovery.

For Ngati Kahungunu this exhibition is a celebration of their tipuna (ancestors) and a reminder to the rest that they are still a strong people.

You will not find a detailed history written here. That history is known only by the descendants of Kahungunu and can only be given directly from their mouths.

This exhibition is a celebration of the mana of Ngati Kahungunu. It is an attempt to alert you to the mauri (the life essence), the ihi (the power) and the wehi (the awe) which Ngati Kahungunu feel from their taonga. Taonga are addressed in whaikorero as the living past. Respect the taonga for what they are – a living and powerful dimension of Ngati Kahungunu culture.

The Nga Tukemata opening was a great occasion; the past and the present were united in the people. When Maori people talk about the Te Maori

Exhibition they emphasize the *whaikorero* of the welcome, the *karakia* of the ceremony, the people they met, and the excitement of being part of the *ope* (group) present on great occasions.

Part of the continuing challenge of Nga Tukemata is to keep it alive by involving the *tangata whenua* in welcoming people to the exhibition. The active presence of *tangata whenua* to support their *taonga* must be a primary objective of future planning. To achieve this end the institution must be prepared to commit resources as well as words.

Sandy Adsett's perspective as a Maori artist has produced an exhibition unlike anything previously seen in New Zealand. The environment created by painting the entire gallery *tutaewhetu* (blue, a traditional East Coast colour), including the ceiling, and laying blue carpet on the floor, conveys a spirit appropriate to a place where tribal *taonga* are to live. The primary message of the exhibition, to celebrate the *mana* of Ngati Kahungunu, is emphasized by focusing on a relatively small number of art works. This required the simplification or removal of many of the didactic features a curator would normally want to include. This exhibition was not the place to write another textbook on the wall; it is a spiritual place where the works of the great Ngati Kahungunu tribal artists can communicate directly with their descendants, a place where people will acknowledge the presence of the ancestors.

To non-Maori the exhibition also brings a unique message. The *taonga* convey the particular identity of *Kahungunutanga* to the viewer without mediation. Museums often weaken the reality of cultural difference by leading the visitor to believe that an understanding of another culture can be gained by reading a series of labels. There is a place for these words, but they must not stand between the *taonga* and the observer. The *ihi*, excitement, fear, and mystery of the *taonga*, should work directly on the mind of the visitor. The exhibition labels provide information about type of artefact, date, location, and use in a brief form. Other labels include *whakatauaki* (proverbs) and *whakapapa* (genealogies).

In introducing viewers to the wealth of Ngati Kahungunu art, this exhibition aims to create a sense of respect for Ngati Kahungunu culture. How we see the past of a culture influences how we view that culture today and in the future. Hence it is a positive step for museums to de-emphasize their traditional concerns with primitive technology and subsistence economics and to highlight such elements of Maori culture as art, *karakia*, *whaikorero*, *waiata*, and dance. This is not to say that artefacts not considered to be 'art' should be left in the storerooms. They too have a place in such exhibits. Traditionally these artefacts are seen behind lengthy labels that explain how to make an adze or a fishhook, or emphasize material typologies. This type of explanation would be better explored through the wide range of audiovisual techniques now available.

For whom are collections of *taonga Maori* exhibited? Do Maori and European expect or derive the same things from exhibitions? One group of Ngati Kahungunu elders made it clear that their generation seldom visits museums but saw Nga Tukemata as a valuable part of their children's education, particularly those living in the cities away from their *marae*.

Greater Maori involvement in museums has recently been urged by Dr Ngahuia Te Awekotuku of Waikato University. The resultant change that she anticipates would be fundamental:

> No more a rua koiwi, a death house, a sad repository of plunder and grief, a cave of relics; but instead a place of joy and laughter and memory; a haven of inspiration and hope, the silent sleeping seeds of life itself.   (Te Awekotuku 1985)

Nga Tukemata is a first step toward this change. It is the curator's role to facilitate, advise, and listen. Maori curators will eventually fill most of the positions dealing with collections of *taonga Maori*. To operate effectively they too will need to be facilitators, advisers, and listeners, working closely with their own people. No matter who fills the curatorial role, they cannot work in isolation.

The role of archaeology in the museum context also deserves re-examination. In New Zealand, it has long influenced museum anthropology, particularly that of the Maori. To this day, most curators of important Maori collections in New Zealand museums are trained predominantly in prehistoric archaeology. Lacking adequate backgrounds in social or cultural anthropology, they are ill equipped to deal with an anthropological understanding of a living culture. None of them (myself included) has a fluent command of *te reo Maori* (Maori language). As students, these people had been led to believe that a degree in archaeology constituted sufficient training for curatorial positions. What they find when they take up such positions is that further education is required, often involving a radical revision of many preconceptions.

The past five years have seen some changes. The contributions of two social anthropologists in charge of Maori collections have been significantly progressive. Changes in academic training are also conducive to such sensitivity. In the past, the concentration of archaeology departments on New Zealand prehistory de-emphasized the value of understanding living Maori culture. Until recently, Otago University had no Maori language course, the anthropology department had no Maori lecturers, and there was little opportunity to study contemporary Maori culture. The university now has one Maori teaching the Maori language and another in the anthropology department teaching archaeology. At several other New Zealand universities, Maori language and Maori studies courses have been available for some years.

Maori attitudes to archaeology are varied – some positive, some extremely negative. Much of the negative reflects recollections of early fossicking and of early archaeological research done without reference to local Maoris. In recent decades archaeologists have shown a growing sensitivity to the need for consultation and involvement with local Maori, and there are many instances of close co-operation. But many Maori still hold negative images of archaeologists. They lump them with Pakeha scholars who study Maori cultural heritage to advance their own careers and give local people little in return.

How traditional Maori oral history can best be combined with archaeological information is a problem needing closer attention. Curators of Maori collections are moving towards closer involvement with Maori communities which sympathetically view their past in terms of their own traditions. Archaeological information can add an important dimension to such traditional history, but the archaeological information needs to be integrated with traditional history in interdisciplinary *iwi* (tribally based) programmes. Such integration is now becoming common for the later prehistoric and protohistoric periods (e.g. Barratt 1987), but is more difficult to implement farther back in time.

The growing intensity of contact between museum curators and Maori communities seems likely to make museum exhibitions important stimuli for innovation in New Zealand archaeology. Museum archaeologists will increasingly be required to show that their research is significant in local Maori terms. I am sure that archaeology has a great deal to offer Ngati Kahungunu and vice versa. As the dialogue between museum staff and *kaumatua* continues, newly acquired archaeological information may either be incorporated into the Ngati Kahungunu exhibition or into a supplementary gallery.

In conclusion, I want to consider the role of the Pakeha majority and the indigenous Maori in the control of cultural property. As O'Regan (Ch. 7, this volume) shows, Maoris are now strongly challenging Pakeha control over cultural resources in realms ranging from land and fishing rights to welfare and education. Many Maoris see museums as memorials to the Pakeha conquest of Aotearoa and challenge such museums' control over an important dimension of the Maori heritage.

For museums, two major questions arise. Is it more important for *taonga Maori* held in museums to be used by Maori people for their own needs, or for more general educational and research purposes? And is there a solution that can satisfy both needs?

Many Maoris are still distanced from collections in the museums. Many of the older Maori do not visit them willingly, and probably never will. School visits and television exposure give the younger generations greater familiarity with the role of museums, but resentment and reserve persist. Only through the progressive involvement of Maoris in all aspects of museum work, as board members, directors, and curators, will museums become an integral part of Maori life. Plans for a *Wharetaonga o Nga Tangatawhenua* as part of the National Museum indicate the positive influence that Maori leaders have had in calling for a change in museum administration in New Zealand.

It is now harder – and rarer – for Pakeha scholars to publish on Maori topics without the close involvement and consent of relevant Maori. The awesome responsibility involved in conserving Maori collections in public institutions is more widely recognized, and greater resources are being brought to bear. Four Maori students are studying the conservation of cultural property at the Canberra College of Advanced Education in Australia, made possible by studentships provided by the Cultural Conservation Advisory Council. These and other signs of change reflect the will to advance the process of increasing Maori control over their heritage.

At a *marae* on the Mahia Peninsula in northern Hawke's Bay in 1987, I attended the unveiling of the gravestone of a man who had been buried the previous year. He had been determined to take part in the opening ceremony of Nga Tukemata. He had worked closely with the other *kaumatua* and museum staff in the planning of Nga Tukemata. He participated in welcoming back the *taonga* on loan from the metropolitan museums.

I remember this man, who would sit and talk for hours; he travelled hundreds of kilometres with me visiting Ngati Kahungunu *marae*. His concern for the future of his people was paramount; it was he who translated Nga Tukemata as 'The Awakening'. The sense of loss when *kaumatua* like John Tangiora and Kuini Tamaku King die is overwhelming and the gulf they leave is vast. It is this sense of loss that causes us to treasure with such *aroha* those who remain, along with the memory of those who have returned to their 'homeland'.

Ngati Kahungunu have given the people of Hawke's Bay a very special gift: Nga Tukemata. With a gift one accepts responsibilities, ties, and reciprocity. The exhibition still grows and widens its sphere of influence as people continue to discover it. More *taonga* to be added soon are likely to generate new issues for debate.

Acknowledgements

I wish to record my gratitude to Ngati Kahungunu *kaumatua* who guided the creation of Nga Tukemata, and to my museum colleagues who have always been encouraging and supportive. I am indebted to Fay Butts for her support and assistance.

Note

1 This process continues: in 1988 Auckland Museum returned the *whakawae* (carved door posts), which had been cut into sections by a private collector and eventually came to the museum from different collections. Their incorporation into the exhibition has required some modification of the original design. It is hoped that other carvings from this house will be identified in the future and eventually incorporated in Nga Tukemata.

References

Barratt, G. 1987. *Queen Charlotte Sound, New Zealand: the traditional and European records 1820*. Ottawa: Carleton University Press.

Buchanan, J. D. H. 1973. *The Maori history and place names of Hawke's Bay*, D. R. Simmons (ed.). Wellington: Reed.

Butts, D. J. 1984. Co-operative redevelopment planning: first steps. *Art Galleries and Museums Association of New Zealand Journal* 15(4), 23–4.

Davidson, J. M. 1984. *The prehistory of New Zealand*. Auckland: Longman Paul.

Gathercole, P. 1979. Changing attitudes to the study of Maori carving. In *Exploring the visual art of Oceania*, S. M. Mead (ed.), 214–26. Honolulu: The University Press of Hawaii.

Kawharu, I. H. 1975. *Orakei: a Ngati Whatua community*. Wellington: New Zealand Council for Educational Research.

Mead, S. M. 1985. Concepts and models for Maori museums and cultural centres. *Art Galleries and Museums Association of New Zealand Journal* 16(3), 3–5.

Mitchell, J. H. 1972. *Takitimu: a history of the Ngati Kahungunu people*. Wellington: Reed.

Neich, R. 1985. Interpretation and presentation of Maori culture. *Art Galleries and Museums Association of New Zealand Journal* 16(4), 5–7.

O'Regan, S. 1984. Taonga Maori mana Maori. *Art Galleries and Museums Association of New Zealand Journal* 15(4), 15–18.

O'Regan, S. 1990. Maori control of the Maori heritage. In *The politics of the past*, P. Gathercole & D. Lowenthal (eds), Ch. 7. London: Unwin Hyman.

Te Awekotuku, N. 1985. He Tuhituhi Noa Iho . . . *Art Galleries and Museums Association of New Zealand Journal* 16(4), 8.

Thomson, K. W. 1981. *Art galleries and museums in New Zealand*. Wellington: Reed.

9 God's police and damned whores: images of archaeology in Hawaii

MATTHEW SPRIGGS

The title of this chapter, lifted from a work on images of women in Australia (Summers 1975), describes well the ambiguous or even liminal position of archaeologists in Hawaii. An archaeologist might be seen as an unnecessary evil to a real-estate developer anxious to get a project started and, at the same time, a useful ally to Native Hawaiians or environmental groups seeking to stop the same project; the same archaeologist might also be seen as having been 'paid off' by the developer depending on what is found on a parcel of land slated for development, and what is recommended to be done with the finds. A new discovery by an archaeologist might be seen as providing a fascinating window on the past or as sacrilegious grave robbing. Archaeological sites themselves partake of an ambiguous status: as fragile cultural resources to be preserved and revered, or as having more sinister character-istics. One recent headline in relation to sites discovered in the path of the proposed H3 freeway read 'Archaeological sites threaten H3'.

This chapter deals with media images of archaeology and archaeologists in Hawaii (for a recent survey of archaeology in Hawaii, see Kirch 1985). It is based on archaeological items appearing in Hawaii's two major news-papers during the years 1970–85 (see Table 9.1), viewed in their social and political context. A variety of limitations make this study far from com-prehensive. Reliance on print alone skews our viewpoint, as more people are directly affected by electronic media and their styles of reportage differ substantially. Hawaii has many radio stations, five major television stations, and at least one cable television station that carries some local programming; but, as far as I am aware, news items, talk shows, and the like are neither archived nor easily accessible after they have been on the air. We are better off with print media in terms of archiving, but not in terms of indexing. The two major Honolulu newspapers, the *Honolulu Advertiser* ('A' in references) and the *Honolulu Star-Bulletin* ('S' in references), have indexes compiled by the State Library,[1] but the local daily and weekly newspapers on the different islands do not. Archaeological stories might also appear in various specialist and trade publications, monthly feature magazines, and airline in-flight magazines.

Even the two major daily newspapers on which I have chosen to concen-trate present problems. Short articles of a few lines, including many

Table 9.1 Summary of archaeological news items in the *Honolulu Star–Bulletin* and the *Honolulu Advertiser*, 1970–85

Year	New finds	Hawaiian concerns over historic sites	Kaho'-olawe sites	Archaeo-logists vs. state & developers	*Heiau*	Burials/ bones	Petro-glyphs	National or state register	Other stories
1985	1	3	—	8	1	—	—	—	—
1984	4	—	3	2	4	1	—	—	4
1983	3	14	—	4	3	3	2	—	1
1982	—	4	4	—	1	—	—	—	—
1981	—	1	9	—	1	4	—	—	2
1980	2	—	12	—	2	2	3	—	7
1979	1	—	8	2	2	3	3	1	4
1978	—	—	7	—	4	3	2	—	4
1977	—	—	22	—	4	—	—	2	2
1976	1	—	6	—	4	—	—	—	4
1975	3	—	—	—	2	—	1	1	4
1974	—	—	—	—	1	—	2	—	—
1973	—	—	—	1	1	4	6	14	1
1972	—	1	—	—	12	3	3	4	—
1971	1	—	—	—	3	1	3	—	2
1970	4	3	—	—	11	6	—	—	18

archaeological stories such as the discovery of human bones, are not always indexed. Sometimes an archaeological component is not clear from the title and is not referred to in the indexes.

A story or event is considered newsworthy, a media guidebook claims, when it is new, involves conflict, relates to famous persons, is directly important to great numbers of people, involves mystery, is considered confidential, pertains to the future, and/or is funny (cited in Ho 1985, p. 7). Archaeological stories covered in the Hawaiian newspapers fit this categorization well. Stories abound of new and exciting finds, often with an element of mystery.

Aside from wire-service news of finds overseas, the vast majority of discoveries reported in the press relate to three classes of Hawaiian sites: *heiau*, petroglyphs, and human burials. *Heiau* are the structural remains of pre-Christian Hawaiian temples. They are often physically impressive both in location and size; indeed, many of them have never truly been 'lost'. Press stories about *heiau*, the largest architectural remains of ancient Hawaii, have been common since early this century. Many Native Hawaiians, and immigrants too, stand in some awe of them because of their spiritual associations. Some rebuilt or restored *heiau* have recently become the focus of religious revival activities.

Petroglyphs, most of them newly discovered, are also often reported in the press as presumably the most durable and accessible on ancient Hawaiian art forms. Prehistoric human remains eroding into visibility on beaches or uncovered by construction crews are also news. Other classes of Hawaiian sites are rarely reported. An exception is extensive prehistoric irrigation terraces recently found, but they are newsworthy mainly because they are located in the path of a controversial freeway.

Conflict is, indeed, the main thing that makes archaeology newsworthy. The image of archaeologists has been set since the 1970s in terms of conflict over archaeological activities or the disposition and control of archaeological sites. It is closely linked to the Hawaiian Renaissance, a reawakening of Hawaiian cultural pride and political power since about 1970, which has set segments of the Native Hawaiian community increasingly at odds with developers, government, the military, and, on occasions, archaeologists. Conflicts with archaeologists have involved differing interpretations of the past, charges of sacrilege and/or grave robbing in particular archaeological investigations, and disputes over preserving particular archaeological sites and areas.

Archaeological responses have not been monolithic. Hawaiian activist political groups hire or solicit help from archaeologists, who are often found on both sides of such disputes. Archaeologist may confront archaeologist over the significance or management of particular sites or the professional adequacy of an archaeological operation. One or two private archaeological consultant companies are alleged to minimize site significance to obtain jobs from developers unsympathetic to historic preservation.

Archaeologists also often differ with government agencies and developers over the fate of archaeological sites in areas slated for development, and over the failures to enforce historic preservation laws in the state's historic preservation programme.

Neither a scholarly nor a popular interest in Hawaii's past is a new phenomenon nor exclusively the domain of archaeologists. A Hawaiian view of prehistory, to be found in oral traditions collected mainly by Native Hawaiian scholars in the mid to late 19th century and codified in such works as Fornander's *Account of the Polynesian race* (1878–80), long preceded archaeological enquiries. The potential for indigenous critique of purely archaeological research was thus formed early from a rich corpus of oral tradition (see Finney *et al.* 1978).

Until the late 1960s, archaeology was almost exclusively associated with the Bernice P. Bishop Museum, established in 1889. Although the first 'scientific' archaeological excavation took place in 1913, the major emphasis before 1950 was on surface survey of structural remains such as *heiau* and petroglyphs.

Beginning in 1950, the museum, in association with the University of Hawaii, undertook excavations on various islands to gain evidence of whence and when Hawaii's earliest settlers had come. The first newspaper-index volume, covering 1929–67, is full of stories of new finds, early dates, and links to Tahiti and the Marquesas, particularly during the 1950s and

1960s. Only three articles warn that indiscriminate digging by amateurs or pothunters was destroying archaeological sites, notably on the island of Kaua'i.

After statehood in 1959 the pace of economic development in Hawaii quickened. Contract or salvage archaeology began in 1964, when the Bishop Museum was called in to locate archaeological sites where the Mauna Kea Beach Hotel was to be constructed. Beginning in 1956, the museum had already helped the National Park Service develop archaeologically significant areas. At this time archaeology had a high profile and a positive image in the press.

Increasing public concern in the United States over the destruction of archaeological sites led to the National Historic Preservation Act of 1966, which has helped to protect sites and mitigate the adverse effects of government funded or approved projects. The State of Hawaii in the late 1960s set up a Historic Sites Section within the State Parks Office to oversee efforts to protect historic sites, established a State Register of Historic Places, and prepared a state-wide inventory of such sites for planning purposes. Up to 1973, State Register site designations were news items, but thereafter interest in the topic declined, partly perhaps because the 'Historic Hawai'i Foundation' started distributing a monthly publication covering news of this kind.

The first hints of controversy over archaeology came in 1970, in a series of articles on the increased trafficking in Hawaiian antiquities removed by looters from archaeological sites. While all agreed that the important sites should be excavated, artefact collectors argued that the museum already had large numbers of antiquities stored away and did not need any more (S&A, 25 January 1970, A12; A, 26 January 1970, A8; A, 27 January 1970, C1; A, 28 January 1970, A5). The looting of burial caves by collectors seemed deplorable from a Hawaiian perspective, but columnist Sammy Amalu (A, 13 February 1970, A13) saw no ethical difference between artefact removal from caves by scientists and by looters. After hikers in 1973 discovered a looted historic-period burial cave (A, 14 May 1973, A12), the *Advertiser* presented prominent Hawaiians' views deploring the situation. A characteristically emphatic response to looting came from Richard Paglinawan (A, 16 May 1973, B4):

My feeling is a strong reaction against people going to these caves. Hawaiians have a strong dislike of exposing the bones of ancestors. That's why they did their best to hide them. Putting it in the newspapers and on TV only brings attention.

The reburial issue has not yet become the major conflict between archaeologists and indigenes that it has in the mainland United States, but Hawaiian attitudes clearly differ from those of many archaeologists, who stress the scientific value of bones and seek to curate them rather than to reseal burial caves or rebury skeletons.

The beginning of the Hawaiian Renaissance can be dated back to two speeches by the Reverend Abraham Akaka, a respected Hawaiian church leader (Ho 1985, p. 4). In January 1970 Akaka urged the revival of the Hawaiian heritage; in March he launched Operation Hawaiian Uplift, a 'plan for preserving and developing our cultural and religious activities, the spirit of Aloha, our language and literature, our music and dances, our arts and crafts, our ancient arts, our historic sites and artifacts' (S, 26 March 1970, A22). With cultural awakening came interest, also fuelled by the archaeological discoveries of the 1960s, in preserving historic sites, and in interpreting and using them in line with distinctly Hawaiian perspectives. In 1970, Hawaiian scholar Alika Cooper challenged the National Park Service's historic interpretation of Waha'ula Heiau as geared only for tourists, and also decried public access to the temple's sacred precincts (S&A, 1 November 1970, A4).

Ancient *heiau* have always been important symbols of Hawaiian cultural heritage. But in 1979 former National Park Service historian Russ Apple recalled the 1969 rededication of the Hale O Keawe Heiau at Honaunau (a Hawaiian religious and political centre, now a national park) as a milestone in the rebirth of interest in Hawaiian culture. He quoted the then president of the State Association of Hawaiian Civic Clubs as saying that, to modern Hawaiians the restored *heiau* 'means an anchor to their heritage, a visual link to the civilization from which they come and a means for all people to understand and appreciate the traditional Hawaiian culture before modification by the invading western culture' (Pilipo Springer in S, 20 February 1979, III: 27).

Restoration of ancient *heiau* has continued to provide Native Hawaiians with a symbolic focus. 'This is more than a physical restoration', as the administrator of Kamehameha Schools said of plans for restoring Kuilioloa Heiau in Wai'anae; 'It is a psychological rejuvenation for our people. Development has devastated so much of the Leeward coast already. In this spot we must say hold the bulldozers back' (Fred Cacholain in A, 2 August 1975, A13).

Many Native Hawaiians view both particular historic sites and the landscape as a whole from a spiritual perspective quite unlike that of the professional archaeologist. The mystical association between themselves and the *'aina* (land) goes beyond simple property rights:

> Hawaiians see themselves as an integral part of the cosmos and the *'aina*, the land. We belong to this and everything in it is living and everything is conscious and everything intercommunicates. This means when anything bespoils the land – such as freeways or buildings – it destroys our *'aina* which is the source of our sustenance, our livelihood, our source of political power, and it pains us and we must cry out in pain and do something about it. (Kekuni Blaisdell in S&A, 1 December 1985, A15)

Mandating archaeological surveys ahead of development made archaeology a business in Hawaii. The early 1970s saw the first of several private archaeological consultant companies, in competition with the Bishop Museum and the University of Hawaii's academic approaches to prehistory. As environmental impact laws and associated public hearings brought the development process under public scrutiny, conflict surfaced between archaeologists and developers, and between archaeologists and Native Hawaiian and environmentalist groups.

Opposing development, Native Hawaiians fought to retain, take over, or gain access to land, starting in the early 1970s with the occupation of Kalama Valley on O'ahu. In 1975 the Moloka'i Hawaiian group *Hui Alaloa* ('group of the long trail') held marches along ancient trails across private land in West Moloka'i to open up access to the island's beaches.

A Native Hawaiian campaign (Protect Kaho'olawe 'Ohana) to stop the US Navy from using Kaho'olawe Island as a bombing range and to have it returned to Hawaiians came to the fore in 1976. Kaho'olawe had formed part of the Crown and Government lands seized by the Federal government after the overthrow of the Hawaiian Kingdom in 1893 (A, 19 July 1978, A3), and for Hawaiians this dispute represented the continuation of an ancient land struggle. Hawaiian activist occupations of Kaho'olawe starting in January 1976 focused attention on the many historic sites on the island that were threatened by bombing. 'I always thought it was the hotels that desecrated our islands, but now I know that the bombing is the desecration', said Noa Emmett Aluli, after seeing bombed sites including shrines on the first activist occupation of the island. 'We saw huge boulders – you know Hawaiians worship boulders – split. If our grandparents had seen that they would have cried.' Another activist representative, Charles Maxwell, likened 'the bombing of the *heiaus* . . . to the bombing of white men's churches' (A, 7 January 1976, A1).

Archaeological knowledge of the island was at that time limited to a short Bishop Museum monograph of 1933, by Gilbert McAllister (S&A, 11 January 1976, D1). In response to charges of historic-site destruction by Aluli and others, the State Historic Preservation Officer recommended, and the Navy acceded to, an archaeological survey of the island. Archaeologists at once began to turn up previously unrecorded sites, and by September it was reported that the Navy had temporarily stopped using some target areas owing to their proximity to archaeological sites. One of the archaeologists, Farley Watanabe, reported finding some sites previously recorded in March 'blown to bits', but another, Rob Hommon, found little evidence of direct ordnance landings and thought the sites had been damaged mainly by erosion caused by the grazing of wild goats; in his view, if bombing were controlled it would not be necessary to designate the entire island as a federally protected historic site (A, 4 September 1976, A3).

Evaluation of the Navy's role in site destruction divided activists and archaeologists from the start. In October 1976 the activists filed a class-action suit against the Federal government; the first occasion on which Native Hawaiians had invoked Federal historic preservation laws to further their cultural and political aims. They claimed that 'continued use of live ordnance on Kaho'olawe pollutes the environment, endangers lives, interferes with religious practices and destroys historical sites' (A, 14 October 1976, A6), and that in failing to file an environmental impact statement describing the impact of military use of the island's archaeological sites, the Navy had violated the National Environmental Protection Act.

In some ways, 1976 marked the peak of the Hawaiian Renaissance. Activist action had led to the archaeological exploration of Kaho'olawe, the Navy had granted permission for Native Hawaiian religious ceremonies to be held there, and public support for ending military use of Kaho'olawe and returning it to state ownership was widespread. Beyond these island conflicts, the double-hulled sailing canoe *Hokule'a* made its first voyage to Tahiti and back, re-establishing the ancient Polynesian voyaging tradition.

Conflict between the Protect Kaho'olawe 'Ohana (PKO) and archaeologists over the significance and interpretation of Kaho'olawe's sites arose in 1977, but as a newspaper noted, 'the basic division between the preservation office and Hawaiians dates back to the old split between science and spiritualism or religion' (A, 17 January 1977, A2). Sites of spiritual and cultural importance to Native Hawaiians may have little research value to archaeologists or lend themselves poorly to public interpretive display; indeed, some are natural features which do not even come within the usual definition of a historical site. State Historic Preservation Officer Jane Silverman agreed that archaeologists' failure to consider *wahipana*, the *mana* or spiritual power of a place commonly revered by Hawaiians, had led to valid PKO objections. Insisting that Hawaiian *kupuna* (elders) play a role in the study and interpretation, activists raised the spectre of an alternative prehistory to be constructed from the memories of respected *kupuna* rather than the research of university-trained archaeologists.

New archaeological discoveries in 1977, revealing Kaho'olawe's great archaeological potential, pleased long-time opponents of military use. Because the bombing was 'depriving the State of a historically significant property', Maui mayor Elmer Cravalho saw a greater likelihood of ending it (S, 27 January 1977, B6). A cultural anthropologist sympathetic to Native Hawaiians, Dr Stephen Boggs, testified that native access to and an indigenous perspective on the Kaho'olawe sites were essential, for Hawaiian *kupuna* were 'uniquely qualified to identify them, analyse their function, and relate them to oral traditions' (S, 1 March 1977, A8). Hearings on the PKO lawsuit highlighted the differing archaeological and Hawaiian perspectives: state archaeologist Hommon asserting that the sites and the military could co-exist if bombing accuracy could be assured; the PKO that all military use should cease because the land was sacred to the Hawaiian people (S, 2 September 1977, B4). In the end the PKO won the lawsuit but failed to get the military off the island (S, 15 September 1977, A2). Archaeological studies continued, but at first the Navy would not allow Hawaiian *kupuna* to accompany the archaeologists to validate findings or give an alternative perspective. The past was to remain the domain of the 'objective' scholar.

Responsibility for the island survey passed from the state to Hawaii,

Marine Research, a private consultant company headed by geologist Maury Morgenstein. Hints that prehistoric Hawaiian land-use practices had played a part in devastating the island's vegetation and landscape now started to appear in the press, perhaps as rejoinders to the PKO's stress on the Hawaiian value of *Aloha'aina* ('love for the land'). 'Kaho'olawe has been misused and abused for hundreds of years', stated Morgenstein (A, 17 July 1978, A3), and its sites were 'not any stranger or more unique or less than those found on other islands' (A, 19 October 1978, C4). Where the PKO stressed military impacts, especially bombing, the archaeologists tended to see prehistoric slash-and-burn agricultural practices and subsequent over-grazing in the historic period as the major destructive agents.

PKO members were allowed to accompany archaeological survey visits for the first time in June 1979. On this occasion Aluli stated the view that 'only *kupuna* can verify sites, because they know from their *kupunas* what the sites were used for' (A, 18 June 1979, A2). But the Navy was still unwilling to accept that such visits could aid archaeological studies or help determine site significance, and since 'the visit by *kupuna* is considered a religious visit by the Navy, . . . the elders will have to find their own way to the island' (A, 23 June 1979, D4).

Having completed the survey the consulting firm agreed with the PKO that the island should be put on the National Register of Historic Places as an integral archaeological district (Hommon 1980a, b), 'if not as "a matter of science" ', as PKO members stated, then as 'a decision of the heart' (S&A, 9 November 1980, A2). Against Navy opposition, the entire island was in the end placed on the National Register. This has not, however, abolished military use, still protested by the PKO who are allowed monthly access for religious and cultural purposes.

Since then the PKO has come into open conflict with archaeologists. The conflicts concern the Draft Cultural Resource Management Plan, prepared by part-Hawaiian archaeologist Hamilton Ahlo (1981) for Science Management Inc. (the successor company to Hawaii Marine Research), and the coverage of Kaho'olawe in a historic preservation film prepared by the Society for Hawaiian Archaeology (SHA), the professional organization of archaeologists in Hawaii formed in 1980.

The management plan played down the scholarly significance of the archaeological sites and gave scant attention to their religious significance:

Many historical sites on the island contain information of a limited variety and some of these can be used to answer only a few questions . . . The wealth of fire-cracked rock features is an example of this. They contain important information in part because they have never been investigated before. It is probable, however, that after thorough recording and investigation of a small number of these features we will find that the information they contain is redundant and that we are able to predict the data that other sites of a similar nature would yield.   (quoted in S&A, 4 October 1981, A8)

By implication, little was to be gained by safeguarding more than a few such sites. PKO spokespeople charged that the plan trivialized the island's cultural and spiritual importance. 'What they talk about is the importance of Kaho'olawe . . . as a museum showcase. They're looking at it in the most narrow way. The way the 'Ohana looks at it the whole island is a resource' (Puanani Burgess, quoted in S&A, 4 October 1981, A8). Ultimately, a cultural anthropologist was brought on to the scene to address Kaho'olawe's contemporary cultural significance, in a report (Keene 1983) that has also generated controversy because it is seen by the PKO as being unsympathetic to their beliefs.

The second dispute affected the entire archaeological community, deeply divided the Society for Hawaiian Archaeology, and soured PKO relations with many archaeologists. In 1982 SHA produced an educational film, *Hawaii's Endangered Past*. The film gave prominence to Native Hawaiian views on the importance of prehistory, although these were almost exclusively the views of Moloka'i activists. But the film also bent over backwards to present a neutral, balanced view of the issues. The PKO were angered by the segment that dealt with the Navy-sponsored archaeological work on Kaho'olawe, which made no mention of its own efforts to have the sites studied and preserved. In the newspaper report on the premiere of the film (S, 27 May 1982, A2), a photograph of archaeologist Hommon (a SHA member involved in making the film) was captioned 'Didn't consider political angles', and Emmett Aluli was pictured as saying 'You haven't told the truth'. PKO supporters charged, 'It's a distorted film. You are consciously setting forth the doctrine that the U.S. Navy out of the goodness of its heart is taking care of archaeological sites' (David Stannard, University of Hawaii professor); 'People died to force the Navy to save the Island' (Haunani Trask, University of Hawaii professor); 'It if weren't for the 'Ohana archaeologists would never have gone to Kaho'olawe' (Bo Kahui, O'ahu PKO leader).

For the first time, archaeologists were really confronted *en masse* with the political implications of their work. 'Archaeologists have never been political', said Rose Schilt, chair of the committee that made the film. In the end, SHA voted to include a statement in the film about PKO efforts, but some members resigned over this issue, and the activists who had publicly embarrassed the archaeologists faced much resentment in the organization. As a result, archaeologists in Hawaii began to recognize the political nature and implications of their archaeological practice, however distasteful they may have felt it to be.

Increasingly in the 1980s the media have depicted archaeological concerns as conflictual. Contested case hearings and other litigation calling into question the conduct of archaeological contract surveys have become numerous. Development is the underlying issue: Should sites be preserved by developers? If so, which kinds of sites and how many? Native Hawaiian groups (often PKO offshoots) act in concert with various environmental organizations as litigants. Archaeological ethics and standards of performance are often debated, and archaeological assessments of site significance are attacked. Whether archaeologists should give weight to cultural and spiritual site significance as opposed to strictly scientific concerns often comes to the fore. Alternative prehistories often emerge from Hawaiian *kupuna* and from archaeologists. But in many hearings archaeologists testify against other archaeologists. Some cases (Kapua and Puna geothermal projects on Hawai'i Island) air genuine differences about correct archaeological procedure, such as how much of an area needs to be surveyed to serve as a representative sample. Elsewhere (projects at Kawakiu and Kaiaka Rock on Moloka'i, West Beach on O'ahu) serious charges of inadequate or even fraudulent work have been made.

At Kawakiu Bay, West Moloka'i, Native Hawaiians opposed plans for a condominium development as despoiling an isolated beach. The adequacy of the private consultant's archaeological report came under scrutiny by SHA, who were asked to review it by the Hawaiians (A, 25 February 1982, A3). After verifying 'the *kama'aina* [native] historical perspective' on the site given by *kupuna* Harriet Ne, Patrick Kirch of SHA reported that 'On a one day survey . . . we found six significant sites missed by the developer's archaeologist'. The Hearing Officer recommended hiring a new archaeologist to complete the study.

Another dispute pitting archaeologists against Native Hawaiians was the affair of Hawaiian *kahuna* (religious practitioner or priest) Sam Lono. Lono applied in 1980 under the Native American Religious Freedom Act to rebuild a fishing *heiau*, destroyed in the Second World War, in the grounds of Kaneohe Marine Corps Air Station. The Marines sought the opinion of Kenneth Emory, dean of Hawaiian archaeologists. He expressed scepticism about the 'springing up of *kahunas*' and doubted that the temple could have been associated with the deity Ku as Sam Lono had claimed; Emory's own express concern was 'merely to protect the integrity of the knowledge that has been passed down to the Museum by scholars, Hawaiian and otherwise, of the past' (A, 7 September 1980, A3). Backed by Emory's advice, the Marines refused Lono and his followers permission to rebuild the *heiau*, although they were later allowed to hold a religious gathering on the military base. Lono's followers retorted that 'the information in Museum books is often in error because it is gathered by *haoles* (whites) to whom Hawaiian informants did not tell the truth'; they said that neither the Marines nor the Bishop Museum should tell them how to worship. One follower called the Marines' action cultural genocide; another added, 'What about our Hawaiian culture and religion? If you ain't got nothing to worship at, you ain't got a culture.' Lono later started to construct a *heiau* at Kualoa Regional Park, another site with religious significance, but was cited for camping without a permit and his structures were removed by the police.

A freelance archaeologist's discovery of a religious shrine and prehistoric burials in a lava tube on Hawai'i Island, originally dubbed 'the most significant find of Hawaiiana yet recorded', led to conflict of a different kind (S, 6 June 1983, A1). The site included a large rock formation closely resembling a vagina, associated with a probable *heiau* and interpreted by the archaeologist to be the origin of the legend of Kapokohelele ('Kapo of the flying vagina'). Kapo saved her sister Pele, the volcano goddess, from rape at the hands of the pig-god Kamapua'a by detaching her vagina which flew away enticing the assailant to follow. The discovery was announced at a large press conference. But instead of it being hailed as a great find, as its discoverers (hastily formed into the 'Institute for Hawaiian Antiquity') had hoped, many Native Hawaiians expressed outrage at desecration of a major religious site (said to be known to, but kept secret by, the local community) and at the 'vulgar translations' of the legend of Kapo. The Society for Hawaiian Archaeology joined the chorus of criticism, charging the institute with providing no documentation for its statements about the cave's sacred, religious, or secular use, announcing the cave's discovery and location in a way that 'may only attract possible vandals or curiosity seekers to the area', taking no steps to preserve the cave's ecosystem, and generally outraging the Hawaiian people (S, 10 June 1983, A11). The society had obviously learned some political lessons since the previous year. Both institute announcement and media coverage of the find were held responsible for exacerbating local feelings 'to the point where a cultural treasure may be jeopardized' (Jordan 1983, p. 34).

The most recent archaeological conflict story covered at length by the media has an archaeological site rather than archaeologists as the villain or hero of the piece. In 1984 (A, 31 July 1984, A5), the Kane'ohe Historical Society announced the discovery of a large and well-preserved taro irrigation system amidst banana plantations on O'ahu, and the Bishop Museum was called in to conduct a survey. Test excavations showed 'the most extensive early (mid-12th century) wetland agricultural complex known on the island of O'ahu [with] a stratigraphic sequence reflecting a long period of continued use and development'. The site was right in the path of the proposed H3 freeway, a project held up for more than 25 years because of opposition from environmental groups. Late in 1985 a congressional bill was introduced to exempt the freeway from all environmental controls, including historic preservation. Meanwhile, the museum's report had been submitted to the Federal Highways Administration but was not released to the public. Preparing to testify before congressional hearings, opponents of H3, including a local state legislator, tried to obtain copies of the museum's study in order to evaluate the significance of the newly recorded sites. On the grounds that publicity might lead the archaeological site to be vandalized, the Highways Administration refused to issue the report to the state's Historic Sites Section, to professional archaeologists, or to the Federal Advisory Council on Historic Preservation. The term 'Bananagate' was coined and a cover-up charged (A, 15 November 1985, A20).

Increasing pressure from local government agencies, politicians, and environmental groups (S, 15 November 1985, A3) finally got the report released and included in testimony at the congressional committee. The site's significance became the major stumbling block in the way of plans to exempt the freeway from environmental controls and a boon to freeway opponents. Although the exemption bill was passed by Congress late in 1986, the Highways Administration plans to forestall further opposition by diverting the freeway around the site.

Archaeology in Hawaii has become controversial since the mid-1970s; archaeologists are in the centre of that controversy. The image of the discipline has changed dramatically. Formerly arcane knowledge of the past dispensed by a few academic researchers at the museum or the university, it is now a commodity, owing to the proliferation of contract archaeology and private consultancies. The Hawaiian cultural and political renaissance has provided interpretations of the past that sometimes contest previously unchallenged academic views. Many more people in Hawaii now have a stake in the past than did ten years ago. Archaeologists are no longer its sole guardians, nor other archaeologists their sole audience and critics. But changes in the social context of Hawaiian archaeology have outstripped archaeologists' attitudes and practices. This may help to explain their liminal and ambiguous image.

Note

1 Much of the source material from indexes was compiled for me by Mikilani Ho (1985), on whose material I have drawn and somewhat expanded.

References

Ahlo, H. 1981. *Kaho'olawe: a cultural resource management plan*. Honolulu: Science Management Inc.

Finney, B., R. K. Johnson, M. N. Chun & E. K. McKinzie 1978. Hawaiian historians and the first Pacific history seminar. In *Studies in Pacific history*, N. Gunson (ed.), 308–16. Melbourne: Oxford University Press.

Fornander, A. 1878–80. *An account of the Polynesian race, its origin and migrations and the ancient history of the Hawaiian people to the times of Kamehameha I*. London: Trubner, 3 vols.

Ho, M. 1985. Newspapers' attitudes toward archaeology. Paper prepared for Anthropology 460E course, Spring 1985, University of Hawaii at Manoa, Honolulu.

Hommon, R. J. 1980a. *Multiple resources nomination form for Kaho'olawe archaeological sites*. Washington, DC: National Register of Historic Places.

Hommon, R. J. 1980b. Kaho'olawe: final report on the archaeological survey. Typescript, Hawaii Marine Research Inc. Prepared for US Navy, Pacific Division.

Jordan, T. 1983. Covering Kapokohelele. *Honolulu*, August 1983, 30, 34.

Keene, D. T. P. 1983. Ethnography and cultural values. Part 2 of *Kaho'olawe cultural study*. Honolulu: Environmental Impact Study Corporation.

Kirch, P. V. 1985. *Feathered gods and fishhooks: an introduction to Hawaiian archaeology and prehistory*. Honolulu: University of Hawaii Press.

McAllister, J. G. 1933. *Archaeology of Kahoolawe*. B. P. Bishop Museum Bulletin 115. Honolulu: Bishop Museum Press.

Summers, A. 1975. *Damned whores and God's police: the colonization of women in Australia*. Ringwood, Victoria: Penguin.

10 *Aboriginal perceptions of the past: the implications for cultural resource management in Australia*

HOWARD CREAMER

History should not be written with bias and both sides must be given, even if there is only one side.   John Betjeman, *First and Last Loves*

The popular concept of history in Australia is strikingly one-sided. Ignoring Aboriginal views, it has adopted a colonial perspective, concentrating almost exclusively on the past 200 years (Fig. 10.1). This chapter seeks to show how the past is re-created through a subjective selection of data and events, then interpreted to suit the interests of the majority. Thus minority and lower-status groups in society are marginalized in history, as they are in the present. The chapter examines distortions in the presentation of Aboriginal history and suggests how Aboriginal views of the past could be included in the interpretation of cultural sites to provide a more balanced picture of history.[1]

The management of Aboriginal sites in Australia devolves on three main groups: professional archaeologists, government staff, and Aboriginal people. Competing interpretations of the Aboriginal past emerge in the different viewpoints – scientific, educational, and cultural – from which each group assesses the significance of these sites. Scientific data and other information based on archaeological research provide the main basis for site interpretation designed to enlighten the public about the Aboriginal past. Aboriginal people have other views of the past and attach different cultural meanings to their sites, views seldom included in site management. Many Aboriginal people are now demanding that their points of view be heard. For them, and others not so vocal, sites have become important symbols of identity and links with a past of which they are proud (Fig. 10.2). Integrating traditional with scientific pathways to knowledge of the past could yield a creative and meaningful interpretative synthesis.

Figure 10.1 Celebrating 200 years of white Australia, a minute sliver of the ancient Aboriginal heritage.

Figure 10.2 Lake Mungo: sacred Aboriginal site of great antiquity (*c.* 32 000 BP) in south-eastern Australia.

Aboriginal culture and the past

The indigenous world view can best be incorporated into interpretation through an explicitly Aboriginal perspective to site management. In that perspective, present-day culture is firmly based on the past. A conceptualization of the past, however idealized, is an essential component of any culture. As Geertz remarks, cultural patterns are 'historically created systems of meaning in terms of which we give form, order, point and direction to our lives' (1965, p. 116). Moreover, 'men unmodified by the customs of particular places do not in fact exist, have never existed, and most important, could not in the very nature of the case exist' (*ibid.*, p. 96). To understand the role of the past in people's ideas, actions, and creations involves recognizing that the notions they hold about their past are sure to change, just as their cultures are changing. Yet in spite of change, reference to the past is constant. Australian Aborigines have never lost touch with their heritage, notwithstanding all the losses their culture has endured since contact.

As cultural interpreters, anthropologists seek out the meanings given to the past and to its tangible remains, including traditionally valued sites. Yet in obtaining our data primarily from what people say about sites, we should be mindful that 'what we call our data are really our own constructions of other people's constructions' (Geertz 1975, p. 9). Thus what I say in this chapter about the Aboriginal view of the past is my own interpretation, and no adequate substitute for what Aboriginals have to say for themselves.

Both archaeologists and anthropologists subjectively interpret whatever is gleaned from physical remains and oral history. Professional research has added much to our collective knowledge of the Aboriginal past and helped to change many outdated and demeaning white Australian stereotypes about Aborigines, but our work has by no means always been helpful to them.

Re-framing the past

A white, Western, colonizing ideology has provided the intellectual framework for interpreting indigenous cultures the world over. How does the Aboriginal world view, particularly perceptions of the past, differ from that held by non-Aborigines? For one thing, Aboriginal creation beliefs run counter to scientific understanding of human evolution. Instead of finding their origins in a series of migrations from south-east Asia. Most Koories[2] believe in a localized creation, the Dreamtime. They are quick to point out that white people have not always believed in evolution. Many of them are confused, having also received the Genesis mythology from missionaries. Aboriginal rejection of evolutionary and diffusionist theories is not simply a matter of insufficient exposure to Western scientific concepts. The Dreamtime reflects the survival of traditional Aboriginal beliefs, all the more precious in the present circumstances of new-found self-awareness and pride. As Koories strive to validate the distinctiveness of Aboriginal Australian identity, they find the view that humans originated in Africa and Asia, but not in Australia, especially unwelcome. Now, information on sites has to be presented to the public as parallel interpretations of reality, reflecting the viewpoints of both archaeology and Aborigines.[3]

Many distortions in the popular view of the past can in part be attributed to the methods, concepts, and models of archaeology and anthropology. The paucity of the surviving archaeological material record, omitting much of what we understand by the term 'culture', and the attention devoted in ethnographies to religion and spirituality, suggest to many that Aboriginal people are primitive. Like those who criticize anthropology as a servant of colonialism, Aborigines now see archaeology as providing the powerful with a picture of the past that suits their own interests: 'There can be no doubt that your science of archaeology is white organised, white dominated, and draws its values and techniques from a European and Anglo-American culture and devotes much of its time to the study of non-white people', as Rosalind Langford puts it (1983, p. 2). 'As such it has within it a cultural bias which has historically formulated an equation between non-white races and primitiveness.'

The equation of 'old equals best' often implied in archaeology and the anthropological emphasis on the pre-contact past both detract from the integrity of modern Aboriginal culture and diminish the importance of cultural change. The impression the public gets is that Aboriginal culture stopped happening in south-eastern Australia in 1788 when the British arrived. Moreover, there are several demographic misconceptions in the popular view of the past. The common image of first contact is one of a virgin land with but few inhabitants, who chiefly followed a nomadic way of life in remote desert areas, without traditional land ownership or use. Such a model of the past has served to legitimize the invasion of Australia, as Koori people often term it, for nearly 200 years.

Many white Australians still voice these misleading clichés about the Aboriginal past, and sometimes they even form the basis of political policy, as in a recent statement by the leader of the National Party in New South Wales:

> The nomadic Aboriginal races in Australia, years ago, did not occupy specific areas of land. They wandered all over the continent . . . they had no specific area of land to which they were specifically identified, and therefore the concept of land rights so often espoused today bears little or no relation to the true historical situation.   (Murray 1984, p. 6)

The perception that archaeology and anthropology are in part responsible for the stereotypes of Aboriginal people as primitive nomads from a remote time and place has led some Koori activists to call for control over research. 'If we Aborigines cannot control our own heritage, what the hell can we control?' asks Langford (1983, p. 4). As Sharon Sullivan points out (1985, p. 139), 'whoever controls research into . . . sites controls, to some extent, the Aboriginal past'.

To change what they see as a distorted picture of the past, Koori people refer to archaeological and anthropological research that stresses the intimate understanding Aborigines have of their environment and the subtlety of their social organization and cosmology. More work remains to be done in post-contact history, for what has been omitted from images of the past is often as significant as that which has been included but distorted. Few white

Australians know that Aboriginal people were often ruthlessly murdered during the early years of white settlement, or that between 1883 and 1961 as many as one out of six Aboriginal children were forcibly removed from their parents and placed in institutions or sent to work as apprentices and domestic servants (Read 1982).

Aboriginal attitudes to knowledge and sites

Site presentations offer one of the best opportunities for changing popular perceptions about the Aboriginal past and concomitant attitudes towards Aborigines today. Aboriginal views about their sites are expressed within a set of attitudes towards knowledge which is profoundly unlike our own. To most Westerners, knowledge is for free exchange. Apart from matters of national security and a few arcane aspects of law and medicine, there are few socially sanctioned restrictions on the diffusion of knowledge in the community. We encourage our children to ask questions about everything; in our culture curiosity is a virtue. Not so in Aboriginal society. Here cultural tradition safeguards knowledge, allowing it to be used only sparingly, restricted according to age, gender, and status. Like a currency, knowledge bestows power and is not to be given away carelessly for fear of retribution. One implication of this is that older Aborigines sometimes consider site recording as dangerous. Helping researchers to document the location and significance of certain sites in New South Wales has been held partly responsible for the deaths of old people.

'Who is supposed to know what?' becomes an important question for Aboriginal site management. Traditional constraints on knowledge, such as rules of secrecy, frequently conflict with the need to make knowledge public, for example notifying local councils where sites exist so that they can be protected from development.

To Koories sites have intrinsic value as symbols of their own identity. They are seen as ends in themselves, their meaning inherent in their very being, reflecting an emotional commitment and spirituality. As two Aboriginal students commented after visiting an art site near Armidale in 1985:

Nellie Blair:
The feelings I experienced when I first saw the paintings were a bit wary and strange, as if no one was allowed there or to touch. I felt as if someone was standing over the big granite boulder watching us all, I have never seen anything so fascinating in all my life.

Betty Wright:
My feeling about the visit to the site is a feeling close to the land and its natural beauty. I also feel that I am at peace and very close to my ancestors.

Aboriginal attitudes to burials reflect particularly strong attachments to the past. Whites puzzled by intense Koori reactions to the treatment of skeletal remains need to understand that the bones, far from being culturally inert, are powerful links with the past. They are the bones of ancestors. They stand for all ancestors: those who enjoyed the idyllic life before contact and those who endured the suffering of invasion. They resemble 'symbolic artifacts which, once historically created, are recharged over time with new permutations of symbolic meaning and relevance' (Martin 1983, p. 28).

To archaeologists, by contrast, sites serve mainly to answer historical questions: How long have humans been in Australia? Where did they come from? What was their life like? In terms of usefulness to research, some types of site (occupation deposits, middens, burials) rank higher than others (scarred trees, natural features, mission cemeteries). To Aboriginal people, this hierarchy makes no sense – all sites are important. Many whites now accept items of Aboriginal material culture, such as didgeridoos and boomerangs, and even early Aborigines, as part of the nation's heritage, but they still have a long way to go before accepting present-day Aborigines and their heritage needs:

> There is an interest in curios such as King Plates, and the more spectacular or unfamiliar items of material culture, and commonly, romanticized mythology about noble savages, kindly land-holders and the 'last full blood'. This interest is rarely related to the present descendants of the 'dusky tribesmen'. In fact any claim for cultural continuity by Aborigines at a local level, is often met with shock and disbelief. (Sullivan 1985, p. 144)

Aboriginal involvement in site management

The cultural productions (MacCannell 1976) – the signs, brochures, videos, interviews – through which the past is presented at Aboriginal sites, should interpret them in a holistic environmental, cultural, and historical context reflecting the indigenous world view. One way to achieve this is through greater Aboriginal involvement. Increased employment of Aboriginal staff and consultation with the Koori community are current policy in the New South Wales National Parks and Wildlife Service.

The Service has employed several Aboriginal sites officers since 1973, although bridging the two cultures often arouses conflicting loyalties. For example, Koori staff recommendations to salvage sites prior to their destruction by development may run contrary to local community wishes. But increased involvement generally offers greater Aboriginal say about how sites should be managed. As an expression of their perceived congruence with the past, Aboriginal staff are often better equipped than their white colleagues to reflect the different views of the past and its material remains. Visitor behaviour consistent with site conservation and with respect for Aboriginal feelings is often best achieved through the knowledgeable mediation of Aborigines themselves.

Incorporating indigenous perceptions of the past and publicizing the meanings that Aboriginal people accord to sites thus have important implications for site management. Site protection priorities are revised and different written information about sites is provided. Some sites no longer have public access at all, such as the Serpentine stone arrangement site on the eastern New England Tableland, which was closed at the request of local Aboriginal elders in 1985.

A popular tourist destination at Mootwingee in western New South Wales was closed in 1984 following a blockade organized by the Western Regional Aboriginal Land Council. Calling for a new approach to site management, the Council sought employment of Aboriginal staff and revision of guidebooks to the site. It is also demanded an end to access to cave paintings said to have been traditionally sacred to men and forbidden to women and to the main rock engraving slope, then deteriorating under the impact of too many visitors:

> Mootawingee is a very special place for us. Our people have camped here for thousands of years . . . Whites have not shown respect for this sacred place. The National Parks and Wildlife Service have turned it into a tourist attraction. People who have no right here have disturbed this land. The pamphlet . . . is insulting; [it tells] tourists that people from this area no longer exist.[4]

Changing the spelling of Mootwingee – first to 'Mootawingee', then to 'Mutawinttji' – was a symbolic step in the campaign to persuade whites to recognize Aborigines as the rightful owners of the site. 'The significance of the Mootwingee blockade is that this is the first time in over 100 years that a group of Aboriginal people have camped [there] and reaffirmed its cultural and spiritual significance to themselves', wrote the Western Region's archaeologist in a report to the Parks Service. The new management plan meets many of the Aboriginal Council's demands. Aboriginal control over access to sites has been affirmed. No longer will the public be able to go to the Snake Cave or wander unescorted over the engraving slope. Guided tours will be led by Aboriginal rangers.

The 'Mutawinttji' lesson is that many conflicts between site use and preservation, public display and tribal sanctuary, can be resolved through co-operation with the Aboriginal community. Managers must learn to accept the possibility that there is more to the site than they admit knowing, that the site is sacred and should be managed with respect, that the ancestors are watching.

In asserting their belief in Dreamtime, in seeking to correct misleading models of Aboriginality, in exerting influence over presentations of the past through site research and interpretation, Koori people are using the past for their own purposes. Their goal is political, and to this end, they are following the common dictum that the past should serve the present. Yet at the same time there is an insistent personal quest in the rediscovery of Aboriginal identity that transcends the collective motive of increased access to power and resources. One is reminded of T. S. Eliot's 'Little Gidding':

> And the end of all our exploring,
> Will be to arrive where we started,
> And know the place for the first time.

Ownership and control

There is an emerging Aboriginal consensus that their past, which many had feared lost through the ravages of contact, can be recaptured. To foster this new relationship with the past and its material expression, Aborigines need to gain more control over the sites. While the past itself cannot be controlled, reconstructions of the past can be used to help achieve present needs and aspirations. As Langford says (1983, p. 2), 'it is our past, our culture and heritage, and forms part of our present life. As such it is ours to control and it is ours to share on our terms.'

In terms of cultural identity, Koori people are the living descendants of pre-contact Aboriginal society. This link with their past validates their claims to own sites as part of a distinctive cultural property. But some archaeologists, as Allen (1983, p. 8) points out in a reply to Langford, 'believe that no one can own the past. Philosophically they argue that the past only exists in the sense that it is created by people in the present . . . In this sense there can be many "pasts" which depend ultimately upon the belief systems of the people who create those pasts.'

Other arguments countering radical Aboriginal claims to the ownership and control of cultural heritage include the appeal to academic freedom to justify total access by any scholar researching the past, as if intellectual enlightenment gives them a divine right to study any other peoples and their cultural sites. There is a sense in which all human history is the rightful inheritance of all human beings, which everyone is entitled to share. But the present overriding concern is to secure greater equality of access to the past and control over its re-creations for the Aboriginal minority long deprived of both.

Ownership and control have many dimensions – moral, cultural, legal, and material – that require consideration. Questions such as who owns a 30 000-year-old camp site on private land involve complex answers and raise yet more questions. How far back, for example, can living people claim to speak for? On what criteria could a cut-off point, suggested by some researchers, be based? In northern New South Wales several trees carved by Aborigines, brought to a farm many years ago, still stand on the lawns of the homestead. Who should own them and where should they be kept? Legally they are the landowner's property. On the other hand, local Aborigines believe the trees belong to their community, while white museum conservators are concerned about how such vulnerable survivals can be best protected.

Aboriginal claims for effective control and ownership of their heritage are based on moral principles. To facilitate Aboriginal involvement and representation in decision-making, as well as to provide more effective communication of research results, the law needs to be made more responsive to Aboriginal demands. Land rights, access to education, museum funding, and many other realms play a part in securing greater Aboriginal control over their own heritage and, notably, their sacred sites.

Conclusion

It is widely maintained that today a sense of belonging, once common in Western society, has been lost. Indigenous peoples the world over are often distinguished from their mainstream modernized neighbours by their possession of a strong sense of locality, which is pivotal to an enduring sense of the past. In building such a model of their history, Aboriginal people may thus be in a stronger position to face their country's future problems than many other Australians. The latter might heed Christopher Lasch's warning (1978, p. xviii) that 'a denial of the past, superficially progressive and optimistic, proves on closer analysis to embody the despair of a society that cannot face the future'.

This chapter has looked at some reasons for, and efforts towards, incorporating an Aboriginal world view into public presentations of the Australian past. There is, of course, no one coherent Aboriginal view; there is variety in Koori culture as in any other: differences between young and old, men and women, in the way the past is imagined or remembered. Much of the past is invented or idealized, many see it as a golden era by contrast with their present helplessness. Koories yearn to establish contact with their heritage. Aboriginal sites are for them more than just physical relics; they are powerful symbols, laden with meaning, saying things about the way the world was, and is, and perhaps will be.

The challenge for archaeology is to assist in this search for meaning from the past for both black and white in Australia. Aboriginal attitudes toward archaeology are changing. Many Koories now see its value in providing information to buttress claims for greater respect for Aboriginal people and their culture. It is not uncommon for Koories to ask for excavations to help them reconstruct detailed pictures of the past in their localities. To integrate all Australian history from 40 000 years ago to the present, it is essential to achieve an archaeological orientation that embraces both white and Aboriginal perspectives (Trigger 1984). Archaeological evidence will assist Aboriginal people in maintaining their awareness of identity over time, against pressures to conform in Australia's complex, culturally plural society.

Notes

1 This chapter owes much to discussions with many Aborigines. Other sources of inspiration and guidance include Geertz (1965, 1975) on culture theory, Trigger (1984) on archaeological reconstructions of the past, MacCannell (1976) on the impact of ethnography and prehistory on tourism, and Langford (1983) and Sullivan (1985) on local issues in the politics of cultural resource management. While my contribution draws on experience in New South Wales, many of the issues are also relevant elsewhere in Australia, and have parallels in other countries with colonial histories (see, for example, O'Regan, Ch. 7, and Butts, Ch. 8, this volume, on Maori expressions of cultural identity).
2 In line with increasing practice, I use the term 'Koori' as an alternative for Aboriginal. As Miller (1985, p. vii) explains, 'The word Aboriginal is a Latin-derived English word which . . . did not give my people a separate identity [and] always has derogatory connotations.' The word Koori, indigenous to much of southeastern Australia, is gaining vernacular acceptance, especially in that part of the country.
3 Much Aboriginal Dreamtime mythology has a possible foundation in historical reality (Hiatt 1975, p. 3). There are stories of landscape features being submerged by rising sea levels that may reflect interglacial periods, and the giant beings of the Dreamtime may have a connection with now extinct megafauna.
4 Extract from publicity released by the Land Council at the time of the blockade.

References

Allen, J. 1983. Aborigines and archaeologists in Tasmania. *Australian Archaeology* **16**, 7–10.
Butts, D. J. 1990. Nga Tukemata: Nga Taonga o Ngati Kahungunu (The Awakening: The Treasures of Ngati Kahungunu). In *The politics of the past*, P. Gathercole & D. Lowenthal (eds), Ch. 8. London: Unwin Hyman.
Geertz, C. 1965. The impact of the concept of culture on the concept of man. In *New views on the nature of man*, J. R. Platt (ed.). Chicago: University of Chicago Press.
Geertz, C. 1975. *The interpretation of cultures.* London: Hutchinson.
Hiatt, L. R. 1975. *Australian Aboriginal mythology.* Canberra: AIAS.
Langford, R. F. 1983. Our heritage – your playground. *Australian Archaeology* **16**, 1–6.
Lasch, C. 1978. *The culture of narcissism: American life in an age of diminishing expectations.* New York: Norton.
MacCannell, D. 1976. *The tourist: a new theory of the leisure class.* New York: Schocken Books.
Martin, B. 1983. *A sociology of contemporary cultural change.* Oxford: Basil Blackwell.
Miller, J. 1985. *Koori: a will to win.* Sydney: Angus & Robertson.
Murray, W. 1984. The concept of rural land rights is a myth. *Northern Magazine*, 7 October.
O'Regan, S. 1990. Maori control of the Maori heritage. In *The politics of the past*, P. Gathercole & D. Lowenthal (eds), Ch. 7. London: Unwin Hyman.

Read, P. 1982. *The stolen generations: the removal of Aboriginal children in N.S.W. 1883–1969.* New South Wales Ministry of Aboriginal Affairs.
Sullivan, S. 1985. The custodianship of Aboriginal sites in southeastern Australia. In *Who owns the past?* I. McBryde (ed.), 139–56. Melbourne: Oxford University Press.
Trigger, B. 1984. Alternative archaeologies: nationalist, colonialist, imperialist. *Man* **19**, 355–70.

11 Search for the missing link: archaeology and the public in Lebanon

HELGA SEEDEN

> The past is the present in the sense that our reconstructions of the meaning of data from the past are based on analogies with the world around us. (Hodder 1982a, p. 9)

This chapter is based on developments witnessed in Lebanon during the past 14 years of civil war and social turmoil, while I was conducting field archaeology in predominantly rural areas and teaching the subject to university students in urban Beirut. One limitation of the views expressed here is that they were gathered by an outsider whose personal experience and preferences in archaeology have influenced the choice of data and ideas presented. Although frequent periods of insecurity imposed restrictions on their scope, my continuing research and fieldwork have given me an awareness of the sophisticated and appropriate knowledge possessed by rural people who were my partners in learning. The resulting perspective on Near Eastern archaeology offers a new approach to the subject and increases its relevance to Lebanese society. Attempting to understand the development of society from its village origins in antiquity by means of ethno-archaeological field research likewise promises to revitalize the subject.

The role of the past in a divided nation

Public attitudes toward archaeology

Developments during the civil war suggest that the old archaeology, imported from the West, is now out of touch with the public in Lebanon's socially fragmented society. The various surviving archaeological activities can be listed thus: the collection and trade of antiquities; the preservation of monumental sites and buildings as tourist attractions; object- and site-oriented excavations; biblical archaeology; and the publication of scientific reports addressed to a small and mostly foreign group of specialists. None of these has been able to generate any significant interest among the population at large, except for the widespread view that the country is full of treasures of monetary value to be sold off.

In a country lacking a properly functioning social security system and suffering debilitating unemployment and ruinous inflation (*Nouvelle Observateur* 15–21 May 1987, p. 3; cf. Nasr 1985a, pp. 313–16), this attitude is hardly surprising. It is a view found from the shopping centres of towns to the marketplaces of remote villages. For example, antiquities are a recurring and rather vexing subject of conversation with the ordinary taxi driver, whose chief concern is to pay his children's school fees. Should the question of one's profession be asked, and answered, the ensuing stereotypical dialogue begins with the driver's recitation of his first-hand knowledge of many archaeological sites in the country. He then evokes nostalgic memories of the tourist boom of the 1960s and inevitably ends with a question about the identification of antiquities – the purported role of the archaeologist – and how to reach that well-to-do Western clientele who will buy anything old from copper pots to bronze figurines. Perplexity and frustration result when the beleaguered archaeologist claims to lack any interest in 'robbing' archaeological objects for cash. This dialogue is so predictable that it can induce an almost pathological reluctance to reveal one's profession.

The following encounter adds another dimension. In 1983 I had an enlightening technical discussion with the adventurous guardian of an Arab castle in the 'Akkar, an underprivileged rural province whose feudal history (Gilsenan 1982, pp. 96–110; 1984) had earned it the legendary name of brigands' land. My ignorance of the Arabic term for 'metal detector' generated a lengthy and expert description of the appearance and internal mechanism of such an essential instrument for the treasure-hunt. Further proposed discussion was accompanied by an invitation home, the preparation of a sheep for a meal, and other customary rituals of traditional Arab hospitality.

As these experiences show, the practice of clandestine digging reaches the far ends of the country. People untouched by any knowledge of archaeology and whose view of the past is inspired by oral tradition and religious instruction can be well informed about aspects of modern mechanics and technology. Modern archaeology has adopted a panoply of sophisticated technical equipment for use in fieldwork and scientific analysis, but here, on quite a different practical level, technical know-how has reached the broadest general public; one indication that rural societies are indeed receptive to new technology and information. At the same time, scientific archaeological investigation in Lebanon is confined to academic practitioners, who communicate with a restricted audience (cf. Hodder 1984, p. 29, Cleere 1984).

Training and research in archaeology

In the 1960s, archaeological training was available only at the Lebanese University and at the American (Protestant) and French (Jesuit) universities of Beirut. Although instruction at the Lebanese University was in Arabic, the degree offered in archaeology was based on an outdated French history of art programme. The languages at the other two universities were foreign. Archaeology at the American University, taught in combination with ancient history, was oriented towards objects and sites. The French University offered a programme in the history of the classical period. Though the staff included several outstanding scholars in the Greco-Roman and prehistoric Levant, not a single Lebanese prehistorian has been trained to this day.

Excellent libraries were available at the universities, at the Institut français d'archéologie (IFAPO 1980), and at the Orient-Institut of the Deutsche Morgenländische Gesellschaft. Although they were mainly research centres for foreign students, these institutions did provide some scholarly interchange with local specialists. However, since they gave no formal instruction, they reinforced local students' dependence on the Western 'mother countries' for specialized training. Recent events have effectively closed the Beirut branch of IFAPO, and the centres of activity have shifted to Syria and Jordan. Perceptive members of the Orient-Institut have stressed the need for a drastic change in the outlook and objectives of foreign research centres in the area (Rotter & Köhler 1981).

The archaeological activities of foreign and local scholars and amateurs have formed several useful study collections, such as the prehistoric flaked industries at the Université Saint Joseph and the archaeological exhibits of the American University of Beirut (AUB) Museum – the first museum in the area, established 120 years ago (Woolley 1921). For example, Rudolph von Heidenstam, a Swedish engineer in charge of a main water-pumping station near the prehistoric sites of Antelyas and the Dog River (Mackay 1951, p. x), contributed samples of stone industries to the museum. His absorption with implements of the human past did not stop with collecting but led him to engage in 'experimental' and 'reconstruction' archaeology as well.

Not until 86 years after its foundation, however, did the AUB Museum get its first Arab curator, Dimitri C. Baramki (1959, 1967), a British-trained Palestinian. He sought to introduce archaeology into the AUB curriculum and to transform the museum into a viable teaching collection for training local archaeologists. His Master of Arts programme in archaeology was the first to be established in Lebanon. Practical training, including fieldwork, was given priority. One of AUB's first teaching excavations was begun in 1956 in the Biqa' Valley (Baramki 1964, pp. 47–8).

Archaeological excavation and related activities in Lebanon are characteristically undertaken by foreigners or by local groups remote from the concerns of the majority of its inhabitants. Thus information about an important collection of artefacts from Kamid el-Lōz, ancient Kumidi, in the Biqa' Valley, excavated by the University of Saarbrücken between 1963 and 1981, is available only in' an exhibition catalogue published in German (Hachmann 1983). Hence knowledge of the site and its rich materials is inaccessible to most Lebanese. In a different context, the International

Association for the Preservation of Tyre, founded in 1980 by some wealthy Lebanese, has succeeded in getting Tyre declared a *patrimoine universel* (UN Security Council Res. 459 §5), but it has staged most of its highly advertised cultural activities in Paris (*Tyr* 1985) and elsewhere abroad, remote from the people of Tyre themselves.

Archaeology in Lebanon is mainly perceived as an occupation of the well-to-do and educated, oriented primarily toward art objects, monuments, and sites. Its clientele evinces a general lack of concern for the interests of the population at large and contempt for its understanding of, and contributions to, the subject. For example, the conscientious reporting of a chance discovery in 1974, during construction work in a refugee village near Tyre, met with total silence from official quarters. The villagers who reported the discovery received no credit in the subsequent archaeological publication of the find (Doumet 1982, cf. Hachmann & Will 1983, p. 4). That villagers living in the midst of archaeological remains commonly resort to clandestine digging and antiquity dealers partly reflects the neglect with which they are treated by governmental agencies.

Museums in Lebanon

That the Department of Antiquities in Lebanon remains part of the Ministry of Tourism reveals its primary orientation. The National Museum of Beirut, opened in 1937, is the chief depository of archaeological material excavated in the country (Chehab 1937; n.d.). It has never been popular in the wider sense and was visited by few from outside the cities. Between 1963 and 1966 it received only one-fifth as many visitors as another public museum, the Ottoman period palace of Beit ed-Din (Saidah 1967, p. 180). (A similar situation exists in Damascus, where attendance at the 'Azm Palace ethnographic museum far exceeds that at the larger National Museum. School classes and university students go to both Damascus museums, in line with the Syrian educational policy stressing the national heritage.)

The National Museum of Beirut is no longer open to the public. Located on the dividing line between East and West Beirut, it was badly damaged by artillery, and has endured military occupation since 1976. The Director General of Antiquities succeeded in removing portable pieces to places of greater safety, while the larger exhibits were protected by sandbags and cement casings wherever possible (*Monday Morning* 20 June 1983, pp. 58–62; and Emir M. Chehab, pers. comm. 1984).

The museum at Beit ed-Din, in the 19th-century palace of the Shihab dynasty, representing Lebanon's more recent history, is ethnographic in character. Although recently in danger, it is still intact and open to the public. However, as a result of the continuing conflict, it remains inaccessible to many Lebanese.

Hassan Salamé-Sarkis, who was then the department's archaeologist in charge of northern Lebanon, created the country's first two regional museums prior to 1975. They accommodated local archaeological finds from excavations at the castle of Tripoli (Salamé-Sarkis 1980) and at al-Mina, the city's harbour, together with Islamic materials (Salamé-Sarkis 1973, pp. 91–2). The al-Mina museum was built at relatively low cost with the help of local craftsmen, whose interest made the project possible. Unfortunately, the exhibition and work rooms, laboratory, and offices (including most of the records) did not survive the subsequent turmoil in Tripoli. These museums have practically ceased to function and are effectively closed to the public.

The only museum still regularly accessible to the public is the American University collection, but the average visitor finds its holdings difficult to assimilate owing to the large number of items and crowded display methods. Regular lecture series, special exhibitions, and children's classes launched by the present curator have enhanced the museum's popularity.

The Beirut open-air exhibit of models of important historical monuments entitled 'Libanorama' has not survived the war, nor has the exhibition at the Greek Orthodox monastery of Deir Mkalles, east of Sidon. The monastery's valuable icon collection can now be seen, however, at the Beit ed-Din palace museum (*Daily Star* 15 September 1985, p. 1). Plans for other museums projected at Beit ed-Din and on the site of ancient Tyre remained unconsummated when the war broke out.

The widespread penchant of wealthy Lebanese for displaying antiquities and art treasures in their elegant mansions has resulted in the establishment of several substantial collections in historically and architecturally important Beirut residences. Some homes have become veritable museums. The Sursock Collection, maintained by the municipality of Beirut, is predominantly an art gallery. The collections of Henri Pharaon combine archaeological and historical objects from most major periods of the Near East. To this day the owner has been able to guard his palace with extraordinary tenacity. His is, in fact, the only 'museum' in the form of a private residence at present inhabited. While it may be visited at the discretion of the owner, it is naturally not open to the general public.

The Qaṣr Musa in the Shūf district, built and equipped by another private citizen, is a curious Disneyland version of a castle and a museum of a different kind. It contains a heterogeneous series of displays, foremost among them being an extremely popular, crowded, and animated reconstruction of traditional Lebanese village life and activities. Open to the public for a low admission fee, it is a children's paradise, frequently visited by large crowds from accessible areas. Qaṣr Musa easily heads the list of Lebanon's museums in general popularity.

A small wax museum of regional village life was set up through private initiative at Byblos, in conjunction with the Department of Antiquities' restoration of the town's Ottoman sūk area. Its exhibits were mainly conceived to add local colour to the archaeological ruins of Byblos, which used to attract many visitors. Such displays, intended primarily for tourists, point to the lack of a wider vision for reconstructing aspects of local cultural heritage for the Lebanese public.

Conflicting views of the past: causes and cures

Sectarian biases and archaeology

Ascending political and social movements commonly choose 'their own' historical periods, dividing the past into highlights of 'glorious achievements' and more or less neglecting intervening 'dark ages'. Thus in Egypt and Iran, the emphasis in archaeological research has shifted from pre-Islamic to Islamic times. In Egypt, when political movements favoured a pan-Islamic or pan-Arab orientation, interest in pre-Islamic history and archaeology waned. In Iran, interest has shifted away from the history of Achaemenid Persia to hostility towards this period and its monuments (Gaube 1982, Trigger 1984).

In both past and present, dominant ideologies have often gone further in their emphasis on a chosen period by building up claims for descent from 'superior' ancestors in support of cultural or racial chauvinism. Archaeology is then expected to substantiate such claims, notwithstanding firm evidence to the contrary (for example, Diakonov 1972, Liverani 1980), while dissenting texts are declared dangerous, withdrawn from the market, or the publication forbidden.

Claims to legendary origins are even graver when used to justify territorial hegemony. Thus in Israel efforts are being made to deduce legitimacy from the results of 'biblical' archaeological research in order to substantiate the 'greater antiquity' and 'superiority' of the group in its Arab environment and to justify expansive or suppressive policies (Gaube 1982, p. 99). During the 1982 Israeli invasion of Lebanon this view found exemplary expression. Despite heavy shelling and loss of life the Israeli army posed as the liberator of Lebanon's National Museum from 'barbarians or terrorists who understood little of art and civilisation'. Judged incapable of comprehending archaeological objects, they were termed 'ignorant forever', evoking the stereotypes of 'the steppe which does not appreciate culture' (*Révue du Liban* **1186**, 1982, p. 14).

The emphasis given by Maronite Christians in Lebanon to 'Phoenician' links, assigning supreme importance to this ancient era while neglecting more than a millennium of the Muslim past, exacerbates sectarian antagonisms and politicizes archaeology. Their exclusive focus on this period has been detrimental to the archaeology of Lebanon's Arab and Islamic past. How are Muslim Lebanese supposed to develop an interest in a 'national' past that substantially ignores their own cultural heritage? As one consequence, Islamic fundamentalist ideology is, in turn, generally dismissive of archaeology altogether. These dogmatically exclusive ideologies are uncritically accepted by many in the respective communities.

Nonetheless, historical common sense has led some Lebanese to conclude that they live in the same country and are the heirs '*à part entière de la totalité de son passé, sans aucun complexe de quelque nature que ça soit* (Salamé-Sarkis 1986, p. 62, cf. Beydoun 1984, pp. 9–22). Throughout Lebanon's history,

Figure 11.1   Shams ed-Din 1974: mudbrick villages and a neolithic settlement excavation threatened by the artificial Euphrates Lake. The two villages in the flood plain have since disappeared under water.

institutions and practices in the various communities have deeply influenced one another or even fused (e.g. Chevallier 1971, p. 174). A valid archaeology would reflect the varied historical traditions of all sections of Lebanese society. Such a perspective stimulates new inquiries into the recent past: the past within living memory.

An ethnoarchaeological approach

Ethnographic enquiries in the Near East can engender mutual comprehension between local inhabitants and visiting archaeologists. Unfortunately, the field archaeologist (unlike the anthropologist, who often comes to the village alone and as a guest) has little experience of working with the inhabitants of rural areas. His predominant interest in the past cuts him off from his host environment by a gap of anything from a few decades to several millennia.

One productive way to bridge this gap, thereby enhancing both local communication and research results, is to study modern as well as ancient settlement patterns at archaeological sites. For instance, a one-season rescue excavation in the mid-1970s at a neolithic village site in the Taqba dam area of the Euphrates (al-Radi & Seeden 1980; Fig. 11.1) necessitated communal living arrangements with dry-land farmers and animal herders in a half-

Figure 11.2 Shams ed-Din 1974: empty grain silos and sun-drying mudbricks.

Figure 11.3 Shams ed-Din 1982: building a new house of stone, mudbrick, tin, and wood.

Figure 11.4 Shams ed-Din 1982: grain silo abandoned in 1974 (details of silos in Figure 11.2).

Figure 11.5 Shams ed-Din: remnant of Neolithic grain silo excavated in 1974.

abandoned mudbrick settlement. The mutual concern of archaeologists and villagers about the immediate threat of the rising level of the Euphrates led to conversations between foreigners and villagers that in turn prompted discussion of the advantages and disadvantages of ancient and contemporary forms of housing and storage (Figs 11.2–3), farming, animal husbandry, irrigation, and cash crops.

Archaeologists returning to the site in 1980 met old friends settled in a new (post-1976), but traditional, mudbrick village, located at a safe distance from the artificial lake. Archaeologists and villagers again observed, discussed, and compared modern architectural features with remnants of the ancient village (Seeden 1982). A complete architectural and ethnographic study of the new village ensued. Villagers' experiences with cement architecture during their stay in the towns of Taqba and Raqqa and their selective adoption of materials such as metal doors were noted. They had found the urban provision for domestic space inadequate to their needs but were pleased with such innovations as electricity, water pumps, and irrigation (Seeden & Kaddour 1984). They welcomed many modern changes and chose to adapt them in ways appropriate to their traditional technology, essentially without the interference of outsiders and their development schemes.

Ethnoarchaeologically, the study of contemporary grain silos suggested the function of a comparable neolithic structure (Figs 11.2, 4, 5). The rescue archaeologists' mental horizon was broadened to include settlement patterns and agricultural strategies in a modernizing, yet still traditional, rural environment. Their initial narrow concern with artefactual data expanded into a 'contextual archaeology' of the present (Hodder 1982b, p. 217) which included material, social, economic, and historical factors vital for shaping a rural community, present and past. Most beneficial was the growing recognition that the villagers were often more knowledgeable than the urban experts. Involving rural people as partners in learning helps to divest archaeologists of entrenched stereotypes of technological superiority (Chambers 1983, pp. 75–102).

After 1975, the civil war made fieldwork in Lebanon dangerous, particularly since it involved mixed groups of students from several sectors of their fragmented society. To bring such groups together was far less difficult on a neighbouring Syrian site. Two specific ethnographic and archaeological village projects were planned. That in the village of Buṣrā (southern Syria) was completed in 1984 (Seeden & Wilson 1984, Seeden 1985). (The Lebanese sister project at Batrūn-Kubbe, in co-operation with the French and Lebanese universities, cannot yet be undertaken, owing to the division of the country into separate areas controlled by opposing militias.) For Lebanese students and professional participants alike, the Buṣrā project was a salutary exercise in peace-time living. Interaction with the different culture of the villagers highlighted intra-group prejudices which the war had entrenched. Indeed, communication with members of the rural community was sometimes easier than between some of the students, who, although

Figure 11.6 Beirut 1981: Buṣrā exhibition: press report after the exhibition's closure (as-Safir **2553**, 7 June 1981, p. 12).

from similar urban backgrounds, professed different group ideologies. More than once, members of the village community eased and even mediated student dissensions (cf. Hodder 1982a, p. 212).

Following the first Buṣrā field season of 1980, archaeologists and students held public meetings to raise funds and ascertain the level of public interest in such research. Lectures on 'village archaeology' from geographical, historical, archaeological, and ethnographic perspectives were given in Beirut, Batrūn, and Tripoli. In 1981 the American University sponsored an exhibition of the first season's work. The Buṣrā team's enthusiastic interest stimulated wider participation on the part of the general student body, and volunteers from the fields of architecture, agriculture, anthropology, and art and photography helped to mount the exhibit.

This was an extraordinary achievement, given the disturbances of the time. Indeed the exhibition had to be postponed because of an outbreak of heavy fighting. Yet the official opening was attended by one of the Buṣrāwi community's most esteemed elders, who had risked travelling by service taxi from Buṣrā to Beirut despite the hazards. The official Lebanese representative, the former Minister of Tourism, gave considerable support to the exhibition, which received both Arabic and foreign press coverage (Fig. 11.6) and drew 2000 visitors over ten days. The overall response, directed primarily toward the ethnographic sections of the exhibit, was most encouraging. Its scheduled display in Damascus and Buṣrā, however, was prevented by the invasion of Lebanon in 1982.

Urban–rural cleavages

Despite the almost daily experience of fear and frustration during the heavy shelling of Beirut, including parts of the AUB campus, in February 1984, a student-aided newspaper series concerning traditional Lebanese village life and crafts appeared shortly afterwards (Daily Star March–July 1984). Data previously collected (students were no longer able to return to their family villages) from many different areas revealed basic village similarities and major disparities between rural and urban sectors. Students of village origin had an excellent knowledge of local geography and a sure grasp of sources of information. Those who had grown up and been educated in Beirut, by contrast, showed keen emotional and intellectual motivation, but lack of direct association with a village background flawed their understanding.

These urban–rural cleavages are mirrored in the attitudes of the Lebanese generally. The increasing isolation of the population within beleaguered enclaves has intensified old prejudices. Urban animus against the hinterland remains entrenched, and the more remote the rural area the greater the prejudice. It is practically impossible for any Lebanese, however urbanized, to deny his village origins. But while the inhabitants of one's original village may be upheld as hard working, thrifty, orderly, responsible, and eminently worthy of emulation, villagers elsewhere are denigrated and viewed as strangers.

Old-established inhabitants of Beirut are today baffled by the changed face of the crowds in the capital's streets, where inhabitants of the rural areas and the poor southern suburbs of the city mingle with others dressed in traditional costumes from the central mountains. Repeated bombing and military raids forced both town and country people to flee in the hope of finding safety. The destination of these people was often the overcrowded and impoverished suburbs and 'camp' settlements of large towns (Beirut, Saida, Tripoli, and Ba'lbek) (*Daily Star* **8787**, 23/24 June, 1984, p. 7). The influx of village traits surprised urbanites and revealed their unawareness of the state of affairs in a country of great social inequalities and rapidly mounting urban poverty (Nasr 1985a, pp. 310, 329–30, n. 13).

My own field experience in the 1960s in Lebanon's hinterland confirmed these social disparities (cf. Marfoe 1979, pp. 5, 7, Nasr 1985b, pp. 88–91). Contact during excavations with village labourers and the treatment they received revealed that urban prejudice against rural inhabitants was widespread, and there was an unspecified 'fear' of folk from more distant villages on the eastern side of the Biqa'. These villages were underdeveloped by comparison with those on the western foothills of the plateau, nearer larger town centres. Many of the eastern villages lacked electricity, elementary schools, medical dispensaries, and roads. Economic difficulties were exacerbated by wealthy landowners who controlled labour and could limit wages. These controls, along with urbanite prejudices toward the villagers, inhibited productive co-operation and cut off most channels of communication. By contrast, appropriate explanation on site has gone far in changing potential 'treasure thieves' into informed guardians and reporters of antiquities.

The erosion of tradition

The continuity of traditional culture with the past has been rapidly eroded by wartime upheaval. Most Lebanese village crafts and industries are dying out. Several of the five surviving traditional pottery-making workshops at Rashaya al Fukhar, in the Biqa', which once supplied wide areas of the Near East with distinctive household wares (Figs 11.7–8), have been damaged by bombing (*Daily Star* **8794**, 3 July 1984, p. 2), and Israeli occupation has made it impossible to market what is still produced. Beit Shebab, in the central Christian mountains, had a thriving industry making storage jars for wine, olives, and oil, and bottles for 'arak and other local products (Hankey 1968, p. 27). But the 'mountain war' of 1983 cut off its major market in the neighbouring, mainly Druze, agricultural areas. Prior to the war, Jisr al-Qadi, in the Shūf district, with a tradition of mostly glazed pottery, had begun to cater for tourists; it too has practically closed down. Only in some remote areas do crafts still flourish. In Assia, in the district of Batrūn, women continue to produce domestic pottery of ancient types for local use (Fig. 11.9) (*an-Nahar* **5244**, 15 May 1985, p. 4). Pockets of basketry production survive in areas where such containers are still in demand during harvests and other traditional uses.

Figure 11.7 Rashaya al Fukhar (Biqa') 1980: painting jars at the workshop of Sa'id al-Gharib.

Figure 11.8 A group of painted jars at Sa'id al-Gharib.

Figure 11.9 Modern pottery from Assia resembling ancient types.

Koubba - un petit village du Liban
the little village of Koubba in Lebanon

Figure 11.10 Batrūn area: village of Kubbe 1979. (From *Landmarks of Lebanon*. Beirut: Ill. Publ.)

Traditional Lebanese architecture, one of the most characteristic creations of village and city alike, has been doubly devastated, by wartime destruction and by redevelopment, and is perhaps beyond salvation. Although artists and architects have sung its praises (Kalayan & Liger-Belair 1966, Ragette 1980; Fig. 11.10), the romantic interests of the connoisseur have had little effect on the private building sector and investors bent on modernization.

A popular base for discovering the heritage?

The pride most Lebanese display in their home villages is one of the greatest assets of their cultural consciousness. Many schoolchildren, and not only those from rural backgrounds, know the practical uses of products of local craftsmanship. The construction of a traditional village house in any classroom evokes spontaneous responses with a wealth of specific information. The latent curiosity of many Lebanese about ancient things, often engendered by the archaeologically rich environment of their natal villages, could provide a basis for correcting misconceptions about 'treasures' engrained from school age on. An appreciation that still-living traditions are an important part of the country's heritage in need of protection could enable Lebanese to re-evaluate the material remains of their past as a non-renewable and endangered cultural resource (Cleere 1984, p. 128).

Some of Lebanon's dedicated researchers are professional archaeologists and teachers blessed with a non-sectarian perspective on their country and its past; others are amateurs and antiquities collectors whose interest in objects stems not merely from aesthetic or monetary considerations but from keen scientific curiosity. To effectively broaden participation in the heritage, and to curtail the illegal trade in antiquities, communication has to be established between these researchers and the public.

Increased awareness of the recent past can be used to bring out latent public concern with the past in general. The public at large may not share the private collector's interest in *objets d'art*, but its interest in the archaeological traces everywhere observable can be tapped, as educational values shift the learning process from zest for treasures to an appreciation of cultural continuity. The involvement of Lebanese villagers, whose access to higher education has been enhanced by the large-scale emigration of wealthy urbanites (Bourgey 1985, p. 19), can mobilize a particularly rich source of understanding.

Despite continuing civil unrest, the data on surviving traditional village techniques, equipment, and tools in agriculture, architecture, pottery, and the like are being collected and published. It is planned to analyse the toponyms of Lebanese village settlements and thus throw light on their origins. Present-day changes in traditional village institutions as well as their origins and history are under study. A proposed ethnographic centre would generate considerable interest among people of all ages and backgrounds. The re-creation of artisans' workshops, techniques, and experiences could serve as a focus for the collection and preservation of rapidly disintegrating

Lebanese crafts and industries. Plans have been drawn up for the rehabilitation of artisans' schools in old Beirut (Salman 1984). Such a 'museum' may be a step towards reuniting the divided public with its neglected recent past.

Lebanese archaeologists must find and meet the public, especially the larger public passed over by conventional archaeological approaches. Greater awareness of contemporary traditional culture would benefit the people, the researcher, and the country. It would serve to spread knowledge of skills and traditions in danger of extinction and engender mutual appreciation of a complex past of interest to all.

References

Baramki, D. C. 1959. *The Archaeological Museum of the American University of Beirut.* Publications de l'Institut historique et archéologique Néerlandais de Stamboul IV. Leiden: Nederlands Historisch-Archaeologisch Instituut in het Nabije Oosten.

Baramki, D. C. 1964. Second preliminary report on the excavations at Tell el Ghassil. *Bulletin du Musée de Beyrouth* 17, 47–103.

Baramki, D. C. 1967. *The Archaeological Museum of the AUB.* Beirut: American University of Beirut centennial publication.

Beydoun, A. 1984. *Identité confessionelle et temps social chez les historiens libanais contemporains.* Université Libanaise, section des études philosophiques et sociales XV. Beirut: Librairie Orientale.

Bourgey, A. 1985. Importance des migrations internationales de travail dans l'Orient arabe. In *Migrations et changements sociaux dans l'Orient arabe*, 11–35. Beirut: Centre d'études et de recherches sur le Moyen Orient contemporain.

Chambers, R. 1983. *Rural development: putting the last first.* London: Longman.

Chehab, M. 1937. Le Musée de Beyrouth. *Bulletin du Musée de Beyrouth* 1, 1–6.

Chehab, M. n.d. *Le Musée National.* Beirut: Imprimerie Catholique.

Chevallier, D. 1971. *La société du Mont Liban à l'époque de la révolution industrielle en Europe.* Institut Français d'Archéologie de Beyrouth, bibliothèque archéologique et historique 91. Paris: Geuthner.

Cleere, H. 1984. World cultural resource management: problems and perspectives. In *Approaches to the archaeological heritage*, H. Cleere (ed.), 125–31. New Directions in Archaeology. Cambridge: Cambridge University Press.

Daily Star 1984. Nos. 8712–8809, weekend issues from 24/25 March to 21/22 July.

Diakonov, I. M. 1972. Die Arier im Vorderen Orient: Ende eines Mythos. (Zur Methodik der Erforschung verschollener Sprachen.) *Orientalia* 41, 19–20.

Doumet, C. 1982. Les tombes IV et V de Rachidieh. *Annales d'Histoire et d'Archéologie* 1, 89–135.

Gaube, H. 1982. Geschichte, Altertümer und Archäologie in den Kernländern des Islam. In *Archäologie und Geschichtsbewußtsein*: Kolloquium zur *Allgemeinen und Vergleichenden Archäologie*, vol. 3, 85–103. Munich: Beck.

Gilsenan, M. 1982. *Recognizing Islam: religion and society in the modern Arab world.* New York: Pantheon.

Gilsenan, M. 1984. A modern feudality? Land and labour in north Lebanon, 1858–1950. In *Land tenure and social transformation in the Middle East*, T. Khalidi (ed.), 449–63. Beirut: American University of Beirut.

Hachmann, R. (ed.) 1983. *Frühe Phöniker im Libanon, 20 Jahre deutsche Ausgrabungen in Kamid el-Lōz.* Mainz: Philipp von Zabern.

Hachmann, R. & E. Will 1983. *Rapport. Mission de l'Unesco à Tyr, protection et présentation des sites et monuments.* Unesco report, 22.

Hankey, V. 1968. Pottery-making at Beit Shebab, Lebanon. *Palestine Exploration Fund Quarterly* **100**, 27–32.

Hodder, I. 1982a. *The present past: an introduction to anthropology for archaeologists.* London: Batsford.

Hodder, I. 1982b. *Symbols in action: ethnoarchaeological studies of material culture.* Cambridge: Cambridge University Press.

Hodder, I. 1984. Archaeology in 1984. *Antiquity* **58**, 25–32.

IFAPO 1980. *Institut français d'archéologie du Proche-Orient* (exhibition booklet). Paris: Ministry of Foreign Affairs, University of Paris, and IFAPO.

Kalayan, H. Y. & J. Liger-Belair 1966. *L'habitation au Liban* I & II. Beirut: Association pour la Protection des Sites et Anciennes Demeures.

Liverani, M. 1980. Le 'origini' di Israele. Progetto irrealizzabile di ricerca etnogenetica. *Rivista biblica* **28**, 9–32.

Mackay, D. 1951. *A guide to the archaeological collections in the University Museum (AUB).* Beirut: Imprimerie Catholique.

Marfoe, L. 1979. The integrative transformation: patterns of sociopolitical organization in southern Syria. *Bulletin of the American School of Oriental Research* **234**, 1–42.

Monday Morning (Beirut), 20 June 1983. Lebanon's wars and Lebanon's treasures. Interview by M. es-Said with Emir M. Chehab, 58–67.

Nasr, S. 1985a. Guerre, migrations vers le Golfe et nouveaux investissements immobiliers dans le Grand Beyrouth. In *Migrations et changements sociaux dans l'Orient arabe*, 309–30. Beirut: Centre d'études et de recherches sur le Moyen Orient contemporain.

Nasr, S. 1985b. La transition des chiites vers Beyrouth: mutations sociales et mobilisation communautaire à la veille de 1975. In *Mouvements communautaires et espaces urbains au Machreq*, 87–116. Beirut: Centre d'études et de recherches sur le Moyen Orient contemporain.

al-Radi, S. & H. Seeden 1980. The AUB rescue excavations at Shams ed-Din Tannira. *Berytus* **28**, 88–126.

Ragette, F. 1980. *Architecture in Lebanon.* Delmar, NY: Caravan Books.

Rotter, G. & W. Köhler (eds) 1981. *Orient-Institut der Deutschen Morgenländischen Gesellschaft in Beirut.* On the occasion of its 20th anniversary.

Saidah, R. 1967. Chronique. *Bulletin du Musée de Beyrouth* **20**, 155–80.

Salamé-Sarkis, H. 1973. Chronique archéologique du Liban-nord II: 1973–1974. *Bulletin du Musée de Beyrouth* **26**, 91–8.

Salamé-Sarkis, H. 1980. *Contribution à l'histoire de Tripoli et de sa région à l'époque des croisades.* Institut Français d'Archéologie de Beyrouth, bibliothèque archéologique et historique 106. Paris: Geuthner.

Salamé-Sarkis, H. 1986. L'arbre généalogique: essai sur quelques aspects irrationels dans le discours historique libanais. *Annales d'Histoire et d'Archéologie* **3**, 35–66.

Salman, R. 1984. Ain el-Mreisse: Rehabilitation. Beirut: American University of Beirut, Bachelor of Architecture final project.

Seeden, H. 1982. Ethnoarchaeological reconstruction of Halafian occupational units at Shams ed-Din Tannira. *Berytus* **30**, 55–90.

Seeden, H. 1985. Buṣrā 1983: an Umayyad farmhouse and bronze age occupation levels. *Annales Archéologiques Arabes de Syrie* **33**(2), 161–73, 267 (Arabic summary).

Seeden, H. & M. Kaddour 1984. Space, structures and land in Shams ed-Din Tannira on the Euphrates: an ethnoarchaeological perspective. In *Land tenure and social trans-*

formation in the Middle East. T. Khalidi (ed.), 495–526. Beirut: American University of Beirut.

Seeden, H. & L. J. Wilson 1984. Buṣrā in the Hawran: AUB's ethnoarchaeological project 1980–1985. *Berytus* **32**, 19–34.

Trigger, B. 1984. Alternative archaeologies: nationalist, colonialist, imperialist. *Man* **19**, 355–70.

Tyr, Patrimoine universel en danger. 1985. Association Internationale et le Comité Français pour la Sauvegarde de Tyr (ed.). Opéra de Paris programme of 2 May 1985.

Woolley, C. L. 1921. *Guide to the Archaeological Museum of the American University of Beirut*. Beirut: American University of Beirut.

12 *The legacy of Eve*

SÎAN JONES & SHARON PAY

> Who controls the past controls the future: who controls the present controls the past. (Orwell, 1949, p. 199)

Terms like 'our past' and 'heritage', both denoting some form of ownership, are commonly used with reference to the study and presentation of prehistory. To whose past, however, do we refer? The notion that history in some way belongs to, or is a concern of, ordinary people is not, of course, new, but it *is* a new development for them to wish to take control of their own past, and thereby their present and their future.

The need to examine the role of women in the past stems from a political movement through which women seek to take control of their own lives. Feminist historians conceptualize afresh the construction of knowledge in women's own terms and values, explicitly the need to end women's oppression in their own society. This requires the recognition that male descriptions of the world are incomplete.

> Masculine ideologies are the creation of masculine subjectivity: they are neither objective, nor value free, nor exclusively 'human'. Feminism implies that we recognize fully the inadequacy for us, the distortion, of male created ideologies, and that we proceed to think and act out of that recognition. (Rich 1980, p. 207)

In this chapter we argue that, in archaeological and historical terms, the exclusion of women's experience is most evident in the public arena of the museum. Museum personnel have a responsibility to 'collect, document, preserve and interpret material evidence for the public benefit' (Museums Association 1984, p. 14). But in their selection of material to illustrate aspects of the past, museums in fact serve the interests of only *some* of the public.

Horne (1984, p. 4), in his survey of European museums, found the

> continuing legitimation of male authority . . . so consistent as to be almost universal . . . With exceptions such as The Virgin Mary or Joan of Arc, women simply are not *there*. They make their appearance as dummies of sturdy peasant women in folk-museum reconstructions of peasant kitchens, or in other useful supporting roles.

The representation of women is equally limited where history is reconstructed as heritage. Many who are critical of museums and the heritage industry for neglecting the social dimensions of class and race (Wright 1985, p. 215f., Hewison 1987, p. 10) allow issues of gender and the presentation of gender roles to go without comment. Using heritage to preserve and assert social values, notably those of the family, conditions visitors' views of gender relations in the past.

In discussing such biases we first examine the process of selection in presenting the past in museums, then discuss the archaeological ideology, and finally suggest how gender imbalance in both might be rectified.

Gender in museum presentations of the past

It is recognized professional practice that 'museum objects on public display, with all forms of accompanying information, should present a clear, accurate, and balanced exposition . . . and must never deliberately mislead' (Museums Association 1983, p. 4). But this aim is little more than an abstraction. The experience and beliefs of all museum professionals influence the questions they ask and the answers they find. Current ideologies not only influence how the past is interpreted but determine which topics are considered worth representing and how to present them to the public.

In museum archaeology, display transforms the context of excavated objects.

> Once the material dug up is presented to the public, the entire presen-
> tation, not just the actual facts about the past, or excavation, or
> analytical techniques, becomes an entirely new artifact, a piece of
> modern material culture, one to be analyzed for what it tells about the
> culture creating it, not about the past per se.   (Leone 1981, p. 5)

The image of a past society represented in a museum is necessarily distorted and incomplete, divorced from its original meaning by artificially created temporal and spatial contexts. Selection and juxtaposition within displays give objects new meanings.

In our view, museum curators mislead the public about gender roles in the past through the deliberate omission or misrepresentation of women's experiences. For example, Ivor Noël Hume, in commenting on a colonial Virginia inventory that lists several axes in a lady's bedchamber, is said by Deetz (1980, p. 43) to have remarked, '*quite correctly*, that no curator would ever dream of including them in a bedchamber re-creation' (our emphasis). Because axes are not what the public, or Hume, or Deetz, would expect to find in a woman's bedroom, Hume deems their deliberate exclusion justified, even though historically inaccurate. The 'no axes in the bedchamber' attitude is symptomatic of a wider mental set that imposes 20th-century norms and values on past societies.

This attitude is especially apparent in representations of the family; neither curator nor visitor is able to comprehend the domestic organization of past societies and gender roles. In the Jewry Wall Museum of Archaeology, Leicester, the figures in the nuclear family tableaux spanning the historic and prehistoric past are firmly moulded into their respective gender roles. Each male clutches his symbol of power or authority; each female watches anxiously over a small child. Ironically, despite years of criticism from within the profession, the museum's reluctance to dispose of the figures is largely a response to public demand. These families are what visitors expect: the images are easy to understand, comfortable, and unchallenging.

At the Jorvik Viking Centre in York, the intentions of the interpreters should be compared with the reality of the exhibition. 'The first element is an orientation area where the various correct perceptions that average people have about the Vikings are subtly confirmed, while many appalling misconceptions are unostentatiously corrected' (Addyman & Gaynor 1984, p. 11, Addyman, Ch. 20, this volume). So visitors are presumably correct in thinking that all Viking men are tall, fair, and incredibly good-looking, while women exist mainly as victims. The woman-as-victim imagery is vividly confirmed by the last scene in the time tunnel, where a woman in tattered garb flees from a Norman soldier.

And how do the crones of reconstructed Viking York, bartering in the marketplace or weaving in their smoky huts, accord with recent research showing women in this period as possible warriors, emigrants, inheritors and holders of land, skilled embroiderers and weavers, mothers and carers, and servers of food and drink (Fell 1984, pp. 129–47)? Events and activities at Jorvik are selected and displayed according to the ideologies of their creators, who then place them in the objective settings of a museum and of an historic time. Authenticity as such is less important than the creation of an environment where objects and events can be perceived as real.

The powers of the museum curator go beyond the images they choose to display; curators influence the nature of the evidence available to a museum through their acquisitions policies. Porter (1987) has shown how criteria for collecting artefacts in history museums result in gender bias. She argues that artefacts are collected, in the first instance, to document technological changes in extractive and primary industries with a predominantly male work force. Women's work, being located largely outside the central production process, is not recognized under these criteria.

The collection of artefacts related to women's work is inhibited because that work is undervalued, even by women. Lack 'of pride and power' impedes the donation and collection of relevant artefacts (Porter 1987, p. 12). Moreover, objects used in the domestic and reproductive roles of women tend to be impermanent and hence, at least until recently, have rarely survived.

Among those artefacts that do reach museums, systems of classification and documentation serve further to conceal women's experience (Porter 1988). Among manufactured objects, for example, the bias is towards categories identified with males. Objects tend to be classified in terms of production rather than consumption or use. Thus archaeologically derived ceramics are often exhibited in terms of production rather than use, of stylistic analysis rather than iconography (Vanags 1986).

Differential artefact survival also affects museums' acquisitions of material culture. Audiences are usually familiar with the stone implements ascribed to Man-the-Hunter. Curators must explain the reasons for the absence of artefacts available to Woman-the-Gatherer. Research on microwear and plant residues suggest that some of her work involved the collection and grinding of seeds and the dressing of skins, few of which have survived.

The construction of knowledge

Many factors determine how knowledge is constructed. Among these, the concepts of value, perception, and objectivity are influential in hiding women's experience. Some 40 years ago Margaret Mead (1949, p. 159) drew attention to the universal bias favouring male values:

> In every known human society, the male's need for achievement can be recognised. Men may cook, or weave or dress dolls or hunt humming-birds, but if such activities are appropriate occupations of men, then the whole society, men and women alike, votes them as important. When the same occupations are performed by women, they are regarded as less important.

The marginalization, if not exclusion, of women's experience manifested in archaeological interpretation is now widely recognized (e.g. Conkey & Spector 1984, Gero 1985, Coontz & Henderson 1986, Lerner 1986). Conkey & Spector (1984, pp. 2, 7) find the archaeological literature 'permeated with assumptions, assertions, and statements of fact' about gender, which derive more from contemporary experience than scholarly analysis. The Man-the-Hunter model of human evolution

> includes a set of assumptions about males and females – their activities, their capabilities, their relations to one another, their social position and value relative to one another, and their contributions to human evolution – that epitomize the problem of androcentrism. In essence, the gender system presented in the model bears a striking resemblance to contemporary gender stereotypes.

Gender arrangements are not only depicted as unchanged since prehistory, but the *value* of women's experience in the past is regarded as similar to the present.

To examine women's past experience, theories and methodologies must be developed that incorporate the world as seen through women's eyes, rather than classifying their views as subjective and contrasting them with objective knowledge (Spender 1980, p. 61) – a dichotomy between the invalid subjective and the valid objective that cannot be accepted by feminists.

Oral testimony offers women an opportunity to express their lives and experiences as they perceive them. Although oral testimony is accepted as a form of historical expression, it has been criticized in ethnoarchaeological studies for failing to give a comprehensive picture of artefact use, since 'participants in any behavioral system simply do not encode in their memories an amount of detail about all events and activities sufficient to form the basis of sound behavioral generalizations' (Schiffer 1978, p. 235).

Much of our language endorses and reinforces the values of patriarchal society. For example, it excludes or hides gender difference; the use in English of the words man and mankind to designate the whole human race demonstrates male dominance. 'The very language used to describe or refer to males and females differs to the disadvantage of women', note Conkey & Spector. 'There is a striking absence of the word *activity* used with reference to women . . . Passive verb forms are typically used for females' (1984, p. 10).

In view of women's lack of status, prestige, and control in archaeological work, it is not surprising that gender issues and the archaeology of women have received such superficial attention. The sexual division of archaeological labour is as marked today as in the past.

> The archaeologist is MALE, he works out-of-doors, sometimes far from civilization but always remaining public and visible; he is physically active, rugged, exploratory, dominant and risk taking; and he brings home the goodies . . . Inextricably intertwined with Man-the-Hunter, . . . he takes his data raw . . . [Meanwhile the woman is] secluded at the basecamp, sorting and preparing the goodies for consumption. If traditional economic and cultural stereotypes prevail, she will be indoors, private and protected, passively receptive, her 'feminine' skills and traditional roles supported as she neatly orders and systemizes, without recognized contribution to production processes . . . She does the archaeological housework; she cooks the data. (Gero 1983, p. 51; see also Arthur 1985, Gero & Root Ch. 2, this volume)

In considering feminist archaeology, Lerner's account of feminist historiography offers a useful guide (1976, p. 357ff). At the start, a 'compensatory history' focused on the Florence Nightingales and Mary Seacoles of the past as isolated exceptions within the male paradigm of history. This was followed by a 'contribution phase' exploring women's participation in male-constructed history, for example, political and social movements.

Significantly, feminist historiographers have placed women in the centre of their studies, thereby refashioning the agenda for research and critical comment. Some feminist historians have identified the private sphere as the prime location of women's experience, as opposed to the public world of men. Women's work and procreation, the connections between sexual self-determination and control over production, the effect of work in the family and on women's position in society, and power and gender dynamics in the family itself are among the topics feminist scholars address. Many of these studies also reveal the extent to which males depend on the private world of women to sustain them in their public roles (Davidoff & Hall 1987, p. 33).

Gender roles considered from various conceptual standpoints could form a basis for new perspectives on the archaeological past. Kelly (1979, p. 221), referring to the public–private paradigm, observes that 'social relations arising from each sphere structure experience in the other'. In revising family history theory, Hareven (1974, p. 325) divides women's lives into 'family times' (marriage, childbirth, maturation) and 'social times' (occupation, migration, and legislation). Criticizing the public–private dichotomy as too restrictive for pre-industrial periods, Barker & Allen (1976) propose a broader classification of sexual division.

A new construction of archaeological knowledge

The feminist critique in archaeology today 'has moved from the more blatant examples of male dominance to the more subtle forms of the reproduction of gender asymmetry as naturalised in the everyday and mundane features of the modern world' (Miller & Tilley 1984, p. 8). But feminist theory and methodology remain undeveloped and often vague; they are not yet part of mainstream archaeology.

To identify material culture directly related to women's lives, Conkey & Spector have devised a 'task differentiation framework' that records the sexual division of labour, detailing the artefacts used for specific tasks in particular contexts. Such a data bank may also be of use in identifying archaeological evidence about the sexual division of labour.

Funerary remains have always allowed archaeologists to make generalizations on gender status and roles. Shennan (1975, pp. 279ff) has shown that equating rich grave goods with high status, particularly among males, is too simplistic an approach. The assumption that rich female burials are the expression of male wealth and status likewise lacks validity. Instead, a variety of social relations should be postulated. When found in association with a male burial, even the most ordinary domestic equipment is assigned an important function. Winters identified pestles in female graves with ownership and food processing; in a male context, he suggested that the men had either made them or used them as hammerstones (in Conkey & Spector 1984, p. 11).

Palaeopathological evidence may provide a broader base for analysing changing cultural forms. In North America, skeletal remains from the Woodland group of the Lower Illinois River region reveal changing patterns in the diet of males and females. Trace-element analysis showed differences in bone strontium levels for males and females in the Late Woodland period which were not evident earlier. Females had significantly higher levels of strontium at the later time, which 'may indicate differential consumption of animal protein between the sexes' (Buikstra 1984, p. 229). Do such changes in food consumption during the transition from gatherer-hunter to an agricultural society reflect changes in the productive roles of men and women, in social customs, or in both?

In ceramic studies, typology, fabric analysis, form, and decoration have traditionally dominated archaeological analyses. Although Hodder (1982), Brathwaite (1982), and others have begun to explore the symbolic dimensions of pottery usage and production, the everyday use of ceramics by women and the effect of consumer demand on design and form remain little studied.

In a number of recent archaeological studies, the feminist critique has made gender relations central to an understanding of past social organization (Brathwaite 1982, Hodder 1982, 1984, Welbourn 1984, Lerner 1986, Arnold et al. 1988). These writers have focused on the sexual division of labour, the social relations that surround it, and the way ideologies are legitimated through the symbolic decoration of material objects. Social change, they argue, can be seen in terms of the changing relations between men and women and in the degree of power women have to negotiate their positions.

Hodder (1983, p. 157) suggests that in small-scale societies concerned to increase labour power, 'the control of women by men, and the negotiation of position by women will become the dominant feature of social relations and will often involve cultural elaboration of the domestic sphere'. From studying the decoration of material objects and the nature of tombs and house types, Hodder (1984, p. 62) has hypothesized social relationships in the North European Neolithic which focused on gender competition for control of reproduction.

Classic anthropological findings show that women have produced their own symbolic codes, often in opposition to the dominant male symbols (Ardener 1975 especially Okely 1975, pp. 70–1). These studies place women in active interaction with men in the social relations of the past. But in interpreting gender differences and gender relations many problems remain unresolved.

A study of the relationship between ideology, representations of power, and material culture among the Endo of Kenya examines the means by which men gain and keep control by setting up specific structural oppositions, e.g. symbolic versus functional, permanent versus temporary (Welbourn 1984, p. 24). Among the Nuba of Sudan, the form and type of decoration on pots are seen to transmit both explicit and hidden meanings. Hodder (1982, p. 189) suggests that 'women in a subordinate position to men may be able to form group solidarity and achieve social strategies through the silent discourse of their decorated pots or calabashes' (see also Brathwaite 1982).

Women continue to invest material culture with their own symbolic meanings, but these meanings are often lost through non-recognition. For instance, the women of Greenham Common Peace Camp, Newbury, Berkshire, have created their own canon of material and expressive symbols, notably the snake, the web, and the moon. But since the women's culture is not valued and possibly not even recognized, their artefacts are not being collected by the local museum, on the ground that 'outside of the camp objects will lose their significance' (WHAM! 1984, p. 24). This is true, but beside the point; for the objects say something about the women who have created them. They need to be collected.

Towards a new emphasis in museums

Female museum professionals are moving towards a wider and more profound feminist perspective and towards an exploration of women's lives in past societies. To date, museums have focused on individual women, on the design of exhibitions specific to women's experience, and on presenting gender in all exhibitions (WHAM! 1984, 1985). Women curators' attention, mirroring the compensatory and contribution models of women's history, has concentrated on post-industrial societies. Little attempt has been made to challenge the existing male framework or to reassess collection strategies.

Durbin (1983), for example, was commissioned to re-present collections at two Norwich museums for an Open University women's studies course. Her guide identified objects made or used by women, but she failed to analyse or explain their functions in the context of domestic economic activity. Elsewhere, examinations of material culture have been more rigorous.

At Bruce Castle Museum, 'Her-story' traces the history of Haringey from a gender-specific and anti-racist perspective (Hasted, pers. comm. 1987). North West WHAM!, using visual, material, and other sources in a new interpretive framework, has produced 'Fit Work for Women', which assesses working-class women's contributions to local industry (WHAM! 1985, p. 27).

At Lancaster Maritime Museum, the role of women in the traditionally male fishing industry has been given new emphasis. Oral evidence has been used to identify aspects of material culture usually neglected by traditional research designs.

> The record of the men's activities is illustrated by the nets, netting needles, sailmakers' palms, model yachts, balls of twine, boilers and the prawner boats themselves . . . [The] unorganized labour [of women] is often very difficult to trace. The material culture it leaves behind is ephemeral. Pulling the shells off shrimps requires nothing except skilled fingers, an oil cloth and bowls on the table, a sack in which to put the 'slough' (shells) and, occasionally a pocket scale or measuring jug to weigh out the picked shrimps . . . Only a single shrimp picker's

bonnet and a jug out of all this material culture has yet come to light
. . . (Whincop 1986, p. 47)

Oral testimony has made it possible to document visually women's activity
in the reconstructed cottage of a fishing family.

Most such gender-inclusive or gender-specific views of the past bear on
recent history; the more remote archaeological pasts have as yet received
little attention. Woman-the-Gatherer, however, is the subject of one of the
University of Aberdeen's Anthropological Museum displays that focus on
the social rather than the material aspects of culture (Hunt 1986).

At the British Museum, Vanags has examined the image of women
portrayed in Greek black and red figure ware. She cites the label for a pot
depicting two naked women washing, which states 'The women are probably *Hetairai* [courtesans]' (1986, p. 2), and suggests 'that for the uninformed observer this selection of female Greek images is *not* susceptible of
further questioning or analysis without additional information' (p. 3). She
doubts whether enough information could be provided for visitors to
discover for themselves something of women's life in Greek society and
suggests that 'socially-orientated displays, more so than traditional art-
historical displays, need interpretation for visitors to use them successfully'
(p. 3). She has devised a worksheet for sixth-form students that provides
additional information about images of women depicted on pottery, which
enables its users to examine both male and female attitudes toward women
in Greek society.

In Southampton, extensive archaeological excavations have ensured the
widespread recovery of materials from the medieval walled town (Platt &
Coleman-Smith 1975, Oxley 1986). An exhibition, designed to highlight
areas of women's experience, gave equal weight to public and private
spheres but emphasized the value female work ascribed to the domestic
sphere. Where possible, objects were linked to known individuals and occupations; elsewhere artefacts from other archaeological contexts were used
along with contemporary visual and documentary sources. Textual information was limited to short, simply written panels, also reproduced in
leaflets; visual stimuli in the form of reconstructions and manuscript illumi-
nations created a positive, active female image.

The principles applied in the Southampton exhibition could be advan-
tageously used elsewhere. Where contemporary sources show the participation of both sexes in a specific activity, the female should be identified.
Where an artefact cannot be restricted to either gender, it should be accepted
practice to demonstrate hypothetical use by both female and male.

This catalogue of activities demonstrates that a re-examination of extant
collections is taking place within a loosely feminist context. Without the
development of a coherent theoretical framework, however, women curators will continue to work in isolation, producing exhibitions that can do
little more than contribute to 'women's history'. Any fundamental change
in museum policies needs to encompass gender as well as class and race, and

to recognize the very different pasts, and perspectives on the past, these categories define. To achieve this, existing structures and disciplinary divisions within museums need to be changed radically.

Conclusion

In this chapter we have discussed some strategies through which women are beginning to assume control over their own past. Unless research strategies are devised to examine the dimensions of gender more fully, curators will continue to present a past devoid of women. Since the past reflects and reinforces the present, a re-evaluation of gender is also critical for change today. To that end, a feminist perspective is indispensable. It is also not remedial, because it questions what has long been labelled important, and is a political protest against making the past solely one of men.

References

Addyman, P. 1990. Reconstruction as interpretation: the example of the Jorvik Viking Centre, York. In *The politics of the past*, P. Gathercole & D. Lowenthal (eds), Ch. 20. London: Unwin Hyman.

Addyman, P. & A. Gaynor 1984. The Jorvik Viking Centre: an experiment in archaeological site interpretation. *International Journal of Museum Management and Curatorship* 3, 7–18.

Ardener, S. (ed.) 1975. *Perceiving women*. London: Malaby.

Arnold, K. *et al.* (eds) 1988. Women and archaeology. *Archaeological Review from Cambridge* 7(1).

Arthur, J. 1985. Women in archaeology. Paper presented at WHAM! [Women, Heritage & Museums], Southern Conference, November.

Barker, D. L. & S. Allen 1976. Sexual divisions and society. In *Sexual divisions and society: process and change*, D. L. Barker & S. Allen (eds), 1–24. London: Tavistock.

Brathwaite, M. 1982. Decoration as ritual symbol: a theoretical proposal and an ethnographic study in southern Sudan. In *Symbolic and structural archaeology*, I. Hodder (ed.), 80–8. Cambridge: Cambridge University Press.

Buikstra, J. E. 1984. The Lower Illinois River region: a prehistoric context for the study of ancient diet and health. In *Palaeopathology at the origins of agriculture*. M. Cohen & G. J. Armelagos (eds), 215–34. London: Academic Press.

Conkey, M. W. & J. Spector 1984. Archaeology and the study of gender. In *Advances in archaeological method and theory* 7, M. B. Schiffer (ed.), 1–38. London: Academic Press.

Coontz, S. & P. Henderson (eds) 1986. *Women's work, men's property: the origins of gender and class*. London: Verso.

Davidoff, L. & C. Hall 1987. *Family fortunes: men and women of the English middle class 1780–1850*. London: Hutchinson.

Deetz, J. 1980. A sense of another: history museums and cultural change. *Museum News* 58(5), 40–6.

Durbin, G. 1983. *Women's work and leisure: a guide to the Strangers Hall and Bridewell Museums*. Milton Keynes: Open University Press.

Fell, C. 1984. *Women in Anglo Saxon England*. London: British Museum Publications.

Gero, J. M. 1983. Gender bias in archaeology: a cross cultural perspective. In *The socio-politics of archaeology*, J. M. Gero, D. M. Lacy, & M. L. Blakey (eds), 51–7. Research Report no. 23. Department of Anthropology, University of Massachusetts, Amherst.

Gero, J. M. 1985. Socio-politics and the woman-at-home ideology. *American Antiquity* **50**, 342–50.

Gero, J. & D. Root 1990. Public presentations and private concerns: archaeology in the pages of *National Geographic*. In *The politics of the past*, P. Gathercole & D. Lowenthal (eds), Ch. 2. London: Unwin Hyman.

Hareven, T. 1974. The family as process: the historical study of the family cycle. *Journal of Social History* **7**, 322–9.

Hewison, R. 1987. *The heritage industry: Britain in a climate of decline*. London: Methuen.

Hodder, I. 1982. *The present past: an introduction to anthropology for archaeologists*. London: Batsford.

Hodder, I. 1983. Boundaries as strategies: an ethnoarchaeological study. In *The archaeology of frontiers and boundaries*, S. W. Green & S. M. Perlman (eds), 141–59. London: Academic Press.

Hodder, I. 1984. Burials, houses, women and men in the European Neolithic. In *Ideology, power and prehistory*, D. Miller & C. Tilley (eds), 51–68.

Horne, D. 1984. *The great museum*. London: Pluto.

Hunt, C. 1986. New displays in Aberdeen. *Scottish Museum News*, Spring, 6–7.

Kelly, J. 1979. The doubled vision of feminist theory: a postscript to the women and power conference. *Feminist Studies* **5**, 216–27.

Leone, M. P. 1981. Archaeology's relationship to the present and the past. In *Modern material culture: the archaeology of us*, R. A. Gould & M. B. Schiffer (eds), 5–14. London: Academic Press.

Lerner, G. 1976. Placing women in history: a 1975 perspective. In *Liberating women's history*, B. Carroll (ed.), 357–67. Urbana: University of Illinois Press.

Lerner, G. 1986. *The creation of patriarchy*. New York: Oxford University Press.

Mead, M. 1949. *Male and female: a study of the sexes in a changing world*. London: Gollancz.

Miller, D. & C. Tilley (eds) 1984. *Ideology, power and prehistory*. Cambridge: Cambridge University Press.

Museums Association 1983. *Code of conduct for museum curators*. London: Museums Association.

Museums Association 1984. Code of practice for museum authorities. *Museums yearbook*, 5–7. London: Museums Association.

Okely, J. 1975. Gypsy women: models in conflict. In Ardener 1975, 55–86.

Orwell, G. 1949. *Nineteen eighty-four*. Harmondsworth: Penguin.

Oxley, J. 1986. *Excavations at Southampton Castle*. Southampton: City Museums.

Platt, C. & R. Coleman-Smith 1975. *Excavations in medieval Southampton 1953–1969*. Vol. 1 *The excavation reports*. Leicester: Leicester University Press.

Porter, G. 1987. Gender bias: representations of work in history museums. *Museum Professionals Group Transactions* **22**, 11–15.

Porter, G. 1988. Putting your house in order: representations of women and domestic life. In *The museum time machine: putting cultures on display*, R. Lumley (ed.), 102–27. London: Routledge/Comedia.

Rich, A. 1980. *On lies, secrets and silence: selected prose, 1966–1978*. New York: Norton.

Schiffer, M. B. 1978. Methodological issues in ethnoarchaeology. In *Explorations in ethnoarchaeology*, R. A. Gould (ed.), 229–47. Albuquerque: University of New Mexico Press.

Shennan, S. 1975. The social organization at Branc. *Antiquity* **49**, 279–88.

Spender, D. 1980. *Man made language*. London: Routledge & Kegan Paul.

Vanags, P. 1986. Looking for housewives and finding Amazons: Greek women on display. Paper given at the symposium 'Making exhibitions of ourselves: limits of objectivity in the representation of other cultures', British Museum, 13–15 February.

Welbourn, A. 1984. Endo ceramics and power strategies. In D. Miller & C. Tilley 1984, 17–24.

WHAM! 1984. Collecting peace camp material. *Women, heritage and museums.* [Proceedings of the 1984 conference.] Bradford: Social History Curators Group.

WHAM! 1985. *Working for women's heritage.* [Proceedings of the 1985 conference.] Portsmouth: WHAM!

Whincop, A. 1986. Using oral history in museum displays. *Oral History* **14**(2), 46–50.

Wright, P. 1985. *On living in an old country: the national past in contemporary Britain.* London: Verso.

13 *Museums: two case studies of reaction to colonialism*

FRANK WILLETT

Museums help to promote a sense of identity at various levels of society: national, regional, tribal, local, and individual. In this chapter I contrast the functions they have served and are currently serving in two quite different lands long under British suzerainty: Nigeria and Scotland. Different histories of subordination, different relations between rulers and ruled, and differing priorities of public needs have enforced different museum roles. Yet in both Nigeria and Scotland the nature and purpose of museums is now clearly, if not always overtly, political.

Nigeria

The roots of the Nigerian museums service go back to 1943 when Kenneth Murray, an artist and teacher, was seconded by the Education Department to 'report on the practical steps to be taken to preserve the known antiquities of Nigeria' (Anon. 1947). As a result he was asked to start the Nigerian Antiquities Service in 1943. Since Nigeria became independent only in 1960, the present National Museums and Monuments Board, which has succeeded it, is clearly a creation of the British colonial regime. Fortunately for his successors, Murray was a far-sighted man. He planned to have

> a national museum network. In every major urban area that was fifty or so miles from another was to be a museum in which would be represented material culture from every other region of the country. It was in this way that he could justify the withholding of export permits for seemingly common items and the bulging storerooms of the Nigerian Museum.   (P. Stevens, in Willett 1973, p. 92)

Nigerian identity was Murray's overriding aim at the opening of the Nigerian Museum in Lagos in 1957 (Fig. 13.1). The absence of tribal names from the labels was striking. In Britain at that time it was usual to identify African sculpture by its tribal name; here only the name of the town or village of collection was given. The dangers of promoting tribalism were apparent to Murray before it became a political hazard in Nigeria. Local identity likewise mattered to Murray. He spent a great deal of his time

Figure 13.1 The Nigerian Museum, Lagos, at the time of its opening in 1957.

finding out and recording the historical traditions recalled by local chiefs, cult leaders, and artists.

Getting so close to 'the natives' was viewed with suspicion by most other whites and with hostility by some. It was Murray's determination to disregard these prejudices that laid the foundations of success for the Nigerian museums service. His records and informants proved invaluable when archaeologists and ethnographers began to work in such centres as Ife and Benin and helped them to carry out investigations in these places with proper respect for local feelings.

The first Nigerian museums were collections of archaeology and traditional art and were mainly located in important archaeological and art-historical centres. As early as 1937 the local teacher, J. D. Clarke, had provided a shelter for the stone figures of Esie; the local museum opened in 1970 (Stevens 1978, pp. 3–11). Ife's museum was planned from 1940 but not begun till 1948; its formal opening was delayed until 1956. A museum set up in Benin in 1946 in the old local government lock-up was transferred to the old post office in 1960 (Anon. n.d., pp. 37–8) and to a purpose-built museum in the 1970s. The Oron *ekpu* figures, temporarily stored in the old Waterside Rest House in 1948 (Anon. 1949), were moved to a purpose-built museum in 1959, which was damaged during the Civil War, rebuilt, and reopened in April 1977 (Nicklin 1977, Ch. 23, this volume).

Nigeria's first permanent museum building, in 1952, was the Jos Museum (Anon. 1952), not far from the area of the Nok terracottas that were its

Figure 13.2   The Jos Museum at the time of its opening.

principal glory (Fig. 13.2). The Nigerian Museum in Lagos was opened in the Federal Capital in 1957, with material drawn from the whole country. Museums at Owo, Kano, and close to Igbo–Ukwu were conceived in 1957–8 (Anon. 1961, p. 3). Museums were opened by the Native Authority at Argungu in 1958 (Anon. 1961, p. 3, 1963, p. 4), and in 1959 at Kaduna in the entrance hall to the Premier's Office (Anon. 1963, p. 20).

It was thus the practice for museums to be based on local collections rather than on materials from all the country's major centres, as Murray had planned. One Ife and a few Benin works, together with a selection of recent sculpture from all parts of Nigeria, were shown in Jos, and one Nok and one Benin work in Ife. Only the Lagos museum attempted to be truly national in scope.

Museums became popular with local people. Nigerian women coming to market in Jos would visit the museum, although relatively few Europeans did. The latter preferred the zoo, which Bernard Fagg had established in order to use as much land around the museum as possible. His collection there of buildings in the styles of different areas of Nigeria has been expanded into the Museum of Traditional Nigerian Architecture (Fig. 13.3), and on the same site are museums of pottery, of mining, and of transport.

In the late 1950s local authorities clamoured to have museums as prestigious institutions. The Yoruba have always had a strong sense of their own history, and every major Yoruba town aspired to have its own museum. In

Figure 13.3 A reconstructed entrance gate in the Kano City walls, in the Museum of Traditional Nigerian Architecture at Jos.

1959 I conducted a rescue excavation in Ilesha that disturbed a royal grave below a pit filled with terracotta sculptures (Willett 1960). I was asked by the King in Council to replace everything in the grave, 'including', one chief added, 'all the terracotta sculptures'. 'No!' thundered the King. 'We want to keep those for a museum!'

The first indication of how politically prestigious museums were came in 1958, when within a year of gaining regional autonomy, the Western Region government acquired the Ife Museum from the Federal government. As its curator from 1958 to 1963, I was in the anomalous position of managing a Western Region budget to run a Western Region museum, while simultaneously as a Federal government officer being in charge of a Federal budget for archaeological fieldwork. Among my less happy memories is one of a long spell in 1958–9 during which Western Region civil servants refused to make payments for materials I had ordered. They did this on the grounds that the Federal Department had spent the money, whereas it had simply set enough aside to meet such commitments as salaries for the whole year. Once this difficulty was ironed out, the system worked perfectly well, although some years later argument arose over whether a Federal officer could be stationed in a Western Region museum! (To resolve this problem, I believe the museum has since reverted to its Federal status.[1])

Regional strife in the 1960s, which came to a head with the military coup of 1966 and the abortive secession of the old Eastern Region, wholly altered the perceived role of museums in Nigeria. To counter the dominance of the Muslim north in the Federal government, the country was divided repeatedly; it is now split into 21 states plus the Federal Territory of Abuja. To some degree these states follow the old colonial administrative provinces, which in turn to some extent reflected supposed 'tribal' boundaries.

In undermining Northern dominance, the new states have tended to revitalize those feelings of identity that are widely condemned as tribalism in the nation-states of modern Africa. The national boundaries established by colonial powers usually divided traditional societies and are meaningless in terms of group identity. How can tribalism be contained and a sense of nationhood promoted within these artificial former colonial territories such as Nigeria?

In Nigeria it was recognized that museums had an important role to play. Unconsciously reverting to Murray's original intention, a 'Museum of Unity' was planned for each state capital in the Federation (Nicklin 1977, p. 14). The art from several ancient Nigerian centres – Nok, Igbo-Ukwu, Ife, and Benin – having achieved international fame, was to be displayed in these new museums, which would not only emphasize local history and culture but also represent the heritage in which all Nigerians may take pride. The guidebook to the museum in Kaduna in the Muslim north, for example, refers to displays on Nok, Ife, Igbo-Ukwu, and Benin (Anon. n.d., cover, pp. 8, 10–13, 25, 30).

The immediacy with which every major sale of a Benin antiquity is reported in the Nigerian press both reflects and promotes the feeling that Benin belongs to the whole of Nigeria. When the four Benin pieces bought back at Sotheby's in June 1980 were displayed in the exhibition 'The Lost Treasures of Nigeria', at the National Museum in Benin City, the King of Benin, while expressing gratitude at their retrieval, said:

> We are naturally sadly disappointed that they are not back here for good. . . . I want . . . to appeal to the National Commission [of Museums and Monuments] and the Federal Government that is responsible for purchasing these works of art to allow themselves to be constantly reminded that the home of these works of art is not in Lagos, but here in Benin City. (Omoruyi n.d., pp. 1, 3)

We can all sympathize with the King's feelings. For my part, I have always been glad that the great bulk of Ife art is still in the Ife Museum. I do not relish the prospect of having to travel widely throughout Nigeria to check on details of individual pieces for the *catalogue raisonné* of Ife art on which I have been working for decades. Yet the promotion of national unity is of paramount importance for Nigeria's future peace. Distributing the products of the national heritage from these important art centres to museums in every state of the country is a policy which deserves to succeed.

The future augurs well, if gauged by the international impact of the travelling exhibition, 'Treasures of Ancient Nigeria' (Eyo & Willett 1980). This consisted of 100 sculptural antiquities drawn from the national collections of Nigeria, selected by Michael Kan of the Detroit Institute of Arts from a larger exhibition mounted in Lagos by Dr Ekpo Eyo, the Director of Antiquities (Eyo 1977), for the Second Festival of Black Arts and Cultures. The exhibition had been seen by Congressman Charles Diggs of Michigan, who thought that black Americans would appreciate some of their ancestors' greatest artistic achievements. Visiting Detroit, San Francisco, and New York in 1980, the exhibition resulted in a striking recognition of black African achievement among both black and white Americans, and later among Europeans as well.

So great was the impact that the tour was extended to Washington, DC, Calgary, Atlanta, Los Angeles, Philadelphia, Oslo, London, Stockholm, Hildesheim, Leningrad, Sofia, Florence, Paris, and Zurich, returning to Nigeria only at the end of 1984. Such an impact abroad suggests that these works of art should also be capable of stimulating a sense of nationhood within Nigeria. The internationally recognized quality of these museum collections does not, however, guarantee that this objective will be achieved. The prosperity of Nigeria in the 1970s led to a great expansion of the staff of the national museums, but owing to the subsequent fall in oil prices, staff salaries now absorb practically the entire budget. Field archaeology and ethnology, once the life-blood of the museum service, have been all but abandoned.

The display of the national cultural heritage is now substantially reduced, even in the nation's capital. The main exhibition gallery has been truncated, another gallery converted to temporary exhibitions not necessarily related to Nigeria, and a planned extension has been subjected to long delays. In the museum's grounds are a small historical museum displaying 'Nigerian Governments: Yesterday and Today' (Anon. 1979), a craft centre, and a restaurant and bar with a space for dance and dramatic performances (Mimiko 1978). Yet the whole seems to lack coherence, as if a succession of opportunities had been seized without any overall design. The plan for museums of national unity may well be overtaken by other ideas or suspended for lack of funds.

Yet the ideal of national unity persists and remains a partial reality. Nigerian museums are being used to instil a sense of pride in all the achievements within its colonial-derived boundaries in order to promote a sense of nationhood. Ife, for example, is no longer merely the ancestral home of the Yoruba peoples; it has become an artistic centre in which all citizens of Nigeria can take pride. Thus museums serve a sense of heritage translated from tribal and regional settings to a national stage.

Scotland

The Scottish museum situation affords an interesting contrast with that of Nigeria. A glance at Scottish history will help to explain the difference.

Scotland and England had existed as wholly separate kingdoms for five centuries. With the death of Queen Elizabeth I of England in 1603 the two kingdoms came to share a single king, James the Sixth and First. Scotland was thereafter ruled from London: James returned to Scotland only once in his 22 years on the English throne. Tension mounted between the Scots and their rulers over modes of religious observance and the exclusion of Scotland from the benefits of overseas trade. An Act of Union in 1707 merged the two parliaments, but the Scottish legal and educational systems continued to be independent of the English, as they still are. Although Scotland gained equality of opportunity in foreign trade, the Union was not one of equals. Scotland was regarded merely as an appendage of England and subjected to crippling taxation. Discontent with the Union became and remained widespread.

The defeat of 'Bonnie Prince Charlie' at Culloden in 1745 led to the suppression of Scottish culture: many estates were confiscated, the wearing of the kilt and plaid was proscribed, the playing of the pipes was banned, and clan chiefs were stripped of judicial and military authority over their followers. Little wonder that during the American and French revolutions Scottish sympathy lay with the American colonists and the French people, and that parallels were drawn with the parlous plight of the Scots. The indignities visited on the Scots are exemplified in the Highland Clearances that forcibly removed small farmers from the land to make way for sheep. Some moved to the industrial areas in the central lowlands; many emigrated

Figure 13.4 The Hunterian Museum, Glasgow University, opened in 1807. It was the first museum in a Classical style to house non-classical collections, and set the style for museum architecture in the Western world for almost a century and a half.

to North America, Australia, and New Zealand. The clearances continued well into the Victorian era.

However, Scottish achievements in many walks of life during the 19th century helped not only to restore the confidence of Scots in their own culture and traditions but also to project abroad an image of Scotland as a land of romance and beauty. Walter Scott and Robbie Burns achieved international literary fame. The expanding British Empire allowed Scots such as Mungo Park and Hugh Clapperton, David Livingstone and Mary Slessor to seek fame if not fortune abroad. Their share in the imperial enterprise gave Scots an increasing sense of participating in the vision of Great Britain. A succession of parliamentary reforms increased Scottish representation, and Scottish participation in both world wars further strengthened the feeling of national unity. Today, however, economic stress – as during the depression of the 1930s – again undermines that sense of union. Once again, the British government is perceived as sacrificing Scottish interests for the sake of the English Home Counties.

The Scottish National Party has, however, made little headway. Aware that Scotland is too small to go it alone, the majority of Scots seek not independence but greater control over their own affairs. This reflects their enduring sense of separate Scottish identity. Despite almost four centuries under an English Crown and almost three with a common parliament, Scots manifest a strong sense of national identity. In terms of heritage awareness, Scottish national feeling currently manifests itself in a great efflorescence of new museums.

The movement began slowly. The first public museum in Scotland was the Hunterian (Fig. 13.4). Dr William Hunter, who found success in London as an anatomist and physician, bequeathed his wide-ranging collection to his alma mater in 1783, and it was opened in 1807 (Willett 1983). The Perth Art Gallery and Museum, originally the private property of the Perthshire Literary and Antiquarian Society (founded 1784) admitted the public in 1824. The following year the Northern Institute inaugurated the Inverness Museum, while the Elgin and Morayshire Museum commenced in 1836. The first national museum, the National Museum of Antiquities of Scotland, was established in 1851, when the Society of Antiquaries of Scotland presented its collection to the nation. Three years later the Industrial Museum of Scotland was founded; in 1904 it became the Royal Scottish Museum. The City of Glasgow launched its Art Gallery in 1856, while the National Gallery of Scotland began in Edinburgh in 1859.

Museums grew at an increasing pace. It appears that seven museums opened in Scotland between 1807 and 1849; by 1899 there were 31, and by 1948, 63 (information based mainly on Markham 1948). In 1981 an official guidebook cited 'almost 350 facilities' (Council for Museums and Galleries in Scotland 1981, Introduction), while the revised edition only five years later refers to '400 institutions' (Bain 1986, p. 3).

Some of these museums were founded to commemorate such famous Scots as Robbie Burns, Thomas Carlyle, Andrew Carnegie, and David Livingstone. Before the Second World War, a great many collections made by private individuals were given to the local authorities for the benefit of the community, while others put together by scholarly societies, which fell on hard times, had to be taken over by a public authority. Apart from those that honoured individuals, the museums were mostly wide-ranging in both subject matter and geographical area. The more recent ones, however, have been much more sharply focused. The Scottish Museums Council, through which central government funds are channelled to the non-national museums, records that between 10 and 20 are currently being founded every year, many supported primarily by government agencies that aim to promote employment or tourism rather than the heritage as such.

As in Yorubaland during my Nigerian residence, every Scottish town and village seems to want to express its own historical and cultural identity by establishing a museum of its own. Many of these are intended to preserve the remains of the industry that once made the community prosperous. Others aim to record a rural way of life that is now changing rapidly. One colleague found the Scottish National Party in his district especially sympathetic to museum needs, presumably because museums promote a sense of cultural identity; another tells me that in his 2000-square-mile administrative district no fewer than 18 Community Councils have asked him to provide branch museums. Currently Scotland has at least one museum for every 15 000 residents, twice as many museums per capita as for the United Kingdom as a whole!

These grass-roots Scottish museum foundations are closely bound up with their immediate localities and aim to promote a sense of pride in local achievement and culture. Beyond the local scene, the Williams Committee Report on the national museums of Scotland (Williams 1981, p. 13) saw the need to project a broader image of Scottish culture both to Scots at home and to visitors from overseas, many of whom take pride in their Scottish ancestry. The National Museum of Antiquities of Scotland and the Royal Scottish Museum have been combined under a single administration. Whether this union will be able to present Scottish culture as the Williams Committee desired is yet to be seen.

The wish to identify and to study Scottish culture is manifested also in recent developments in secondary education in Scotland. Oxford and Cambridge were the only universities in England until the 19th century, whereas Scotland, with a much smaller population, has four universities founded in medieval times: St Andrews (1427), Glasgow (1451), Aberdeen (1494), and Edinburgh (1583). Despite this antiquity, 'the continuous neglect of Scottish culture in the [present-day] educational system must be quite unparalleled in any other country . . . in the developed world. Everywhere else it is an axiom that children should learn something of their own national history [to] better understand who they are and their place in the world' (Grant 1982, p. 22). But not in Scotland. The independent Scottish educational system, always greatly admired throughout Britain, has been undermined, and its certification scheme for secondary education has become totally colonial in character. Corrective efforts are now at last in train. The changes now beginning to be implemented in the Scottish secondary school curriculum place far greater emphasis on local studies and on the investigation of primary data. This will afford local museums abundant opportunities to serve their communities as educational resources for use by the schools.

Conclusion

What can we deduce from these two different responses to English colonialism? Nigeria was not one people but many before being brought under British rule. As an artefact of colonial rule with artificial frontiers, evolving Nigeria needs to promote a sense of national identity, pride, and unity. It has begun to use museums to help do so by redistributing material from all parts of the country to museums throughout the land. In this way, Nigerians of different languages, cultures, religions, and allegiances can begin to appreciate how the past has made them one as well as many peoples.

The Scottish experience has been very different. Most of its frontier is a sea coast, and despite regional differences of culture, the Scots are an ancient people with a strong sense of national identity. Scotland was absorbed rather than colonized *sensu stricto*, but the attempt to suppress its culture in the 18th century was far more deliberate and punitive than the changes forced on Nigeria. Although the repressive legislation was repealed by the end of the century, Scotland became subsumed under the image of 'England' by which name Great Britain is still universally known abroad – the great English confidence trick. Because Scotland never lost the unity it achieved in the 11th century, local pride (notwithstanding continuing suspicion between the Macdonalds and the Campbells) is not seen as a threat to national unity. Through their museums and primarily at the local level, Scots are now recovering and re-expressing the history and culture of Scotland. The promotion of local pride is today a significant mode of throwing off the English cultural yoke, yet paradoxically many of those active in founding local museums are English incomers. Some Englishmen, at least, have seen the light. For the rest, those of us who live in Scotland cannot fail to respond in sympathy with the words of the King of Benin: 'We want to appeal to people in Lagos to endeavour occasionally to look beyond the Lagoon to the Hinterland of Nigeria' (Omoruyi n.d., p. 4).

Note

1 There are two other museums in Ife, both at the university. One was founded as part of the university's Institute of African Studies with archaeological material derived from university excavations as well as ethnographic material, whereas the other deals with natural history. Other universities, too, have established museums; the museum service in Nigeria is far from being monolithically state-controlled.

References

Anon. [Murray, K. C.] 1947. *Annual report of the Antiquities Section for the year 1946.* Lagos.
Anon. 1949. *Annual report on antiquities for the year 1948.* Lagos.
Anon. 1952. Nigeria's first National Museum of Antiquities. *Man* **52**, 107–8.
Anon. 1961. *Annual report of the Antiquities Service for the year 1957–58.* Lagos.
Anon. [Fagg, B. E. B.] 1963. *Annual report 1958–62.* Lagos: Nigerian National Press.
Anon. 1979. *Nigerian governments yesterday and today.* Lagos: Nigerian Federal Department of Antiquities.
Anon. n.d. *Guide to the National Museum, Kaduna.* [Lagos: Department of Antiquities.]
Bain, Alice (ed.) 1986. *Scottish museums and galleries guide.* Edinburgh: Polygon and the Scottish Museums Council in association with the *Glasgow Herald.*
Council for Museums and Galleries in Scotland and Scottish Tourist Board 1981. *Museums and galleries in Scotland.* Edinburgh.
Eyo, E. 1977. *Two thousand years: Nigerian art.* Nigeria: Federal Department of Antiquities.
Eyo, E. & F. Willett 1980. *Treasures of ancient Nigeria.* New York: Alfred A. Knopf for The Detroit Institute of Arts.
Grant, N. 1982. *The crisis of Scottish education.* Edinburgh: The Saltire Society.
Markham, S. F. 1948. *Directory of museums and art galleries in the British Isles.* London: The Museums Association.
Mimiko, J. 1978. Nigerian domestic arts. *Nigeria Magazine* **126–7**, 66–72.

Nicklin, K. 1977. *Guide to the National Museum, Oron*. [Lagos: Department of Antiquities.]

Nicklin, K. 1990. The epic of the *Ekpu*: ancestor figures of Oron, south-east Nigeria. In *The politics of the past*, P. Gathercole & D. Lowenthal (eds), Ch. 23. London: Unwin Hyman.

Omoruyi, A. (ed.) n.d. *Benin series. A new dimension in Benin studies. Nigerian Review of Art, Culture and History* [first issue].

Stevens, P. 1978. *The stone images of Esie, Nigeria*. Ibadan: Ibadan University Press/Lagos: Nigerian Federal Department of Antiquities.

Willett, F. 1960. Recent archaeological discoveries at Ilesha. *Odu, A Journal of Yoruba, Edo and Related Studies* 8, 4–20.

Willett, F. (ed.) 1973. Kenneth Murray through the eyes of his friends. *African Arts* 6(4), 2–7, 74–8, 90–3.

Willett, F. 1983. The Hunterian Museum, its founder and its ethnographic collection. *Museum Ethnographers Group Newsletter* 14, 10–15.

Williams, A. 1981. *A heritage for Scotland. Scotland's national museums and galleries: the next 25 years. Report of a Committee appointed by the Secretary of State for Scotland under the chairmanship of Dr Alwyn Williams*. Edinburgh: Her Majesty's Stationery Office.

POLITICS AND
ADMINISTRATION

Introduction

This part of the book deals with the functions of certain institutions in Africa and Oceania. These institutions, largely European in origin and structure, were translated wholesale to colonial realms, but have since developed characteristics of their own in response to local needs. They have come to articulate indigenous attitudes, as well as official policies, towards archaeological research and publication, museum development, and public education. These chapters show, for example, how such institutions deal with problems arising from the desire to preserve and to extend the understanding of local culture histories. Financial constraints in new nation-states make it especially difficult to cope with such needs. In some cases overseas aid is offered for cultural projects; in others tourism may generate economic benefits; but both threaten the cultural integrity of the people thus assisted.

Nzewunwa (Ch. 14) discusses how archaeology, as part of cultural education in West Africa, especially Nigeria, has been developed through universities, museums, and the media. Communication with the urban middle class has generally been more successful than with the rest of the population. The growth of archaeology at the university level has been hampered by its continuing elitist stance and its junior status within history departments. In museums, however, archaeology is better placed. As Willett (Ch. 13) demonstrates, museums in Nigeria have grown spectacularly during and since the run-up to independence. Nzewunwu remains cautious, however, about the future of archaeology in all these institutions in West Africa.

The next two chapters deal with specific museum problems in southern Africa. Are museums as relevant to public needs as are more broadly based cultural centres? To what extent should such needs be met locally, rather than through national museums?

At the core of the state, culture is seen as a force to be harnessed for national development. At the periphery, however, culture is often regarded as a way to protect local interests against outside encroachment, and national officials are apt to castigate local museums as reactionary for this reason. Such tensions occur in Botswana, where MacKenzie (Ch. 15) considers museum policy from the conflicting viewpoints of the National Museum and Art Gallery at Gaborone and of the two independent district museums. In Chapter 16, Grant, the director of one of them, criticizes the National Museum for regarding his museum as an expression of antinational tribalism and maintains that fostering tribal pride does not detract from national feeling.

In Chapter 17, Foanaota, Director of the National Museum of the Solomon Islands, surveys the growth of his museum from colonial roots somewhat similar to those described by Nzewunwa. Since the Solomons lack an autonomous university (it has a branch of the University of the South Pacific, based in Fiji), the National Museum is the Islands' major cultural institution, responsible for the promotion of archaeological research and the maintenance of a National Site Survey. The museum relies on outside support for staff training and for development grants. While its present emphasis is on central growth, one can foresee a time when culture centres, which now exist in rudimentary form, may emerge as major instruments of regional policy.

The last chapter (Ch. 18) discusses tension between centre and periphery from a very different viewpoint. Rapu, the Provincial Governor as well as Museum Director of Easter Island, examines the history of archaeological survey, excavation, and site protection on this remote and tiny appendage of Chile. He emphasizes the extent to which archaeology, the island's major tourist resource, depends on outside personnel and finance. Yet the romantic European vision of the ancient Polynesians brings in much needed cash. This chapter is a commentary on the changing attitudes of a colonial administration towards a Polynesian culture linked to Chile only by the latter's desire for a strategic presence in the Pacific.

A capacity for either cultural destruction or cultural resurgence persists in the aftermath of colonialism. One is left to query whether the institutions discussed in this section will ever command sufficient support, including outside aid, to attain an autonomy that could encourage cultural resurgence at both national and local levels.

14 *Cultural education in West Africa: archaeological perspectives*

NWANNA NZEWUNWA

West African archaeologists, like many colleagues elsewhere, provide five basic cultural services. They engage in research to recover artefactual materials and analyse and interpret finds to aid our understanding of past ways of life. They curate and display artefacts for public education and entertainment. They help to establish a cultural-chronological framework. Finally, they increase people's awareness of their cultural heritage. Thus the West African archaeologist is situated – both formally and informally – within cultural education, which I define as the development of taste and the creation of awareness and appreciation of the national cultural heritage. Its aim is knowledge of the past for its operational value in the present, and as a source of hope for the future (Okita 1981, 1985).

When discussing cultural education, we must consider training in knowledge of the past through archaeology as it inspires West Africans today as well as in the future. Cultures discovered through archaeology represent the prehistoric baseline of man's creative ability, conveyed through tangible or visible materials. Thus education through archaeology should occupy a unique place in the education of West Africans. This role requires some knowledge of the history of West African archaeology, of colonial attitudes towards it, of its relationship to African culture history, and of its place in the West African education system. Finally, consideration must be given to the successes and failures of cultural education overall.

Early archaeological research

Archaeological material from West Africa was first mentioned by M. de Beaufort in 1851 (Obayemi 1970). French interest in cultural objects from the region continued wherever their military and commercial assignments took them. In 1893 Laurent Mouth, a government engineer engaged in constructing a road inland from Conakry in French West Africa, noticed the cave of Kakimbon (Guinea). Mouth's limited excavations at the site have gone down in archaeological history as the first of their kind in West Africa. He discovered pottery, oyster shells, and ashes. The Kakimbon excavations were continued by MacLaud in 1896, who sent his finds to E. T. Hamy in France for study.

In 1897 Colin found stone artefacts at Messa-Mbombo near Dubreka (Guinea), which were also sent to France. In the same year a French army officer, Captain Florentin, excavated some tumuli between Tendirma and Saia, some 30 km south of Goundam in Mali, finding pottery and a copper bracelet. This was the first inland excavation in West Africa. In 1900 extensive work was undertaken at Kakimbon by Mouth, his brother Albert (also an engineer), and Roux, a financial officer; and the French captain J. I. Moreau reported polished stone axes at Dadokho in the upper Faleme Valley. Thus it was the French who blazed the trail of archaeological research in the region.

The British were slower to engage in such pursuits, but in the year following their punitive expedition to Benin in 1897 Captain J. W. M. Carroll reported finding circles of sculptured stone pillars from the area of Lamin Koto on the upper Gambia River. Meanwhile, Nigerian works of art became popular with European collectors. Highly esteemed plundered objects from Benin Palace came to adorn private and public galleries. Speculation about their origin and workmanship gave rise to such publications as C. H. Read and O. M. Dalton's *Antiquities from the city of Benin in the British Museum* (1899), Lieut.-General A. Pitt Rivers' *Antique works of art from Benin* (1900), and F. von Luschan's *Die Altertümer von Benin* (1919). But early writings on West African culture history by Sir John Lubbock, Hamy, and Pitt Rivers did not reflect first-hand knowledge of the region; indeed, none of these authors visited it, relying solely on West African materials that had come to Europe.

Colonialism and cultural development

Three different colonial policies operated in West Africa: French, British, and Portuguese, the latter confined to Guinea Bissau and the small Atlantic islands. The French viewed their West African territories as an extension of metropolitan France and intimately involved themselves in their affairs. They expected qualified Africans, as French citizens, also to be involved. The British, on the other hand, saw it as their sacred mission to civilize primitive peoples. But the latter, in the British view, could never rise to their own level, because God had not endowed them with the virtues and potential to do so. The British therefore felt that to give recognition to local ingenuity and achievement would unduly aggrandize the status of African peoples and legitimize their place in world affairs.

While European Christian missions were busy denouncing native ways of life and destroying the physical manifestations of their world views, metropolitan governments sanctioned missionary activities by keeping the natives in check. However, the missionary viewpoint often differed from that of colonial administrations, especially in cultural matters. Indeed, some individuals in the colonial services sought to articulate and protect the local cultural heritage. They attempted to excavate and recover artefacts, to collect works of art, and to preserve, display, and publicize them. More often than not, colonial officials denied that indigenous West Africans had created the objects they admired and instead attributed them to foreign peoples and agencies. But although few acknowledged the significance of West Africans and their past, such recognition was the ultimate result of their efforts.

Archaeology and West African culture history

From the 1930s, colonial governments showed increasing interest in indigenous cultural resources. Thurstan Shaw began excavations in the Gold Coast (now Ghana) in the 1930s. The French established a research institute (IFAN) in 1938, with headquarters in Dakar. The increase in private art and artefact collections put colonial governments under pressure to permit official collection and preservation of works of art. For instance, Kenneth Murray, appointed to the Nigerian Education Department in 1927, built up a considerable private collection which he later gave to the Nigerian Museum. Works of art and antiquities also received publicity in *Nigeria Magazine* (see Nicklin, Ch. 23, this volume).

In the 1940s the British colonial government established antiquities services in Nigeria (1943) and Sierra Leone (1947). Archaeological fieldwork, however, remained the pastime of trained and untrained officers in the colonial service, soldiers, public works engineers, teachers, and administrators. Until the 1950s archaeology aimed mainly to supply artefacts for museums and to increase knowledge about political centres such as Ife and areas with spectacular accidental finds such as Nok.

In West Africa, as in other parts of the continent, historical understanding – largely stored as orally transmitted tradition – is viewed as both the anchor and mooring of society. Anthropological studies sponsored by colonial governments, especially of the 1940s, relied extensively on oral sources, but the information acquired served practical rather than scholarly purposes. Indeed, academics subjected these traditions to such derision that for a time they hardly counted as historical sources.

The 1950s marked a turning point in West African cultural education, and it was then that museum development began (Table 14.1). Colonial governments enacted cultural legislation. Antiquities ordinances were passed by Sierra Leone in 1946, Nigeria in 1953, and Ghana ten years later. The establishment of antiquities centres and museums followed. However, these developments were not necessarily intended primarily for the benefit of West African nationals (Nzewunwa 1984b).

During the 1960s the emergent nations of West Africa formally recognized the significance of archaeology. They attached great importance to their people's origins, to their contributions to history, and to their desire to

Table 14.1 Museum development in West Africa

Country	Location	General	Art/ethnography	History	Archaeology	Other
Senegal	Gorée			1954		1961
	Dakar		1960			
	St Louis		+			
The Gambia	Banjul			1980		
Guinea Bissau		×	×	×	×	×
Guinea	Conakry	+				
Mali	Bamako	+				
Burkina Faso	Ougadougou	+				
Sierra Leone	Freetown	1957			+	
Liberia	Monrovia	1957				
Côte d'Ivoire	Abidjan	1957				
	Zaianon		1960			
Ghana	Accra	1952				
	Legon				×	
Togo	Lomé	1979	1960		+	
Benin	Porto Novo		1960			
	Abomey			×		
Nigeria	Esie		1945			
	Jos	1952				×
	Ife		1954		+	
	Lagos	1957				
	Oron		1958			
	Angunu		1958			
	Kano			1960		
	Nsukka				1965	
	Owo		1968			
	Nri		1972			
	Benin		1946			
	Kaduna	1959				
	Port Harcourt	1986			1981	
	Yelwa				1982	
	Zaria	1986				
	Sokoto			×		
Niger	Niamey	1986				
Chad	Fort Lamy	1986				

+ indicates that facility exists in some form
× indicates that facility exists in that form, but date unknown

see both accepted as rooted in antiquity. Since archaeology has the potential to substantiate, enrich, and date aspects of oral traditions, as well as to recover evidence of earlier periods, it could become central to cultural education and historical studies, but its results have not yet been substantial enough to influence them significantly.

The mass media

In order to promote popular appreciation of prehistory, it has been suggested that formal and informal education in archaeology be pursued simultaneously (Posnansky in Calvocoressi 1970, pp. 57–8). But the subject has not yet made any significant inroad into informal cultural education. Being orally literate, West Africans could best benefit from archaeological education through the mass media, adult education, and exhibitions. Only an appropriate use of such forms of communication can make any cultural policy effective (see Unesco OAU 1975, p. 17). Of the mass media (television, radio, and the press), television potentially has the broadest appeal. Audiovisual messages are particularly effective among people sensitive to the power of words and pictures. Unfortunately television is unavailable in many communities, and even where the service exists sets are rare since, as luxury items, they attract high taxes in all West African states.

In Nigeria, where the television service is best developed, it has been used for cultural presentations during national celebrations, state occasions, and festivals. But such programmes are too infrequent and too oddly timed to have had any appreciable impact. The few cinematographic recordings of the cultural heritage have mostly been prepared by foreigners or government ministries of information or culture. Access to these recordings is restricted, and they seldom feature in public cinema houses. Radio is the most effective means of spreading news rapidly in West Africa, since most households have access to some type of receiver. Most people consider radio an indispensable companion at both work and leisure. However, radio rarely presents archaeological programmes.

On the other hand, newspapers do feature archaeology, although the coverage is often trivial and sensational (Cleere 1984). This weakness arises from two factors. First, archaeologists seldom invite media representatives to visit excavations, and the response from those who have been asked has not been encouraging. Second, archaeologists do not write for the popular press; the feature articles that do appear are usually badly written by ill-informed non-professionals. Archaeologists continue to confine themselves to writing traditional professional reports that are too technical to interest even a highly literate public. In this respect West African archaeology remains largely elitist. Such archaeological journalism as exists has been geared towards tourism, aimed at the foreigner rather than the West African consumer. This is most evident in francophone West Africa and anglophone Gambia, where government policies encourage tourism.

In essence, archaeological education through the media has not properly begun in West Africa. Television services are inadequate; the media in general seldom cover archaeological themes; when archaeological features appear at all they are presented unprofessionally. A more positive educational approach by the mass media might encourage people to report archaeological finds and to pass on to museums artefacts they discover or already possess.

Adult education

In the early 1970s Nigerian governments were strongly urged to institute cultural-heritage education at school and post-school levels (Alagoa & Awe 1972). They failed to do so. Adult education programmes remain non-existent in most rural areas. Those that do take place are confined to teaching basic skills in reading, writing, communication, and mathematics. History, though a traditional school subject, is not now considered a priority, so the cultural dimension of education is omitted. In the early 1980s the Nigerian government promoted local education through what was known as the Open University, and the time seemed ripe to expose more Nigerians to cultural education through archaeology. However, when the Open University was suspended in 1984, the archaeology programme went into cold storage, thus eliminating the only teaching of archaeology in West Africa so far to a wider public.

Museums and exhibitions

It is somewhat ironic that the colonial masters made their greatest contribution towards cultural education in the realm of museum development, before the West African nations attained independence (Ikwueme 1980, Nzewunwa 1984a, Okita 1985). Obichere (1981, p. 2) has described museums as necessary blocks in nation building because they are 'valuable instruments for the preservation and dissemination of the ideals of society, even in a plural society like Nigeria'. Promoting acculturation and culture contact, museums also teach cultural dynamism and stimulate national consciousness and a sense of unity in diversity. Museum societies in the capital cities of Sierra Leone, Ghana, and Nigeria, and also in Jos, Nigeria, organize tours, lectures, and visual presentations, but are so isolated from national life that their impact is minimal. Their membership is largely drawn from foreigners and urban elites, and the larger public is unaffected by their activities. Even the middle-class West African image of a museum is a negative one; it is seen as a storehouse of antiquated, obsolete artefacts (Nwabara 1972). Hence Nigerian museums strive to make themselves more inviting through such attractions as restaurants, hairdressing shops, craft shops, even bandstands. Use of museums as social and cultural centres has given Nigerian museums a new lease of life and could be emulated by other countries. In francophone West Africa, however, museum development is linked only with tourism (Fabre 1979).

Travelling exhibitions, whether international or intercontinental, are not yet a feature of West African life. The largest exhibition of artefacts from the area, 'Treasures of Ancient Nigeria', toured America, Europe, and parts of Asia between 1980 and 1984, but not Africa, despite the obvious benefits of such a step. Sadly one must observe that Nigerians, though they own these objects, are hardly aware of their existence. This is also true of other West African nationals who could profit from such exhibitions to reinforce common cultural elements and to record cultural diffusion (Biobaku 1972). Most West African museums, including those of Nigeria, display only indigenous works of art from their own nation. Only the Ghana Museum in Accra and IFAN Museum in Dakar exhibit collections from other African countries.

Local travelling museums, rather than one-off exhibitions, play an important role in children's cultural education. The Nigerian National Museum has operated a school service since the 1960s. Travelling personnel take artefacts and ethnographic materials to secondary and primary schools (Emeruwa 1975). They use films and slides to demonstrate aspects of Nigeria's past and encourage the children to handle the specimens (Nkanta 1976).

Formal archaeological education

One might ask why archaeology should become an aspect of formal cultural education at all. The professional literature avoids this question. But by the late 1960s, organized archaeological education had become a matter of concern to practitioners working in Africa, most of them foreigners. The topic was discussed at the conference of West African archaeologists at Fourah Bay, Sierra Leone (1966); at the First International Conference of African Archaeologists, Fort Lamy, Chad, in the same year; at the Sixth Pan African Congress, Dakar, Senegal (1967); and at the Third Conference of West African Archaeologists, Accra, Ghana (1969).

Three objectives were seen for formal archaeological education (Calvocoressi 1970). One was to train African archaeologists for field research in little-known parts of the continent. A second was to educate the public to appreciate, and policy-makers to implement, protective measures to stop the destruction of sites by development projects and to halt trafficking in antiquities. A third objective was to consolidate archaeological knowledge as an important research tool for a deeper and clearer understanding of history.

It is strange that West African archaeology, in which fieldwork began in 1893, was not considered to be worth teaching to West Africans at any level until some 70 years later (Nzewunwa 1983b). Cultural education (and the place of archaeology within it) was at best peripheral to the aims of colonial rule. Since it did not contribute to imperial economic well-being, it was generally neglected. Archaeology was conceived initially as a field disci-

Table 14.2 Archaeology education in West Africa

Country	Location of institution	Type of institution	Status of archaeology	Number of courses offered now	When started	Number of lecturers
Senegal	Dakar	university	within history	4	?	3
The Gambia	—	—	—	—	—	—
Guinea Bissau	—	—	—	—	—	—
Guinea	Conakry	école normale	within history	3	?	2
Burkina Faso	Ouagadougou	university	within history	1	1978–9	1
Sierra Leone	—	—	—	—	—	—
Liberia	—	—	—	—	—	—
Mali	—	—	—	—	—	—
Côte d'Ivoire	Abidjan	university	within history	2	1976–7	1
Chad	Fort Lamy	university	within history	1	1979–80	1
Ghana	Legon	university	full department	undergraduate and postgraduate	1963	5
Togo	Lomé	university	within history	2	1982	1
Benin	(same as above)	university	within history	2	(1975–6) 1982	1
Niger	Niamey	university	within history	3	1982	1
Nigeria	Ibadan	university	full department	undergraduate and postgraduate	1966, 1978	7
	Ilorin	university	within history	2	1980	1
	Nsukka	university	full department	undergraduate and postgraduate	1963, 1983	4
	Zaria	university	full department	undergraduate	1981	4
	Ife	university	full department	undergraduate	1978, 1984	3
	Port Harcourt	university	within history	4	1979	2
	colleges of education (all over the country)	higher education	within history	service	various	external (part-time lecturers)

pline, whose results would serve only museums and art galleries. Formal training was considered unnecessary even for the few archaeologists in field research, and hardly any institutions offered such training before the 1960s. Moreover, the 'dustpan and trowel' discomforts of archaeological fieldwork ran counter to the perceived value of higher education as a mode of entry to white-collar jobs. A few foreign professionals and local volunteers satisfied supposed archaeological needs. Archaeological education also lagged because the subject was seen to be elitist. It long remained an educated urbanite preserve, dominated by foreigners who came and went, only to be succeeded by other foreigners.

The dismissive attitude of West Africans towards archaeology reinforced colonial neglect into and beyond the first years of independence. Most local people took the view that they *knew* their own histories, of which their elders were the repositories. It seemed odd to them to be asked to search for this history by digging at their ancient habitation sites. They did not fancy such a preoccupation, even though discoveries aroused their curiosity.

Policy-makers and education planners in post-independence West Africa often speculated about their culture and its long past, but they did not initiate archaeology courses or other training programmes at home or sponsor students to study abroad. Thus there were few, if any, African nationals involved in the subject.

Ghana was the first West African nation to train archaeologists locally (Table 14.2). The archaeology unit there dates back to 1952, though only as a research group. An archaeology department was established in 1963 (Shinnie 1965) to carry out field research, to offer postgraduate courses for a diploma and a master's degree within African studies, and to provide a course for undergraduate history students. In Nigeria, Nsukka and Ibadan universities acquired independent departments in 1963 and 1966 respectively, followed by others at Ife (1978) and Zaria (1981). At other universities in Nigeria the discipline has been tied to history departments. Since history had achieved full manhood before this unholy and unhealthy wedlock was contracted, archaeology has remained the underdog (Nze-wunwa 1981, 1983a,b). It is unfortunate that more West African archaeologists did not strive for an independent status.

Archaeological education would be useful at teacher training colleges, for by educating future teachers it could reach school children. But the paucity of both archaeologists and history teachers with any archaeological training makes this suggestion merely a dream. Some colleges of education in Nigeria do include courses in archaeology or prehistory in their history programmes, but normally these are taught by history teachers untrained in archaeology who have at best read some of the archaeological literature on their own. Only a few colleges, such as at Port Harcourt and Owerri, use the services of professional archaeologists.

Apart from receiving passing mention, archaeology as such is not taught below the tertiary level in any West African country. One Nigerian professor of history, A. E. Afigbo, suggests that inclusion of the subject in the secondary school curriculum could make history more relevant and attractive. He sees archaeology as useful because it requires handling objects, experimentation, and a shift from 'the use of books at the expense of boots in the study of history' (Afigbo 1985, p. 131). He stresses the archaeologists' 'duty to distil and disseminate the essential information from and about their work in the interest of society generally and of the schools and colleges in particular' (ibid., p. 136). Unfortunately, most archaeologists are still locked in their ivory towers, using incomprehensible terminologies and issuing indigestible technical reports that frighten potential consumers away from the fruits of their research. There is nothing in Nigeria comparable to the Council for British Archaeology's activities for schools (Corbishley 1983).

The diffusion of knowledge

Archaeologists have a responsibility to disseminate knowledge among professionals and non-professionals alike. Until recently archaeological research in West Africa has been the preserve of foreign archaeologists, who found their outlets in learned journals, newspapers, and other publications. Most of them were peripatetic public servants. Until recently francophone and anglophone researchers saw no need to collaborate or come together to form a unified professional group (Nzewunwa 1980). However, a welcome change occurred during the early 1960s, when tenured academic posts in archaeology were established, and imperial barriers began to give way. Archaeological collaboration moved from informal meetings to formal conferences, the exchange of information and ideas, and joint action. As far back as the 1940s the French had established IFAN, which disseminated research information through *Notes Africaines* and the *Bulletin de l'Institut Français d'Afrique Noire*. In Ibadan in 1964 Thurstan Shaw's *West African Archaeological Newsletter* began reporting the preliminary results of current projects. Its successor from 1971, the *West African Journal of Archaeology*, demonstrated that the subject had come of age. Subsequent publications devoted in whole or in part to archaeology include *Sankofa* and *Archaeology in Ghana* from Legon, *Godogodo* from Abidjan, *Zaria Archaeology Papers*, and *Banda* from Conakry.

    These publications have their own sad stories. Some have been phased out, passing away without even a requiem; others have limped on even if badly in arrears. In sum, poor editorial and financial management, low funding, and inadequate distribution systems have lost them their readers' confidence and prevented any increases in subscription income. The resulting information flow is so meagre that not even archaeologists can keep track of what their colleagues are doing. Government policy also adversely affects this flow. A dearth of foreign exchange makes it difficult for archaeologists to obtain foreign publications and keep up to date about overseas developments. This further reduces their ability to fulfil their responsibilities in archaeological education.

However, more books on West African prehistory and archaeology are now on the market than in the 1960s (e.g. Shaw 1961). These range from specialized site reports on Igbo-Ukwu (Shaw 1970) and Benin (Connah 1975) to regional studies on the Lake Chad Basin (Connah 1981) and national syntheses on Senegal (Thilmans *et al.* 1980), Ghana (Anquandah 1982), and Nigeria (Shaw 1978, Nzewunwa 1983a). Regrettably, workers have not yet transcended national boundaries, although francophone researchers have reviewed the state of research in their own areas (CNRS 1978). But no up to date general survey exists comparable to Oliver Davies' bold synthesis of 1967.

Conclusion

In West Africa those who make and implement policy tend to see archaeology as an aspect of history, and thus fail to recognize that its aims and methods are quite different. Their approach curtails resources and facilities – personnel, hardware, materials, and infrastructure – which archaeology needs. No more than one archaeologist has been hired for each university department concerned, and fieldwork has been starved for lack of money and equipment.

The hopes of the 1970s for cultural revival in Africa and the black world that gave rise, for example, to FESTAC 1977, the Black and African Festival of Arts and Culture, have not been realized. In some countries they evaporated as the festivals wound up; in others they lingered on for a short time; in a few they have survived on a reduced scale. In the currently worsening economic climate, developing countries in Africa emphasize the roles of science and technology in the quest for economic self-reliance, still further downgrading cultural studies and the humanities, including archaeology. Yet it is the cultural heritage which offers a vantage point for assessing a new self-realization.

Mass ignorance about the importance of art, history, ethnology, and archaeology as repositories of culture is still a major problem. One may ask: who needs cultural education? Everyone needs it, particularly urban dwellers who have been severed from their rural roots. This is the group from which policy-makers and executors are drawn. They, above all, need cultural education to help them plan the future of West Africa.

Nonetheless, the region has made some progress in cultural development. Before 1960, only 10 museums and exhibition areas existed in 6 countries, whereas now more than 30 such institutions are established in 15 countries (Table 14.1). These centres, located in large cities and on university campuses, play a major educational role. Archaeological teaching arose within the context of tertiary education less than three decades ago (Table 14.2). Although fieldwork has recently dwindled and many basic pedagogic facilities are lacking, the number of archaeology courses offered in these institutions is currently increasing (for a study of their curricular content, see

Nzewunwa 1984b). Perhaps this offers a ray of hope that, at least quantitatively, growth may continue. Regrettably, however, several newly advertised archaeological posts have failed to get either local West African or foreign responses. This has compounded the difficulty of expanding existing projects, let alone initiating new ones.

The spread of museums and exhibition facilities and the distribution of pedagogic centres and personnel are highly uneven. In some countries nothing is happening and, given their economic weaknesses, no improvements may be expected in the near future. Although urgently needed in such countries as The Gambia, Guinea-Bissau, Guinea, Liberia, and Sierra Leone, international cultural co-operation and aid from international agencies appear no longer to be forthcoming. One can only hope that the gloomy picture painted here does not persist for too long into the future.

Acknowledgements

This chapter owes its inspiration to an archaeological expedition across 12 West African countries in 1981. The project was initiated by Professor Thurstan Shaw and sponsored by the Wenner-Gren Foundation of New York and the University of Port Harcourt. I owe an immense debt to the sponsoring bodies, to Thurstan Shaw, to my colleagues on the expedition, Keith Ray and Marion Barnett, and to other colleagues and respondents in West Africa who gave their time and facilities and provided information which amplified my understanding of the topic treated here.

References

Afigbo, A. E. 1985. History, archaeology and schools in Nigeria. In *Museum and nation building*, A. E. Afigbo & S. I. O. Okita (eds), 128–38. Owerri: New Africa Publishing Co.

Alagoa, E. J. & B. Awe. (eds) 1972. *Nigerian antiquities*. *African Notes*, Special No. Ibadan: Institute of African Studies.

Anquandah, J. 1982. *Rediscovering Ghana's past*. Accra: Longman & Sedco.

Biobaku, S. O. 1972. Introduction. In *Nigerian Antiquities*, E. J. Alagoa & B. Awe (eds), 9–11. *African Notes*, Special No. Ibadan: Institute of African Studies.

Calvocoressi, D. 1970. Report of the third conference of West African archaeologists. *West African Archaeological Newsletter* **12**, 53–90.

Cleere, H. 1984. World cultural resources management: problems and perspectives. In *Approaches to the archaeological heritage*, H. Cleere (ed.), 125–31. Cambridge: Cambridge University Press.

CNRS 1978. *Les recherches archéologiques dans les états d'Afrique au Sud Sahara et à Madagascar*. Valbonne: Centre régional de frappe de Sophia-Antipolis.

Connah, G. 1975. *The archaeology of Benin*. Oxford: Clarendon Press.

Connah, G. 1981. *Three thousand years in Africa*. Cambridge: Cambridge University Press.

Corbishley, M. J. (ed.) 1983. *Archaeological resources handbook for teachers*. London: Council for British Archaeology.

Davies, O. 1967. *West Africa before the Europeans*. London: Methuen.
Emeruwa, A. El Amin 1975. The ontological role of the museum in education: its tacit dynamism. Nsukka (mimeo).
Fabre, P. 1979. *Méthodologie de la planification tourisme internationale et projets touristiques dans les pays en développement*. Paris: Centre de Documentation, Ministère de la Coopération.
Ikwueme, P. I. O. 1980. The growth and organisation of the Federal Department of Antiquities, Nigeria. Unpublished MA (Museum Studies) thesis, University of Leicester.
Nicklin, K. 1990. The epic of the *Ekpu*: ancestor figures of Oron, south-east Nigeria. In *The politics of the past*, P. Gathercole & D. Lowenthal (eds), Ch. 23. London: Unwin Hyman.
Nkanta, M. 1976. Federal department of antiquities: present position and perspectives. Keynote address to Conference on Museology, Zaria.
Nwabara, S. N. 1972. Statement to open the first working session. In *Nigerian antiquities*. E. J. Alagoa & B. Awe (eds), 18–21. *African Notes*, Special No. Ibadan: Institute of African Studies.
Nzewunwa, N. 1980. The organisation of prehistoric research in Nigeria. In *Focus on history, Kiabara* (special issue), E. J. Alagoa (ed.), 203–15. Port Harcourt: University of Port Harcourt.
Nzewunwa, N. 1981. Reflections on West African archaeology. Paper delivered at the third conference of the West African Archaeological Association, Dakar, Senegal, December.
Nzewunwa, N. 1983a. *A source book for Nigerian archaeology*. Lagos: National Commission for Museums and Monuments.
Nzewunwa, N. 1983b. West African archaeology: uneven development, Part II. Paper delivered at the Ninth Pan-African Congress, Jos, Nigeria, December.
Nzewunwa, N. 1984a. Nigeria. In *Approaches to the archaeological heritage*, H. Cleere (ed.), 101–8. Cambridge: Cambridge University Press.
Nzewunwa, N. 1984b. Archaeology education in Nigeria. Paper delivered at the 29th Congress of the Historical Society of Nigeria, Sokoto, April.
Obayemi, A. 1970. Archaeology in West Africa till 1939: a critical history of its origins and development till 1939. MA thesis, University of Ghana, Legon.
Obichere, B. C. 1981. Museums and nation building. Paper delivered at the ICOM/ICOMOS Conference, Owerri, Nigeria, April/May.
Okita, S. I. O. 1981. The role of archaeological collections in cultural education. Paper presented at the fourth conference of the Archaeological Association of Nigeria, Zaria, June/July.
Okita, S. I. O. 1985. The emergence of public museums in Nigeria. In *Museum and nation building*, A. E. Afigbo and S. I. O. Okita (eds), 1–31. Owerri: New Africa Publishing Co.
Shaw, T. 1961. *Excavations at Dawu*. Edinburgh: Nelson.
Shaw, T. 1963. Editorial. *West African Archaeological Newsletter* **2**, 1–3.
Shaw, T. 1970. *Igbo-Ukwu: an account of archaeological discoveries in eastern Nigeria*. 2 vols. London: Faber.
Shaw, T. 1978. *Nigeria: its archaeology and early history*. London: Thames & Hudson.
Shinnie, P. L. 1965. The Department of Archaeology of the University of Ghana. *West African Archaeological Newsletter* **3**, 10–13.
Thilmans, G., C. Descamps & B. Khayat. 1980. *Protohistoire du Sénégal. Recherches archéologiques. Vol. I. Les sites megalithiques*. Mémoires de l'Institut Fondamental d'Afrique Noire 91. Dakar: IFAN.

Unesco OAU 1975. *Intergovernmental conference on cultural policies in Africa, 27 October – 6 November 1975: final report.* Accra.

15 *The development of museums in Botswana: dilemmas and tensions in a front-line state*

ROBERT MacKENZIE

In 1980 I was seconded from the Institute of Adult Education at the University of Botswana to act as co-ordinating secretary for the experimental National Museum Open Week. As an adult educator trained in history, I became intrigued by the potential significance of cultural institutions, such as museums, in the process of national development.

Before Botswana achieved full independence from Britain in 1966, the country had no official museum, though such a proposal was being mooted. Twenty years later Botswana boasted a National Museum and Art Gallery (NMAG) in the capital, Gaborone, and two independent district museums in the traditional 'villages' of Mochudi and Serowe, which, in colonial times, had been respectively the seats of the Bakgatla and Bamangwato chieftaincies. Since independence, attempts have been made to set up other museums in Kanye and Tati Town, a colonial mining centre in the north of the country. Museums have also been proposed for Maun and Molepolole. In addition to these central and local government ventures, several independent attempts have been made to set up museums, some on a commercial basis.

The general uncertainty and disagreement about the role of museums in national development, implicit in the work of MacCannell (1976) and evident in Botswana in 1966, continue to prevail. Despite discussion stimulated by the National Museum's Open Week and three subsequent consultants' reports (Oram & Nteta 1983, Agren & Carlson 1984, Oram 1984), a co-ordinated policy for museum development has yet to emerge. For all the rhetoric now associated with them, museums in Botswana remain relatively marginal institutions.

Why is this so? Superficially one can point to numerous administrative difficulties. Those who provide the resources, especially finance, and those who administer the services often have abrasive relationships. In addition, the central planners – often expatriates or visiting consultants – have different priorities and are unimpressed by, or indifferent to, culture as an element in national development.

Compared with other development expenditure, allocations to museums are meagre enough to ensure their continuing low status. The disinclination to invest in museums means that there are still too few qualified indigenous museologists (Omolewa 1979, p. 177). On the other hand, museologists often take as axiomatic the importance of their institutions to the nation and are surprised when others do not share their enthusiasm. It may be for this reason that they are often less vigorous than they should be in promoting an understanding of their activities by government and among ordinary citizens. These contrasting attitudes have exacerbated competition between national and local museums and strained relations between all museums and government departments.

Museums and cultural policy

Such conflict between national and regional museums, often expressed as nationalism versus tribalism or as progress versus tradition, is not unique to Botswana, however. Nor are clashes between significantly placed individuals. In many parts of black Africa the conflict is specifically cultural, rooted in the colonial period, when levels of cultural awareness were often closely accordant with degrees of resistance to colonial domination.

Crowder (1977) has distinguished four cultural layers in Africa: black African culture, national cultures, ethnic cultures, and imported cultures. The first three each contain opposing elements: an active one embracing adaptation and change, and a passive one associated with conservatism and preservation. But as Jones (1974) has pointed out, elements within African cultures are oppositional in yet another sense. Within each culture, groups compete for access to resources. It is to be expected, therefore, that cultural awareness, today no less than in the colonial period, would vary greatly depending on the strength of these competing elements.

This competition (often a hidden item on the agenda of museum controversies in Botswana) is illustrated, on the one hand, by the National Education Commission's recognition of the importance of culture as mediated through the education system (Botswana 1977, p. 177), and, on the other, by the radical symposium on 'Culture and Resistance', held at the University of Botswana in July 1982, which examined culture's potential value in the struggle against apartheid and other forms of political and cultural domination.

The importance of culture in the development of national identity in African states has been recognized by such international bodies as Unesco and the Organization of African Unity, which have provided forums to encourage cultural programmes (Unesco/OAU 1975). Countries as ideologically different as Nigeria and Mozambique include cultural studies in their formal educational programmes. After attaining independence, several African states institutionalized cultural activities through ministries of culture, centres for African studies, and national performing companies. Some museums established during the colonial period have become national institutions (Masao 1975, p. 103). More recently, the Southern African Development Co-ordination Conference, a regional grouping of front-line states to which Botswana belongs, identified Culture and Society as one of 17 key interest areas requiring members' attention (Jones 1985, p. 185).

Youngman (1981) has noted the lack of official backing for cultural affairs in Botswana compared with other African states. Few people are employed in developing the cultural heritage (Grant 1986, p. 9), but not many Batswana appear concerned about this weak cultural position. One person who *is* concerned is B. Nfila, who has stressed the need 'to find ways of developing the culture of Botswana which is fast giving way to foreign cultures' (Nfila 1982, p. vii). Given the country's colonial experience as the Bechuanaland Protectorate, its former though now diminishing role as a labour reserve for neighbouring white-dominated regimes, its export of primary products in exchange for manufactured goods, and the disintegration of the traditional ways of life of its various ethnic groups, Nfila's view reflects the cultural anxieties of a front-line state that is picking its way gingerly across the boundary between 'non-modern' and 'modern' worlds (MacCannell 1976, p. 8).

However, the cultural problems of Botswana today do not arise solely from difficulties of transition to independence. The chequered history of attempts to set up museums during the colonial period is also significant.

The background to present-day museums in Botswana

From 1885 to 1966 Bechuanaland (as Botswana was then called) was under British colonial rule. Until the Nationalist Party came to power in Pretoria on an apartheid ticket in 1948, it was generally supposed that South Africa would eventually incorporate Bechuanaland within its borders. Significantly, the country's administrative headquarters were located across the border at Mafeking in South Africa. Until full independence became unavoidable, the Protectorate's infrastructure was little developed, and during the colonial period museum collections were few and privately owned. Given the policy of minimal investment in the country, it is hardly surprising that official circles had little enthusiasm for a subsidized or outright government-funded museum. Moreover, outside institutions, particularly in South Africa (e.g. Witwatersrand University), were already carrying out museum-related research in Bechuanaland, especially in anthropology and archaeology; in effect the Protectorate was treated as a human laboratory, and museum collections were exported rather than retained.

Local officials, however, voiced concern about the removal of Bushman relics, antiquities, arts, crafts, and the results of research (MacKenzie 1982, p. 10). Even so, it was some 50 years into the colonial period before regulations were enacted to attempt to protect and preserve the material record.[1] The Historical Monuments Commission, composed of chiefs, magistrates, the Director of Education, and interested Europeans, was set up in 1935 (V. F. Ellenberger, District Commissioner, Serowe, to Assistant

Resident Commissioner, Mafeking, 7 October 1935).[2] But it was not until 1938 that Ellenberger raised with his superior the question of building a museum. He sought funds through the Colonial Office from the Carnegie Corporation in New York and proposed sites at Mafeking, or at Gaborone or Mahalapye in Bechuanaland (29 July 1938). Eventually Mafeking was chosen (16 August 1938). The application, however, was blocked by the British government on the grounds that other colonial territories had priority (Secretary of State [D.O. London] to High Commissioner, Cape Town, 25 May 1939). The outbreak of the Second World War postponed any further discussion.

Chief Bathoen of the Bangwaketse tribe had also cherished hopes for a local museum at his capital, Kanye (16 August 1938), where the old London Missionary Society tribal church was the chosen site. This museum functioned fitfully without the benefit of a permanent curator, but Bathoen confessed difficulty in amassing an adequate collection to justify his project (Bathoen to G. S., Mafeking, 1 February 1961 [S.406/11 or 7384/9]).

It has been pointed out that two distinct interest groups in the 1930s formed a loose alliance to try to manage changes that were taking place. Colonial administrators were 'generally indifferent to those aspects of local life that did not enter directly into policy matters. In their turn, Batswana leaders were concerned to secure the best possible advantage for themselves and their people in this externally imposed system' (Wilmsen 1985, p. 175). A comparable alliance seems to have been involved at the early stages of promoting museum development.

Botswana emerged to full political independence in 1966 as one of the 25 poorest countries of the world. Political power was exercised by a coalition of rich cattle-owning peasants and small trader-capitalists, whose power derived from their connections with traditional sources of authority. Since independence a notable feature has been the growth of central government powers, with a gradual but deliberate erosion of chiefly authority and a vigorous commitment to development planning. The centralizing tendency detected by Grant (1986) towards museums is part of a more general policy.

In the transition from colonialism, African scholars reoriented their intellectual and ideological views away from the concerns of Western-based research. African archaeologists now 'tend to be concerned more with recent prehistory than Palaeolithic archaeology and with problems that relate to their national history . . . anthropology is not well regarded and archaeological research is being increasingly aligned with history, just as ethnological studies are being redefined as sociology' (Trigger 1984, p. 363). The first post of Lecturer in Archaeology at the University of Botswana was advertised in 1985 within the Department of History. For its part, the government has expressed concern that the Basarwa (previously called the Bush People, a term increasingly regarded as offensive) are being over-researched by anthropologists and is trying to direct attention into other fields. However, governmental aims to exert greater control have not yet been matched by resources for achieving this (MacKenzie 1989, pp. 12–17).

As independence approached, senior government officers and an indigenous elite marked the occasion by jointly urging the creation of a national museum. Senior Game Warden Alec Campbell, who had collected more than 1000 historical and cultural items relating to southern Africa (Campbell, pers. comm. 28 July 1981), and was a driving force behind this initiative, became the first director of the National Museum and Art Gallery (NMAG). The museum's shifting organizational arrangements, detailed elsewhere (MacKenzie 1982, pp. 7–9), show that portfolio responsibility has changed several times, indicative of the government's difficulty in narrowing down this remit to the confines of a single department or ministry. It is interesting to notice that the social composition of the NMAG Board, at least in the late 1960s, differed little from that of the Historical Monuments Commission of 1935.

NMAG had ambitious plans for growth as an important national and international institution. In the words of the Annual Report for 1967 (p. 1):

The intention is to build up a Museum and Art Gallery which will eventually be able to take its place among the museums of the world, providing a centre for research, particularly in the fields of Natural History and Archaeology, a repository for the preservation of museum material and an institution of cultural education for both child and adult.

NMAG has developed links with certain museums and organizations abroad, for example, the Denver Museum of Natural History, Colorado, USA. At the same time, voluntary and business support, especially from expatriates, has been an important feature of the museum's survival.

By late 1980, NMAG's position was as follows. Its purpose was 'to develop an educational and cultural institution, providing a visual record of man's achievements and his effects on the natural environment in Botswana'. This would be done 'by building up national collections of ethnographic, historic and plant material, by permanent and temporary displays, a mobile exhibit, the protection of the national monuments, and by research'. Current displays portray historic and contemporary life in Botswana, changes in the environment, and government development programmes (Botswana 1980, V, pt 5, pp. 161–2). All of this is part of an attempt to reflect the country's national aspirations.

Launching the Open Week on 28 November 1980, the responsible minister referred to NMAG's standing as 'one of the newest Government Departments and one of the most prestigious institutions in our country'. This statement may be true for international scholars, tourists, local expatriates, and school parties; it may even be true for students and staff at the University of Botswana. I doubt very much, however, if it is yet true for the majority of citizens. The problem of how to make NMAG more attractive and relevant to ordinary Batswana – which prompted the organization of the Open Week – is heightened by the sheer size of the country and the uneven distribution of its one million population. But there are more profound reasons. Social and economic changes have removed many Batswana from their past. By the early 19th century new tribal groupings had begun to emerge. All accounts suggest they had thriving cultures, but these are not illustrated in museum collections, which reflect episodes in southern Africa's settlement history. Nfila's complaint (1982) concerning the decay of Botswana culture demonstrates concern about the neglect into which they have fallen.

Although independence brought major socioeconomic advances, as measured by the enormous growth in annual expenditure on development, inequity is growing between those who have benefited materially from the process and the 40 per cent or so of households that were below the officially determined poverty line in 1981. The degeneration of traditional cultural life is therefore a matter of deep concern for the country's small artistic and intellectual elite.

The present position of museums

Sandy Grant, the director of the Phuthadikobo District Museum, describes a situation of 'neglect' and 'deadlock' in museum development and contends that government policy is ill-defined for its own cultural departments and non-existent for independent district museums (Grant 1986, pp. 9–12). He offers four main reasons for the current confused and inert state of affairs: (a) an inexorable centralizing tendency of the Botswana government; (b) a dogmatic view that district museums are incompatible with development; (c) the ambivalence generated by the absence of a coherent government museums policy; (d) individual personality factors.

Grant's first point was anticipated by MacCannell (1976, p. 25), who argued that although ownership of cultural production is not yet organized by a historically distinct class, 'governments at all levels and of all types are becoming increasingly interested in controlling cultural production'. This attitude is illustrated in Botswana by the creation of NMAG as a department of a ministry and by plans to make culture an explicit part of a ministerial portfolio. But the desire for control is not matched by resources to give it firm direction. Insofar as museums are concerned, control seems to come by the denial of resources. There is not much consistency in either policy or programmes. At present, the latter continue without clear guidelines, and contending elements co-exist, albeit uneasily.

Grant believes that the case for independent local museums is unassailable. He distinguishes between a government 'museum service' and district museums serving local communities. He sees a potential conflict between 'top-down' and 'bottom-up' approaches to decision-making and dismisses as unfounded three recurring sets of objections to local museums in Africa: their too specific focus lends itself to tribalism and undermines national unity; their ethnographic displays detract from the modern state by publicizing the crudities of an earlier way of life; and such institutions represent an attempt to freeze people in the past. To Grant these claims are nonsense, because no museum in the world has the power to stop the massive complexities of change (Grant 1981, pp. 17–18).

The limitations of the National Museum and Art Gallery have been set out in three consultants' reports (Oram & Nteta 1983, Agren & Carlson 1984, Oram 1984). They identified insufficient funding, inability to meet the nation's museum requirements, inadequate professional standards, and the lack of sufficient planning and commitment to secure the necessary resources. They concluded that NMAG was not so much a national museum serving the whole country as a parochial institution specifically rooted in Gaborone.

As almost a lone voice, Grant has argued strenuously in favour of independent local museums. He was gladdened by the general tenor of these reports and disappointed by their evident failure to persuade government of the need to establish independent local museums. Instead NMAG has plans to establish local outposts, but these would be quite different from Grant's concept of local community museums, even if resources were available to staff and supervise them properly. In his view, local museums must cater for the needs of local inhabitants as well as visitors, set up a display centre, record events as they happen, provide a research base for scholars and development planners, and act as a service and extension centre, especially for schools (Grant 1976, pp. 14–15).

The triangular contest between the Ministry of Home Affairs (the Ministry responsible for NMAG), NMAG, and the Phuthadikobo Museum highlights the general issues involved in an attempt to formulate a national approach to museum development. In the debate about the proper role of muesums in Botswana, Phuthadikobo Museum, which has survived (often precariously) by its own efforts for more than ten years, can be taken as a useful guide to the underlying reasons for the current difficulties. No doubt the museum's siting and historical associations help to explain why it is the first local museum in Botswana to have lasted a full decade. Its current policy is based on the twin planks of self-help principles of community involvement and the contention that 'the missing dimension of Development is the historical one' (Grant, pers. comm. 9 August 1981). In Grant's view, at a time when rapid change in a developing economy causes confusion of identity, it is imperative to create a historical reference point. Thus the museum is organized around two major themes: the development of Mochudi, and the process of change (Grant 1981, p. 16).

Grant has strong views about the role of local museums in fostering development: 'We seek to support, to underpin, the Government's own development initiatives but also to assist and publicise the achievements of the local community' (*ibid.*). He is baffled by the failure of government and foreign donors to accept and support his position. Any right-thinking planner could not fail to see its logic. And yet, patently, the arguments are not having much impact. Grant writes and argues cogently and forcefully, so one can only assume that underlying issues of government policy are not yet part of the public debate.

One of the underlying issues could be the status of ethnic groups. When Chief Linchwe revived initiation rites among the Bakgatla in 1975, the then President, Sir Seretse Khama (himself Paramount Chief of the Bamang-wato) was swift to react with charges of tribalism and retrogressive ethno-centrism (Grant, Ch. 16, this volume). On a more academic plane, Hall (1984, p. 456) has argued that different interest groups perceive the past differently. Black nationalist governments tend to reject research emphases on ethnicity, while researchers in southern Africa remain preoccupied with tribal diversity. In controversies over cultural origins, Hall detected an ambiguity and dualism which has developed between increasingly polarized black and white nationalists. White liberal scholars are trapped in the middle; many who object to the abuse of history and prehistory to justify white nationalist policies 'are probably also opposed to black nationalism which threatens existing social and economic orders and therefore the institutions from which archaeological research is conducted' (*ibid.*, pp. 461–2).

Museum development in Botswana is unlikely to remain aloof from these struggles; there is some hostility – as elsewhere in Africa (see, for example, Garlake 1984, pp. 121–2) – to foreign scholars' interpretations of the country's past, especially to those who seem preoccupied with uncomfort-able questions of ethnicity. Pointing to the declaration of the 1983 Azanian Peoples' Organisation that ethnicity and tribalism play right into the hands of apartheid, Hall concluded that 'ethnic emphasis is not currently a political option' (1984, p. 464). Despite protestations to the contrary, local museums still have to contend with a strongly held view within government and planning circles that local equals ethnic. It is not surprising, therefore, that local museums are regarded with considerable ambivalence.

Perhaps it is indicative of the problems facing Botswana museums that no director of NMAG to date has been indigenous (which, incidentally, is also true of the director of Phuthadikobo Museum). Well-qualified and experi-enced local personnel are snapped up by government, industry, and com-merce, while the direction of museums has been left in the hands of 'paper Batswana' or expatriates. Their services have been sterling, and without them there would probably have been no museum service at all, but this state of affairs is a further indication of the relatively low priority accorded to museums by government.

Relationships between the various museum directors have not always been cordial, which matters more than usual in a country where most of the political, cultural, and commercial elite know each other. These cultural custodians have found it difficult to present a common front to government. Even acting jointly, they have failed to market their institutions suc-cessfully.

Museums have also failed to convince central planners that culture and the past are relevant to national and local development. Botswana has an international reputation for sophisticated development plans, with the Ministry of Finance and Development Planning acting as a kind of super-ministry, advising the Cabinet on how national resources should be distributed. Senior expatriate planners within this ministry have tended to be economists not noted for their interest in indigenous cultural affairs. This has added to the difficulties of museum directors in getting through to government.

Conclusion

Historical, economic, social, bureaucratic, and individual factors have shaped and constrained museum development in Botswana, but they have been little analysed. It may be that they are simply 'growing pains' (Grant, Ch. 16, this volume) that will disappear once the foundations of Botswana's infrastructure, economy, and future are firmly set. In that utopia museums will be marginal no longer, and in their various forms they will receive adequate resources within the framework of a sound cultural policy.

However, the dilemmas and tensions that I have described are unlikely to disappear quickly. Against huge odds, committed individuals within the museum service strive to make their institutions more relevant and responsive, and to bring them nearer to the centre of national consciousness. There have been some excellent initiatives, but the power to give direction is concentrated in the hands of a small number of planners, who do not put museums high on the agenda of development. I strongly subscribe to Grant's belief that the past is the 'missing dimension of Development'. But try telling that to the planners.

Acknowledgements

I would like to thank Dr Q. N. Parsons for introducing me to relevant archival material, and Louis Taussig, a former colleague at the Institute of Adult Education, University of Botswana, for making helpful suggestions on the first draft of this chapter.

Notes

1   In fact, measures were taken in 1910 (Proclamation No. 40: Ancient Ruins and Bushman Relics) and 1929 (Bushman Relics Proclamation). But it was not until 1934 (Proclamation No. 68: Bechuanaland Historical Monuments Commission) and 1935 (Bushman Relics Act) that an official body supported by legislation was set up to have systematic oversight of the problem.
2   Most archival references in the text are to files lodged in the Botswana National Archives (S.406/12/1–2 BNA) or in the Bechuanaland Protectorate Secretariat 7384/10 (1935). Subsequent dates in the text refer to these archives.

References

Agren, P. & G. Carlson 1984. *National Museum and Art Gallery Botswana Extension Project: a consultancy report.* Gaborone.

Botswana, Republic of 1977. *Education for Kagisano.* Gaborone: National Commission on Education.

Botswana, Republic of 1980. *National development plan 1979–85.* Gaborone: Ministry of Finance and Development Planning.

Crowder, M. 1977. Culture and development – the West African case. Lecture to the Centro de Estudios Economicos y Sociales del Tercer Mundo, Mexico City, 24 September.

Garlake, P. 1984. Ken Mafuka and Great Zimbabwe. *Antiquity* **58**, 121–3.

Grant, S. 1976. The case for district museums. *Kuthwano* **15** (12) December. Gaborone.

Grant, S. 1981. The Phuthadikobo Museum – evolution and issues. Paper presented at the Botswana National Cultural Council Conference on Cultural Activity at the District Level. Phuthadikobo Museum, 30 May.

Grant, S. 1986. Neglect as policy: ten years of deadlock: museums and government in Botswana. In *Archaeological 'objectivity' in interpretation.* World Archaeological Congress, Vol. 2 (mimeo).

Grant, S. 1990. A past abandoned? Some experiences of a regional museum in Botswana. In *The politics of the past*, P. Gathercole & D. Lowenthal (eds), Ch. 16. London: Unwin Hyman.

Hall, M. 1984. The burden of tribalism: the social context of southern African Iron Age studies. *American Antiquity* **49**, 455–67.

Jones, B. 1974. *The politics of popular culture.* Occasional Paper 12, Centre for Contemporary Cultural Studies, University of Birmingham.

Jones, K. 1985. A select bibliography of Botswana material for 1983. *Botswana Notes and Records* **17**, 183–6.

MacCannell, D. 1976. *The tourist: a new theory of the leisure class.* London: Macmillan.

MacKenzie, R. 1982. The development of Botswana's museums. Unpublished discussion paper, Department of Adult Education, University of Southampton.

MacKenzie, R. 1989. Botswana's research policy: a contextual analysis. In *Research in Botswana: proceedings of the Botswana Society Symposium on Research Development*, R. Hitchcock *et al.* (eds). Gaborone: Botswana Society.

Masao, F. 1975. National Museum of Tanzania: post-Independence progress. *Tanzania Notes and Records* **76**, 103–12.

NMAG [National Museum and Art Gallery] 1967. *The National Museum of Botswana: annual report.* Gaborone.

Nfila, B. 1982. *The evaluation of phase I of the cultural development project.* Gaborone: University of Botswana, Institute of Adult Education.

Omolewa, M. 1979. Supporting institutions: libraries, museums, exhibitions, fairs, shows and festivals. In *A handbook of adult education for West Africa*, L. Bown & S. Tomori (eds). London: Hutchinson University Library for Africa.

Oram, J. 1984. Museum development in Botswana: brief synopsis of proposals. Unpublished report for the Ministry of Home Affairs, Gaborone.

Oram, J. & D. Nteta 1983. Interim report: towards a national policy for museum development. Unpublished report presented to the Permanent Secretary, Ministry of Home Affairs, Gaborone.

Trigger, B. 1984. Alternative archaeologies: nationalist, colonialist, imperialist. *Man* **19**, 355–70.

Unesco/OAU 1975. *Intergovernmental conference on cultural policies in Africa, 27 October – 6 November 1975: final report*. Accra.

Wilmsen, E. 1985. Conversations with Mr. Tommy Kays of Maun. *Botswana Notes and Records* **17**, 175–8.

Youngman, F. 1981. *Adult education in Botswana 1960–80: an annotated bibliography*. Gaborone: National Institute for Research.

16 *A past abandoned? Some experiences of a regional museum in Botswana*

SANDY GRANT

In 1974 it was agreed to abandon the old Bakgatla National School (Fig. 16.1) on Phuthadikobo Hill, in Mochudi, Botswana. The building was in a poor state of repair, without room for expansion, and with insufficient space for toilets, football ground, or garden. It was difficult for the children to walk up the hill each day to school. During 1974–5 a new primary school was constructed elsewhere in Mochudi, and in August 1975 the pupils were transferred to the new building.

Sometime before this event, during 1972 or 1973, I had proposed that Mochudi should establish its own museum but had made no attempt to identify available buildings, to investigate sources of funding, or even to determine who might be in charge of such a venture. In 1975, when I was out of the country, there was some correspondence about initiating the project by using the old school. On my return to Botswana the secretary of the Kgatleng District Council wrote to say that the old building would be available for the museum but did not promise anything in the way of council support. An *ad hoc* committee met in December 1975. The minutes state cryptically that 'the Council's offer of the old National School building be accepted and that the museum be established there. The ambitious nature of this decision, given that the Committee possesses not one cent, was understood and accepted.'

The assumption, which I did not question, was that I would get on with the job. The immediate prospects were immensely challenging and overwhelmingly daunting. The old National School, formally opened by Prince Arthur of Connaught in July 1923, had been – with 700 square metres of floor space – for many years the largest building in the country. But it had never had an access road; all the materials for its construction and later repair had been carried to the site by head and hand. Nor had it had a water supply, and, not surprisingly, lacked electricity, telephone, and toilets. If it were to become a museum, or indeed used for any purpose at all, these facilities would be needed. But how were they to be provided? From where was the necessary support likely to come? By the mid-1970s non-government aid agencies in Africa were less interested in Botswana, which was no longer one of the poorest countries in the world, and were transferring their attention to Mozambique and Zambia, where public need was arguably

Figure 16.1   The Phuthadikobo Museum, Mochudi, Botswana, formerly the old Bakgatla National School.

greater. The District Council would presumably do what it could to help; but local government in Botswana is operated on a centrally subsidized deficit system, so the council had only limited resources at its disposal.

Despite the bleak financial prospects, the opportunity presented was too unusual to pass up. The primary issue was not the unexpected availability of a large, suitable, and centrally located building. Rather it was the opportunity to demonstrate how to reach the heart of the development problem, which was very much a matter of concern at that time in Botswana. Here was a chance to go beyond the provision of the necessary infrastructure, such as better public facilities, roads, clinics, schools, and water supplies, by developing a project in which the local people were directly involved.

The construction of the old National School had been an immense self-help project directed by the Regent of the Bakgatla tribe, Isang Pilane, who between 1920 and 1929 had attempted to transform his society through a spectacular and purely tribal effort to move from the lowest to the higher levels of education in a single leap. The fact that the school only spasmodically achieved some form of post-primary education was not its own failing. The tribe could build the school, but it could not alone achieve the purposes for which it was built. Yet the intention and the building were triumphs in themselves, and the vision that inspired this project is evident in the fact that it was another 40 years before the British administration opened the first government secondary school in 1965. For much of the 1930s, 1940s, and 1950s, the administration viewed the Bakgatla as the most progressive tribe in the country. This reputation was primarily based on Isang's astonishing modernization programmes in the 1920s, of which the creation of the National School was his finest achievement.

By 1974 circumstances were very different. Local experts advised that the old school was no longer suitable and that funds were available for a new one. This, as it turned out, largely fallacious advice was accepted, and the National School was left forlorn and decayed, a home for owls and a place of depredations by young vandals.

Let us consider the implications of the move. For 52 years the old school had stood proudly on its dramatic site overlooking much of Mochudi, the visible symbol of tribal effort in the past and, through education, of its investment in the future. How could the school be abandoned? What forces for change were at work in the community that could bring this about? What were the new values that could so blithely cast away so much of the community's past? What would be the psychological effect of ripping out its heart, leaving an abandoned and collapsing edifice in place of the previous hill-top symbol of progress? One district councillor perhaps understood the implications of such a dismal scene when he suggested that the building be demolished. But the proposal for its demolition represented that type of official thinking that sees the advantages of an old building only in making space for a new one.

The past disguised

By 1975 these modes of thought were regularly being invoked in Botswana for traditional old towns such as Mochudi. The thrust of national development was on the new towns, the capital Gaborone, the copper town of Pikwe, and the diamond town of Jwaneng. These were the symbols of post-independence progress. The old, traditional towns and tribal capitals were consciously or otherwise pushed into the less sharply focused corners.

Unusually in Africa, the Batswana have been town builders. The remains of their towns, covering a period of perhaps 800 or 900 years, are scattered throughout Botswana and the Transvaal in as yet unrecorded numbers. Early 19th-century European travellers, on encountering Batswana towns for the first time, remarked on their unusual size and substantial character. Trüter and Somerville in 1801 estimated the circumference of old 'Leetako' to be

> fully as large as Cape Town, including all the gardens of Table Valley; . . . it was concluded . . . that [the number of houses] could not be less than two or more than three thousand . . . The whole population, including men, women and children, they considered to be from ten to fifteen thousand persons.   (Barrow 1806, pp. 390–1)

The naturalist William J. Burchell described his reactions to the BaTlhaping in 1812:

While surveying with rapidity the new character of this bustling crowd of Africans and admiring the social appearance and magnitude of a town so different in every respect from those of Europe . . . [and accustomed], as I had been, for so many months, to the sight of only the frail moveable huts of Hottentot and Bushmen, I rejoiced at finding myself at length arrived among a nation whose dwellings claimed the name of buildings. (Burchell 1952, p. 359)

In 1820 the Reverend John Campbell described the Hurutse settlements of 'Kureechane'. 'The plain, which extended between the hill we were descending and that on which the city stood, was soon covered with people . . . ' (Campbell 1967, p. 221).

Some 150 years after these first European travellers had expressed their delight and astonishment at finding genuine indigenous Tswana towns, not one exists which can similarly intrigue a visitor from abroad. Only 'villages' seemingly remain as evidence that the Batswana were once town builders. Yet the actual towns today are much the same; it is only the perception of them that is bizarrely different.

Botswana today has five traditional settlements with populations of more than 20 000, another five over 10 000, and seven over 5000, figures strikingly similar to those of the 'towns and cities' visited by Trüter, Somerville, Burchell, and Campbell early in the last century. But these contemporary settlements are termed 'villages', as ordained by administrative order long antedating codification in 1955 that towns could exist only on Crown (now state) land. It followed, therefore, that tribal lands contained only villages. Curiously, this perversion has persisted through the 20 years of post-colonial history. The reason is quite simply that the Batswana have so thoroughly lost any awareness that they now neither know nor care about their own extraordinary historical achievements. The colonial legacy has left some strange imprints in Africa, but surely few so remarkable as the total unawareness on the part of both the ordinary man and the Cabinet minister that the ancestral 'village' of 20 000 or so people is actually a town; the former because the 'village' has no resemblance to the modern urban model; the latter because he has no wish to be associated with either. Only visitors from elsewhere in Africa show an astonishment comparable to that of early 19th-century European travellers. But today's African visitors marvel not at finding an indigenous town but at discovering that it is called a village.

The colonial process commonly reduced native kings to chiefs, and it was at least consistent similarly to reduce the status of Botswana capitals from towns to villages. The traditional town in Botswana is therefore something of a political anomaly. Its existence owes nothing to modernizing policies; its roots are tribal, its base rests in chieftancy. The paradox exemplifies the tensions between the past and the future, between historical and contemporary power, between inherited and adapted tradition and culture that characterizes much of post-colonial Africa.

So Mochudi, a village, decides to start a museum in an abandoned building possessing immense historical, cultural, and political implications. And Mochudi itself is representative of all those conjoined social forces that alike contribute to the making of a new nation and yet can so easily be interpreted as opposing the national genesis.

The past revived

Several opposing forces were sweeping through this traditional community in the mid-1970s. The newly installed Chief Linchwe II had abandoned his father's house in 1965 to build his own on the site of his great grandfather's on Phuthadikobo Hill. His move back to a historical base contrasted sharply with the District Council's decision in 1974 to abandon the National School on the same hill. As one went back to the historic hill, the other marched away from it, symbolic perhaps of the conflicts within the community.

The most dramatic development in terms of revitalization was Chief Linchwe's revival in 1975, backed by the tribe, of the old initiation rites, including the circumcision of men, which had been abandoned in 1902. Until 1963 these rites had survived in reduced form, but by then the process by which an age group was constituted had become a matter of formal routine only. However, the status of the traditional age group had remained extremely high. The decision to revive full initiation rites was the first major intrusion by the old into the new anywhere in Botswana since independence in 1966. The President, Sir Seretse Khama, reacted strongly against it:

> One is tempted to remark about the renaissance of wasteful and long forgotten tribal rituals such as Bogwera [initiation]. In my view Bogwera is a divisive ritual. It smacks of the seeds of disunity coming as it does, at a time when we thought we were winning the battle against tribalism . . . all it does is to encourage tribal identities and ethnocentrism at the expense of national identity and national unity . . . There are more useful things to do than running around naked in the forest. (Khama 1975, p. 2)

Undeterred by the President's disapproval, the tribe conducted initiation rites for men, with circumcision, in 1975, 1976, 1980, 1982, and 1985, and for women, without circumcision, in 1975, 1976, 1979, 1981, 1982, and 1985. The purpose of these adapted and humane initiation rites is to underpin an individual and community sense of identification. That this identification is tribal and achieved through the chieftancy may be a matter of regret to the national government, but having insisted that there should be no coercion and no fatalities, the government has provided discreet assistance, while allowing itself sufficient room for dissociation should this later seem desirable. Whether the revival of initiation is reactionary or an advance remains debatable, but that it has been a dramatic quest for identification can hardly be in doubt.

The past conserved

These events provided the setting for the establishment of the Phuthadikobo Museum in 1975–6. But although they occurred in the same year, the revival of initiation and the birth of the new museum were strictly coincidental. The museum was not Chief Linchwe's specific initiative, but he actively supported it from the start, and the background and setting bore directly on the role perceived for the museum from its earliest days. It was strongly felt, for instance, that the museum should continue the educational tradition associated with the old school building. What was intended was the creation of a community education centre whose activities would revolve around those of the new district museum. Acquisitions were to play a central part in that educational process, extending the museum's classic roles of collection, classification, storage, and display. There was a conscious decision that the museum should strengthen the sense of local pride and achievement; hence its objective of illustrating the processes of change and urban growth in Mochudi. The museum's achievement over the period 1976–86 will now be assessed in terms of the three categories originally used to cover its main activities: the educational role, the local museum project, and containing costs.

The educational role

The Phuthadikobo Museum's displays are simple and inexpensive, and, somewhat unusually, are often deliberately subjected to public handling. No entrance fee is charged, for it was felt that to turn away people who had no money (the great majority) would work against the museum's aims. Display themes were largely determined by what existed in the collection. The fact that acquisitions were normally restricted to artefacts from within the district made it relatively easy to achieve coherence and some sense of chronology in displays.

Having no organizational capacity to undertake its own education programme, the museum instead lent substantial support to other agencies, offering a physical base for those who lacked it. Two such partners are the district's departments of Non-Formal Education and In-Service Training, both in the Ministry of Education. Since 1982 the Non-Formal Education Department has held training courses for new literacy teachers in a restored traditional homestead which is part of the museum. The In-Service Primary Teachers Training Unit was accommodated between 1979 and 1985 in two old classrooms and subsequently in an old prefabricated bank building donated to the museum. These arrangements enhance a healthy sense of co-operation and provide the museum with desperately needed income. The District Council and Land Board also use museum facilities for seminars, training sessions, and meetings, and two High Court murder trials have been held in its building. All these events mark the museum's revitalization of the old building and forge new links within the community.

The museum has also sought more active popular involvement. In 1976 it produced an ambitious plan for a graphics training and publishing centre. Because the proposal never received outside support, the museum decided to winch itself up by its own bootstraps and, with minimal external assistance, created a silk-screen workshop printing on both textiles and paper. The workshop employs a dozen local people, all of whom have learned their skills on the job. In addition, it has provided training for dozens of other people eager to embark on their own home-based printing projects. Early on, the workshop also experimented with art education classes for primary school children, an attempt that may soon be revived.

The local museum project

Had the museum been wrong in believing that a settlement of 20 000 people must have enough material for such a project, the result would have been disastrous. In the event, the museum's modest collection is sufficient to mount the largest display of Tswana cultural objects in the country. The policy is to collect anything that has been made or used within the district. A similar approach has been adopted by the silk-screen workshop, where local designers have been encouraged to use local themes, thereby closely relating their work to the objectives and contents of the museum proper.

Above all, the creation of a genuine museum project required the renovation of the old building, the first attempt by any community in Botswana to conserve a building of major historical and cultural importance. What is interesting is that such an ambitious undertaking arose in the context of the conflicting responses to tradition and modernity, illustrated by the chief's return to his family home on Phuthadikobo Hill and by the District Council's departure from it. Apart from the immediate difficulty of persuading the District Council to support the renovation of a building that they themselves had just abandoned, the museum confronted a long-term need to build an image blending the new and the old, the traditional and the modern. The past had somehow to be projected into the future. This could not be achieved merely by creating an orthodox museum, for many people were eager to write off the project as reactionary and tribalistic.

Somehow the museum has managed to step delicately through this minefield. Moreover, its apparent success over a ten-year period must be seen as the key factor that has stimulated similar initiatives in the Khama III Museum, Serowe, Botswana, and in the museums now planned for Francistown, Maun, and Molepolole, as well as in the Nayuma Museum, Zambia. Future museum development in Botswana is bound to remain hazardous, however, and one or two dubious steps could stifle these initiatives. The experience of the Phuthadikobo Museum could well be decisive for the future of Botswana's museums.

Containing costs

One means of determining how deeply a project is locally rooted is to examine the proportion of its funds so derived. The Phuthadikobo Museum's total income from donations and grants over the ten years since 1976 makes revealing reading:

Donations	Pula 13 300	
Kgatleng District Council	16 450	
Ministry of Home Affairs	25 000	
Grants external to Botswana	67 900	
Grants within Botswana	48 600	
(a) approved by external authorities		28 600
(b) approved by internal authorities		20 000
Total	P171 250	

Adopting a total notional figure of P10 000 for *non-cash* contributions, donations exceed the support received from the District Council, and fall only slightly below the amount provided by the Ministry of Home Affairs. An attempt to separate foreign from domestic money is likely to be somewhat dubious, but a rough picture emerges by identifying grants approved by foreign authorities (P28 600) as opposed to those internally approved (P20 000). Using the higher donations figure (P23 300), a crude breakdown shows that, remarkably, the museum has achieved near parity in domestic compared with overseas sources of funding: P84 750 from Botswana sources and P96 500 from abroad. Had the District Council been able, and the Ministry willing, to provide more support, the picture would have been even more impressive.

Over the ten years, the museum has deliberately sought to minimize expenditure and maximize income, as the following figures show:

	1983	1984	1985	1986
Expenditure	21 989	19 170	19 240	15 769
Income	14 512	15 875	16 221	17 615

Such figures suggest a situation of bare survival, necessary perhaps to pave a way for establishing other museums, but in the long run self-defeating. Costs may be trimmed to such an extent that a museum can no longer employ the staff needed to provide the services for which it was brought into being. Prudent accounting is the essential requirement for all local projects; impoverishment benefits nobody.

Future museum development in Botswana

The past ten years have been beset with imponderables. Circumstances have required the Phuthadikobo Museum to grow slowly through trial and error. This has been frustrating, but as a development process it does have something to be said for it. The museum had no model to follow, no policy or guidelines to provide a framework. Each step was a matter of exploring and testing. An extraordinary range of individual support has helped to make up for the paucity of official backing. Relationships with the government-owned National Museum in Gaborone and with the Ministry of Home Affairs have been ill-defined, confusing, and sometimes strained (see MacKenzie, Ch. 15, this volume). On the larger stage, the government has appeared to be preoccupied with plans to co-ordinate cultural activity in order to embellish its own image; hence the grandiose plans for a national cultural centre in the capital. Such preoccupations may simply reflect growing pains; in the next ten years a different pattern may emerge. But some difficult questions must first be answered.

How, for instance, will the non-government district and town museums relate to the government-owned National Museum and to the Ministry of Home Affairs? What levels of expenditure and sophistication will be acceptable, and to whom? What support will the National Museum be able to provide? How will the district and town museums relate to each other? Will they be able to create a common resource pool, and of what services and resources? Will government and aid agencies seek to establish some uniformity of standards, or will there be a free-for-all with each project prospering according to its ability to secure external support? What will be the relationships between the community-owned museums and the town and district councils? What governmental sensitivities should local museums be aware of? Will new projects be able to sustain themselves, or will they be absorbed within a centralized and government-controlled national programme? That the Phuthadikobo Museum has survived these difficult ten years, and even prospered, suggests that it may provide a helpful guide for the future.

Two key requirements need further emphasis. First, local museum projects in Botswana (and doubtless in other African states) must be locally rooted, and secondly, they must achieve a balance between the old and the new. It can be assumed that a local museum will have a board of trustees drawn from interested local citizens, and that its collection will come largely from the local community. By themselves, however, these factors are insufficient to ensure local success; management and funding should also be as local as possible. In countries such as Botswana, with a dearth of trained people, it may be essential to use foreign personnel. Sensitivity on both sides, then, is vital.

Foreign aid usually comes as a package deal, with cash and manpower provided together. Great care must be taken to ensure that the museum's relationship with the aiding agency does not flourish to the detriment of links with the local community. If foreign experts brought in to administer and use aid rely on sophisticated standards involving high capital and recurrent expenditure, a dependent relationship ensues that takes the museum from the local social environment in which it should be set.

Foreign aid and manpower provide temptations to take dangerous short cuts. Foreigners working with local museums should be conscious of the risks inherent in their short-term contracts – the continual changes of policy and practice, the difficulty of grasping within a short time all the nuances of a complex social, cultural, historical, and political milieu. Local histories and local cultures have inherently political dimensions. It may not be possible to avoid all the problems, but it helps to know that they exist, and to display a well-mannered sensitivity to local understanding.

How can a balance be struck between the opposing pulls of the new and the old that impinge on all communities? The experience of the Phuthadikobo Museum suggests that orthodox museum development must be accompanied by projects transcending conventional roles, directed towards specific local needs. Such museums should function as community education centres for all age groups. But non-income-generating activity of this kind is possible only if funding is made available from outside. Otherwise, museums can seek to create employment through craft activities, ideally by providing for the revival of traditional crafts. The skills required to start and manage such initiatives are not usually to be found among trained museum workers, and maybe their recruitment should be confined to larger, national museums. Few local museums have an economic base that would justify such expensive expertise. Indeed, levels of sophistication that are unlikely to be sustained in the long term should not be adopted in the first place. Local museum projects necessarily involve a series of compromises enforced by local circumstances. Outside aid can circumvent this process, but at what cost? And to whom?

References

Barrow, J. 1806. *A voyage to Cochinchina, in the years 1792 and 1793: . . . to which is annexed an account of a journey, made in the years 1801 and 1802, to the residence of the chief of the Booshuana nation : . .* London: Cadell & Davies.

Burchell, W. J. 1952. *Travels in the interior of southern Africa*, Vol. II. (Reprinted from the original edition of 1822–24; edited by I. Schapera.) London: The Batchworth Press.

Campbell, J. 1967. *Travels in South Africa – undertaken at the request of the London Missionary Society, being a narrative of a second journey in the interior of the country*, Vol. I. London: Johnson Reprint Corporation. (Originally published in 1822 by Westley.)

Khama, S. 1975. *Towards ten years of peace, stability and progress, His Excellency the President's Independence Day message to the nation*, 30 September. Gaborone: Government Printer.

MacKenzie, R. 1990. The development of museums in Botswana: dilemmas and tensions in a front-line state. In *The politics of the past*, P. Gathercole & D. Lowenthal (eds), Ch. 15. London: Unwin Hyman.

17 *Archaeology and museum work in the Solomon Islands*

LAWRENCE FOANAOTA

The Solomon Islands is a sovereign state in the South Pacific with a total land area of about 11 500 square miles. There are six major islands plus numerous smaller raised limestone and volcanic islands and low coral atolls, divided among seven provinces (Fig. 17.1). The Melanesian, Polynesian, and Micronesian population comprises a variety of distinct cultures, with some 87 different languages. The island of New Guinea is 350 miles away; the next nearest land mass is the northern tip of Australia, 1000 miles to the west.

The Solomon Islands National Museum (Figs 17.2,3) is situated on Guadalcanal in the centre of Honiara, the capital. It is supported by grants from the Solomon Islands government through the Ministry of Education, Training and Cultural Affairs and by overseas agencies such as the South Pacific Cultures Fund of the Australian government, the South Pacific Commission, Unesco, and, most recently, the Cultural Aid Fund of the Japanese government. When the museum was first opened in June 1969, its chief aim was to collect ethnographic material. Today its national collection and exhibitions promote knowledge of Solomon Islands' cultures and its staff documents the nation's languages and traditions in order to encourage the restoration of its rich cultural heritage (Foanaota 1980). Services provided for the general public include exhibitions, radio programmes, school visits, and festivals of traditional and contemporary music, dance, and song. The museum is open to all ideas, including the most recent, and is conceived as a forum for the discussion and exchange of views. Technical advice is given to islanders wishing to preserve their cultures, and to advocates of legislation for the protection of the cultural heritage.

The museum was manned by a caretaker without formal training in field research until mid-1973 (Foanaota 1974b), when a technical co-operation curator, Anna Craven, arrived from the United Kingdom. She introduced new projects into the museum's development plan, many of which were successfully implemented before her term of service expired early in 1979. At present, all ten staff members are Solomon Islanders, though only three have academic training or fieldwork experience in archaeology or social anthropology. One of the museum's main drawbacks is its lack of trained staff in museology and associated subjects.

The museum consists of sections for administration, archaeology, conservation, education, ethnography, and photography, under the overall

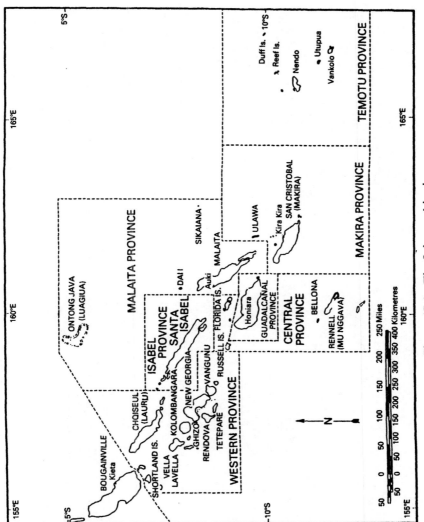

Figure 17.1 The Solomon Islands.

Figure 17.2 The main museum gallery, which houses exhibitions and an artefact shop.

Figure 17.3 The technical wing, where all administration and conservation activities are carried out and where the national ethnographic collection is kept.

co-ordination and supervision of the Director, who also heads the Administration Section. The Archaeology Section consists of two full-time staff members responsible for carrying out archaeological surveys throughout the islands and for collecting oral traditions associated with archaeological sites. The Conservation Section has one full-time employee assisted by a volunteer from Japan. The Education Section has one full-time qualified teacher. One education project entails circulating to all secondary schools a Mobile Centre Learning Kit consisting of folding panels, historic photographs, publications, artefacts, a teaching guide, and pre-recorded cassettes of stories, music, dances, and songs. The one staff member in the Ethnography Section collects, documents, and records items in the collection. There is a Photographic Section head, a full-time attendant, and two gardeners who maintain the museum's grounds.

The museum's policy is to encourage the use of new media; its own audiovisual centre is in many ways better suited to demonstration and analysis than are traditional methods. Staff research programmes help to update and enrich exhibitions and amplify public knowledge and appreciation of them. The National Museum is the main centre for the dissemination of technical and scientific advice to people from other islands aiming to set up and manage new cultural centres. In 1984 a student from another province was seconded for training in museology, with the intention of his returning to establish a cultural centre in his village.

The architecture and natural setting of the museum are modern, although the thatched roofs of the main gallery (Fig. 17.2) and the Canoe House (Fig. 17.4) retain a traditional air. The scattered layout of the buildings – the open-air theatre (Fig. 17.5) and the Canoe House are outside the main site, which contains the technical block and main gallery – presents a minor security problem. Lack of space restricts future expansion of the whole complex. In most of the buildings, lighting and temperature are maintained naturally. Air conditioning and artificial lighting are provided only in the ethnographic and equipment stores, exhibition halls, laboratories, cataloguing room, and photographic darkroom. Overall, the museum has reached its third stage of development and expansion. The government is slowly realizing its importance, and each year makes provision for its recurrent expenditure. The sums are inadequate, but it is recognized that economic realities must constrain the budget.

Like many other fields of scientific study, archaeological research was begun in the Solomon Islands about 20 years ago by external researchers and expatriate amateurs, ranging from surveyors, administrative officers, and farmers to trained linguists, botanists, physical and social anthropologists, and archaeologists. Some of this work, undertaken before archaeological operations were systematized, suffered from insufficient funds and lack of proper training in excavation techniques. However, it was this work that opened up a new area of study for Solomon Islanders. Excavations of the Poha Cave on Guadalcanal were carried out by W. H. Davenport in 1968 and subsequently by T. Russell and J. L. O. Tedder; religious and burial

Figure 17.4 A canoe house containing different models and full-size canoes from all the provinces.

Figure 17.5 An open-air theatre used for presenting cultural shows to the general public.

sites on Vella Lavella (Western Province) were surveyed by L. Wall in 1972 and Foanaota in 1973 (Foanaota 1974a), as were old village sites on New Georgia (Western Province) by Tedder in 1973.

The first major systematic fieldwork began in 1970 under Roger Green of the Department of Anthropology, University of Auckland, and Douglas Yen, then of the Bernice P. Bishop Museum, Honolulu. Green intended 'a two to three year programme of investigations in the south-east Solomons to obtain information on the prehistory and early history of this region' (Green & Cresswell 1976, p. 6). In fact, this project continued until early 1978. Experienced researchers carried out site surveys, excavations, comparative language inquiries, and studies of pottery manufacturing techniques, agricultural activities, and horticultural systems. They also collected oral traditions, and made other archaeological and ethnological investigations. The project trained some local people in fieldwork and provided much short-term local employment.

The investigations covered the early prehistoric sequences for the Reef/Santa Cruz group (Green 1976); Anuta (Kirch & Rosendahl 1973, 1976, Kirch 1982); Tikopia and Vanikoro (Kirch & Yen 1982), and the Duff Islands (excavations by J. Davidson and F. Leach in 1977–8); and the late sequence for Nendö Island, Santa Cruz (McCoy & Cleghorn 1979, Foanaota in prep.). The main achievement of the project was to build up a cultural sequence for the south-east Solomons, beginning about 3500 years ago. Evidence from the distribution of Lapita pottery clearly linked the Santa Cruz Islands (Temotu Province) with other island groups to the east, including Vanuatu, New Caledonia, and Fiji, and to the west, for example, Watom and Ambitle Islands, Buka, and the New Britain archipelago (Green 1978, 1981, 1982). These investigations provided the archaeological data to demonstrate that Solomon Islands' history began well before the Spanish explorer, Alvaro Mendaña, 'discovered' the main chain of the Islands during his expedition in 1567–8 and attempted to set up a Spanish settlement on Nendö Island in 1595 (Allen & Green 1972, Allen 1976).

The commencement of the National Sites Survey project at the National Museum in 1976 heralded another major change in archaeological work. Funded by the Australian South Pacific Cultural Fund, a continuous site recording scheme has begun to survey all sites throughout the islands (Foanaota 1979, Miller 1979, Roe 1979, in prep. (a)). Daniel Miller, a volunteer archaeologist from the United Kingdom, undertook the implementation of the project, followed in 1978 by another volunteer graduate archaeologist, David Roe. But his appointment in 1981 as director of the Guadalcanal Cultural Centre, which preserves as well as records cultural material and archaeological sites on Guadalcanal, has restricted his activities to that island alone. Once again the archaeology of the rest of the Solomons has been neglected.

The National Sites Survey staff carry out salvage operations, establish contacts with companies involved in large-scale development, visit schools in the provinces, assist provincial assemblies to draft by-laws to protect the cultural heritage and archaeological sites, and inform the public about the importance of archaeology. The educational programmes include radio talks, slide shows, exhibitions in the National Museum, talks to schools, and involving the public, in particular senior school students, in the museum's oral tradition project (Roe in prep. (b)).

In trying to operate large-scale national projects of this nature, developing countries such as the Solomon Islands are constrained by lack of time, finance, and trained local people. The survey has had to restrict its activities to areas under immediate threat and concentrate on salvage operations, including test excavations, at the expense of problem-oriented research.

It is important to persuade large companies to appreciate the need for preserving sites as necessary ingredients for understanding local history. Some companies have supported these efforts, notifying staff of new areas they propose to develop, so that preliminary survey work can first be carried out. The Archaeological Section of the museum has benefited from such co-operation on Kolombangara and north New Georgia in the Western Province, and the Guadalcanal, Isabel, Makira/Ulawa and Western provinces have passed by-laws to protect some of their sites. A list of individuals and groups who have undertaken archaeological work at various times and places is published in the Research Register of the University of the South Pacific Centre in Honiara (Chick 1977).

Archaeology is still far from being accepted as integral to the cultural heritage of the Solomon Islands. Some Solomon Islanders appreciate it only as a useful tool in land disputes. Many areas still need to be investigated before a proper history can be written of the islands' various cultural and language groups. Green (1977) has summarized all the data from the south-east Solomons research project in a non-technical publication. But further elaboration and clarification are needed to put the information across to a wider audience in a suitable way. This is no easy task!

Archaeology and museum work in the Solomon Islands are progressing very slowly, owing to insufficient funds and lack of trained staff, including experts and managerial personnel. Only the injection of substantial resources can make possible further large-scale co-ordinated projects such as that by Green and Yen in the south-east Solomons, and only continuity in such projects can provide the wider coverage needed before an overall view of the islands' prehistory and history can be established. Undiscovered coastal sites on the larger islands could almost certainly produce much earlier dates than those so far recorded, yielding hypotheses concerning, for example, the date of initial settlement. Inland areas have likewise been insufficiently studied.

As in many other developing countries in the Pacific and elsewhere, senior civil servants do not understand or recognize the importance of archaeology or museum work for the management and protection of the people's cultural heritage. As a result we still depend on outside agencies for funding to attain these objectives. However, the museum is now firmly established and has contacts with the outside world concerning such matters as the exchange of information and the return of archaeological and ethnographic materials from institutions and individuals overseas. At the same time, we foster cultural communication within the Solomon Islands and provide information not easily available elsewhere. The museum is now being used more and more as a driving force to promote cultural understanding at both national and international levels.

References

Allen, J. 1976. New light on the Spanish settlement of the south-east Solomons: an archaeological approach. In Green & Cresswell (1976), 19–29.

Allen, J. & R. C. Green 1972. Mendaña 1595 and the fate of the lost Almiranta: an archaeological investigation. *Journal of Pacific History* **7**, 73–91.

Chick, J. 1977. *Solomon Islands Research Register* **6**, 18–49. University of the South Pacific, Solomon Islands Centre, Honiara, Solomon Islands.

Foanaota, L. 1974a. Burial sites on Vella Lavella Island. *Journal of the Solomon Islands Museum Association* **2**, 22–33.

Foanaota, L. 1974b. Solomon Islands Museum 1971–1973. *South Pacific Bulletin* **24**(3), 24–7.

Foanaota, L. 1979. The Solomon Islands national site recording system. In *Archaeological resource management in Australia and Oceania*, J. R. McKinlay & K. L. Jones (eds), 29–33. Wellington, NZ: Historic Places Trust.

Foanaota, L. 1980. Solomon Islands. In *Preserving indigenous cultures: a new role for museums*, R. Edwards & J. Stewart (eds), 144–53. Canberra: Government Printer.

Foanaota, L. in prep. Prehistoric sequence for Nendö Island, Santa Cruz, south-east Solomon Islands.

Green, R. C. 1976. Lapita sites in the Santa Cruz group. In Green & Cresswell 1976, 245–65.

Green, R. C. 1977. *A first culture history of the Solomon Islands*. Auckland: University of Auckland Bindery.

Green, R. C. 1978. *New sites with Lapita pottery and their implications for an understanding of the settlement of the western Pacific*. Working paper no. 51.' Department of Anthropology, University of Auckland.

Green, R. C. 1981. Location of the Proto-Polynesian homeland: a continuing problem. In *Studies in Pacific languages and cultures*, J. Hollyman & A. K. Pawley (eds), 133–58. Auckland: Linguistic Society of New Zealand.

Green, R. C. 1982. Models for the Lapita cultural complex: an evaluation of some current proposals. *New Zealand Journal of Archaeology* **4**, 7–19.

Green, R. C. & M. M. Cresswell (eds) 1976. Southeast Solomon Islands cultural history: a preliminary survey. *Royal Society of New Zealand Bulletin* **11**.

Kirch, P. V. 1982. A revision of the Anuta sequence. Ms. on file, Department of Anthropology, Bernice P. Bishop Museum, Honolulu.

Kirch, P. V. & P. H. Rosendahl 1973. Archaeological investigation of Anuta. In *Anuta: a Polynesian outlier in the Solomon Islands*, D. E. Yen & J. Gordon (eds). *Pacific Anthropological Records* **21**, 25–108. Honolulu: Bernice P. Bishop Museum.

Kirch, P. V. & P. H. Rosendahl 1976. Early Anutan settlement and the position of Anuta in the prehistory of the southwest Pacific. In Green & Cresswell 1976, 225–44.

Kirch, P. V. & D. E. Yen 1982. *Tikopia: the prehistory and ecology of a Polynesian outlier*. Bernice P. Bishop Museum Bulletin 238. Honolulu: Bishop Museum Press.

McCoy, P. C. & P. L. Cleghorn 1979. Summary report of recent archaeological investigations on Santa Cruz (Nendö). Ms. on file, Department of Anthropology, Bernice P. Bishop Museum, Honolulu.

Miller, D. 1979. *National sites survey summary report*. Honiara: Solomon Islands National Museum. [The second printing carries the correct title: *Report of the national sites survey 1976–1978*.]

Roe, D. 1979. Wanem nao 'archaeology'? *Waswe* **11**, 6; **12**, 8; **13**, 6; **14**, 6.

Roe, D. in prep. (a). Report of the national sites survey 1978–1980.

Roe, D. in prep. (b). Teaching archaeology in Solomon Islands. *Bulletin of Archaeology for Schools*.

18 *Fifty years of conservation experience on Easter Island (Rapa Nui), Chile*

SERGIO RAPU

In Easter Island the past is the present, it is impossible to escape from it; the inhabitants of to-day are less real than the men who have gone; the shadows of the departed builders still possess the land. Voluntarily or involuntarily the sojourner must hold commune with those old workers; for the whole air vibrates with a vast purpose and energy which has been and is no more. (Routledge 1919, p. 165)

Katherine Routledge visited Easter Island (Rapa Nui, Fig. 18.1) in 1914. For seven months she carried out the first systematic and professional archaeological research on the island. At that time more than 85 per cent of the island comprised a foreign-owned ranch. More than 10 000 head of livestock – sheep, cattle, and horses – grazed freely. Amid the numerous archaeological sites, the foreign company built stone fences and reservoirs, often using not only natural lava but the dressed stones that had formed the foundations of prehistoric houses. Along the coast, windmills were erected above underground reservoirs, which had been lined with stone by pre-historic people several hundred years before. Eucalyptus trees were planted to supply the ranchers with posts for fencing and to protect the livestock from the hot summer sun and the strong winds and rain of winter.

Thus, amid the ruins of an industrious society now gone, the newcomers developed a profitable wool business. In the process, they drastically changed the island's environment with apparent indifference to the magnificent archaeological heritage that lay silently at their feet. The great stone works of prehistoric man were often dismantled, so that the labours of times past could be re-used for the ranchers' needs.

In a sense, the local population was indeed 'less real', as Routledge described in the passage above. At the time of her visit the remnants of that prehistoric population consisted of no more than 300 people. They had left their original 'kainga' land, held by different lineages, and were settled in a small village, Hanga Roa, on the west coast. Periodically, the men were employed as company labourers. Many years before, their native religion

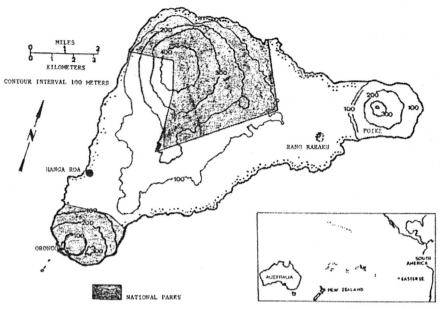

Figure 18.1   Easter Island, showing archaeological sites and National Park areas.
(After Porteous 1981, Figs pp. 110, 197.)

had died with the last native priests, and subsequent generations had
become Christians (McCall 1976). In great part, the past for them was
gone, and the shadow of their ancestors' way of life endured primarily in
the form of a few oral traditions and the ever-present monuments of
stone.

Routledge's perception of Easter Island's past was genuine. Even today,
the past is the present. Fifty years ago Easter Island was declared a
national park and a historical monument. Indeed, a trip around the island
is like visiting a museum. In every open-air showcase, one can appreciate
the magnificent works of the ingenious artists who left for humanity a
valuable testimony of man's ability to survive on a remote island in the
Pacific.

The modest goal of this chapter is to present a historical account of the
steps taken during the past 50 years to conserve Easter Island's archaeological
heritage. These steps will be described in terms of the relationship between
the most important decisions made about the island's development and the
attitudes and actions of the government agencies that are responsible for the
conservation of monuments.

The archaeological heritage

The archaeological survey begun by McCoy (1976) and continued by Cristino Ferrando *et al.* (1981) represents the most detailed inventory of sites and monuments available. More than 70 per cent of the total surface has been mapped, and every archaeological site and feature has been carefully documented. At least 6927 sites and 11 913 features are recorded, but more remain to be added to the inventory. McCoy's studies of prehistoric settlement patterns indicate that occupation was concentrated along the coast, probably because fresh water, a scarce resource, could be obtained from underground streams that were intercepted at the coastline. Coastal settlement permitted access to food resources from both sea and land. Ceremonial structures also bordered the coast, while some domestic structures and agricultural activities were located inland.

The ceremonial structures, known as *ahu*, are the most outstanding archaeological sites on the island. More than 350 of them are located along the coast or a short distance inland. Archaeologists have classified these sites into several basic types according to their shape, architectural features, and the presence or absence of the large prominent statues, which have brought the island its fame.

The most common type of *ahu* consists of a long rectangular platform made of carefully worked basalt stones, which sits on an earthen ramp above the level of the surrounding landscape. The large statues, *moai*, stood on top of these platforms facing inland. The *ahu* were owned by different lineages and were considered to be the focal points of various religious ceremonies. According to oral traditions, the *moai* represent the 'living faces' of the ancestors (Métraux 1940, Englert 1948). Many of the *ahu* exhibit successive reconstructions of their walls and platforms. Today these ceremonial sites are in a state of ruin. The statues were overturned during conflicts in late prehistoric times. Erosion, tidal waves, and vandalism in the early 1900s have added to the damage.

Further inland, more than 1881 house foundations of worked basalt were recorded during the archaeological survey (Cristino Ferrando *et al.* 1981). These stones were generally laid in an oval shape similar in form to a long narrow boat. Holes at regular intervals on the upper surface of these stones supported the poles which formed the frame of a house. These houses, known as *hare paenga*, are only one of several house types. Less impressive are the circular, semicircular, and rectangular structures, known as *hare oka*, whose foundations are marked by a single or double course of unworked stone.

Other domestic structures, such as chicken houses, called *hare moa*, are commonly found associated with prehistoric houses. They have thick walls of unworked stone. Inside, small, narrow chambers served as places to keep chickens. These structures were real fortresses built to protect domestic animals from thieves. More than 200 *hare moa* have been recorded in the area surveyed.

The archaeological inventory also includes more than 700 other domestic and economic structures. Some are circular stone walls, frequently clustered near prehistoric villages. Known as *manavai*, they were probably used to protect crops that could not otherwise survive the destructive effects of the wind. In addition, hundreds of freshwater reservoirs, ancient pathways, and remnants of prehistoric agricultural activities were recorded. Stone towers and habitation caves with added masonry are also found around the island.

Rock art is one of the most impressive aspects of the rich archaeological heritage. The prehistoric artists used various techniques and designs. Perhaps the most remarkable are the birdman motifs carved in bas-relief at the ceremonial village of Orongo. Many types of fish and other sea fauna, birds, and mythological characters are depicted on vertical and horizontal rock panels, on walls of caves, and on prominent stones. Petroglyphs are engraved on the walls of *ahu*, on the large stone statues, and on their top-knots; indeed they are everywhere, even on small, seemingly insignificant stones.

These same artists also made paintings on the walls of caves and on slabs forming inside walls and ceilings of the houses at Orongo. Some of the larger painted slabs from this site were removed during restoration of the village in 1984 for preservation at the local museum. Certainly these paintings comprise one of the best collections of rock art in eastern Polynesia.

There are several prehistoric quarries for different kinds of stone. The most magnificent of these is the statue quarry at Rano Raraku, one of many small volcanic cones. Within its crater lies a small freshwater lagoon covered with totora reeds. Both the inside and outside slopes of the south-east side formed the only quarry for the monolithic statues of volcanic tuff. The statues (*moai*) were carved *in situ* in various styles and sizes. Many are unfinished and reveal different stages of production. Mounds of debris at the base of the exterior slope attest to the tremendous amount of work accomplished at the site by the carvers. At least 396 statues remain around the quarry area.

Steps towards conservation

One of the first important steps taken towards conservation by the Chilean government was to register the whole island as state property in 1933. This settled a long legal dispute between the government and the private company that claimed ownership of most of the land, and allowed the government to implement rules to protect the interests of the small native population. Regulations were also established to safeguard the island's antiquities and to prohibit the export of the monuments, unless permission was granted by a decree from the President. The law states:

Article 72: The Authority will maintain the strict preservation and care of the historical monuments of the Island, adopting all the measures which it deems proper towards this objective.

Article 73: The Authority will not allow for any reason the export from the Island of monuments unless it has been so authorized by decree by the President of the Republic and this decree has been officially communicated to it by the direction of the Coastal Authority and the Mercantile Marine Authority.

Article 74: The Authority must keep a special book with an inventory of the monuments in which it will indicate their characteristics, sizes, state of preservation and location and assigning them a reference number. (translated from Vergara 1939, p. 239)

In 1935 the government took more direct action towards heritage protection. A law, known as Decreto No. 103 of the Ministry of Lands, declared the whole island to be a national park, in order to protect the native flora. At the same time the Ministry of Education declared Easter Island a historical monument, to safeguard the archaeological heritage under control of the National Council for Monuments. The two laws gave public recognition to the need to protect the endemic flora, the natural environment, and the archaeological monuments. But these measures were only partly successful. As Porteous points out, 'the continued use of the land as a sheep-ranch, however, effectively prevented the proper preservation of both trees and monuments' (1981, p. 196). Today the role of the national park has greatly expanded, protecting historical monuments along with the natural environment.

The growing interest in Rapa Nui culture among scholars, notably at the University of Chile, led to the appointment of a Capuchin pastor and scholar, Father Sebastian Englert, in 1935. From the island he broadcast lectures on Rapa Nui culture to mainland Chile. He lectured in the United States to help raise funds to conserve and investigate the monuments (Englert 1970), and made an inventory of the statues and the *ahu*. His interest also encompassed the islanders' language and oral traditions. During his 34 years of residence he served as a continual guardian of antiquity, performing his duties in the spirit of the laws of the 1930s concerning historical monuments and national parks. He strongly influenced the local population and government agencies to be sympathetic towards the conservation of the island's heritage.

Throughout Englert's time, the island remained isolated from the outside world, with only an annual visit by a cargo ship bringing supplies. This infrequent transport limited the visits of potential researchers to the island. Only a Franco–Belgian expedition in 1935 and a Norwegian expedition in 1955, which had private transport arrangements, were able to carry out long-term scientific research (see Heyerdahl & Ferdon 1961).

This isolation also rendered impossible the development of tourism. Thus livestock remained the only viable economic enterprise. Between 1935 and 1965 livestock increased from 10 000 to more than 50 000, with sheep predominating. However, the continual efforts of the naval authorities administering the island, the work of Father Englert, and the interest of academics at the University of Chile at Santiago strongly supported the view of planners and administrators that the island needed to be developed as a tourist attraction.

A 1966 law (No. 16.441) improved the administrative status of the island and provided the necessary budget for the construction of an airport, a new school, and facilities for several public services. For the islanders, this law became a catalyst for stronger and closer ties with the mainland. Further steps were taken to conserve monuments; for although laws safeguarding the archaeological heritage had been passed in the 1930s, it was only in 1966 that specific proposals were formulated to develop the whole island as an open-air museum. With assistance from Unesco and the International Fund for Monuments (now the World Monuments Fund), the government 'hoped to conserve the antiquities of the island in the face of modern developments' (Peterson 1966, p. 2).

A report by Charles Peterson under the aegis of Unesco made valuable recommendations for the general development of the island. Though Peterson's main concern was the conservation of antiquities, he sought to harmonize diverse interests to make Rapa Nui 'a safe, accessible, convenient, educational and enjoyable place . . . The serious student of archaeological remains, the Pacific vacationer, the native population, and its government all need to be accommodated' (ibid., p. 3). The government has diligently followed these recommendations. Lands considered rich in archaeological remains or possessing topographical features of scenic or scientific interest are designated part of the national park.

Also under Unesco's aegis, two prominent archaeologists studied 'the nature and significance of the archaeological monuments of the island and proposed means and methods for their conservation and restoration in order to record permanently as an island-wide museum an important segment of Polynesian prehistory' (Mulloy & Figueroa 1966, p. 1). In their view, archaeological monuments were the island's most important economic resource and should be developed as a profitable tourist industry. Rapa Nui could be made an

> island-wide museum . . . by relatively modest long term projects of archaeological conservation and restoration carefully organized to coordinate . . . with agricultural and other kinds of land use and with other projects for development of other aspects of the resources of the island . . . In addition to the obvious scientific value of such an island-wide museum, it would quickly become world famous and, with transportation facilities available, would attract tourists in such numbers that land so used would quickly come to have much greater value than might be developed by any other means of exploitation. (ibid., p. 27)

These recommendations coincided with Peterson's suggestions for developing the island into a national park or island-wide museum for tourism, in harmony with the various interests of the population. The government was urged to complete a survey of the island, to encourage salvage archaeology, to continue specific restoration projects, and to protect scenic features and archaeological sites by regulating land use. A programme of archaeological restoration was then prepared by another specialist (Angelini 1968).

These authoritative recommendations ended the emphasis on using the island primarily as a sheep ranch. The ranch, which had covered 14 000 hectares, was reduced to 5500 hectares. Thousands of sheep were replaced by 1500 head of cattle – a sufficient number for local consumption – which reduced the erosion of the monuments and soil. National park land was increased from less than 3000 hectares to 6600 hectares.

Up to this time the government's predominant policy had been to preserve the island's rolling grasslands, eminently suitable for grazing. However, it was now proposed to reafforest grasslands with endemic species. This would help to prevent further soil erosion and provide timber for local use, e.g. for wood carving, building, etc.

Representatives of the National Council for Monuments, staff at the national park headquarters, and archaeologists now permanently resident ensure that direct legal action can be taken locally in response to any threat to antiquities. The ongoing training of park rangers enables the national park continually to expand its control of the archaeological heritage, ensuring the maintenance of official interest in conserving the archaeological patrimony.

The list of projects undertaken since 1966 (see Appendix) clearly demonstrates the government's intense concern to increase research on, and to conserve, the island's archaeological heritage, showing that the recommendations of Peterson, Mulloy & Figueroa, and Angelini have been put into practice. Sponsored by the United Nations Development Programme, the World Monuments Fund (New York), and the government, and advised by specialists in archaeology and conservation from ICCROM (see Stanley Price 1984, Ch. 22, this volume), conservation programmes are using the most up to date techniques and concepts.

Two research institutions have been established on the island, the museum and the University of Chile Study Centre. Both are directed by university-trained archaeologists, ensuring that archaeological research can be developed on a permanent basis. A new and welcome trend is the training of local archaeologists in university departments specializing in Polynesian archaeology in places such as Hawaii, New Zealand, and perhaps in the future Australia.

Conclusion

During the last 50 years, the socioeconomic emphasis on Easter Island has shifted from the extensive exploitation of the land for grazing sheep to the protection of archaeologically important national park lands. These changes have been brought about by legislation and development plans incorporating the results of extensive studies in archaeology, ethnology, social anthropology, and other disciplines, following the implementation of recommendations by specialists.

The value of archaeological resources is now seen to be more than purely scientific. In addition to being a priceless treasure for humanity, and a unique laboratory for scientists, archaeological heritage is a practicable and potentially profitable economic resource for the small local population. Archaeology is a highly respected profession on Easter Island, and archaeologists actively contribute to the planning of the island's development. Thus the future of archaeology on Easter Island seems to be more hopeful than ever before.

References

Angelini, S. 1968. *Rapa Nui – Isla de Pasqua. Programma di restauro*. Report to The Easter Island Committee, International Fund for Monuments.

Cristino Ferrando, C., P. Vargas Casanova & R. Izaurieta San Juan 1981. *Atlas arqueologico de Isla de Pascua*. Santiago: Corporacion Toesca.

Englert, S. 1948. *La tierra de Hotu Matu'a. Historia, etnologia y lengua de isla de Pascua*. Santiago: Imprenta y Editorial 'San Francisco', Padre Las Casas.

Englert, S. 1970. *Island at the center of the world: new light on Easter Island* (translated and edited by William Mulloy). New York: Charles Scribner's Sons.

Heyerdahl, T. & E. N. Ferdon (eds) 1961. Reports of the Norwegian Archaeological Expedition to Easter Island and the East Pacific. Vol. 1. Archaeology of Easter Island. *The School of American Research and the Museum of New Mexico*, no. 24, pt 1.

McCall, G. 1976. Reaction to disaster: continuity and change in Rapanui social organisation. Unpublished Ph.D. dissertation, Australian National University, Canberra.

McCoy, C. 1976. *Easter Island settlement patterns in the late prehistoric and protohistoric periods*. New York: Easter Island Committee, International Fund for Monuments, Bulletin 5.

Métraux, A. 1940. *Ethnology of Easter Island*. Bernice P. Bishop Museum Bulletin no. 160. Honolulu.

Mulloy, W. & G. Figueroa 1966. *The archaeological heritage of Rapa Nui (Easter Island)*. Paris: Unesco.

Peterson, C. E. 1966. *Contributions towards a master plan for the proposed Rapa Nui national archaeological monument on Rapa Nui, Isla de Pascua or Easter Island, Chile*. Paris: Unesco.

Porteous, J. D. 1981. *The modernization of Easter Island*. Western Geographical Series, 19. Department of Geography, University of Victoria, Victoria, British Columbia.

Routledge, Mrs Scoresby [Katherine] 1919. *The mystery of Easter Island: the story of an expedition*. London: Sifton, Praed.

Stanley Price, N. P. 1984. *Conservation of the archaeological heritage of Easter Island (Rapa Nui)*. A report prepared for the Centro Nacional de Restauración, Santiago.

Stanley Price, N. P. 1990. Conservation and information in the display of prehistoric sites. In *The politics of the past*, P. Gathercole & D. Lowenthal (eds), Ch. 22. London: Unwin Hyman.

Vergara, M. de la P., V. M. 1939. *La Isla de Pascua: dominación y dominio*. (Memorio de Prueba, Universidad de Chile.) Santiago: Instituto Geográfico Militar.

Appendix: Archaeological conservation projects on Easter Island, Chile

Date	Project description	Participants
1966–8	master plan for development programme for restoration	Unesco Chilean government
1968	archaeological site survey	University of Wyoming Chilean government
1968	investigation and restoration of Tahai complex	University of Wyoming Chilean government
1969	official establishment of Easter Island museum	Chilean government
1969	training of first native islander as museologist	Chilean government
1970	investigation and restoration of Tahai complex, phase II	Chilean government
1972	consultations on stone consolidation	Unesco
1972	investigation and restoration of Ahu Huri a Urenga and Ahu at Hanga Kio'e	Unesco Chilean government University of Wyoming World Monuments Fund
1973	training of first native islander as archaeologist	Chilean government
1974	investigation and restoration of ceremonial village of Orongo	University of Wyoming Chilean government
1974	management plan for the Rapa Nui National Park and appointment of park rangers to sites	Chilean government
1975	initial construction of Easter Island museum	Chilean government
1976	investigation and restoration of Orongo and Ahu 'O Kava	
1976	training of two archaeologists in the Pacific culture area	University of Wyoming Chilean government
1977–86	continuation of archaeological survey	Chilean government
1978	investigation and restoration of Ahu NauNau at Anakena	Chilean government Fundacion del Pacifico World Monuments Fund
1979	establishment of the University of Chile Study Centre	University of Chile
1979	investigation and restoration of Ahu Tautira at Hanga Roa	Chilean government

Appendix continued

Date	Project description	Participants
1979	construction of cultural centre in modern village of Hanga Roa	Chilean government
1979	United Nations Development Programme CHI.79/013	Unesco Chilean government
1981	salvage of osteological materials from open tombs at archaeological sites	Chilean government University of Wyoming University of Chile
1981–6	investigation and inventory of petroglyphs	University of California, LA University of Chile
1982	plan for construction of a new and larger museum	Chilean government
1982	study of consolidation of statues	Chilean government
1982	investigation and salvage archaeology in Vai 'A Tare	Chilean government
1983	partial stabilization of Orongo restoration	Chilean government World Monuments Fund
1985–6	construction of new exhibition hall, Easter Island Museum	Chilean government
1985–6	experimentation on statue consolidation	Chilean government UN Development Programme
1985–6	courses on conservation directed to public employees	Unesco World Monuments Fund Chilean government
1985–6	consolidation of rock paintings	Chilean government UN Development Programme

ARCHAEOLOGY AND THE PEOPLE

Introduction

Chapter 20 contains a sentence by Addyman which should make every museum curator and archaeologist ponder: 'Having established the low knowledge threshold of most potential visitors to the Jorvik Viking Centre and the fallacies needing correction, [the Trust] decided to begin the visitors' tour with an orientation area to implant the requisite knowledge and to remove misinformation.' As Addyman shows, the Centre's reconstruction of Anglo-Scandinavian York is a popular success, visited in 1985 by nearly 900 000 people. Did they benefit from the removal of misinformation and its replacement by correct knowledge? Were they reoriented in their understanding of the Vikings, despite the fact that most 'have difficulty in chronologically placing anything much older than their own grandmothers'? These questions imply no criticism of Addyman. He is no doubt correct in claiming that 'the Jorvik Viking Centre is probably the most systematic and successful purveyor of archaeological information in Britain'. His Trust is doing a superb job of selling a slice of archaeologically wrought history. Entrance fees help to finance further excavations, which, together with the Centre itself, make York perhaps the most historically self-conscious city in England.

Economic influences, often with political overtones, inevitably pervade the museum profession. Market forces increasingly affect the economics of museum administration: the size and effectiveness of staff, storage facilities, and displays. Hitherto curatorial competence was assessed largely in terms of scholarly standards. Nowadays success is the watchword, in considerable part measured by the ability to sell heritage to the consumer. The honest brashness of the Jorvik Centre may engender criticism, but at least it tackles the problem of how to educate its visitors. Many museums just open their doors, start the show, and hope that the public will benefit. They assume that people have a thirst for knowledge about the natural, environmental, and cultural past, as attendance figures bear out. But in today's world of mass communications, as this book shows, those responsible for portraying the past need to be more sensitive to the political and social influences that impinge on their work.

Along with Addyman's discussion of Viking York, three chapters deal with the political and social contexts of historical reconstructions. In Chapter 19, Mikołajczyk discusses the changing emphases of policy and practice in the Archaeological and Ethnographical Museum in Łódź, Poland. He shows how the museum reflected the growth of an independent nation for two decades after 1918. In 1939 the situation changed suddenly. The turmoil of the Second World War, the subsequent establishment of a Stalinist government, and its ideological consequences brought politics directly into the museum. Mikołajczyk's discussion of 'didacticism' in museum education reveals some of the difficulties that have faced the Polish intelligentsia since 1945 in trying to reconcile public historical understanding with the forms of education demanded by the state.

In Chapter 21 Kuttruff discusses the history and excavation of Fort Loudoun, Tennessee, before it was inundated by dam construction. This 18th-century British fortification was then re-created on an adjacent site as an educational exhibit, thus at least minimally fulfilling the requirement under Federal law to protect the site and promote knowledge about it. Kuttruff takes the reader through the process of excavation, reconstruction, and the provision of interpretive information, and considers their political salience for the governmental, educational, and other agencies that favoured or opposed this operation.

Reconstruction on a broader scale is the theme of Stanley Price's chapter (Ch.22). Focusing on the discrepancy between what archaeologists do and what the public believes they do, he reviews some of the problems connected with preservation. To what extent should sites be restored, by what criteria, and in whose interests? Does the minimum of interventionist reconstruction sought by the archaeologist leave the site intelligible to the public? Should the present-day interests of either side be allowed to pre-empt the needs of future publics? These questions, as Stanley Price shows, are seldom as straightforward as they seem.

Some of the consequences of non-conservation are touched on by Nicklin (Ch. 23). He examines the changing perceptions of both experts and the Oron people of south-east Nigeria towards the latter's *Ekpu* figures. These have been at various times venerated ancestor carvings, objects of art and ethnography, trophies during the 1967–70 civil war, illegal exports prized by collectors, and symbols of cultural identity. Each new role has been costly to their survival. In 1944, 1296 carvings were known to exist, of which about half were subsequently taken to the Oron Museum. Today that collection numbers only 116, though some others are held elsewhere. This surviving remnant continues to express Nigerian cultural aspirations at the national level. Nicklin's sobering account of the history of these figures illustrates what can happen to the material symbols of a culture caught up in the power struggle between contending cultural groups in which minority interests receive scant attention.

19 Didactic presentations of the past: some retrospective considerations in relation to the Archaeological and Ethnographical Museum, Łódź, Poland

ANDRZEJ MIKOŁAJCZYK

The subject of this book encourages me to discuss didactic presentation concretely rather than in ideal or theoretical terms. I have chosen to concentrate on the experiences of the Archaeological and Ethnographical Museum in Łódź, an institution with more than 50 years of experience. I have disregarded the co-existence of the archaeological and ethnographical components of the museum (which are somewhat different but complementary), and I also omit discussion of the mass media, since it has never tried to play a constructive role in promoting archaeology in Poland. Instead, I concentrate on the Łódź Museum's role in the presentation of prehistory and early history.

The museum is situated in Plac Wolności in the very centre of Łódź (Fig. 19.1), now a city of almost one million. The city received its municipal charter as early as the 15th century, but only in the second quarter of the 19th century did it grow rapidly, owing to the development of the textile industry. Cultural and scientific institutions in metropolitan centres in this part of the Russian Empire were not encouraged, and the building on Plac Wolności was not erected as a museum. The museum was founded only after Poland regained her independence in 1918 (Fig. 19.2), and some years passed before the new institution was established in the present building.

In 1939 the Nazis conquered part of Poland, and Łódź and its hinterland were incorporated into the Third Reich. The Kościuszko monument in the centre of Plac Wolności was demolished, as were many others. The city itself was renamed Litzmannstadt. One might say that all these events took place outside the museum (Fig. 19.3). What happened inside the museum – then called the Stadtisches Museum für Vorgeschichte – can be illustrated by the exhibitions and lectures (Fig. 19.4) supporting Nazi propaganda about

Figure 19.1 The present view of the Plac Wolności in the central part of Łódź, with the Kościuszko monument in the middle and the Archaeological and Ethnographical Museum on the right.

Figure 19.2 After Poland regained independence in 1918, the building was taken over by the city council (note *Magistrat* inscribed below the roof which is crowned by the Polish flag).

Figure 19.3 The museum building witnessed Nazi ceremonies in occupied Łódź.

Figure 19.4 Notice of a public lecture on 'the prehistory of our Fatherland', demonstrating the strong impact of Nazi politics on archaeology in Łódź during the Second World War.

Figure 19.5   Ceramic medallion issued by the Nazi authorities showing urn with swastika.

the occupied territories. These are excellent examples of the way in which the museum was used for political purposes, and of the role played by inherently political institutions in interpreting the archaeological record for Nazi purposes during those dark years.

The Nazi attitude towards archaeological finds and exhibits in 'Łódź-Litzmannstadt' now seems barely credible. The Nazis sought purely political propaganda to use in the country they had conquered. In such an atmosphere the nearby Ost-Raum Museum became a target for the new managers. A noteworthy example is the earthenware urn excavated just before the Second World War at the cremation cemetery of the 2nd and 3rd centuries AD at Biala, near Łódź. The vessel was distinguished by the interesting decoration engraved on its belly, but only one ornament attracted the Nazis, a swastika, a symbol they saw as evidence of the proto-Germanic character of central Poland. The urn became the main exhibit in the museum, and soon, when the name of the city was changed to Litzmannstadt, a representation of the vessel with its swastika became the city's new coat of arms (Fig. 19.5).

Other holdings in the museum that did not serve these new ideas were used in quite different ways. Some, such as ethnographic items from Africa and South America, were sold to German museums, while artefacts of Slavic origin were either dispersed or destroyed. Fortunately, this gross manipulation of archaeology ended in January 1945, when Soviet troops liberated the city.

The first archaeological exhibition in liberated Poland opened in early May 1945 at the Municipal Prehistoric Museum in Łódź. It was augmented several times, following large archaeological projects undertaken in Łódź as well as in other parts of the country. Under the direction of Professor Dr K. Jacdzewski, who revitalized the museum and was first incumbent of the Chair of Archaeology at the newly established Łódź University, a new archaeological community came into being. The role of the museum was extended to serve academic needs.

From the late 1940s Polish archaeology underwent a rapid and beneficial development. Investigations advanced knowledge concerning early medieval history and culture, throwing new light on the beginnings of the Polish state. The results became merged in the Millennium celebrations in the 1960s. A millennial tradition highlighting the beginnings of the Polish state was felt to be necessary for a people whose country had been ruined by the Second World War. Since Poland had regained some of its western and northern regions in 1945, archaeologists were able to include the early medieval centres in Silesia and Pomerania in their researches.

Archaeology has played an important role in national politics. The millennial celebrations led to some expansion in archaeological institutions, and excavations became routine in both national and regional projects. In Polish museums archaeological departments were established or enlarged. The Łódź Archaeological and Ethnographical Museum was considerably extended in 1962.

Another impact of both politics and ideology on archaeology was reflected in the mid-1950s in a travelling display, 'From a Hoe to a Tractor'. This presented popularized simplifications of the evolutionary development of material culture, an interpretation of the past (and present) fashionable in what later came to be called the years of mistakes and deformities. It was soon abandoned, however, in favour of permanent exhibitions that interpreted the past more didactically. One such exhibition, which opened in 1956, displayed prehistory from the Palaeolithic to the early Middle Ages. But it was the subsequent one, 'The Łęczyca and Sieradz Lands in a Thousand Years of the Polish State', held between 1963 and 1966, that was the Łódź Museum's major contribution to the millennial celebrations.

The main emphasis of these didactic presentations was to *teach* archaeology. A belief in the efficacy of didactics outside the routine school programmes, or in supporting certain elements in these programmes, can be traced back to the positivism of late 19th- and early 20th-century Poland, essentially a time of anti-romanticism. Then the emphasis was on scientific facts, on demonstrating social contexts, and on the significance of science in promoting the cultural and economic development of the country.

The growing didacticism associated with the educational activities of museums was typical of postwar Poland. After the war the concept of a museum changed; besides gathering and studying objects, museums came

Figure 19.6   Archaeology lessons for blind children in the museum.

to be seen as crucial elements in modern education. Didacticism in museum presentations was also promoted by two other factors. First, recent archaeological finds displayed in museums are new sources of evidence about the past with which one should be familiar. Second, most museum visitors were, and still are, young people. In the Łódź Museum young people comprised about 90 per cent of the prewar public; in more recent years they have constituted more than two-thirds of the visitors and make up as much as 90 per cent of those taking part in group excursions.

The Łódź Museum has worked constantly with schoolchildren, teachers, and the school authorities. As early as 1947, teachers were given a basic course in prehistory. New elements introduced into museum practice included such diverse reforms as providing information on the preservation of finds and their role in didactic teaching, and making the museum more accessible to schoolchildren, including the handicapped (Fig. 19.6). Such activities were most intensively promoted during the millennial celebrations of the 1960s.

The most important form of popularization the museum has undertaken has been collaboration with schools and schoolchildren. One reason for this has been the inadequacy of teaching programmes in Polish schools, where little respect was paid to prehistory or to ancient and early medieval history. In 1965 a conference at the Łódź Museum on 'How to Make the Most of Archaeological Achievements in Learning History' was organized for archaeologists and teachers. Three years later another conference on 'Significance of Archaeology for Social and Political Education' was held, summing up the experiences of the millennial celebrations. In 1979 a further conference was devoted to 'The Museum's Role in Education: History Collections as Teaching Aids' (Mikołajczyk 1984), exemplifying the didactic emphasis of the museum's public activities.

The 1965 conference influenced the museum's next permanent archaeological display, open from 1968 to 1976. The most recent permanent exhibition, 'From the Prehistory of Central Poland', held from 1978 to 1986, was arranged to correspond to the history syllabus in the fifth and sixth classes of primary school. Prehistory and early history were presented in a condensed form in four parts, in line with the school programme: (a) the life of early man; (b) the Pre-Slavs; (c) the Slavs; (d) the beginnings of the Polish state.

Some 5000 lessons for schoolchildren, additional sets of archaeological objects prepared for special purposes, and continuous film shows about the exhibitions and excavations, in collaboration with the Houses of Youth Culture, comprised the museum's part in the project. In addition, national and regional essay competitions took place in the museum. Subjects were 'The Millennium of the Polish state'; 'My adventures in museums'; 'The most interesting exhibit'; 'My region'; 'What do you know about the Archaeological and Ethnographical Museum in Łódź and the local museums of the Łódź region?'; and 'What do you know about archaeology?'

In 1970 an organization called the Inter-School Circle of the Lovers of Archaeology was founded in response to the desire of secondary-school children to further their archaeological interests. Throughout the school year, these young people meet monthly in the museum, where they have direct contact with finds and discussions with archaeologists from various institutions. The holidays provide opportunities to participate in fruitful museum-run excavations.

The museum has recently begun collaborative work with the Sieradz Banner of the Union of Polish Scouting (ZHP). The union organizes annual holiday camps in an attractive place on the Warta River. Excavations are carried out by the museum at the nearby Lusatian culture cemetery, dating from the late Bronze Age. The Scouts are as much attracted by the digging as by the material found during fieldwork, which they also help to process.

The museum's archaeological tours, dating from the early 1960s, are arranged annually for secondary-school students from Łódź and neighbouring towns, with financial support from local school authorities. The two-week tours in the summer holidays are popular with the young participants, who excavate known sites, undertake documentation and elementary inventory work, visit local monuments and museums, and search for undiscovered sites, especially in areas threatened by industrial development. The sites in question range from megalithic graves of the middle Neolithic period to early medieval cemeteries, late medieval castles, and early manors.

More than 40 archaeological tours have provided enjoyable holidays for about 1100 secondary-school children. The educative value of these activities includes learning to co-operate, understanding a rural environment (so

Figure 19.7   Excavations of the cremation cemetery (2nd–3rd century AD), discovered at the present Roman Catholic graveyard in Łódź, ul. Szczecinska.

different from the young people's background in an industrial city), and the creation of lasting friendships based on mutual archaeological interests.

Drawing young people's attention to local history and prehistory helps both to generate respect for tradition and to increase popular awareness to protect archaeological finds as part of cultural heritage. The participation of schoolchildren in excavations, notably of the recently discovered 2nd- and 3rd-century burials in the present Roman Catholic graveyard in the western quarter of Łódź, has proved profitable and successful (Fig. 19.7).

Protecting archaeological sites in a large industrial city is complicated. The development of industry and the expansion of residential areas and municipal installations constitute continuing threats. Unfortunately the didactic approach, predominant in presentations aimed mainly at school-children, does not suffice to impress the extent of the danger on Łódź's adult inhabitants. People today face so many difficulties that they have little scope left for attending to the preservation of monuments.

A distinction must be drawn between the museum's immediate and overall tasks, since the latter must be appreciated outside as well as inside the museum. In order to enlarge the public's understanding, which had been over-influenced by the earlier didacticism, a short colour film, *Ancient Łódź*, was recently produced to challenge people's general knowledge of the city's comparatively short history. It shows that archaeological sites have been recorded at what seem to be surprisingly ordinary places and in unusual circumstances.

Figure 19.8   'Prehistoric Fashions' displayed in front of the museum (1980).

The museum's successful experiences with young people have not been repeated with the adult public. Slogans adopted from time to time in the socialist system, such as 'Alliance of the working world with culture', introduced in 1975, have failed to bridge the gulf between the museum's attempts to stimulate the interest of people and the limited response of the majority of Łódź citizens. Co-operative efforts with some big factories and plants, including small on-site archaeological exhibitions, did not bring the anticipated results (Laszczewska 1983). Other types of archaeological presentation, such as one on 'Prehistoric Fashions', which was displayed in front of the museum (Fig. 19.8) where it attracted numerous passers-by, were introduced to give the museum's exhibits a more realistic note.

As has often been the case in the past, history as reconstructed in the museum is influenced by living history visible through the museum's windows. Heavily armoured vehicles once again crossed Plac Wolności in December 1981. Poland's recent political and economic crises also disrupt its cultural life. According to official statistics from 1975 to 1983, the number of people visiting theatres in Łódź fell to 62 per cent, opera-goers to 78 per cent, those going to classical concerts to 63 per cent, cinema attendances to 71 per cent, and museum attendance to 78 per cent (Kwiatkowski 1984). To counteract the public's declining interest, the museum needs to consider all the possible means of seeking support. Daily cares deter people from regular visits to the museum, relegating it to a position where it is in danger of becoming an aesthetic and cultural relic of the past.

References

Kwiatkowski, S. (ed.) 1984. *Rocznik statystyczny województwa łódźkiego.* (The statistical yearbook of the Łódź voivodship.) Łódź.

Laszczewska, T. 1983. Muzeum Archeologiczne i Etnograficzne w Łódźi. Dzieje-zbiory-działalnóść. (Activities related to the history collections in the Archaeological and Ethnographical Museum, Łódź.) *Prace i Materiał: Muzeum Archeologicznego i Etnograficznego w Łódźi,* serjia etnograficzna **21,** 11–39.

Mikołajczyk, A. (ed.) 1984. Rola muzeum w procesie dydaktycznowychowawczym. Zbiory muzealne pomoça w nauczaniu historii. (The museum's role in education: history collections as teaching aids.) *Biblioteka Muzeum Archeologicznego i Etnograficznego w Łódźi* **19.**

20 Reconstruction as interpretation: the example of the Jorvik Viking Centre, York

PETER V. ADDYMAN

The Museums Association of Great Britain, having devoted much discussion and careful thought to the question of what a museum really is (*Museums Bulletin* 1984), eventually promulgated this definition: an institution which collects, documents, preserves, exhibits, and interprets material evidence and associated information for the public benefit. Britain has about 1500 such institutions, which annually attract 54 million visitors. Eighteen institutions attract more than half a million people each, while even the average museum attracts 56 000. Suffice it to say that whatever their role as collectors, documenters, and preservers of the nation's past, museums have an important function and a remarkable opportunity to present the British past. Museums have the power to form attitudes and to alter interpretations about the past. The more effectively they present the past, the more fundamentally they can change people's perceptions not only about their historic environment but also about themselves and their patterns of life.

Museum directors and curators have a responsibility akin to that of newspaper editors and television and radio producers. Indeed, the moral responsibilities may be all the greater, since museums are less obviously interpreters, and their displays last longer. Moreover, the public unconsciously assumes that museums, in presenting the material evidence from the past, are offering something that is somehow objective, not subjective.

The York Archaeological Trust recently confronted these problems for the first time and in an acute form. The Trust is a charitable foundation whose main work is rescue excavation in the city of York, England. Between 1976 and 1981 it carried out extensive excavations in the deep and waterlogged deposits of the Coppergate area (Hall 1984). A sequence of deposits from the Roman period to the present was uncovered, of which by far the majority belonged to the Anglo-Scandinavian period, c. AD 850–1050. At that time York was known as Jorvik, and for some time was the capital of a Viking kingdom with contacts throughout Europe. The excavations revealed part of the commercial area of Jorvik, with street-front shops, workshops behind, and yards beyond them. A nearby riverfront with wharves and warehouses is presumed.

The wet conditions had resulted in the preservation of a far wider range of materials – especially artefacts of organic origin – than is normally found in excavations. It was therefore possible to reconstruct in great detail the layout and conditions of life in the commercial heart of the city. The wooden buildings still stood to a height of 2m, and their contents were largely *in situ*. The artefacts in and around the buildings and the contents of rubbish dumps and pits gave evidence of domestic conditions and practices, a wide range of crafts and industries, and far-flung trade contacts with other parts of Britain and much of the then-known world. Artefacts were found from as far away as northern Norway (walrus ivory), the Indian Ocean (cowrie shells), Ireland, and Samarkand. The amount of archaeological information was staggering: 35 000 archaeological contexts, recorded on 11 000 drawings, producing 20 000 small finds, 230 000 pot shards, 12 tons of soil samples, and 4.5 tons of animal bones. It seemed possible to reconstruct, in archaeological terms at least, almost the entire material environment of Anglo-Scandinavian Coppergate. This will be done in a conventional archaeological report, *The archaeology of York*.

The excavation attracted public and media attention and was visited by well over 500 000 people. Their entry fees and souvenir purchases contributed substantially to the costs of the excavation. They also expressed a desire to see the site preserved. This was eventually done by creating within the excavated area the Jorvik Viking Centre, a display below a new shopping precinct (Addyman & Gaynor 1984). The centre had to be self-supporting, its finance coming almost entirely from commercial funds and private donations.

By the time the decision was taken, the York Archaeological Trust was sufficiently aware of the public's level of understanding (or more correctly lack of it) of archaeology and the Viking age to know that special measures would be needed to convey the detailed and complicated results of the Coppergate excavation. Its task was a problem in communication.

Initially, it carried out market research to find out what typical members of the public knew about the Viking age and archaeology, what misconceptions they harboured, and what they wanted to know. This research showed misconceptions as fundamental as the belief that the Viking age came before the Roman age (because Vikings were 'more primitive'). Horned helmets were still synonymous with Vikings in the popular mind, despite half a century of archaeological publicity to the contrary. Few people could conceive of the length of time which had elapsed since the Anglo-Scandinavian period. Most had only the vaguest ideas about the actual principles and practice of archaeology, which still has a treasure-hunting image in the popular mind. When told that the excavated remains they were seeing represented houses, visitors would listen in polite but evident disbelief. It became clear that the Trust had a vast gulf of misunderstanding to bridge between some of the richest and most complicated archaeological

Figure 20.1 A modern visitor to the Jorvik Viking Centre travels down an alleyway off Coppergate, simulated on the basis of archaeological evidence to give a detailed impression of life in 10th-century Jorvik.

data ever recovered and a public which, though keenly interested, was often quite unable to perceive the message.

The Trust applied simple communications procedures to the task. Having established the low knowledge threshold of most potential visitors to the Jorvik Viking Centre and the fallacies needing correction, it decided to begin the visitors' tour with an orientation area to implant the requisite knowledge and to remove misinformation. Knowing that most people have difficulty in chronologically placing anything much older than their own grandmothers, the Trust designed a short regression sequence, taking people rapidly back through the 30 or so generations that have elapsed since Anglo-Scandinavian times. The device used was a ride in a backwards-moving car, viewing representatives of those generations who seem to be striding forward into the future.

Then there was the problem of converting millions of items of archaeological data into an interpretation that could be understood by the uninformed. The Trust decided to rely on the same modes of sensory input that ordinary people depend on when visiting any new city: their eyes, their ears, and their nostrils. In a word, the Trust rebuilt Anglo-Scandinavian Coppergate with all its sights, sounds, and smells (Fig. 20.1). For many of the details of what Coppergate looked like on an autumn day in the mid- to late-10th century, the archaeological evidence was clear enough. There was evidence for the layout of the buildings, their superstructures, the range of

Figure 20.2 Bone and antler working went on in many parts of Viking-age York. The model depicts a combmaker at work in the Jorvik Viking Centre.

artefacts and commodities in use, and the associated environmental conditions. Direct or dependable indirect evidence also existed for the character of bone and antler working (Fig. 20.2), textiles, leatherwork, dye colours and pigments used to ornament them, and to some extent clothing styles. The domestic animals and the wildlife, the level of hygiene, and by inference the smells, both pleasant and unpleasant, were reasonable deductions. So was the speech, known at least approximately from various contemporary documents and saga sources. However, considerable gaps in knowledge existed: for example, roof types and roofing materials, whether buildings were of one or more storeys.

Where knowledge was completely deficient, academic integrity was in a measure preserved by presenting a series of alternative hypotheses. Thus the roofs of the houses, the originals of which were almost certainly thatched, are variously covered with wheat straw, Norfolk reed, and natural grass. The actual material is still unknown, though further analysis of environmental evidence may point to an answer. With these provisos, however, the reconstruction of Coppergate provides a reasonable and extremely complex suggestion of what a 10th-century neighbourhood was like. The interpretation is in a form that can, in a sense, be appreciated by a five-year-old yet contains levels of information to provoke and stimulate the most expert and fertile archaeological mind. Behind the reconstruction is a database that can be re-interrogated, checked, and re-evaluated academically.

This reconstruction, though informative, exciting, and compelling, is not enough. The public needs proof that the whole thing is not a figment of the archaeologists' imaginations. Such proof is provided immediately afterwards. Here, in what to all appearances is an incomplete excavation, are found the remains of the houses seen in the reconstruction, with latrines, other pits, and decomposed rubbish in the state in which they were unearthed in 1980.

Thereafter, the visitor follows the archaeological process through the finds shed, excavation office, conservation laboratory, and environmental archaeology unit, until the artefacts themselves are encountered, indicating by their presence that domestic conditions and everyday life were as shown, and that the local and international trade did take place. The final element in the educational process is provided by a shop where an extensive range of publications and souvenirs is designed to reinforce the impact of the display.

The Jorvik Viking Centre is probably the most systematic and successful purveyor of archaeological information in Britain. Its subject matter is intentionally limited; the messages conveyed, introduced in a sequence that slowly and logically builds up comprehension, are restricted to about eight. They are mutually confirmatory. Enough evidence is adduced along the way to convince even the least suggestible of visitors of its veracity. The atmosphere is of enjoyment and pleasurable anticipation, and most of the messages are presented to the visitor seated in comfortable dynamic repose in a time car. The use of time cars ensures that everyone has the best possible view of the exhibits.

The result is that visitors leave the centre with several clear messages accurately implanted. Some are about the Viking age in Britain, here seen in quite a different light from the conventional one. Others are about the nature of archaeology. These messages are, of course, received at levels of sophistication appropriate to the individuals concerned; but at whatever level, they seem to be favourably accepted. Almost everybody (94 per cent of a sample of 3025) considers the whole experience good value for money.

To measure the effectiveness of the Jorvik Viking Centre in altering perceptions of Anglo-Scandinavian York and of the nature of archaeology is probably beyond the ingenuity of statisticians, but visitors themselves say their views have been changed. In a small survey (80 people), 81 per cent admitted that they now thought differently of the Vikings, for instance considering them more civilized; 47 per cent gained a new insight into the 'primitive nature' of 10th-century living conditions. Eighteen per cent had discovered that Vikings emanated from Scandinavia, while 11 per cent had learned the date of the Viking age for the first time. The archaeologists' dedication impressed 25 per cent, but 52 per cent doubted that the Jorvik Viking Centre had really changed their view of archaeology. Yet 41 per cent said that they were now more likely than before to visit another archaeological attraction.

In fact, the Jorvik Viking Centre is probably a more effective propaganda machine for the Vikings and for archaeology than these surveys suggest. It certainly reaches large numbers of people (889 056 in its first year, and 894 590 in its second). Moreover, it seems to reach segments of the public that do not go into conventional museums.

All this has ensured commercial success for the centre. Repayment of the development loans is in prospect, with eventual profits to be devoted to further rescue archaeology in York. That is a matter for satisfaction, especially to members of the York Archaeological Trust, who seem to have been constantly fund-raising for the whole 15 years of its existence.

The developers of the Jorvik Viking Centre believe the same subtle techniques of effective and accurate communication can be used to put across almost any archaeological message and to help to alter the nation's perception of almost any aspect of its past. This new approach to archaeological reconstruction and display has, moreover, brought moves to emulate the Jorvik Viking Centre in other places and for other subjects. At York itself the York Archaeological Trust is developing an exposition of life in the late medieval city in two restored timber-framed buildings and is contemplating the creation of an Eboracum Roman Centre below a modern development within the area of the Roman legionary fortress.

Part of the team that created the Jorvik Viking Centre has set up a company, trading under the name Heritage Projects Ltd, that builds on their experience. The company, in a joint venture with Oxford University, has opened 'The Oxford Story' to explain the origins, growth, and present-day position of the university. At Canterbury, in consultation with the Canterbury Archaeological Trust, the company has created 'The Canterbury Pilgrims' Way', an evocation of life in the late medieval city using pilgrimage and the literary tradition represented by *The Canterbury tales*. 'The Edinburgh Story' will similarly explore the nature of the city of Edinburgh in 1594, at a high point in its development.

The Jorvik Viking Centre has inspired the formulation of schemes at a number of other archaeological sites in Britain (the Chester Roman amphitheatre, Verulamium Roman town at St Albans, and the Raunds countryside archaeological park in Northamptonshire) for more imaginative archaeological reconstruction or simulation than has been normal in site interpretation facilities.

In the Jorvik Viking Centre considerable care has been taken to maintain academic integrity. The objective of the exercise has been to convey an accurate impression of what the archaeological evidence seems to say. Of course, the interpretation reflects the archaeological methods employed during the excavation and the experience, background, and predilections of the York archaeologists of the 1970s and 1980s as much as any objective truth. However, it is the result of a careful, thoughtful, balanced and, it is hoped, non-tendentious approach. Whether the developing sequels to Jorvik will be able to maintain archaeological integrity in the face of commercial pressure, the circumstances of the development, or the tenuous nature of the archaeological evidence, must be a cause for concern. Since there is little doubt that the Jorvik methods of communication can implant whatever messages are formulated, it is important that the messages should be worthy and responsible ones.

Critics of the Jorvik Viking Centre have voiced concern on a number of issues (Shadla-Hall 1984). There is the clear possibility that such displays will trivialize archaeology. The prepackaging of complicated information removes the intellectual stimulus and critical safeguards provided by conventional museum displays, which to a certain extent demand that viewers think for themselves. It is also possible that the success of such expositions, which restrict their activities to the popular aspects of the museum's role, will weaken the desire of museum sponsors to support the unglamorous, expensive, but ultimately most important parts of a museum's work – collection, documentation, and presentation. The organizers of the Jorvik Viking Centre are aware of these and other dangers but find it impossible to stand aloof. In an age of increasing skill and sophistication in communication, some new form of presentation is called for to which people can easily and readily respond.

References

Addyman, P. & A. Gaynor 1984. The Jorvik Viking Centre: an experiment in archaeological site interpretation. *International Journal of Museum Management and Curatorship* **3**, 7–18.

Hall, R. 1984. *The excavations at York: the Viking dig*. London: The Bodley Head.
Museums Bulletin 1984. What is a museum? **24**(3), 49.
Shadla-Hall, R. T. 1984. Slightly looted: a review of the Jorvik Viking Centre.
  Museums Journal **84**, 62–4.

21 *Fort Loudoun, Tennessee, a mid-18th century British fortification: a case study in research archaeology, reconstruction, and interpretive exhibits*

CARL KUTTRUFF

Fort Loudoun is the location of an 18th-century British fortification on the lower Little Tennessee River near Vonore, Tennessee. It is one of several archaeological and historic sites acquired by the State of Tennessee for the preservation and interpretation of its past. Excavations had taken place at various times since 1936, but the projected construction of the Tellico Dam, to be completed in 1979, and the flooding of the lower 30 miles of the river, meant that the site was to be submerged. It would be necessary to create a landfill over the area of the fort, on which a partial reconstruction could be built. Extensive excavations were therefore undertaken in 1975–6 in order to mitigate the impact of construction, to obtain the information required to carry out this reconstruction, and to present the history of the site to the public. The operation provided an excellent opportunity for the state's Department of Conservation to test some current theories concerning public education (see Kwas 1985).

In this chapter I argue that the methods adopted to portray the overall history of Fort Loudoun are a viable way to present archaeological information to the public. Traditionally, research results have been available primarily through specialist archaeological reports located in a few university or large public library repositories, where they are inaccessible to most people. Technical reports are even more difficult to locate. Although these publications satisfy professionals, they often fail to give the type of information that the public wants. The few popular summaries of archaeological research, either site-specific or for regions or states, help to ameliorate the situation but are insufficient. Research results are also discussed through courses in schools and universities but do not reach the public to the degree required. Television has made considerable advances in recent years in presenting archaeology on a mass scale and seems likely to have the most success in disseminating archaeological information to the widest and most varied audience.

Regional and site-specific interpretations, such as those at Fort Loudoun, allow visitors to relate archaeological information directly to the site. They also provide a resource for school groups and others studying local history and commemorate the culture history of an area by providing an awareness of the historical past.

At Fort Loudoun, the information available is particularly rich and of considerable public relevance. Before the Tennessee Valley Authority (TVA) could build the Tellico Dam, with the consequent extensive flooding, Federal law required an assessment of the cultural resources of the area. It therefore funded a 15-year project of survey and excavation by the University of Tennessee, which located hundreds of sites; large-scale excavations at many of these sites were carried out to represent the prehistoric sequence (Milligan 1969b, Salo 1969, Chapman 1973, 1977, 1981, 1982, Schroedl 1978). Extensive excavations were also undertaken at the seven historic Cherokee Indian towns located in this part of the valley, which figure prominently in the history of Fort Loudoun (Milligan 1969a, Polhemus 1970, Cornett 1976, Guthe 1977, 1979, Newman 1977, Guthe & Bistline 1978, Chapman 1979, Russ & Chapman 1984, Schroedl 1986).

The Fort Loudoun project, undertaken by the Tennessee Department of Conservation, has been fortunate in the continuity of its staff from the beginning of the mitigation planning through the excavations to the building of the exhibits and the reconstructions. I have been responsible for providing the background information for virtually the entire project over the past decade and was the principal investigator for the 1975–6 excavations, the subsequent analysis of the materials, and the preparation of the final report, now nearing completion (Kuttruff in prep.). My tasks included accumulating the relevant documentation, planning the reconstructions and the research needed to ensure their authenticity (Kuttruff 1978), designing the interpretive plan for the visitors' centre and reconstructions (Kuttruff 1981a, b), and providing documentation, artefactual materials, and sources of information for the exhibits in the interpretive centre. The exhibits section of the Department of Conservation researched, designed, constructed, and installed the exhibits, created two audio visual presentations integral to the interpretive programme, and produced the outdoor signs.

The Tennessee Valley Authority was responsible for parts of the reconstruction as part of their mitigation programme. Their work included construction of the palisade, moat and parapet, the powder magazine, and several stone features within the fort. The other structures and features within the fort have been built, or are planned to be built, under the direction of the State Parks Division Area Manager for the Fort Loudoun State Historic Area.

History

Fort Loudoun was the westernmost of a series of colonial fortifications, created by the government of South Carolina and the Board of Trade in England, which extended westwards from Charleston, South Carolina, and included Fort Ninety-Six and Fort Prince George. Work began on 5 October 1756 and was essentially completed by 30 July 1757. The British needed a fort in the area to deter French encroachment from Fort Toulouse, near present-day Montgomery, Alabama, and from Fort Massac, on the Ohio River in what is now southern Illinois. In addition, a permanent British installation in the area would solidify the sometimes tenuous alliance with the Overhill Cherokee (those Cherokee located west of the Appalachian Mountains in the Little Tennessee River Valley) and serve as a place for recruiting them to fight against the French. The Overhill Cherokee Indians also wanted the fort built, as a refuge for their women and children while the warriors were away fighting with British expeditions against the French, and as a centre for trade.

Two companies of South Carolina provincial militia and one company of British regulars, commanded by Captain Raymond Demere, were sent to build the fort. John William Gerard DeBrahm, an engineer in the service of South Carolina, selected the location on a narrow ridge adjacent to the Little Tennessee River and for a time supervised construction (De Vorsey 1971). The provincial militia erected the fort, while the regular troops provided garrison duty.

DeBrahm's fort was planned with an outer work of ditch (or dry moat) and earthen parapet, within which was to have been a square log palisade with diamond-shaped bastions in the opposing corners (Fig. 21.1). After DeBrahm departed, Demere quickly abandoned this concept. The palisade line was taken down and placed against the inside of the earthen parapet. The original plans had called for a hornwork on the river side of the fort, and although this was begun in the autumn of 1756, work halted in January 1757 (Hamer 1925, Kelley 1961a, McDowell 1970). Other constructions within the fort, known from contemporary documentation and archaeology, included gun platforms in the four bastions, houses and barracks for officers and men, storehouses, a blacksmith's shop, powder magazine and guardhouse, and Officer of the Day's quarters (Kuttruff in prep.).

In August 1757, Captain Paul Demere replaced his brother as commanding officer, and the two companies of provincial militia were disbanded. Thereafter the fort was manned by one company of British regulars, with occasional reinforcements. Relations with the Cherokee remained relatively friendly and mutually beneficial until the autumn of 1759. Subsequently they deteriorated, and the Cherokee began to harass the garrisons at Fort Loudoun and Fort Prince George. Throughout the spring and summer of 1760 the siege of Fort Loudoun was tightened to the point where the garrison faced starvation.

Demere surrendered to the Cherokee in early August 1760 (Hamer 1925,

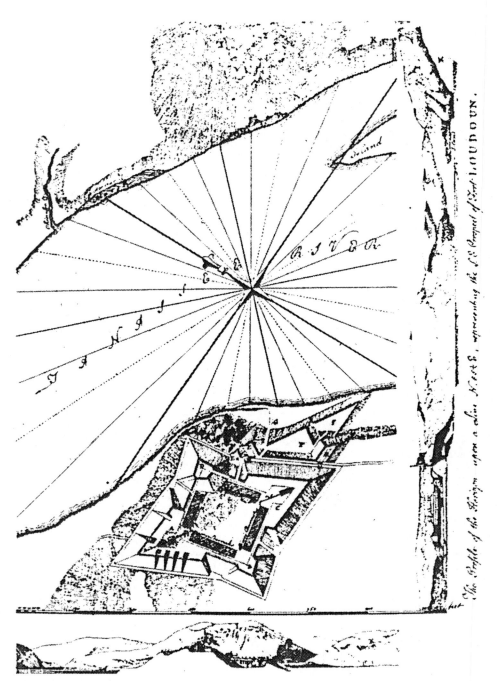

Figure 21.1 'Plan and profiles of Fort Loudoun upon Tanassee River.' The British Library copy of DeBrahm's plan of Fort Loudoun, contained in his *Report of the general survey in the southern district of North America* (1772). (Courtesy of the British Library, King's Mss. 210 f. 27.)

Kelley 1961a, McDowell 1970, Kuttruff in prep.). The garrison abandoned the fort on the morning of 9 August. The following morning it was ambushed by the Cherokee about 15 miles from the fort. Paul Demere, all the other officers except John Stuart, and between 20 and 30 of the men were killed. A few of the troops escaped, but the rest were captured and taken to various Cherokee towns. In November 1760 about ten of the captives were ransomed in Virginia. Thereafter the return of the remainder continued over a period of about nine months, most of them being delivered to Fort Prince George in South Carolina (Alden 1944, Brown 1965, Kelley 1961a).

The state of the fort after the British surrender is not well documented. To date, nothing has been located that describes its condition when abandoned or during the period immediately following the Cherokee takeover. Apparently the Indians occupied it to some extent, and all supplies and the like were removed to nearby Cherokee towns (Kuttruff in prep.). In 1762 Lieutenant Henry Timberlake visited the fort (Williams 1948). In his map of that year he showed its location in relation to the Cherokee towns in the valley but did not provide any description other than that it was then in ruins. The Federal Period Tellico Blockhouse was constructed in 1794 on the opposite side of the river (Polhemus 1979), and descriptions by visitors there indicate that by then the fort was decayed and overgrown (see, for example, Louis-Philippe 1977).

Archaeological investigations

Archaeological excavations began at Fort Loudoun in 1936 when the Federal Works Progress Administration determined the position of the outer palisade line and located several interior structures, particularly the barracks and powder magazine (Cooper n.d.(a), (b)). The Fort Loudoun Association administered the site under trust from the State of Tennessee and opened it to the public with the minimum of interpretation, though certain features were marked. During the 1940s interest waned and it became overgrown, but in 1955 the Fort Loudoun Association carried out limited excavations to obtain information on certain features for reconstruction and interpretive purposes (Brown 1955 a–c, 1958, Kelley 1961b, Myers & Polhemus n.d., Kuttruff in prep.).

In the late 1950s and early 1960s the Fort Loudoun Association sponsored a more comprehensive excavation programme to obtain further details about the site plan and certain structural features (Kunkel 1960; n.d.). Reconstruction of the outer palisade line began at this time and was completed by the end of the decade. The interpretive programme consisted of a display of artefacts and other historical information in the visitors' centre. A brochure provided a limited history of the site and a key to a self-guided walking tour. The Association carried out a great deal of documentary research at this time and published an excellent concise site history (Kelley 1961a, Black 1961, Brown 1971, n.d. (a), (b)).

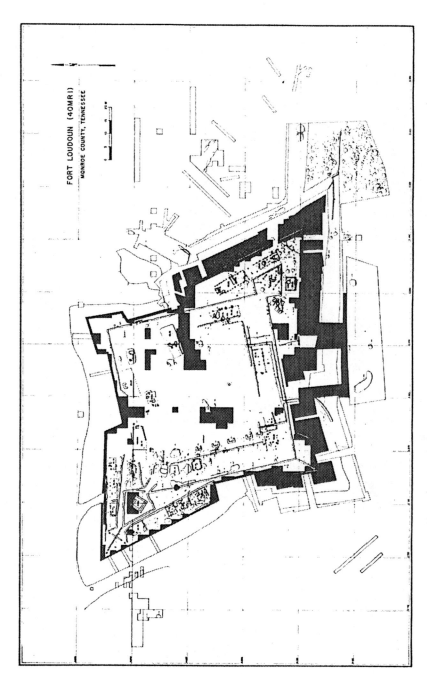

Figure 21.2 Plan of the 1975–6 excavations (darkly shaded areas indicate those areas not excavated).

The final and most extensive excavations commenced in May 1975 and continued until August 1976 under my supervision, with funding from the TVA (Fig. 21.2). The work was urgent because the construction of the Tellico Dam meant that flooding was to occur in 1979. Approximately 8000 square metres (93 per cent) of the interior of the fort was hand excavated in two-metre square units. Trenches were extended across the moat and parapet on the outside of the fort in order to determine their extent and configuration. A series of profile trenches was excavated by backhoe, with a three-foot wide toothless bucket, to verify further the configuration of the moat and the parapet. The remainder of the moat was then cleared by machine and hand on the east, south, and west sides of the fort. Similar excavations were carried out in the area of the hornwork between the east moat and the river.

In addition to the work specifically related to the fortification, an area adjacent to the south-east corner of the moat was cleared with a backhoe to expose the subsurface features and structures in that area. Because of the need for earth to create a landfill over the area of the original fort, we were able to examine a large area to the south for cultural features. Including the area next to the south-east moat, such features were found over 8000 square metres. Twelve structures, 162 pit features, and hundreds of post-moulds were defined and mapped; the pit features were then hand-excavated.

The occupations represented by these features and structures spanned most of the prehistoric continuum and included the Archaic Period (8000–1000 BC), Middle and Late Woodland periods (1000 BC–AD 900), and the late prehistoric Mississippian Period (AD 900–1600). Of particular importance was the location and excavation of three house structures, 19 pit features, one burial, and numerous artefactual materials from the Cherokee Indian village of Tuskegee, settled in about 1757 as a direct response to the establishment of Fort Loudoun. The village lasted until 1776, when it was destroyed, probably by a military expedition led by Colonel William Christian in retribution 'for Cherokee attacks on the Watauga settlements.

Interpretive programme

Although no detailed development plan or interpretive guide was formulated before the final excavations and mitigation action, we knew that the fort would have to be reconstructed and a new interpretive center built (Fig. 21.3) on landfill above the new lake pool level. The overall objectives and themes for the Fort Loudoun State Historic Area, set out in the approved interpretive development guide (Kuttruff 1981b), were to inform visitors (a) why Fort Loudoun was built and what was happening in 18th-century North America to require a British fort in this location; (b) of the nature of the Cherokee–British relationship and its main political and economic factors; (c) how the garrison lived, and (d) about the 18th-century

Figure 21.3   Outside view of Fort Loudoun Interpretive Center.

environment of the Little Tennessee River Valley and how it subsequently changed.

Different levels of information had to be provided for school groups, laymen interested in the history of the area, professionals studying 18th-century history and Cherokee culture, and researchers on various other aspects of the history and prehistory of the area. A brief brochure describes the site, and a concise history of the occupation is available (Kelley 1961a). Copies of all documentary materials and the secondary literature are to hand. The detailed archaeological report will soon be obtainable, to be joined, it is hoped, by a popular volume on the archaeology, history, and reconstructions.

Limits on funding and personnel have necessitated hard decisions about how much information is available for display and how much reconstruction can be carried out. Because the site is now completely artificial, with its original surroundings altered dramatically by the flooding of the valley (compare Figs 21.4–5), special attention has to be given to the natural environment.

The natural environment

Visitor interpretation has to describe the natural setting for the prehistoric and historic occupation of the Little Tennessee River Valley, including its appearance during the 18th century; after the changes brought about by 19th-century Anglo-European settlement and land use; and since the recent destruction of the valley by the impoundment of the river. Interpretation has been achieved by a short slide and tape programme containing photographs of local scenery thought to be pristine, as well as others showing

Figure 21.4 An oblique aerial view of Fort Loudoun, taken in 1975 after the beginning of the 1975 excavations. The photograph shows the location of the fort on a narrow ridge adjacent to the Little Tennessee River. The reconstruction of the palisade dates from the 1960s. (Photograph courtesy of Tennessee Valley Authority.)

various changes. Descriptions of the valley by 18th-century travellers are quoted (Bartram 1791, Williams 1928).

The presentation also places the Little Tennessee River Valley and the fort in the larger perspective of the eastern United States, in order to show the major geographical features that influenced travel, trade, and communications. A composite photograph made from satellite imagery is used to show the topographical features, the distribution of British and French forts and towns, and the theatre of the French and Indian Wars.

Figure 21.5   An oblique aerial view of Fort Loudoun after the landfilling of the fort site and the impoundment of Tellico Lake: compare with Figure 21.4. The palisade is the latest construction of that feature. (Photograph courtesy of Tennessee Valley Authority.)

Culture history

It was decided to emphasize the Cherokee Indian occupation primarily because of its close association with the fort. Much information was available in the form of historical and ethnographic accounts (Adair 1775), 18th-century drawings, and archaeological material.

Cherokee–British relationships are considered mainly in the audiovisual programme on the history of Fort Loudoun. We document the trade between the Indians and the garrison and with British traders in several Cherokee villages. Graphics are used to portray trade-goods lists, and many items of trade recovered archaeologically are displayed. The complicated nature of British–Cherokee relations, including the Cherokee participation in the French and Indian Wars, made a recorded narrative, which reduced the amount of text required, the most advantageous form of presentation. Since the Sequoyah Birthplace Museum is located nearby, we do not have to provide a complete presentation of the Cherokee.

History and occupation

This section of interpretation is designed to summarize the history of Fort Loudoun and to give an understanding of the garrison's way of life. We illustrate the background of the French and Indian Wars and the chronology of the conflict to show its relationship to Fort Loudoun. We depict the principles of fortification and the range of variation in the forts in eastern North America. Aspects of garrison life at other frontier forts are deduced

Figure 21.6 A view in a south-westerly direction across the reconstructed fort. The powder magazine is in the left foreground, and the blacksmith's shop is in the distance.

from evidence at Fort Loudoun. The weapons used by the garrison are described. Day-to-day relations with the Indians and other more general aspects of diplomacy, including the recruitment of Indians for military campaigns against the French, are documented.

To ensure the accuracy of our presentation and to corroborate the archaeological evidence, we studied the primary historical documents, many of which have been published or are on microfilm (McDermott 1965, De Vorsey 1971), and numerous secondary sources (Hamer 1925, Williams 1937, Kelley 1961a, Sirmans 1966, Stone 1969, Brown 1971; n.d.(a), (b), King & Evans 1977). One 18th-century description is available (Hewatt 1779), and two 19th-century historical works provide accounts of the fort (Haywood 1823, Ramsey 1853). Somewhat later, several articles and popular accounts were published (Radford 1897, DeWitt 1917, Henderson 1917, Cook 1921); there is even a novel (Craddock 1899).

Central to the presentation of the background of the French and Indian Wars and to the history of the fort is a 20-minute audiovisual programme using slides of artists' renderings of various events, 18th-century illustrations of certain personalities, photographs of the reconstructed fort (Fig. 21.6) and re-enactment groups, and sketches of the buildings. We considered this the most effective way to present the political and military background information, historical events, and other fort-related activities, including construction, subsistence, person-to-person relationships, and various craft activities. It is also a useful means of portraying garrison–Cherokee contact.

We needed to discuss 18th-century fortifications. Research for this covered primary sources on fortifications and military principles (Muller 1756, 1764, Mahan 1836, Scott 1864), as well as secondary studies (Hunter 1960, Robinson 1977). Maps, plans, and archaeological and other reports were reviewed, including those for Fort Frederica, Georgia; Fort Prince George, South Carolina; Fort Loudoun, Pennsylvania; Fort Ligonier, Pennsylvania; Fort Michilimackinac, Michigan; and Fort Stanwix, New York. We present this information by graphics, including a diagram of the fort with bastions, curtains, and palisades appropriately labelled and explained. Others show several 18th-century fort and archaeological plans illustrating the sizes, shapes, and complexity of frontier forts. A projected model of Fort Loudoun, showing the numerous buildings and other constructions within the fort, will give the visitor an idea of the complexity of the whole installation.

Although it is important to present information on housing and barracks life, financial restraints and security needs mean that the reconstructed buildings generally lack sufficient typical furnishings and accoutrements to provide a lived-in look. A compromise solution has been to create a full-scale cut away barrack room in the exhibition hall, furnished with reproductions of typical furniture and other household items. Alongside are exhibited actual household objects and building hardware recovered from the original fort.

Other topics chosen to illustrate garrison life include food supply, clothing, craft activities, and weapons and armaments. Subsistence information is presented in the audiovisual programme and in a display of faunal remains and culinary artefacts. The clothing display consists of a life-like mannequin dressed in a replicated British military uniform, and a display of buttons and buckles recovered from the fort. Artists' renderings and displays of related artefacts illustrate various craft activities. An original cannon and parts of military muskets and Indian trade guns, all recovered from the fort, are included, as are reproductions of a Brown Bess musket and a cohorn mortar. In the fort reproductions of cannon are mounted on a gun platform in one of the bastions to show their defensive placement. Various living history activities, such as a working blacksmith and occasional military re-enactments and encampments, will supplement this.

Archaeology

A description of the archaeological work forms a small but integral part of the interpretation, illustrating methods of investigation and the nature of the evidence recovered. Photographs of the excavations, arranged chronologically, show changes in excavation techniques since the 1930s and the environmental changes at the site over the same period. The illustrations of archaeological method consist of copies of the archaeological site plan, showing all features and structures (Fig. 21.2), and detailed plans of some of the structures found. Artefacts recovered from the site are displayed throughout the exhibit area.

The contribution of archaeology to the reconstructed buildings and to the historical architectural information is presented by a series of graphics which move from the archaeological plan of the blacksmith's shop and a barrack building to architectural drawings of similar standing structures, an architectural drawing of the reconstructed building, and progress photographs of the reconstruction. By this means we hope the visitor will understand that the buildings are only reconstructions, and will also acquire an insight into the creative process behind the construction of the originals.

Fort reconstruction

The other major part of the interpretation is the reconstruction of the fort. Several factors have had to be taken into consideration, especially the artificiality of its location and the alteration of its surroundings. Because of fiscal and manpower limitations, only six structures and other features could be built in addition to the palisade and powder magazine that were completed by the TVA. We selected structures to illustrate the range of buildings: the blacksmith's shop, two temporary troop quarters, a barracks, an officer's quarters, and a storehouse. A gun platform was installed in one of the bastions. These particular buildings were chosen for reconstruction in part because of their locations, based on archaeological evidence, in different parts of the fort. The model in the visitors' centre is intended to complement our selection and to show a complete reconstruction.

Another important facet of the interpretation is to demonstrate different methods of 18th-century construction. Our work was based on other reconstructions, 18th-century building manuals (e.g. Neve 1969), and more recent studies of 18th-century building techniques (Kniffen & Glassie 1966, Richardson 1973, Historic American Building Survey 1976, Church 1978, Harris 1978). This information is presented in the visitors' centre and is also discussed in the archaeology section.

We had to compromise in the selection of building materials because of the prohibitive cost of such things as hand-hewn timbers and split clapboards, and because of the need for a relatively long life for such materials. Preservative-treated logs were considered absolutely necessary for the palisade. Band-sawn timbers closely resembling pit-sawn wood were used. Reasonable efforts were made to ensure that the constructions were sympathetic to the originals, and attempts have been made to obscure features that would not be in keeping. The constructions give an appearance consistent with the documentation. Steps have been taken to make the visitor aware of these constraints and of the fact that the constructions are neither originals nor necessarily exact replicas.

Motives for reconstruction

Certain points should be emphasized. Long-term continuity of organization and of personnel familiar with the various aspects of a project is essential for efficiency and economy of effort. Archaeologists, historians, architectural historians, and exhibit and interpretive specialists need to coordinate their work. The nature of the audience should be known, so that the interpretations can be designed accordingly. Several different levels of information may have to accommodate a range of audience interests. Information should be presented in many ways, using various media in consistent and complementary presentations. The rationale for the interpretation must be clearly understood by the viewing public. This is particularly true for reconstructions and replications where the underlying principles, be they historical, archaeological, or architectural, need to show how the exhibits were determined. There should be continual re-evaluation of the accuracy, effectiveness, and range of the interpretive programme, with the means for changing the presentations to offer some variety in the programming.

The interpretation of Fort Loudoun attempts to show how local events relate to the wider political and economic interactions of three diverse North American cultures of the mid-18th century: the British colonial empire, the Cherokee Indians of eastern Tennessee, and, to a lesser extent, the French colonial empire. The fort was built by the British with the assent of the Cherokees, owing to the activities of the French. Its rapid demise was due partly to the deterioration of local relations between the British and Cherokee but much more to the results of policies and events quite uninfluenced by the local scene. In hindsight, it is clear that this short-lived British installation was of little importance to the course of events that altered British–Cherokee and British–French relations.

What then is the significance of the fort, occupied for only four years? It was the only British fortification lying west of the Appalachians in southeastern North America, and the presence of the 18th-century participants is reflected in its surviving features, artefacts, and written documents. But neither these facts nor its minor role in 18th-century events are sufficient to account for its present-day status, which led to the activities described in this chapter.

To be sure, the decision endorsing the historical and archaeological significance of Fort Loudoun, ultimately accepted on a Federal level by its designation as a National Historic Landmark, was made well before 1975. But the original justification was superseded by the reasons, primarily local, that made the site important during the various stages of the project. Each of the groups concerned had reasons for promoting its own interests. It is instructive to examine the importance they attributed to the fort in the events leading up to the 1975–6 excavations and later. This can be done by examining their roles in the fight to block the Tellico Dam and in efforts to preserve the valley and its cultural and natural features and resources; in the mitigation of the impact of the dam and the archaeological salvage of the fort; and in its subsequent reconstruction and interpretation.

At the first stage, when construction of the dam was being contested, the fort (along with other historic and archaeological sites in the valley) came to be regarded as equivalent to a natural resource, an entity too precious to be lost to modern development. At this stage, the fort was significant for numerous individuals, conservation groups, the Fort Loudoun Association, the Tennessee Department of Conservation, and certain local political figures. Its existence was one of many things that could be used to justify opposition to the dam. On the other hand, other parties, including the TVA, developers, and some individuals and political figures, saw the fort as an impediment to the likely benefits of the project.

Once certain decisions about the fort's historical and archaeological significance had been made at a Federal level, the various groups, institutions, and individuals adopted different roles. This was the second stage, that of the salvage excavations. Federal law mandated mitigation of the cultural resource prior to its destruction. Thus the TVA's decision to finance the excavations was made because the law required it rather than from any benevolent sense of commitment to preserve cultural remains. However, local individuals, the Fort Loudoun Association, the Department of Conservation, some officials within the TVA, and certain state and local political figures were instrumental in ensuring that the law was adhered to.

Equally, those promoting or supporting the interpretive aspect of the project (i.e. the third stage) were groups, agencies, and individuals compelled to do so by law or contractual agreement and others likely to benefit from its realization. On the other hand, environmental preservationists active in opposing dam construction dropped from the scene after the inevitability of construction removed any benefits they might have derived from continued alliance with the archaeologists.

As an employee of the Department of Conservation, I had no particular brief other than a belief in the need to recover and preserve artefactual and other data. I hoped that the information might be useful in the documentation of what may have happened, when and where, and in the construction of statements about past human behaviour. There was also an anthropological potential for understanding culture contact, intrusive sites, patterns of fortifications, and the like.

Against the interest of the various parties involved in the creation of the recent history of Fort Loudoun, its 18th-century historical importance tends to pale. Fort Loudoun has become a shadow of its own past, just as the physical aspects of sites, with their silences and solitudes, often stand in stark contrast to what they once were. In answer to the question: 'who owns the past?' the recognition of a site as 'archaeological' may in fact indicate that the past no longer belongs to itself but to the present.

References

Adair, J. 1775. *The history of the American Indians*. London: E. & C. Dilly.

Alden, J. R. 1944. *John Stuart and the southern colonial frontier*. Ann Arbor: University of Michigan Press.

Bartram, W. 1791. *Travels through North and South Carolina, Georgia, east and west Florida*. (Reprinted 1980.) Charlottesville: University Press of Virginia.

Black, C. 1961. Fort Loudoun plans and profiles. Manuscript, Fort Loudoun Association.

Brown, E. 1955a, b, c, d, e. Archaeology of Fort Loudoun field report nos.1, 2, 3, 4, & 5. Filed at Fort Loudoun Association and McClung Collection, Lawson McGhee Library, Knoxville, Tenn.

Brown, E. 1958. Archaeology of Fort Loudoun: 1956–57. Filed at Fort Loudoun Association and the McClung Collection, Lawson McGhee Library, Knoxville, Tenn.

Brown, E. 1965. The Fort Loudoun people: a provisional directory based on evidence of residence at the fort between October 4, 1756, and August 9, 1760. Report on file with the Fort Loudoun Association and the McClung Collection, Lawson McGhee Library, Knoxville, Tenn.

Brown, E. 1971. The John Pearson survey. *Tennessee Archaeologist* **27**(2), 46–9.

Brown, E. n.d. (a). Research reports on Fort Loudoun. Filed at Fort Loudoun Association and the McClung Collection, Lawson McGhee Library, Knoxville, Tenn.

Brown, E. n.d. (b). The Virginia fort for the Cherokees at Chota and its relation to Fort Loudoun. Filed at Fort Loudoun Association.

Chapman, J. 1973. The icehouse bottom site (40MR23). *University of Tennessee, Department of Anthropology Report of Investigations*, no. 13. Knoxville.

Chapman, J. 1977. Archaic Period research in the lower Little Tennessee River Valley. *University of Tennessee, Department of Anthropology Report of Investigations*, no. 18. Knoxville.

Chapman, J. 1979. The 1978 archaeological investigations at the Citico Site (40MR7). Filed at Department of Anthropology, University of Tennessee, Knoxville.

Chapman, J. 1981. The Bacon Bend and Iddins sites. The Late Archaic Period in the lower Little Tennessee River Valley. *University of Tennessee, Department of Anthropology Report of Investigations*, no. 31, and *Tennessee Valley Authority Publications in Anthropology*, no. 25. Knoxville.

Chapman, J. 1982. *The American Indian in Tennessee: an archaeological perspective*. Knoxville: The Frank H. McClung Museum, University of Tennessee.

Church, B. H. 1978. The early architecture of the lower valley of Virginia. Unpublished Master's thesis, Division of Architectural History of the School of Architecture, University of Virginia.

Cook, T. H. 1921. Old Fort Loudoun, the first English settlement in what is now the state of Tennessee and the Fort Loudoun massacre. *Tennessee Historical Magazine* **7**(2), 111–33.

Cooper, H. S. n.d. (a). Archaeology of Fort Loudoun site. Hobart S. Cooper papers, C. M. McClung Historical Collection, Lawson McGhee Library, Knoxville, Tenn.

Cooper, H. S. n.d. (b). Archaeological excavations Fort Loudoun, Monroe County, Tennessee. Hobart S. Cooper papers, C. M. McClung Historical Collection, Lawson McGhee Library, Knoxville, Tenn.

Cornett, K. 1976. Excavations at Talassee (40BT8): an historic Cherokee village site in east Tennessee. *Tennessee Archaeologist* 31(1–2), 11–19.

Craddock, C. E. 1899. *Story of old Fort Loudoun*. New York: Macmillan.

De Vorsey, L., Jr. 1971. *DeBrahm's report of the general survey in the southern district of North America*. Columbia: University of South Carolina Press.

DeWitt, J. H. 1917. Old Fort Loudoun. *Tennessee Historical Magazine* 3(4), 250–6.

Guthe, A. K. 1977. The eighteenth-century Overhill Cherokee. In 'For the director: research essays in honor of James B. Griffin, edited by Charles Cleland'. *Anthropological Papers of the Museum of Anthropology, University of Michigan* 61, 212–29.

Guthe, A. K. 1978. Test excavations in the area of Tuskegee, an eighteenth century Cherokee village, Monroe County, Tennessee. *University of Tennessee, Department of Anthropology Report of Investigations*, no. 24, and *Tennessee Valley Authority Publications in Anthropology*, no. 20. Knoxville.

Guthe, A. K. & E. M. Bistline 1978. Excavations at Tomotley, 1973–74, and the Tuskegee area: two reports. *University of Tennessee, Department of Anthropology Report of Investigations*, no. 24, and *Tennessee Valley Authority Publications in Anthropology*, no. 20. Knoxville.

Hamer, P. M. 1925. *Fort Loudoun on the Little Tennessee*. Raleigh, NC: Edwards & Broughton.

Harris, R. 1978. *Discovering timber-framed buildings*. Aylesbury: Shire.

Haywood, J. 1823. *The natural and aboriginal history of Tennessee*. (Reprinted 1973.) Kingsport, Tenn.: F. M. Hill Books.

Henderson, W. A. 1917. The curious story of old Fort Loudoun. *The Lookout* (December).

Hewatt, Rev. A. 1779. *An historical account of the rise and progress of the colonies of South Carolina and Georgia*. London: Alexander Donaldson.

Historic American Building Survey 1976. *The Virginia catalogue*. Charlottesville: University Press of Virginia.

Hunter, W. A. 1960. *Forts on the Pennsylvania frontier, 1753–1758*. Harrisburg: Pennsylvania Historical and Museum Commission.

Kelley, P. 1961a. *Historic Fort Loudoun*. Vonore, Tenn.: Fort Loudoun Association.

Kelley, P. 1961b. Fort Loudoun: the after years, 1760–1960. *Tennessee Historical Quarterly* 20 (December), 303–22.

King, D. H. & E. R. Evans (eds) 1977. Memoirs of the Grant expedition against the Cherokees in 1761. *Journal of Cherokee Studies* 2(3).

Kniffen, F. & H. Glassie 1966. Building in wood in the eastern United States. *Geographical Review* 56, 40–66.

Kunkel, P. H. 1960. Fort Loudoun archaeology: a summary of the structural problem. *Tennessee Archaeological Society Miscellaneous Paper*, no. 6.

Kunkel, P. H. n.d. Final report of project archaeologist on excavations at Fort Loudoun between July 1958 and July 1959. Filed at McClung Museum, University of Tennessee, Knoxville.

Kuttruff, C. 1978. Archaeological and historical documentation for the reconstruction of structures 2, 5, and 16 at Fort Loudoun, Tennessee. Filed at Tennessee Department of Conservation, Division of Archaeology, Nashville.

Kuttruff, C. 1981a. Interpretive proposal for Fort Loudoun Historic Area, Monroe County, Tennessee. Filed at Tennessee Department of Conservation, Division of Archaeology, Nashville.

Kuttruff, C. 1981b. Interpretive development guide for Fort Loudoun Historic Area, Monroe County, Tennessee. Filed at Tennessee Department of Conservation, Division of Archaeology, Nashville.

Kuttruff, C. in prep. Fort Loudoun: historic occupations.

Kwas, M. L. 1985. Archaeological parks and their importance in public education. *Southeastern Archaeological Conference Newsletter* **27**(2), 18–20.

Louis-Philippe. 1977. *Diary of my travels in America* [1797–9]. New York: Delacorte.

Mahan, D. H. 1836. *A complete treatise on field fortification.* Wiley & Long. (Reprinted 1968, New York: Greenwood Press.)

McDermott, J. F. 1965. *The French in the Mississippi Valley.* Urbana: University of Illinois Press.

McDowell, W. L., Jr. (ed.) 1970. *Documents relating to Indian affairs, colonial records of South Carolina, Series 2: the Indian books,* **3**. Columbia: University of South Carolina Press.

Milligan, J. W. 1969a. Tomotley (40MR5). In Salo 1969, pp. 13–25.

Milligan, J. W. 1969b. The Sarnes site (40MR32). In Salo 1969, pp. 166–78.

Muller, J. 1756. *A treatise containing the elementary part of fortification, regular and irregular.* London. (Reprinted 1968, Ottawa: Museum Restoration Service.)

Muller, J. 1764. *A treatise containing the practical part of fortification.* London.

Myers, R. & J. H. Polhemus n.d. Fort Loudoun excavations 1966–1967. Report to Fort Loudoun Association. Filed at McClung Museum, University of Tennessee, Knoxville.

Neve, R. 1969. *The city and county purchaser and builder's dictionary.* (Reprint of 1726 edition.) New York: Augustus M. Kelley.

Newman, R. D. 1977. An analysis of the European artifacts from Chota-Tanasee, an eighteenth century Overhill Cherokee town. Unpublished Master's thesis, Department of Anthropology, University of Tennessee, Knoxville.

Polhemus, R. R. 1970. Chota (40MR2) historical material. In Archaeological investigations in the Tellico Reservoir, interim report 1969. *University of Tennessee, Department of Anthropology Report of Investigations,* no. 8, pp. 81–99. Knoxville.

Polhemus, R. R. 1979. Archaeological investigation of the Tellico Blockhouse site. *University of Tennessee, Department of Anthropology Report of Investigations,* no. 26, and *Tennessee Valley Authority Reports in Anthropology,* no. 16. Knoxville and Chattanooga.

Radford, P. M. 1897. Old Fort Loudoun. *American Historical Magazine* **2**(1), 33–44.

Ramsey, J. G. M. 1853. *The annals of Tennessee.* (Reprinted 1923.) Kingsport, Tenn.: Kingsport Press.

Richardson, A. J. H. 1973. A comparative historical study of timber building in Canada. *Association for Preservation Technology Bulletin* **5**(3), 77–102.

Robinson, W. B. 1977. *American forts architectural form and function.* (Amon Carter Museum of Western Art, Fort Worth.) Urbana: University of Illinois Press.

Russ, K. C. & J. Chapman 1984. Archaeological investigations at the 18th century Overhill Cherokee town of Mialoquo. *University of Tennessee, Department of Anthropology Report of Investigations,* no. 37, and *Tennessee Valley Authority Publications in Anthropology,* no. 36. Knoxville.

Salo, L. V. (ed.) 1969. Archaeological investigations in the Tellico Reservoir, Tennessee, 1967–1968, an interim report. *University of Tennessee, Department of Anthropology Report of Investigations,* no. 7. Knoxville.

Schroedl, G. F. 1978. The Patrick site (40MR40), Tellico Reservoir, Tennessee. *University of Tennessee, Department of Anthropology Report of Investigations,* no. 25, and *Tennessee Valley Authority Publications in Anthropology,* no. 22. Knoxville.

Schroedl, G. F. (ed.) 1986. Overhill Cherokee archaeology at Chota-Tanasee. *University of Tennessee, Department of Anthropology Report of Investigations,* no. 38, and *Tennessee Valley Authority Publications in Anthropology,* no. 42. Knoxville.

Scott, H. L. 1864. *Military dictionary*. New York.

Sirmans, M. E. 1966. *Colonial South Carolina, a political history 1663–1763*. Chapel Hill: University of North Carolina Press.

Stone, R. G., Jr. 1969. Captain Paul Demere at Fort Loudoun. *East Tennessee Historical Society Publications* **41**, 17–32.

Williams, S. C. 1928. *Early travels in the Tennessee country 1540–1800*. Johnson City, Tenn.: Watauga Press.

Williams, S. C. 1937. *Dawn of Tennessee Valley and Tennessee history*. Johnson City, Tenn.: Watauga Press.

Williams, S. C. 1948. *The memoirs of Lieutenant Henry Timberlake 1756–1765*, Marietta, Ga.: Continental Book Company.

22 Conservation and information in the display of prehistoric sites

NICHOLAS P. STANLEY PRICE

Current interest in the objectivity of archaeological interpretation has raised questions about the archaeologist's responsibilities towards both archaeology itself and the general public. As Leone (quoted in Hall 1984, p. 456) asks: 'to what degree does our modern archaeology create the past in its own image?' The present chapter considers this question particularly with regard to archaeological sites on display to the public.

Site conservation and information

In recent years the discrepancy between what professional archaeologists do and what the general public believes they do has become increasingly apparent. This variance, evident in many representations of archaeological activity in popular literature, the press, and other media, has serious implications for the future of the discipline, since archaeology depends to a considerable extent on public support (Cunliffe 1981, Fowler 1981, Fagan 1984). The discrepancy between professional achievement and popular expectation is often evident in responses to the physical appearance of sites. But what the public actually does expect is difficult to ascertain; knowledge of visitors' expectations of, and reactions to, sites remains generally at the anecdotal level.

Prehistoric sites suffer particularly in this respect, because their excavated remains are often meaningless, if not invisible, to the non-specialist. The viewable prehistoric past is therefore heavily biased towards the highly visible, such as Lascaux and Stonehenge, at the expense of sites like Olduvai and Çatal Hüyük. Long-term visitability depends on active maintenance of the site, a point so obvious that it is frequently overlooked in the conflict of responsibilities between excavator and authorizing agency. Recently excavated remains are liable to deteriorate more rapidly than if they had remained buried. Conservation aims to maintain the site in as near its existing state as possible by reducing the rate of decay to which it is inevitably destined. Unless a deliberate decision has been taken to keep the site visible, conservation policy should include appropriate backfilling. But as matters stand, perhaps the majority of excavated sites are completely abandoned after their excavation is over. The decision to leave a site visible makes it in theory accessible both to specialists, who can decipher the cryptic remains on view, and to the interested public. However, even a well-maintained site may not be intelligible owing to the incomplete nature of the remains.

Archaeological sites and ruins, more than most forms of cultural property, are notoriously incomplete. Thus they require additional information to make them intelligible. Such information is commonly provided through physical adjuncts to, or enhancements of, the remains themselves. Such a process of restoration aims to create an image of the monument's original state, so as to render it more intelligible to the observer. Because the observer's subsequent historical experience will continue to build on this interpretation of the past, this puts great cultural responsibility on the restorer's shoulders (Philippot 1980, p. xviii). But it is an illusion to believe that any original state can be re-created. All attempts to produce a 'definitive' restoration, whether out of vanity on the part of the restorers or from a naive trust in new materials or techniques, are misguided.

Contemporary perspectives on conservation and restoration are rooted in negative reactions to excessive 19th-century restoration of objects and monuments (Brandi 1963, Philippot 1976). The earlier national-revival and romantic approaches to restoration have gradually, although not entirely, given way to a scientific approach and a consistent philosophy. The most important principles of present conservation practice, developed mainly in Europe but now applied worldwide, can be summarized thus:

(a) Reversibility: any conservation/restoration process must be reversible without damaging original material or, at the least, must not render impossible any different treatment in the future.

(b) Minimum intervention: the aesthetic appearance and information content (e.g. its potential for dating and analysis) of the material should be altered as little as possible.

(c) Compatibility of materials: the composite formed by the original materials and the modern materials introduced during restoration should merge well under expected environmental conditions (Torraca 1984).

Archaeological site values

Guided by these principles, the character of intervention will depend on a correct understanding of the values ascribed to the site to be preserved. Intervention may aim to enhance certain values at the expense of others. Linstrum (n.d.) has classified values that society uses to justify the preservation of historic buildings and landscapes, while Lipe (1984) has identified the values ascribed to materials viewed broadly as cultural resources. These two schemata have much in common and can be summarized thus (in general following Lipe's terminology):

Aesthetic/artistic values: cultural materials as art and as objects of aesthetic appeal.

Economic/utilitarian values: cultural materials as resources producing an economic return through re-use/rehabilitation or income-generating tourism.

Associative/symbolic values: cultural materials as visible symbols of the past given romantic, folk-traditional, or nationalist/political meanings.

Historic/informational values: cultural materials as unique sources of information about the past to be preserved for future educational and research purposes.

The late 19th and 20th centuries have seen a shift towards an emphasis on authenticity and objectivity in restoration. But this does not mean that values other than historic/informational are neglected in site treatment. On the contrary, economic values – expressed, for example, in the promotion of cultural tourism – have been a powerful force in recent decades. Excavations have been undertaken at sites considered national monuments primarily to present them to the public, an associative/symbolic value not normally considered in the rescue versus research debate. When economic and nationalist motives have predominated, poor excavation techniques and incomplete publication have often detracted from historic/informational values. Paradoxically, the site is then better *known* to the public (because extensively uncovered) but less well *understood* (because poorly excavated) by both archaeologists and the public.

Conflicts of values may also arise when public interest does not coincide with that of professional archaeologists. For example, some people prefer non-rational explanations of archaeological phenomena (the supernatural past), or are prepared to accept the wilful destruction of sites for financial gain (Heath 1973).

Appreciation of a site's beauty may be widely shared; for example, the picturesque, a blend of aesthetic and romantic values, still has wide appeal. Mystery, too (not to be confused with mystification owing to lack of information), contributes to the atmosphere of a site. If a site is to be preserved, the challenge is to find technical conservation measures compatible with appropriate ascribed values. What roles do conservation and restoration play in preserving these values on sites?

When the site is maintained as it is, conservation often suffices to preserve aesthetic and associative/symbolic values, with subsidiary information provided by means other than restoration. Too much information can undermine the uniqueness of picturesque sites or those with their own atmosphere: 'The stimulation of exploring the unknown is forgone if the visitor is deprived of all sense of bewilderment and wonder, or the possibility of losing himself even temporarily' (Beazley 1981, p. 201).

Conservation measures, too, may conflict with the values to be preserved. Vegetation can enhance the aesthetic and romantic values of a site while contributing to its further decay. However, encouraging the spread of climbing species on exposed masonry and planting trees to provide shade can be destructive of historical values, especially if the plant species are alien. Another type of conservation measure, the protective roof or shelter, tends to intrude visually. Rarely can it be said that a roof of imaginative design has contributed aesthetic or artistic values to an otherwise 'flat' site (Stevens 1986).

Restoration, unlike conservation, represents a conscious attempt to enhance site values by making the site more intelligible by increasing the visible information content. Restoration measures may be technically necessary so as to prevent the collapse of structures during excavation, as at Knossos (Evans 1927). Some such measures aim to improve the aesthetic appearance of a site; others reflect economic or nationalist demands, sometimes leading beyond restoration to reconstruction.

Between conservation and reconstruction lies a continuous scale of intervention (Stubbs 1984). The more extensive the intervention, the more we impose our image of the past on a site and condition future interpretations of it. Changing interpretations of sites such as Stonehenge (Chippindale 1983) and Zimbabwe (Hall 1984) are part of the history of ideas; but the restorer bears a heavy responsibility for interpretations given concrete form in alterations to the existing built fabric or environs of a site.

Conservation/restoration theory requires a philosophy and a set of criteria by which to judge restoration work. Basic to the undertaking is a thorough understanding of the site, its history, context, and original 'whole' (Philippot 1976). Careful excavation and recording can ascertain the history. A choice must then be made concerning which phase(s) is to be restored. By definition, sites are *in situ*: their context does not need to be re-created *ab initio* as in the case of museum exhibits. Site context is a valuable asset, not to be squandered by transfer of the remains to another setting except where destruction is imminent. The original 'whole' of the site, to which all restorations should be referred, is more difficult to know. To talk of 'restoring a site to its original appearance' is to refer to an unattainable goal, since existing remains represent the effects of physico-chemical alterations continuing over perhaps thousands of years.

Yet physical intervention in the name of restoration must achieve authenticity, i.e. provide a well-founded and technically proficient image of the past that will conserve the original material in the years to come. Contemporary approaches to restoration emphasize control of agents of deterioration in the monument's environs, rather than, or at least prior to, major interventions on the monument itself. Hence on-site reconstruction may be limited to the re-erection of fallen elements in the positions from which they can be shown to have collapsed, a process known as anastylosis (Dimacopoulos 1985). Examples include the re-positioning of fallen lintels and uprights at Stonehenge, whose positions are known from early prints and photographs (Chippindale 1983), and the re-erection of Easter Island statues on the platforms from which they were toppled (Mulloy 1970).

Restoration, display, and the public

Displays of prehistoric sites governed by restrictive, even purist conservation/restoration theory attempt to minimize the restorer's influence in deciding what image of the past to present, both to this generation and to the next (which will, in any case, evolve its own restoration philosophy). By contrast, the restorer's influence is most evident in such extensive reconstructions as Williamsburg, Virginia, and Louisbourg, Nova Scotia, whose images were designed to reinforce present-day values and myths (Ford 1973, Leone 1973). To accord with public expectations, the sites were sanitized, and did not reproduce the squalor of the time. At carefully conserved ruins of English abbeys and castles conservation policies aim not to re-create past living conditions but to arrest further decay of the monuments themselves (Thompson 1981).

At the other end of the scale from reconstruction, minimal intervention leaves the visitor free to form his own images and assign his own values. At a time when various sites worldwide are objects of conflict between interest groups holding different values, there is much to be said for this policy.

Between the extremes of on-site reconstruction and complete neglect as romantic ruins, there is wide scope for imaginative site presentation without physical modification of the fabric. Visitors should be given information on the present state of the site and how it has evolved both in archaeological terms and as part of a landscape. The more the public is aware of and can participate in the process of making a site known, the more intelligible it becomes to them, and the more likely to be preserved. A site should be viewed dynamically, as the present state of a continuing process of landscape evolution rather than as an isolated and static phenomenon.

Greater public awareness can be achieved through (a) information, (b) exhibition, and (c) participation:

(a) *Information* Excavators increasingly provide information about current work and provide such facilities as viewing platforms and guided tours. Site conservation and restoration methods, now only rarely described, could be no less absorbing for the visitor than excavation methods. Techniques used to distinguish restored areas from original material or used to instal modern structural supports (Thompson 1981, p. 71) are self-evident to few visitors and require explanation. Several museums and galleries now explain such conservation problems as the need to maintain low light levels and the damage that touching can cause exhibits. Notices become explanatory instead of prohibitive. Similar devices could be used on sites; for example, notices forbidding walking on walls could also describe why they are vulnerable.

(b) *Exhibition* Depicting work on a site as one continuous process from excavation through identification, study, and conservation to display helps viewers to understand material remains and information derived from them (see Kuttruff, Ch. 21, this volume). The Jorvik Viking Centre (Addyman & Gaynor 1984, Addyman, Ch. 20, this volume), where the interpretive reconstruction in fact precedes the excavation site on the fixed visitor itinerary, offers a stimulating example. Museum experiments with open storage and visible conservation help to inform the public about the facilities and activities that lie behind an exhibition. Similar initiatives (e.g. Prag 1983) help to explain the archaeologist's post-excavation work to a wider audience. The display – to amateur divers – of marine sites as 'underwater show cases' helps to involve the public in their protection (McCarthy 1986). Off-site replicas (full size or scale models) can convey an idea how the monument might have looked during different phases of its history in a way that is impossible when using original remains alone.

(c) *Participation* The established tradition of volunteer excavators has not led to a similar amateur involvement in technical aspects of restoration. However, a growing number of centres for experimental archaeology enable volunteers to test their perceptions of life in the past against simulated reality (Coles 1979). This type of experience is invaluable since it emphasizes the processes that lie behind the static objects and sites presented to the public as archaeology.

Further involvement of the public along lines indicated in this chapter would enhance general understanding of archaeological sites. The discrepancy between professional achievement and public expectation can be overcome through better understanding of the links between archaeology and conservation, and of the unity of archaeological processes from site discovery through to site display.

References

Addyman, P. V. 1990. Reconstruction as interpretation: the example of the Jorvik Viking Centre, York, in *The politics of the past*, P. Gathercole & D. Lowenthal (eds), Ch. 20. London: Unwin Hyman.

Addyman, P. & A. Gaynor 1984. The Jorvik Viking Centre: an experiment in archaeological site interpretation. *International Journal of Museum Management and Curatorship* 3, 7–18.

Beazley, E. 1981. Popularity: its benefits and risks. In *Our past before us: why do we save it?* D. Lowenthal & M. Binney (eds), 193–202. London: Temple Smith.

Brandi, C. 1963. *Teoria del restauro*. Roma: Edizioni di Storia e Letteratura.

Chippindale, C. 1983. *Stonehenge complete*. London: Thames & Hudson.

Coles, J. M. 1979. *Experimental archaeology*. London & New York: Academic Press.

Cunliffe, B. 1981. Introduction: the public face of the past. In *Antiquity and man: essays for Glyn Daniel*, J. D. Evans, B. Cunliffe & C. Renfrew (eds). London: Thames & Hudson.

Dimacopoulos, J. 1985. Anastylosis and anasteloseis. *ICOMOS Information* 1, 16–25.

Evans, A. J. 1927. Work of reconstruction in the palace of Knossos. *Antiquaries Journal* **7**, 258–67.

Fagan, B. M. 1984. Archaeology and the wider audience. In *Ethics and values in archaeology*, E. L. Green (ed.), 175–83. New York: The Free Press.

Ford, R. I. 1973. Archaeology serving humanity. In *Research and theory in current archaeology*, C. L. Redman (ed.), 83–93. New York: Wiley.

Fowler, P. 1981. Archaeology, the public and the sense of the past. In *Our past before us: why do we save it?* D. Lowenthal & M. Binney (eds), 56–69. London: Temple Smith.

Hall, M. 1984. The burden of tribalism: the social context of southern African Iron Age studies. *American Antiquity* **49**, 455–67.

Heath, D. B. 1973. Economic aspects of commercial archaeology in Costa Rica. *American Antiquity* **38**, 259–65.

Kuttruff, C. 1990. Fort Loudoun, Tennessee, a mid-18th century British fortification: a case study in research archaeology, reconstruction, and interpretive exhibits. In *The politics of the past*, P. Gathercole & D. Lowenthal (eds), Ch. 21. London: Unwin Hyman.

Leone, M. 1973. Archaeology as the science of technology: Mormon town plans and fences. In *Research and theory in current archaeology*, C. L. Redman (ed.), 125–50. New York: Wiley.

Linstrum, D. n.d. *Evaluation of historic buildings and areas.* Lectures to Architectural Conservation course. Rome: ICCROM.

Lipe, W. 1984. Value and meaning in cultural resources. In *Approaches to the archaeological heritage*, H. Cleere (ed.), 1–11. Cambridge: Cambridge University Press.

McCarthy, M. (1986). Protection of Australia's underwater sites. In *Preventive measures during excavation and site protection*, 133–45. Rome: ICCROM.

Mulloy, W. 1970. *Preliminary report of the restoration of Ahu Vai Uri, Easter Island.* Easter Island Committee, International Fund for Monuments Bulletin 2. New York.

Philippot, P. 1976. Historic preservation: philosophy, criteria, guidelines. In *Preservation: principles and practice*, S. Timmons (ed.), 367–82. Washington, DC: Preservation Press.

Philippot, P. 1980. Introductory speech. Conservation and tradition of crafts. In *Conservation of Far Eastern art objects*, xvii–xx. International Symposium on the Conservation and Restoration of Cultural Property. Tokyo.

Prag, A. J. N. W. 1983. Archaeology alive at the Manchester Museum. *Museums Journal* **83**, 79.

Stevens, A. 1986. Structures nouvelles de protection des sites archéologiques du tiers-monde. In *Preventive measures during excavation and site protection*, 225–44. Rome: ICCROM.

Stubbs, J. 1984. Protection and presentation of excavated structures. In *Conservation on archaeological excavations*, N. P. Stanley Price (ed.), 79–96. Rome: ICCROM.

Thompson, M. W. 1981. *Ruins: their preservation and display.* London: British Museum Publications.

Torraca, G. 1984. Processes and materials used in conservation. Paper given at symposium on Scientific Methodologies Applied to Works of Art, Florence, 2–5 May.

23 *The epic of the* Ekpu: *ancestor figures of Oron, south-east Nigeria*

KEITH NICKLIN

> For when all is said and done a work of art must ultimately be judged by
> its visual effect; its appeal must be universal and regardless of its age, its
> function, its maker or what other people have to say about it. Once
> these social criteria take over, it becomes a valuable, an antique, and
> whether it remains a work of art is debatable. Its worth is no longer
> enhanced by purely aesthetic considerations but by its age, its rarity and
> its market value, and this increases every time it changes hands. (Jones
> 1984, p. 1)

The Oron were traditionally a farming and fishing people living on the west
bank of the Cross River estuary in south-east Nigeria (Fig. 23.1). During
the present century, missionary activity, colonialism, and modern communications have precipitated a period of rapid socioeconomic change, but
many Oron people still live in villages and pursue traditional occupations.
The present administrative centre of Oron, a small, thriving, modern
African town with a ferry link to Calabar, capital of Cross River State, is
best known to the outside world for its museum of antiquities.

The archaeological record of the Oron area remains virtually unknown,
although the clay core of a copper alloy casting accidentally discovered by
labourers at a site called Uruc Ntuk Idim has yielded a 17th-century date
(Nicklin & Fleming 1980). No evidence suggests that the present Oron are
other than direct descendants of the autochthonous inhabitants of this
coastal and riverine territory, as they believe themselves to be.

In 1947 Kenneth Murray, Nigeria's first Surveyor, and later Director, of
Antiquities, published the first detailed description of the wooden ancestor
figures of Oron (1947b). Around this time he also initiated efforts to secure
their preservation. Most writers describe the figures as art objects, and
several comment on their austere and dignified appearance. William Fagg,
former Keeper of Ethnography at the British Museum, has referred to the
genre as 'surely among the most deeply impressive of all African styles'
(1968, p. 63), with a 'rhythmical composition of sculptural volumes . . .
hardly . . . surpassed elsewhere' (1965, p. 56).

The Oron name for an ancestor figure is *Ekpu*, a term meaning ancestor or
ancestral spirit. Each *Ekpu* figure is a monoxylous pole-carving of a hard

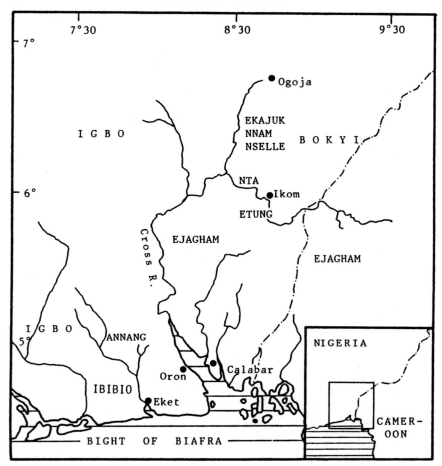

Figure 23.1   Map of south-east Nigeria.

forest timber such as camwood (*Pterocarpus soyauxii*; Oron *ukpa*) or *Coula edulis* (Oron *ekom* or *oko*). *Ekpu* figures are generally around one metre high. They depict deceased Oron elders, all of whom are shown with beards and headgear; most bear emblems of lineage authority in both hands (Figs 23.2, 3). The *Ekpu* corpus contains no known representations of women.

The figures have been the subject of numerous scholarly articles, an art catalogue, a documentary film, a novel (Akaduh 1983), and a monograph (Nicklin in press). They have served as the sacred objects of their original owners, as museum specimens, as victims of the illicit international art traffic, as symbols of Nigerian national unity, and as firewood. I examine these respective contexts in the light of the political and social history of the area.

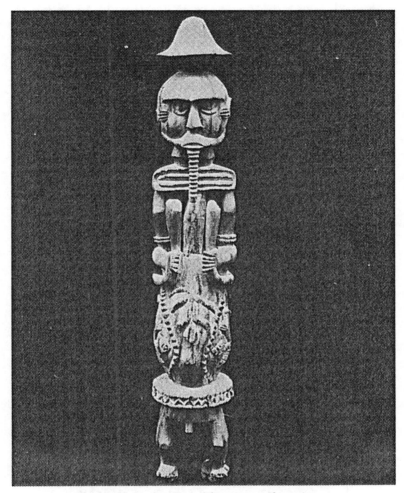

Figure 23.2 An Oron *Ekpu* ancestral carving.

After centuries of commercial activity in the Bights of Benin and Biafra, based initially on the slave trade and, during the 19th century, on the so-called legitimate trade in palm oil, Britain proclaimed the Colony and Protectorate of Nigeria in 1914. Oron was incorporated into Eket District, in the Calabar Province of the Eastern Region. During the early part of this century, the Primitive Methodist Church Missionary Society established several stations in the vicinity of Oron (Ward 1913). The missionaries made every effort to undermine the traditional belief system and to eradicate what they saw as heathen practices. As a result, little is known about Oron

Figure 23.3 Oron *Ekpu* ancestral carvings. (Photograph by K. C. Murray.)

ancestor figures as religious objects, since their production and use died out when European residents were either opposed to, or showed no interest in, the existence of the *Ekpu* cult.

The religious and social significance of the carvings

According to Murray (1947b, p. 313),

When a man died and before his second or ceremonial burial, a carving was made to represent him, the size and elaborateness of which depended on his importance and wealth ... It was believed that the spirit of the dead man had some connection with the carving. It was a shrine where his spirit could be conveniently approached, but it was not itself worshipped. It was a symbol of the deceased and became a thing of great holiness, interference with which might be resented by the ancestral spirits.

Each extended family of *ekpuk* has its own ancestor figures, which were placed against the back wall of the *obio*, the men's meeting house, alongside other sculptures of the same type. Twice a year, during the planting season and at harvest, offerings of food and wine were made to the *Ekpu* figures so that the ancestors might intervene with the great god Abassi to ensure farming success and human health and fertility. The *obio* was kept in good repair and, as important old carvings were destroyed by termites or rotted away, new carvings were made to replace them. And so in the old days, in Murray's words, 'the art lived' (1947b, p. 314).

P. O. Nsugbe (1961), a former curator of the Oron Museum, saw the carvings as monuments to the dead, occupied by the spirits of the ancestors they represent. Since the deceased person for whom an *Ekpu* figure was carved had formerly headed a lineage group, the carving was in fact a perpetuation of the 'lineage rights and claims as were vested in the elder when he was alive'. Because lineage rights and identity were preserved by the *Ekpu* figures, they 'served as an aid to social memory, and therefore as records in wood' that underpinned the authority of living village elders.

The collection of the carvings and the building of the Oron Museum

By the 1940s, the *Ekpu* cult had been in decline for decades, primarily owing to missionary influence, and most of the carvings had either disintegrated or been badly damaged by neglect. Some churches had encouraged their members to destroy the carvings and no new ones were being made. Despite the fact that the Oron no longer appeared to be interested in preserving the figures, they were suspicious and resentful of Murray's interest. A fascinating insight into Oron attitudes at the time is provided by an Oron elder in Akaduh's novel, *The Ancestor* (1983, p. 31):

> Government said these carvings were so valuable to the whole Black Nation that nobody in any family should keep a single stick at home. So we became scared. I thought of an idea. They wouldn't go to the swamps. It was there I buried the sixteen wooden carvings.

However, by 1946 Murray was able to report that the Oron Clan Council had decided on behalf of the people that the carvings should be preserved in a museum 'if Government will build one in Oron' (1946, p. 113).

By this time the colonial authorities were no longer hostile to the study and preservation of certain aspects of indigenous culture, but they were parsimonious in the provision of funds for institutions such as museums. The Nigerian Antiquities Service, later to become the Department of Antiquities, was founded in 1943, but for the first ten years it was run solely by Murray, together with the archaeologist Bernard Fagg, and a handful of junior personnel. Murray gave priority to the Oron sculptures, and in 1944 had conducted an extensive survey of the area, listing some 1296 carvings. Eventually he collected more than 500 specimens; a further hundred were subsequently brought to the museum or acquired by the department's staff. They were housed in the Waterside Rest House, an earth building with a thatched roof made available by the District Officer in Oron (cf. Willett, Ch. 13, this volume).

Most Nigerian antiquities have been procured for the national collections by purchase or gift, but the *Ekpu* figures were only loaned to the museum by the heads of the families who owned them. The owners maintained the right to have regular access to the carvings and to conduct customary rituals, but in practice once they had been handed over to the Department of Antiquities, no such contact persisted.

During the 1940s and 1950s Murray produced publications and held exhibitions aimed at bringing the *Ekpu* figures to public, scholarly and administrative attention in Nigeria and Britain, so that steps could be taken to save them from destruction. At the same time Britain found it politically expedient to stage exhibitions of the art of its colonies. Accordingly, Oron sculpture was exhibited in Lagos in 1946 and in London in 1949 and 1951 (Fagg 1949, Murray 1947a, 1952). Although plans for a permanent museum at Oron were prepared in 1949, construction was delayed for many years, and the authorities criticized Murray for collecting so many carvings (Murray n.d.). Not until the eve of Nigeria's independence in 1959 were the carvings finally housed in modern museum facilities.

Murray's fears for the safety of the carvings were justified. In 1958 the temporary museum building was broken into and up to 30 of the figures stolen. They were smuggled out of Nigeria and offered for sale to private collectors and museums in Europe and the United States. With the aid of

Interpol, an African dealer in Lagos was eventually arrested, charged, found guilty of receiving stolen property, and sentenced to prison. Some of the carvings were recovered, others not; some went underground and have not been seen since. As William Fagg wrote, the Oron sculptural style had become 'more widely known in the most regrettable of ways' (1965, p. 56).

The Civil War

During the Nigerian Civil War of 1967–70, Oron lay within the rebel enclave, and the museum, being in a strategic waterside position, was occupied by Biafran troops. Concrete gun emplacements were built and mines laid within the museum grounds. After Federal forces took Calabar in October 1969, the museum was bombarded. Despite severe damage to the buildings, the collection remained largely intact. The Biafran authorities evacuated the collection with some of the staff to the Igbo heartland, where it was temporarily stored at the Umuahia Government College. With the final capitulation of Biafra, the Federal forces turned the college grounds into a refugee camp. At this time many of the *Ekpu* were used as firewood. Other specimens were looted by the traders and thieves who came in on the heels of the Federal army. At least one European dealer was present during this period. When order was re-established, the number of carvings remaining from the original collection was 116, representing a loss of 545, including many of the best ones. Other fine specimens in the museums at Lagos (Fig. 23.4) and Jos were unharmed. The bulk of the archival and photographic records also survived, having been lodged at the Lagos Museum.

The National Museum, Oron

The Department of Antiquities (which became the National Commission for Museums and Monuments in 1977) aimed to build a new museum with a more national character than the previous one. Reconstruction began on the site of the damaged Oron Museum in 1971, and the official opening of one of Nigeria's first 'Museums of Unity' – the National Museum, Oron – took place in April 1977 (Fig. 23.5). The remaining *Ekpu* collection forms an important focus for the enlarged exhibitions and provides an introduction to the art and material culture of the entire Cross River region. Sadly, Kenneth Murray had died in a motor accident five years earlier. Not long before he died he wrote: 'Any Oron figure which does appear abroad must have been stolen and smuggled from Nigeria and it is most probable that it can be identified among photographs in Nigeria of over 640 of the *Ekpu* carvings which were in the Oron Museum' (Murray n.d.).

Figure 23.4 *Ekpu* ancestral carvings (right) stored in the Nigerian Museum, Lagos.

Conclusion

'The epic of the *Ekpu*' provides a vivid example of a series of artefact value conversions (Fig. 23.6). The following scenario closely reflects Thompson's (1979) model of the conversion of 'junk' into collectable and valued items and Jones's observations (1984) with special reference to the art of eastern Nigeria. The initial effect of European influence in the 19th and 20th centuries on Oron *Ekpu* sculpture was to create a limited edition of the genre simply by removing the necessary cultural conditions for their continued existence as cult objects. Most pieces were destroyed by environmental agencies, while some were burnt in order to secure the spiritual salvation of converts to Christianity. Subsequently, some of the remaining pieces became museum specimens, at which point they took on a potential monetary value, while any remaining spiritual value was lost. Through the

Figure 23.5 The National Museum, Oron.

processes of publication, exhibition, and theft, the monetary value of the collection increased. At the same time a number of specimens were lost to the National Museum, which had become their effective owner.

The *Ekpu* figures were now regarded as international *objets d'art*, part of the cultural heritage of the world. During the Civil War, when the specimens in Nigeria were relocated, many of them were used as firewood. But some were looted and taken abroad. Others were rescued and eventually returned to a rehabilitated museum as symbols of national unity. Both as international *objets d'art* and as national symbols the potential monetary value of the remaining carvings increased and, in Nigeria, the *Ekpu* assumed a new spiritual value. They have now become agents of African nation-building and sacred objects of a different kind.

What, then, are the responsibilities of museum personnel, whether curators, archaeologists, or ethnographers? Murray was a product of British colonial history, but he should not be seen as having worked only in the interest of British colonialism. Indeed, he, and some other colonial administrators (such as P. Amaury Talbot), took considerable interest in indigenous cultures, to the extent that their effectiveness as administrators was sometimes compromised and they were occasionally an embarrassment to the government. Murray was only tolerated by the authorities and, certainly, only reluctantly supported. Support was forthcoming only when government was forced to take a proper ethical and practical stand to preserve the still surviving objects of pre-colonial culture.

Nobody was more aware than Murray of the role of scholarly publication

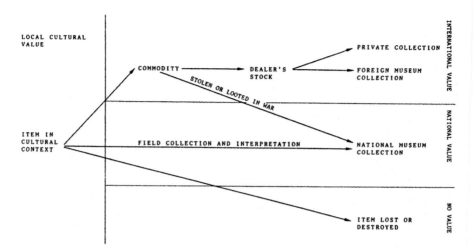

Figure 23.6 Changing values of *Ekpu* carvings.

in increasing the collectability, and therefore the monetary value, of traditional Nigerian artefacts. This is the chief reason why he did not publish a
great deal, although his knowledge was immense. Eventually, he felt compelled to publish and exhibit examples of Oron art in order to convince the
authorities of the desirability of a museum to house them. I myself wonder
whether to publish the results of my field study and collection. This would
be in the interest of the people of the Cross River and of the academic
community, *but* at the peril of the subject of research. If I publish, what form
should an *Ekpu* catalogue take? Should it be a permanent record of a great
collection, a source of pride for the present inhabitants of Oron, and a
charter for the restitution of their cultural property? But such a catalogue
would be welcomed by collectors and institutions that possess *Ekpu* illegally
and that could now authenticate and provenance them accurately. This, of
course, means that the carvings would sell more profitably on the market,
indeed an unfortunate by-product of academic interest.

Perhaps the answer lies not with museum personnel at all, but with such
Nigerians as the novelist Etim Akaduh, who based his story on an *Ekpu*
which went missing in the old days; with painters who create contemporary
interpretations of the ancient images of their ancestors; and with schoolchildren who flock to the National Museum, Oron, to glimpse aspects of the
life of their forebears. If profound mistakes, advertently or not, have been
made in the past, it is to such people that we must now look for vision. If no
'stick' of their wood sculpture had survived into the modern era, their vision
would be the narrower.

Acknowledgements

This chapter, dedicated to the memory of the late Kenneth Crosthwaite Murray O.B.E. (1903–72), is published by kind permission of Dr Ekpo Eyo, Director-General of the Nigerian National Commission for Museums and Monuments. First-hand experience of Oron and the Cross River region was gained in the course of employment as an ethnographer in the NCMM between 1970 and 1978, and from involvement in the rehabilitation of the National Museum, Oron. I should like to thank Dr M. Hitchcock, John Picton, Dr M. J. Rowlands, Brian Stafford, Ken Teague, and Professor Frank Willett for their critical comments. I am grateful for Dr Hitchcock's assistance in designing Figure 23.6.

References

Akaduh, E. 1983. *The ancestor*. Oron: Manson Publishing Company.

Fagg, W. B. 1949. *Traditional art of the British colonies*. London: HMSO.

Fagg, W. B. 1965. *Tribes and forms in African art*. London: Methuen.

Fagg, W. B. 1968. *African tribal images*. Ohio: Cleveland Museum of Art.

Jones, G. I. 1984. *The art of eastern Nigeria*. Cambridge: Cambridge University Press.

Murray, K. C. 1946. The wood carvings of Oron: the need for a museum. *Nigeria Magazine* **23**, 112–14.

Murray, K. C. 1947a. Nigeria's first exhibition of antiquities. *Nigeria Magazine* **26**, 401–7.

Murray, K. C. 1947b. Ekpu: the ancestor figures of Oron, southern Nigeria. *Burlington Magazine* **89**, 310–14.

Murray, K. C. 1952. The colonial art exhibition. *Nigerian Field* **17**(1), 41–2.

Murray, K. C. n.d. *The Oron ancestor figures: their collection, theft of some and loss of most*. Lagos: National Museum.

Nicklin, K. in press. *Ekpu: the ancestor figures of Oron*. London: Ethnographica.

Nicklin, K. & S. J. Fleming 1980. A bronze 'carnivore skull' from Oron, Nigeria. *MASCA Journal* **1**(4), 104–5.

Nsugbe, P. O. 1961. Oron *Ekpu* figures. *Nigeria Magazine* **71**, 357–65.

Thompson, M. 1979. *Rubbish theory: the creation and destruction of value*. Oxford: Oxford University Press.

Ward, W. J. 1913. *In and around the Oron country: the story of Primitive Methodism in southern Nigeria*. London: W. A. Hammond.

Willett, F. 1990. Museums: two case studies of reaction to colonialism. In *The politics of the past*, P. Gathercole & D. Lowenthal (eds), Ch. 13. London: Unwin Hyman.

Conclusion: archaeologists and others

DAVID LOWENTHAL

In manifold ways, the political contexts of archaeology are the concern of every chapter in this book. Our way of grouping them has emphasized certain common themes: Eurocentricity, conflicting majority and minority interpretations of heritage, unequal access to resources, disparities between professionals and the public. But any particular arrangement is inevitably arbitrary and incomplete, and readers may well find equally fruitful or more provocative commonalities of their own. Ours is only one way of structuring these diverse archaeological perspectives on the past.

The past is everywhere a battleground of rival attachments. In discovering, correcting, elaborating, inventing, and celebrating their histories, competing groups struggle to validate present goals by appealing to continuity with, or inheritance from, ancestral and other precursors. The politics of the past is no trivial academic game; it is an integral part of every people's earnest search for a heritage essential to autonomy and identity. In this search, archaeologists form part of a cadre of historians, social scientists, and other scholars increasingly pressed to defend or resist claims to this or that interpretation of the past.

The perspectives discussed in these chapters permeate such conflicts. Thus a Eurocentric legacy dominates modes of valuing the past throughout the world, even among peoples long deprived by, or at odds with, Europeanization. The Western emphasis on material tokens of antiquity as symbols of heritage has been all but universally adopted. International legislation, conservation agencies, and the art and antiquities markets reinforce the primacy of Western views on artefact protection, architectural preservation, and the worth and function of ancient relics. Like archaeological practice, these forces reflect the West's political and economic power and the media's diffusion of Western cultural norms. Deprived of material heritage by imperial and post-imperial plunder and purchase, non-Western cultures that have internalized Western values also deprive themselves of alternative modes of construing their particular pasts.

Within societies long dominated by Western mainstream culture, some minorities – Bretons, say, or Armenians – cling to an idealized past as virtually their sole support for a viable identity (McDonald 1986, Remnick 1988). Lacking political autonomy and often bereft of most elements of their distinctive cultures, they dwell passionately on a past doubly endeared by memory. The origins and traits of the mythic history they glorify lend crucial support to communal solidarity.

A cleavage between professionals and the public affects other perspectives on the past as well as those of archaeologists. In local and oral history, in the current preoccupation with genealogy, in rising support for preserving familiar structures and locales, in the spurt of museum growth and museum-going, a common dilemma confronts conservators and curators pledged to look after and explain the past, and at the same time to accommodate burgeoning public interest in it. Flooded with data, lacking resources to conserve let alone display, and swamped by public demands for access to ever more of the past, professionals become embroiled willy-nilly in partisan disputes.

Majority and minority, elite and folk, rulers and ruled, trained and amateur all differ over how to identify, safeguard, and interpret the past. Increasing public involvement demands new perspectives on collecting and custodial care, display and commemoration. As the 1985 fracas at Stonehenge made all too clear, views about what the past was and how it matters to whom often have their roots in conflict over *whose* past it is (Chippindale 1986).

We all make our history, but as Marx (1852) goes on to say, we do not make it just as we please. Circumstance and culture constrain what we recall or forget, and how we deploy memory and history. All of us confront myriad more or less usable pasts, national, regional, local, familial, personal; what each culture and epoch highlight depends on some unique aspects of identity based now on age, now on class, religion, race, ethnicity, or gender.

How these issues bear on the archaeological dilemmas discussed in this book may be illustrated by three related sets of topics: (a) contrasting British and American views of the past; (b) the politics of history in Poland and in Greece; and (c) campaigns for heritage restitution throughout the world.

The politics of the past: the United States and Britain

Ten-year-old Sarah Rosen of South Bend, Indiana, was named one of *Ms.* magazine's 'women of the year' in 1987, for resisting the exclusion of girls from her school's re-enactment of the American Constitutional Convention. Girls were left out on grounds of historical authenticity, as no women had been present in 1787; for another century and a half American women could not even vote. But the school's authenticity had its limits, for non-white schoolboys *did* participate in the re-enactment. 'They weren't going as life was then', Sarah objected, 'because I don't think Asians were there, and blacks were slaves and I don't think they got to be delegates' (Pogrebin 1988). Not only was Sarah a better historian than her teachers, she underscored the paradox inherent in any historical re-creation: the more authentic it seems the more it reflects the present. Americans often confront this paradox, for they commonly validate the present by reading it back into the past, as though – barring funny clothes and no cars or TV – then and now were much the same.

In making use of the past, cultures vary according to inherited modes of thought so deeply embedded people are seldom conscious of them. Consider Senator Joseph Biden's exit as an American presidential aspirant in 1987, when he was shown to have lifted a figure of speech from British Labour Party leader Neil Kinnock. What is significant is not simply that Biden plagiarized, but the cultural differences that made his borrowing so flagrantly misguided.

'Why is it', Kinnock had rhetorically asked in the spring, 'that I am the first in a thousand generations of Kinnocks to go to university?' 'Why is it', echoed Biden in August, 'that Joe Biden is the first...' Three things made this appropriate in a British context – but *not* for Biden's America. First, the 'thousand generation' phrase. This stretches time a bit even for ancient British universities, but the 'thousand' is a distinctively British way of viewing continuity back to primordial sources; who else has a living heritage of 999-year leases? Secondly, the utterly dissimilar context of class and education; because higher education in Britain has always been a minority privilege, denying that chance to Kinnock's Welsh working-class family made good rhetorical sense. But in America, where half of the school leavers go on to college, it made no sense at all, and coming from Biden was not remotely credible.

Thirdly, the engrained ancestral community implicit in Kinnock's phrasing was quite alien to mobile, restless Americans. Kinnock appealed to a left-wing freemasonry linking a millennium of British folk against gentry. And when he denounced the poll tax being enacted by Parliament as a reversion to 14th-century values, Kinnock conjured up instant empathy with Wat Tyler and the Peasants' Revolt. Labourites no less than Tories inherit an age-old national tradition, a 'continuity of struggles' that calls for a 'Whig history from the bottom up', as Harvey Kaye (1987; see also Wright 1985, pp. 151–7) puts it. 'The image of "lost rights" which inspired movements from the fourteenth to the nineteenth century' celebrates the steady advance of a working class unified not by ideology but by history.

The Biden–Kinnock affair reflects one difference between British and American perspectives on the past. The British social historian Peter Laslett (1986) airs another: 'What strikes me about Americans is that ... the outcomes of the past are part and parcel of their *being* Americans'. For instance, 'it appears to matter enormously [to Americans] that Abraham Lincoln and the North won the Civil War. It is the same with events in which the Founding Fathers were caught up.' History concerns Americans because it still vitally affects them: the past remains an anachronistic, living presence.

By contrast, 'nothing, absolutely nothing, in British history weighs like this', at least for Laslett:

> I don't care a fig that it was Cromwell and his Roundheads who won the Civil War ... because nothing whatever in my present life depends upon it. Magna Carta means even less to me ... The Norman Conquest took place so long ago that it can't possibly count in my experience.

Let us pass by the assumption that the remote in time has little impact on our consciousness (were this so, British historians might as well abandon their trade), and that Britain's 17th-century religious and political struggles had no consequences for present-day life. If Laslett's fellow countrymen are now aloof from their past, how unlike 19th-century Britain, when the 17th century was termed too dangerous to teach because it aroused such strong prejudices, and the 18th was condemned for crude amorality (Burrow 1981, p. 14).

Laslett contrasts his own with contemporary American historical experience. 'I took my British past so much for granted that I was quite unconscious of it. You Americans have a vivider sense of the past than we do. History really matters to you.' So it often seems. The American constitutional bicentenary demonstrates how vitally the supposed purposes and ideals of the Founding Fathers continue to affect Americans.

By the late 19th century the Constitution had become a timeless credo, those who framed it shorn of their historical context, much as its modern celebrants divest them of 18th-century mentalities. But critics of this construction of the Constitution *also* read back the present. To them the framers are not saints but sinners, the Constitution itself almost as evil as William Lloyd Garrison's 1854 characterization of it as a 'covenant with Death and Agreement with Hell' (in Kammen 1986, p. 98). Supreme Court Justice Thurgood Marshall (1987) terms it disgraceful that the white men who wrote it proclaimed 'liberty' in the name of a minority that excluded women and blacks. Another black judge assails the drafters' 'duplicity' for 'high-sounding words about justice while maintaining a system of slavery' as 'a monstrous contradiction' (Higginbotham 1987, see Litwack 1987).

Both sides forget that those who framed the Constitution did not create their society *de novo*; they were born into it, imbibed its values from childhood, and sought to codify most of them. They were folk of their time; for them to see slaves and women as something less than 'men' was not in the common view discordant with professions of liberty (Wood 1988). But the makers of the Constitution now seem like giants in a mythic landscape that resonates with present meanings. As Naomi Bliven (1987) writes, American 'constitutional earnestness is as good as a festival'.

Festivals make the American past usable. 'Catch up on history!' *Connecticut* (1986, p. 100) urges. 'Connecticut is justifiably proud of its history' – unlike other states which 'do not have a history, unless you count the Jurassic, pre-Cambrian and Cambrian eras'. But the region stands for the nation: 'Connecticut's history is more than the background of one small state – it is the history of all the United States.' Hence 'visiting historical Connecticut is a study in patriotism'. But this is 'a history lesson without the boring stuff', as a list of Connecticut's historical firsts proves: 'The lollipop, the hamburger, the cotton gin, vulcanized rubber, and all-night "I-love-Lucy" festivals were all invented in Connecticut. The first American pizza was served in Connecticut.'

On the one hand the Constitution; on the other the pizza and the lollipop.

So indigestible is serious history that it must be Disneyfied into pap. Americans view history schizophrenically: it can be solemn *or* silly, but not both at once. 'History' aspires to be hermetically sealed against 'fiction'. The best bookshop in Harpers Ferry, West Virginia, the famous Civil War locale that has become the headquarters of the US National Park Service, displays no historical novels about the Civil War because, the manager told me in 1987, 'we carry nothing fictitious about the past here; we are only supposed to sell true facts'. Viewing the 'true facts' in the hagiographies of Confederate Commander-in-Chief Robert E. Lee jostling the new certainties of revisionist black historians, the militaristic colouring books shelved with pacifist feminist tracts on 19th-century nursing, underscores the American dilemma. A people still deeply committed to one or another partisan reading of the past cleaves to an ideal of historical truth in which the good guys, whoever they are, will finally be seen to have come out on top.

American heritage seems a partisan minefield. Relative brevity, utter credence in written documents, and glaring and enduring disparities between the lot of colonist and native, white and black, WASP and ethnic, North and South offer much occasion for bitter dispute over historical rights and wrongs. Given such vigorously polarized views, it is no surprise that history in the United States engenders impassioned argument, throws up a profusion of exemplary figures, and lends anachronistic significance to long-dead issues.

By contrast, the British tolerate royal weddings, the Tower of London, and Madame Tussaud's by making ersatz medievalism seem mildly fey (Meades 1987). And Laslett's British heritage is largely taken for granted because it is indubitable, widely shared, and only slowly altered. In this interpretation, bygone feuds between Norman and Saxon, Celt and English, Protestant and Catholic scarcely disturb the unanimity with which the past is apprehended, even from class to class. Given so widespread a consensuality, one would expect history in Britain to arouse little emotion, to require few professions of allegiance or dissociation, and to produce neither heroes nor villains.

But does it? A closer look reveals views of history rife with passion. Angered that Francis Drake would be given only a minor role in the 1988 Armada celebration, a Plymouth city official accused the National Maritime Museum of being 'prissy' so as not 'to offend the Spanish now that they are in Europe' (quoted in Hamilton & Gledhill 1987). (Besides, there is Gibraltar to worry about.) Eminent figures assailed plans to soft-pedal the triumph of Parliament and Protestantism in the tercentenary of the Glorious Revolution as an 'offhand and unpatriotic' demeaning of national history aimed at sparing Catholic feelings. They accused the Prince of Wales, in his anodyne emphasis on Anglo–Dutch friendship, of 'giving his patronage to . . . the sort of rewriting of history practised by undemocratic regimes' (Rae 1987).

In fact, old perspectives on British history co-exist with the new, and nowadays regain increasing favour. The notable debunker of Whig history, Herbert Butterfield (1931), himself during the Second World War re-embraced the old false Whig interpretation (Butterfield 1944) because 'it told much that was significant about the present and about our aspirations for the future'. That 'abominable Whig interpretation of history', *The Times* (1987) recently commented, 'was essential to the maintenance of the nation's spirit'; and we need it still, 'to elevate the human mind and to symbolize profound convictions'.

The politics of official history: Poland and Greece

Each state, each people, employs a unique configuration of pasts in coping with its present. In some states, the present seems so parlous that conflicting versions of the national past become politically crucial. In Poland, the people today defy the official rendering of the past at every turn. Spontaneously erected vernacular memorials labelling the Katyn massacre of Polish army officers in 1940 a Russian atrocity are regularly replaced by official plaques designating the Germans as villains, only to surface elsewhere; historical guerrilla warfare rages throughout the cemeteries of Warsaw. In its church-yard sanctuary the grave of Father Popiełuszko, murdered by the state secur-ity police in 1984, is ringed with memorable quotations from episodes in Polish history, flaunting 'freedom' and 'solidarity' in the face of official re-pression. Schoolchildren from all over the country throng the Royal Castle of Warsaw, restored from rubble in the 1970s; there they declaim credos of Polish autonomy, mirroring the 19th-century history paintings in this anti-Russian citadel. School history texts reinforce the official myth of Polish homogeneity by extending it back into the past, where, it is now said, there never were any Lithuanians, Ukrainians, or Jews; only Poles – and German enemies. Meanwhile, though only a handful of Jews remain out of the former three million, Poles resurrect memories of Jewish grandmothers and revivify Lithuanian links through arts and letters.

A fictitious homogeneity likewise figures in Greek nationalist politics. The Greek state itself is a recent creation, born of Western Europe's philhel-lenic attachment to classical antiquity. Crucial European support for the war of liberation from the Ottoman Empire (1821–9) was predicated on the idea of resuscitating ancient Greece. The Western press reshaped 19th-century Greeks into Homeric heroes and reported the Revolution as a virtual replay of the Battle of Marathon and the Persian Wars. Invoking Miltiades, Themistocles, and Leonidas, the West came to restore Greece to her former classical glory.

Thus the Greeks were made to embrace a romanticized version of their classical identity. But it was a view with which few Greeks were then familiar. They were 'Christians' and called themselves 'Romii' and their demotic tongue 'Romaika'. Philhellenes lumbered Greek nationalist proto-cols with archaistic apparatus; the Constitution of Epidaurus emerged in a classical language that to most Greeks was virtually unintelligible (St Clair 1972, Tsigakou 1981, Just 1987).

The new Greek state excluded many realms of Greek culture, and most Greeks lived beyond its borders. Only gradually, through territorial acqui- sition and the ingathering of refugees, did the nation-state at length emerge as patrimonial Greece. Within it, the Greek heritage was disseminated and cleansed to conform with philhellenic stereotypes of classical life. Classical antiquities were cherished, the ancient language enthroned and revived, and extraneous elements expunged from Greek folklore. Herzfeld (1982, 1985) has shown how Greek nationalists purged village tales of Turkish and Balkan elements in order to strengthen continuity with classical roots and to confute the taunt that modern Greeks were naught but Slavs. And the Greek population too has been made racially homogeneous: officially there are no Turks, Vlachs, Slavs, or Albanians among them.

The politics of heritage restitution

The Greek past today at once signals heritage restitution, a cause now critically significant in the politics of the past. Since 1981 Greece has been in the vanguard of an international crusade to return items of monumental and archival heritage to their lands of origin (Hitchens 1987).

Attachments to national heritage have everywhere intensified efforts to keep it in place or to secure its restitution. First a focus of 19th-century European nationalism, antiquities have since become prime symbols of collective identity all over the world. Architectural and other manifestations of heritage now enhance community and identity in every state. A rich and representative patrimony is said to promote citizenship, catalyse creativity, attract foreign sympathy, and enhance all aspects of national life (e.g. Bator 1983, Lowenthal 1987).

Although these points seem self-evident, for much of the world this awareness is only of recent vintage. Independent nationhood leads the Third and Fourth Worlds, like Europe before them, to emphasize material relics and icons of group identity. For tangible validations of their ancestral antecedents, former colonies have to grub for their roots among relics of which most are still held in Western collections. It is imperative that 'the former mother country restores to the new State not only its sovereignty but also its heritage', as an Algerian expressed it (Tayeb 1979). The chairman of the Unesco committee charged with this issue saw 'the restitution and return of cultural property', embracing architectural structures along with other antiquities, works of art, and archives, as 'one of the key problems of the Third World' (Stétié 1981). The rationale is explicitly anti-colonial: 'The vicissitudes of history have . . . robbed many peoples of a priceless portion of [their] inheritance in which their enduring identity finds its embodiment. [To] enable a people to recover part of its memory and identity', other lands should relinquish these irreplaceable cultural treasures 'to the countries where they were created' (M'Bow 1979).

Some losses are especially grievous. West African artefacts crucial to ceremonial observance were purloined as curios. Oceania was stripped of much of its tangible heritage, most relics ending up in collections thousands of miles away. Few British connoisseurs, dismayed by the sale to Japan of Newcastle University's collection of Pacific tribal art, spared a moment's thought for the Pacific island nations that could not afford to buy back any of the significant items fashioned by their forebears (Horn 1985, Benthall 1986, Specht 1987).

Western political leaders exhort Third World countries to earn a decent living before hankering after a lost heritage; but heritage is inseparable from bread-and-butter practicalities. 'Our culture is everything we do and think', explains a Samoan historian, enabling 'us to become much more self-reliant and self-respecting; . . . looked at in this way, [heritage] is *really* "something we can eat"' (Meleisea 1981). And indigenous and ethnic minorities deprived of all else – autonomy, land, religion, language – may cherish monuments and sites as bastions of communal identity (Williams 1984, McBryde 1985, Lowenthal 1987).

But concern over heritage loss is not confined to poor or new nations. Europeans enriched by centuries of imperial acquisitions nowadays express similar fears. Tax-compelled sales abroad have provoked a loss of British heritage that one antiquities expert terms 'comparable to the damage that Cromwell and his Roundheads caused' in dispersing Charles I's private collection (Leggatt 1978). French antiquities face similar pressures, and exports of the monumental past in Italy and Turkey proceed apace despite draconian prohibitions.

Repatriation alone could neither make good these losses nor stem the outflow of heritage to foreign collectors avid for antiquities. Export bans are flagrantly violated; international sanctions against illicit trade remain dead letters. So numerous and powerful are looters of Mexico's 30 million burial sites that they have their own unions and government lobby. To protect Italy's churches against theft would require a police force larger than the national army; to prevent illicit exports would require customs surveillance that would cripple tourism. Most of the African artefacts now in the West have been acquired *since* African countries gained independence. Under such circumstances, notes Nicklin (1981, pp. 18–19), restitution is 'like trying to fill the bath while the plug is out'.

Retention and restitution are not the only options available in heritage politics. Some states strategically disperse their antiquities instead of hoarding them at home. Given the option of having certain historical relics returned, some New Zealand Maoris recently advised the New Zealand government to leave them abroad so as to enhance international awareness of Maori identity. Rather than viewing antiquities as a finite resource to be zealously guarded at home, Israel disperses them much as early Christendom did with such holy relics as bones, shrouds, and slivers of the True Cross. It disseminates ancient artefacts as symbolic expressions of Israel's modern rebirth in an ancient land. 'Every time an ancient artifact is bought or presented to a foreign visitor' – like the Bronze Age Canaanite scimitar and Iron Age oil jar recently given to Prime Minister Margaret Thatcher – the message of Israel's identity and reason for existence is succinctly conveyed (Silberman 1986, pp. 2–3).

Nationalism and the antiquities market exacerbate strife between those who want relics kept where they are and those who would move them. But the Greek case is especially problematic, as I learned after giving a public lecture on heritage restitution, in 1981. I had used the Elgin Marbles as one point of departure for a general discussion of issues as various as the Sphinx's beard, the Benin bronzes, the Code of Hammurabi, and London Bridge, and I made no recommendations about restitution. Yet my talk generated a flood of response, almost all bearing on whether or not the Elgin Marbles should go back to Athens. To be sure, official renewal of the Greek claim had recently reactivated that issue. But this alone did not explain the intensity of the response. Those who favoured restitution expressed keen interest in the principles I elaborated and told me about their own efforts. Those who opposed restitution focused on details of fact or interpretation but would not discuss the issue on its merits, and some even warned me that as a non-British national I ought to shun touchy matters concerning British property.

What gave this particular issue such salience? Greece is felt to be *different*, both by Greeks and the rest of the world. In Western European eyes, Greece is not some remote or trivial ex-colonial land; it is traditionally seen as the fount of European civilization. And the treasures at issue are not exotic trinkets unrelated to European culture; they are the very emblems of its surpassing excellence. The value of the Elgin Marbles transcends their aesthetic qualities: the Parthenon and the Akropolis are felt to symbolize a civilization at once specifically Greek *and* quintessentially European (Finley 1981, Lowenthal 1985, pp. 75–86, Bernal 1987, Lefkowitz 1987, Lowenthal 1988).

The politics of minority tradition

Like Greece, poorer Third World countries as well as wealthier Western nations can engage in the politics of the past as sovereign states. Ethnic and racial minorities within states lack that leverage. Yet in the absence of autonomy, and with the culture of the majority ever eroding their ways, they may consider the past the only leverage they have left. Hence Native American, Aboriginal, and Maori demands for the return of skeletal remains and artefacts and, as generally shown in this book, for the right to interpret and present their own heritage.

Reinterpreting the past can help minorities secure practical as well as psychic benefits. For example, archaeologists have revised previous views about the implications of Narragansett Indian remains in a Rhode Island cemetery. They now suggest that skeletal postures and grave goods show that 17th-century Narragansetts maintained tribal identity and actively resisted colonial assimilation (Robinson, *et al*. 1985). This interpretation suits present-day Narragansetts, for modern pride in identity and Federal privileges reward *their* continuity with like-minded ancestors. And concurrence with current minority virtues has a practical advantage for the archaeologists, too. Nassaney (1989, pp. 84–5) has noted that it was not only empathy that moved them to posit 17th-century 'group solidarity and cohesiveness' against European pressures; views congenial to the Narragansett Indians of today helped ensure their own subsequent access to the site.

At the same time, minorities may implicitly accept the Western mainstream framework of values even in seeking to bolster their own heritage. Arguing that not only England and France and the Founding Fathers but also other groups have contributed significantly to the making of America, minority students at Stanford University campaigned successfully to restructure the compulsory 'Western Culture' course (now retitled 'Cultures, Ideas, and Values') to include more great figures from their own backgrounds. As a black student leader put it, the implicit message behind the curricular emphasis on white males was 'nigger go home' (Bernstein 1988, Hitchens 1988). But though equal time, in the usual phrase, may spur a search for hitherto unknown or underrated works by women and Africans, this procedural reform essentially reinforces Western notions of tradition. Saul Bellow's taunt at such efforts to raise minority self-esteem – 'Who is the Tolstoy of the Zulus, the Proust of the Papuans?' – is not properly addressed by mounting a search for such heroes, but by realizing that the very query reflects the modern Western bias favouring creativity and innovation. That bias is ever more internalized among minorities the world over. It remains, however, only one view of what matters in tradition, not a universal truth.

Nor do the conceptions of the past these interests quarrel over embody fixed truths. On the contrary, they are changing constructions, continually reshaped by later interpretations that reflect both the outcomes of the past and successive generations' ideas about heritage. The bias with which we approach the past is not to be gainsaid; it is part and parcel of all historical awareness. So too are conflicting aims to magnify certain pasts and consign others to oblivion.

Bias is not to be condoned, however, simply because it is inherent in any view of the past. We should strive to dispel its exclusivist precepts in order to benefit from many possible interpretations of what has taken place. That non-Western and minority viewpoints about their own and other people's pasts diverge sharply from the traditional historical consensus is highly beneficial. They offer new insights about heretofore unsung folk and about their relations with those in power. Interactions between the makers and shakers of history and those bent to their will comprise a vital aspect of history only now beginning to be better understood.

These new areas of historical understanding have their own risks and drawbacks, to be sure. Masses of often incoherent data, much of it apparently trivial, irrelevant, or self-contradictory, must be culled and synthesized. In sifting residues of past reality from later additions, it is all too easy to alienate folk newly concerned to reconstitute their own histories, by too dismissive an application of academic rigour. Yet an approach based on cultural chauvinism or radical chic can warp interpretations no less than the self-aggrandizing views of aristocrats and power elites. Both biases alike universalize or sentimentalize history, to the detriment of us all.

The advantages of incorporating folk pasts none the less outweigh their difficulties. They provide a more comprehensive, if less clear-cut, understanding of how things may have been. They enlarge the scope of evidence that archaeologists, along with other scholars, must now absorb, by not simply adding but synthesizing artefactual with written and oral materials. They illumine for historical inquiry information alien to accepted interpretations and often left out of historical chronicles. Having to recognize present-day descendants or their spokesmen as history-makers brings majority and minority alike face to face with their own ethnic and political biases. People of every kind should be encouraged to join professionals in what is best performed as a collaborative enterprise: understanding and creatively using the whole human past. All of us, rich and poor, rulers and ruled, Europeans and non-Europeans, equally belong to and inherit this past.

References

Bator, P. M. 1983. *The international trade in art*. Chicago: University of Chicago Press.

Benthall, J. 1986. The George Brown collection. *Anthropology Today* 2(4), 1–3.

Bernal, M. 1987. *Black Athena: the Afroasiatic roots of classical civilization*. Vol. 1: *The fabrication of ancient Greece*. London: Free Association Books.

Bernstein, R. 1988. Beyond Plato: Stanford pushed to rethink Western culture. *International Herald Tribune*, 20 January, 1, 6.

Bliven, N. 1987. This constitutional earnestness is as good as a festival. *International Herald Tribune*, 14 September.

Burrow, J. W. 1981. *A liberal descent: Victorian historians and the English past*. Cambridge: Cambridge University Press.

Butterfield, H. 1931. *The Whig interpretation of history*. London: G. Bell.

Butterfield, H. 1944. *The Englishman and his history*. Cambridge: Cambridge University Press.

Chippindale, C. 1986. Stoned Henge: events and issues at the summer solstice, 1985. *World Archaeology* 18, 38–58.

Connecticut. 1986. Catch up on Connecticut! 49(6), 100.

Finley, M. I. (ed.) 1981. *The legacy of Greece: a new appraisal*. Oxford: Clarendon Press.

Hamilton, A. & R. Gledhill 1987. Plymouth defends Drake against new Armada. *The Times*, 17 September, 1.

Herzfeld, M. 1982. *Ours once more: folklore, ideology, and the making of modern Greece*. Austin: University of Texas Press.

Herzfeld, M. 1985. 'Law' and 'custom': ethnography in Greek national identity. *Journal of Modern Greek Studies* 3, 167–85.

Higginbotham, A. 1987. In 'Black Americans and the Constitution: an alternative vision', by J. Tasch. *UCLA Center for Afro-American Studies Newsletter* 10(2), 1, 8–10.

Hitchens, C. 1987. *The Elgin Marbles: should they be returned to Greece?* London: Chatto & Windus.

Hitchens, C. 1988. Whose culture, what civilization? *Times Literary Supplement*, 4–10 March, 246.

Horn, A. 1985. Island cultures reap no reward. *Observer*, 8 December.

Just, R. 1987. Triumph of the ethnos. Paper presented at Association of Social Anthropologists Conference on History and Ethnicity, University of East Anglia, 3 April.

Kammen, M. 1986. *A machine that would go of itself: the Constitution in American culture.* New York: Knopf.

Kaye, H. 1987. Our island story retold. *Guardian*, 3 August.

Laslett, P. 1986. The way we think we were [review of Lowenthal 1985]. *Washington Post Book World*, 30 March, 5, 11.

Lefkowitz, M. 1987. An outstanding debt [review of Hitchens 1987]. *Times Literary Supplement*, 14 August, 865.

Leggatt, H. 1978. In 'Once again, art lovers raise alarm against heritage drain', by R. Reed. *International Herald Tribune*, 11 July, p. 6.

Litwack, L. 1987. Trouble in mind: the bicentennial and the Afro-American experience. *Journal of American History* **74**, 315–37.

Lowenthal, D. 1985. *The past is a foreign country.* Cambridge: Cambridge University Press.

Lowenthal, D. 1987. Where does our architectural heritage belong? In *Old cultures in new worlds*, Proceedings of the 8th General Assembly of the International Council on Monuments and Sites, 685–90. Washington, DC: US/ICOMOS.

Lowenthal, D. 1988. Classical antiquities as national and global heritage. *Antiquity* **63**, 726–35.

McBryde, I. (ed.) 1985. *Who owns the past?* Papers from the Annual Symposium of the Australian Academy of the Humanities. Melbourne: Oxford University Press.

McDonald, M. 1986. Celtic ethnic kinship and the problem of being English. *Current Anthropology* **27**, 333–47.

Marshall, T. 1987. In 'Cracks in the Liberty Bell', by C. Bremner. *The Times*, 22 May, 14.

Marx, K. 1852. *The Eighteenth Brumaire of Louis Napoleon.* New York.

M'Bow, A.-M. 1979. A plea for the return of an irreplaceable cultural heritage to those who created it. *Museum* **31**(1), 58.

Meades, J. 1987. Middle Ages spread. *The Times*, 29 August, 13.

Meleisea, M. 1981. 'Culture is not something you can eat': some thoughts on cultural preservation and development in Oceania. *Museum* **33**(2), 122–3.

Nassaney, M. S. 1989. An epistemological enquiry into some archaeological and historical interpretations of 17th century Native American–European relations. In *Archaeological approaches to cultural identity*, S. J. Shennan (ed.), pp. 76–93. London: Unwin Hyman.

Nicklin, K. 1981. In *Lost heritage*. A Report of the Symposium on the Return of Cultural Property, held at the Africa Centre, 21 May, I. Staunton and M. McCartney (eds). London: Commonwealth Arts Association.

Pogrebin, R. 1988. Sarah Rosen. *Ms*, January, 51, 86.

Rae, J. 1987. Turning a blind eye to history. *The Times*, 16 July, 12.

Remnick, D. 1988. Armenia's struggle to endure. *International Herald Tribune*, 13 September, 4.

Robinson, P. A., M. A. Kelley, & P. E. Rubertone 1985. Preliminary biocultural interpretations from a seventeenth-century Narragansett Indian cemetery in

Rhode Island. In *Cultures in contact: the impact of European contacts on Native American cultural institutions A.D. 1000–1800*, W. W. Fitzhugh (ed.), 107–30. Washington, DC: Smithsonian Institution Press.

St Clair, W. 1972. *That Greece might still be free: the philhellenes in the War of Independence*. London: Oxford University Press.

Silberman, N. 1986. A modern cult of relics. Hanover, NH: Institute of Current World Affairs, NAS-21, 31 December.

Specht, J. 1987. The George Brown affair again. *Anthropology Today* **3**(4), 1–3.

Stétié, S. 1981. The Intergovernmental Committee: mechanisms for a new dialogue. *Museum* **33**(2), 116–17.

Tayeb, M. 1979. Algeria. In 'Viewpoint: The return and restitution of cultural property'. *Museum* **31**(1), 10–11.

The Times, 1987. Whose Armada? 17 September, 17.

Tsigakou, F.-M. 1981. *The rediscovery of Greece: travellers and painters of the romantic era*. London: Thames & Hudson.

Williams, S. A. 1984. Recent developments in restitution and return of cultural property. *International Journal of Museum Management and Curatorship* **3**, 117–29.

Wood, G. S. 1988. The fundamentalists and the Constitution. *New York Review of Books*, 18 February, 33–40.

Wright, P. 1985. *On living on an old country: the national past in contemporary Britain*. London: Verso.

Index

Printed in the United Kingdom
by Lightning Source UK Ltd.
114863UKS00002B/92